This book is dedicated to the Reverend Col. Edward Gell - Corsham's own Unknown Soldier. R.I.P. and also to Miss Doris Chappell who managed the Corsham Maternity Home on a voluntary basis for over thirty years between 1919-1951 for the benefit of the County of Wiltshire.

Giuliano (Julian) Carosi

*The cover shows the Dry Arch's west side Key stone.*

**1827 GENTEEL VILLAGE:** The most genteel village in England is said to be Corsham, in Wiltshire, nine miles from Bath, in which, the newspapers tells us, forty-one families of independent fortune reside, of whom fourteen keep close carriages. It has within it four superb mansions and parks, and sixteen other gentlemen's villas. *[Page 31]*

ISBN 978-1-5272-3910-4

# Corsham Revealed More

First edition published by author in June 2019

Printed by
CorshamPrint Creative Solutions
Unit 4, Leafield Way,
Leafield Industrial Estate,
Corsham,
Wiltshire
SN13 9SW

ISBN 978-1-5272-3910-4

Please do not venture on private land without the proper permission.

© Copyright 2019 Giuliano (Julian) Carosi. All rights reserved.

No part of this book may be reproduced in any written, electronic, recording, or photocopying without written permission of the author.

The exception would be in the case of brief quotations embodied in the critical articles or reviews and pages where permission is specifically granted by the author.

As the author of this book, I have made every effort to ensure that the information was correct at the time of publication. No offence is intended towards anyone or towards any family, as most of the information in this book is already available (and has been for many years) in some form in the public domain. In the event of any error or oversight, my apologies are due to those concerned, and any comment or correction will be most gratefully received. Every reasonable effort has been made to trace copyright holders and to obtain their permission for use of copyright material.

I do not assume and hereby disclaim any liability to any party for any loss, damage, or disruption caused by errors or omissions, or the accuracy of the information contained herein whether such errors or omissions result from my negligence, accident, or any other cause. All the facts have been reported in good faith. No liability is therefore assumed for damages that may result from any of the information contained within this book.

Giuliano (Julian) Carosi.

**Preface:** Following the success of my first book 'Corsham Revealed' published in 2018, I have been asked many times if I intended to write another book about our lovely town of Corsham, Wiltshire. There is so much to know about this little sleepy town, that every time I turn over the leaf of an old book or newspaper, or happen to come across an ancient Corsham story in the bottomless pit of the *Internet* - I want to share it with others. When a new door opens into Corsham's past, it often leads me into other rooms with multiple-doors that revealed *more* facts that have long been lost. In fact, there is still so much more out there to find, that all it needs is time and enthusiasm to collate it all.

In my first book *Corsham Revealed*, I mentioned how the idea about writing a book on Corsham's history came to me over forty years ago, when I surprisingly *beat* my Regis Primary School teacher Mr Williams in a *'Know Your Corsham'* history competition. The prize then, was a small amount of cash. The even bigger prize now - is the joy I see on peoples' faces when they greet me in Corsham High Street with, *"Are you Julian?"* or when they give me even more Corsham facts to digest.

As a child growing up in Corsham, there were no technical contraptions to keep me indoors. We children created our own adventures by delving into every corner (above and below ground) of Corsham that we could - and even some corners that we shouldn't have!

In this, my second book titled *Corsham Revealed More*, my aim is to share with you even *more* of what I have found. You don't necessarily have to read this book from cover to cover; you can dip your toe in from time to time into any chapter that catches your fancy. Inside, you will find *more* hidden, long-forgotten and sometimes mysterious historical snippets of Corsham. You *will not* find much on Corsham's usual subjects, such as Corsham Court or the Alms Houses; information on these can be found in other books. Instead, in this book you will read about our famous and maybe not so famous (but nevertheless very interesting) people. There are anecdotes aplenty - of life spent in the old prefab bungalows. There are forgotten aeroplane crashes and even our own Unknown Corsham Soldier to be proud of. You can find the origin of your Corsham street name or learn how Lloyd George's Principle Private Secretary came to live here in Corsham. Learn about Olga Lehmann's Underground Corsham Murals that still shine with colour in our dark tunnels. It's a shame that our old Town Crier Charlie Bethel is no longer alive to tell you more - but you can read all about his exploits in Chapter 24!

Gathering this information required many hours of research spent *head down* reading, tapping away on my computer and rummaging in the brilliant Wiltshire and Swindon History Centre in Chippenham trawling though their newspaper archives; interrogation of the internet, purchasing historical books, postcards and maps, and even more hours walking around our beautiful town of Corsham. The last effort in putting this book together, required twelve months of sifting through the huge amount of material collected and then piecing it all together; to rewrite and produce this second Corsham Revealed book [Corsham Revealed More]. A book that I hope you will enjoy.

Now, please let me take you on another journey that will hopefully change your perception of Corsham; but I make no apologies for the remarkable and sometimes gruesome findings. Enjoy.

*Julian Carosi*

**Giuliano (Julian) Carosi.**

**Contents of 'Corsham Revealed' More in alphabetical order:**

Chapter  1. Area Map of Corsham Town Centre.................................................................. 4

Chapter  2. Area Street and Place Name Origins. ................................................................ 7

Chapter  3. Around and About Corsham ............................................................................ 24

Chapter  4. Aircraft Bomber Flies over Corsham with Nobody Onboard! ........................... 55

Chapter  5. Arthur Hobbs, WWI Correspondent. ................................................................ 59

Chapter  6. Beechfield House (formerly Pickwick House) including the Goldney Family. ... 67

Chapter  7. Claremont Ladies' College. ............................................................................... 82

Chapter  8. Famous and Notable Personalities of Corsham. ............................................... 94

Chapter  9. Gastard - a history. ......................................................................................... 105

Chapter 10. Ian Logan - a Corsham Lad Done Good. ......................................................... 140

Chapter 11. Mallie Etherds. The Wise Woman of Easton .................................................. 148

Chapter 12. Maternity Hospital, Alexander House. ........................................................... 150

Chapter 13. Mushrooms and Counterfeit Coins. ............................................................... 163

Chapter 14. Neston - Aeroplane Crash 1941. .................................................................... 166

Chapter 15. Neston - Charlie Barnes and his three cows! .................................................. 175

Chapter 16. Neston - Glove Factory................................................................................... 177

Chapter 17. Olga Lehmann's Underground Corsham Murals............................................. 185

Chapter 18. Prefab Bungalows - Married Quarters and Hostel Sites. ................................. 192

Chapter 19. Reverend Edward Gell  Corsham's own Unknown Soldier.............................. 240

Chapter 20. Skating on Corsham Lake ............................................................................... 251

Chapter 21. Station Hotel ................................................................................................. 254

Chapter 22. Stone Quarries - a chronological list. ............................................................. 262

Chapter 23. Sylvester, Albert, James (1889-1989) Corsham. ............................................. 270

Chapter 24. Town Crier - Charlie Bethel. ........................................................................... 283

Chapter 25. Wine Lodge. ................................................................................................... 289

Chapter 26. World's Toughest Job - the Corsham Quarryman. .......................................... 302

Chapter 27. Acknowledgements........................................................................................ 305

Chapter 28. The Author Giuliano (Jullan) Carosi................................................................ 307

Chapter headings of the first, 'Corsham Revealed' book published in 2018. ISBN. No. 978-1-5272-2022-5

Chapter 1. Accident - Fatal accident in Monks Lane 1787.
Chapter 2. Bandstand - in the Recreation Ground.
Chapter 3. Batters.
Chapter 4. Box Tunnel.
Chapter 5. Brewers Yard Quarry.
Chapter 6. Castle - Tumulus/Mound Hartham.
Chapter 7. Cathedral - Corsham.
Chapter 8. Charabanc Trips.
Chapter 9. Cinemas - in Corsham.
Chapter 10. Cricket Club.
Chapter 11. Dry Arch - Corsham Park.
Chapter 12. Farleigh Down Tunnel at Shockerwick Box.
Chapter 13. Fire Brigade - a 200 year history.
Chapter 14. Floods - The Great Railway Flood of 1935.
Chapter 15. Football - Corsham Town Football Club.
Chapter 16. Ghost Stories - Twenty Seven Corsham stories.
Chapter 17. HaHa Wall / Sunken Fence - Corsham Park.
Chapter 18. Highwayman, James Boulter 1748-1778 (alias Baxter) The Flying Highwayman.
Chapter 19. Horsey Tree - R.I.P Corsham Park.
Chapter 20. Hospital - WWI Red Cross V.A.D. Hospital - Corsham Town Hall.
Chapter 21. Ice Houses.
Chapter 22. Libraries in Corsham.
Chapter 23. Lime/Pottery/Brick Kilns and the remarkable Angell Family.
Chapter 24. Lypiatt Hostel No.15 Camp.
Chapter 25. Machine Breakers - and Captain Swing.
Chapter 26. Miscellany Corsham Newspaper.
Chapter 27. Monks Chapel.
Chapter 28. Murder in Swete's Hole, Mynte Mead 4 August 1606.
Chapter 29. Murder of Harry Long 1594.
Chapter 30. Osborne House.
Chapter 31. Parish Chest v Mrs General Lightfoot!
Chapter 32. Pickwick District School.
Chapter 33. Pickwick Motors.
Chapter 34. Police Station - Pickwick Road.
Chapter 35. Poorhouse/Workhouse.
Chapter 36. Porch Entrance of St Bartholomew's.
Chapter 37. Post Office.
Chapter 38. Quarry - Tin Pan Alley - Cross Keys.
Chapter 39. Rising Sun Inn - a 'BLAST' from the past.
Chapter 40. Road Signs - in WWII Wiltshire.
Chapter 41. Roman Coffin and Skeleton find at Hudswell Laboratories in 1942.
Chapter 42. Rossiter's Priory Stores Grocery Shop.
Chapter 43. Skuse - Thomas. Thirty Years Afloat Abroad.
Chapter 44. Small Pox House and Small Pox in Corsham.
Chapter 45. Spackman - Sylvia's Story
Chapter 46. Speke Memorial.
Chapter 47. Starwell (or Holy Well) Corsham.
Chapter 48. Stické Tennis Court at Hartham Park.
Chapter 49. Telephone Exchange.
Chapter 50. Temperance Hotel, Corsham.
Chapter 51. Thingley Junction Rail Crash.
Chapter 52. Toilets - at your convenience.
Chapter 53. Turnpike Road to London - The Great Bath Road.
Chapter 54. Weavern Farm.
Chapter 55. Whores Pond.
Chapter 56. Acknowledgements.
Chapter 57. The Author.

# Chapter 1. Area Map of Corsham Town Centre.

| Street | Grid | Street | Grid | Street | Grid | Street | Grid |
|---|---|---|---|---|---|---|---|
| Academy Drive | C2 | Duke Crescent | A2 | Lypiatt Road | D4 | Sawyers Crescent | A3 |
| Albion Crescent | C2 | Echo Close | A2 | Macie Drive | B3 | Shearwater Way | B4 |
| Alexander Terrace | D2 | Edinburgh Way | B4 | Manor Road | D1 | Silman Close | B2 |
| Allard Avenue | A3 | Edridge Place | C2 | Mansion House Mews | D3 | Smiths Yard | D2 |
| Allen Road | A3 | Elder Court | B3 | Marsh Grove | A3 | South Avenue | E2 |
| Arney Close | C3 | Elm Grove | C2 | Masons Way | B2 | South Street | D3 |
| Arnolds Mead | D2 | Elm Hayes | D4 | Mayo Close | C2 | Southerwicks | D3 |
| Astute Place | A2 | Erneston Crescent | D2 | Meadland | C2 | Spackman Lane | C3 |
| Barn Close | C2 | Ethelred place | C2 | Meriton Avenue | D2 | Spring Gardens | D2 |
| Bath Road | B2 | Freestone Way | B3 | Methuen Way | D1 | Spring Tinings | C2 |
| Bath Stone Crescent | A2 | Front Hill Close | A3 | Middlewick Lane | C1 | Springfield Centre | C2 |
| Beechfield Road | C2 | Fuller Avenue | C3 | Neale Court | C2 | St Barbaras Road | A3 |
| Bellott Drive | C3 | Furzehill | C3 | Newlands Road | D2 | Station Road | D3 |
| Bences Lane | D1 | Gibbs Court | A2 | Nine Acre Drive | B3 | Stokes Road | D3 |
| Bethel Road | B2 | Glebe Way | C2 | Nobles Place | A2 | Stone Close | A2 |
| Black Acre | B3 | Goblins Pit Close | A2 | North Leaze | B2 | Summerleaze | A2 |
| Blossom Drive | A2 | Gorse Place | B3 | Nursery Gardens | D3 | Sumsions Drive | B2 |
| Bluebell Mead | B3 | Groundstone Way | A3 | Oathills | C3 | Swan Road | B2 |
| Bradford Road | A2 | Grove Road | D3 | Oliver Avenue | C2 | Syon Close | C3 |
| Brakspear Drive | C3 | Guyers Lane | B2 | Orchard Road | D1 | Tasker Close | C3 |
| Broadmead | E4 | Hardhams Rise | C3 | Paddock Lane | A3 | Tellcroft Close | D4 |
| Brook Drive | E4 | Hartham Lane | D1 | Park Lane | B2 | The Cleeve | D4 |
| Browns Drive | A3 | Hastings Road | D3 | Partridge Close | C3 | The Crescent | D4 |
| Brunel Close | C2 | Hatton Way | C3 | Paul Street | D2 | The Knowle | C3 |
| Buckthorn Row | B3 | Hazel Way | B3 | Peel Circus | A3 | The Lagger | D1 |
| Burlington Place | A3 | High Street | D2 | Penleigh Close | C3 | The Old School Yard | D3 |
| Burn Road | B2 | Hilly Fields | B3 | Picked Mead | B3 | The Precinct | D2 |
| Burrows Close | C3 | Hitherspring | C3 | Pickwick Park | B2 | The Tynings | D2 |
| Cathedral Grove | A3 | Holly Crescent | C3 | Pickwick Road | C2 | Trafalgar Close | A2 |
| Charles Street | C2 | Home Mead | B3 | Pictor Close | B2 | Tramways | C3 |
| Charlwood Road | D3 | Hornes Mead | A2 | Pockeredge Drive | C4 | Tropenell Close | C3 |
| Chestnut Grange | B2 | Hudswell Lane | A3 | Pockeredge Road | C4 | Tupman Road | C2 |
| Church Street | E2 | Hulbert Close | C2 | Porters Mead | C2 | Upper Potley | B4 |
| Churchill Way | D1 | Ivy Field | D2 | Post Office Lane | D2 | Valley Road | C3 |
| Cleevedale Road | D4 | Jackson Close | C3 | Potley Lane | C4 | Wastfield | D3 |
| Clubhouse Place | A2 | Jargeau Court | D3 | Pound Mead | C4 | Waterhole Avenue | A2 |
| Copenacre Way | A2 | Kings Avenue | D1 | Pound Pill | D3 | Waverley Court | D3 |
| Cottle Mead | C3 | Kinneir Close | D3 | Poynder Road | C2 | Weller Road | C2 |
| Coulston Road | D1 | Kirby Road | C2 | Priory New Road | D1 | West Park Road | B2 |
| Cowslip Bank | B3 | Lacock Road | E3 | Priory Street | D2 | Williams Grove | D3 |
| Cresswells | C3 | Ladbrook Lane | E4 | Privet Way | B3 | Willow Crescent | B3 |
| Cross Keys Road | D1 | Leafield Way | B4 | Prospect | E4 | Woodborough Road | E4 |
| Curlcroft Road | B4 | Lewis Close | B3 | Providence Lane | D2 | Woodlands | C1 |
| Dairy Mews | C1 | Light Close | D1 | Purleigh Road | B2 | Yew Way | B3 |
| Danvers Road | B2 | Limestone Drive | B3 | Queens Avenue | D1 | Yockney Close | C3 |
| Dew Close | D4 | Long Ground | A3 | Randall Court | B2 | York Close | D1 |
| Dickens Avenue | C2 | Lucas Court | A3 | Sandown Crescent | A2 | | |
| Dicketts Road | D4 | Ludmead Road | E4 | Saunders Grove | B2 | | |
| Dovecote Drive | C2 | Lypiatt Mead | D4 | Savernake Road | B4 | | |

Chapter 1. Area Map of Corsham Town Centre.

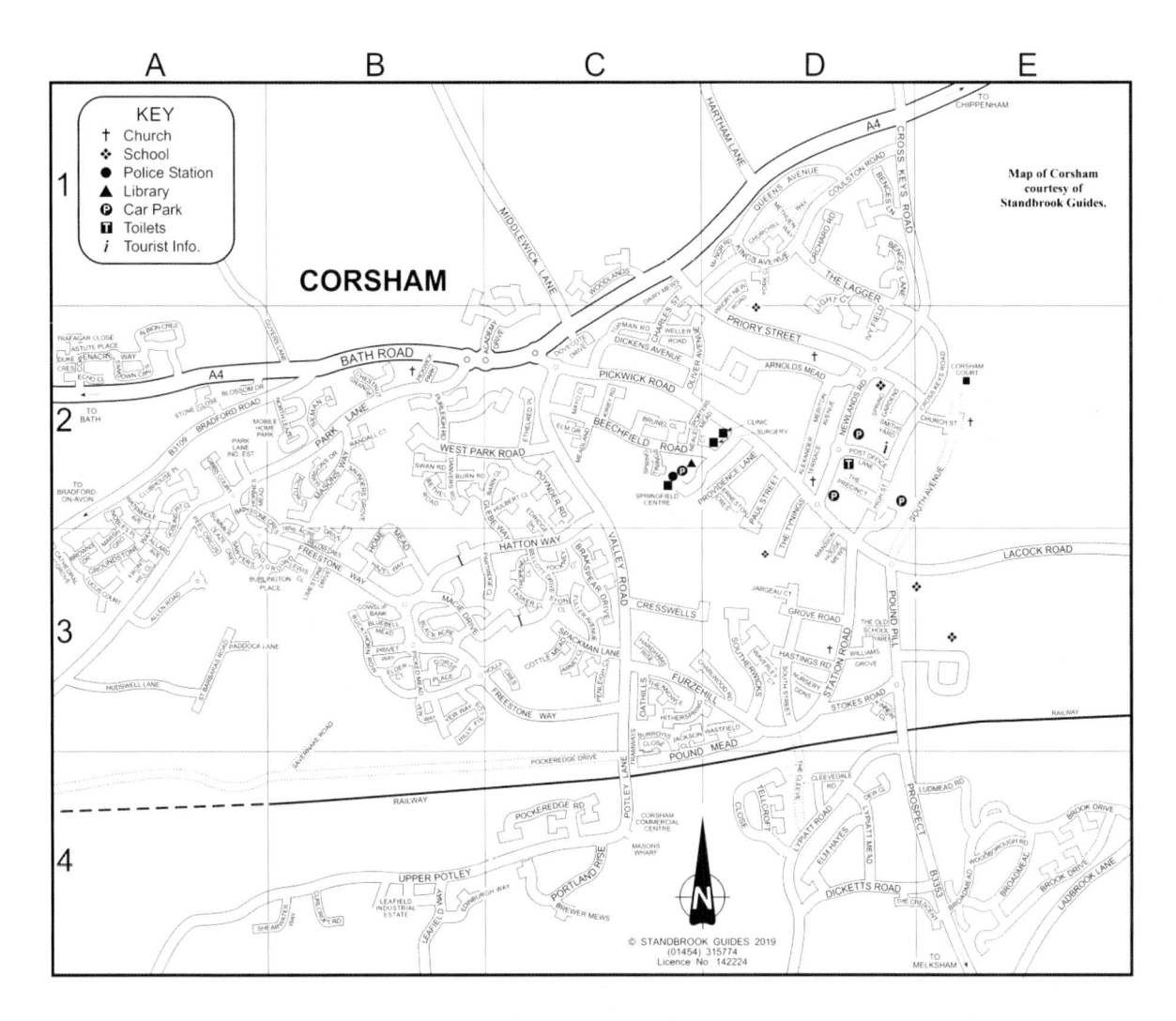

*Above map is licensed by Stanbrook Guides and permission has been granted to produce it here.*

Corsham was historically a centre for agriculture and later, the wool industry, and then became famous for quarrying Bath Stone. During the Second World War and the Cold War, it became a major administrative and manufacturing centre for the Ministry of Defence [now communications], with numerous establishments above ground and in years gone by, underground in the old quarry tunnels.

**CORSHAM - where does our town name come from?:** Gorsan, Cosan-ham, Cusa-ham, Cors-ham, Coseham, Cosseham, Cosham, Cossam, Corsholm, or Cosse-ham……………CORSHAM?

Richard Tomkins, the editor of Wiltshire Place Names (first published in 1983) suggests that the name Corsham is probably derived from Cosan-ham, 'home of Cosa or Cusa or Cossa's ham; this origin also appears on page 62 of 'The Place Names of Wiltshire - Their Origin and History' by Einar Ekblom 1917.

John C. Longstaff [Notes on Wiltshire Names Library Press 1911] suggests that the first element may derive from the Cornish word cos, 'wood' [or from the Celtic name (cors) for bog].

'Ham' is a special English word with the primary meaning of 'home', but can also be used to describe a dwelling-place, village or manor. At one time, the town was called 'Corsham Regis', due to its reputed association with Anglo-Saxon Ethelred of Wessex (King Ethelred) who was a Chief Tenant here [Domesday Book].

## Chapter 1. Area Map of Corsham Town Centre.

The name has changed backwards and forwards many times over the years: 1001 Coseham. 1015 Cosham. 1130 Cosseham. 1086 Cosseham. 1185 Cosham. 1194 Cossam. 1201 Corsholm. 1212 Cosseham. 1225 Corsha. 1230 Cosham. 1310 Cosham. 1316 Cosham. 1334 Cosseham. 1394 Cosham. 1411 it was known again as Cosham or Coshamlond. 1428 Cosham. 1741 Cossum. 2019 CORSHAM.

The letter 'r' in the name of Corsham is a later insertion, possibly caused by the local pronunciation, i.e. due to the local Wiltshire dialect e.g. Yer/Yertiz = here/here it is; and Ark at 'Ee = listen to him, (with incredulity).

It has also been suggested in the past [Notes on Wiltshire Names Library Press 1911 page 56], that it was the home of a man called Gorsan, whose name is also traced to Corston (a small village in North East Somerset). Another suggestion could be that the origin is to be found in the 'Welsh Cors', a marsh. Hence 'the home in the marsh.' This however does not seem to fit the character of the surrounding Wiltshire country.

In his book 'Corsham an Illustrated History', Christopher Hall mentions that the name of Corsham might be a derivation from a Celtic river name, but the absence of a river makes this very unlikely. 'The village of pigs' is another local interpretation in an area that once supported large herds of animals. Or maybe as described by the twelfth-century historian William of Malmesbury, the name 'Corsham' reflects the plot of land opposite Ethelred House in Church Street, where King Ethelred the Unready had a hunting lodge (his Summer Palace), inhabited when he hunted wild boar in the nearby Melksham Forest. The area at the time also had a large forest which was cleared to make way for further expansion.

In her book 'Corsham Facts & Folklore', Patricia Whalley includes the following extract from Leyland's Journey 1540-1542. *'Old Bonhome told me that Coseham appertinid to the erldom of Cornwalle, and that Coseham was a mansion place longging to it wher sumtyme they lay'.* In view of the grammar and spelling in the paragraphs above, it's no surprise that the name of Corsham had many derivatives before its modern title was eventually established.

[Ed: Most likely, it was derived from Cosan-ham, 'home of Cosa or Cusa'.]

**CORSHAM - we love you whatever you're named!**

# Chapter 2. Area Street and Place Name Origins.

**AREA STREET AND PLACE NAMES - THEIR ORIGINS.**

Some Corsham names are simply field names shown on the portions of land identified on the Tithe maps of old, like *Oathills* and *Tellcroft Close*. Others are simple logical references to locations or destinations such as *South Street* and *Lacock Road*. A large number are connected to Corsham's Bath stone quarrying days, such as *Lewis Close* and *Pictor Close*. When they ran out of *quarry type names* for the large Katherine Park estate, they used local tree/shrub names such as Hazel Way and Gorse Place. Quite a few names are in memory of some of Corsham's important inhabitants (including several RAF personalities), for example *Tedder Avenue* and *Bethel Road*. There are quite a few connections to the books of Charles Dickens who used to pass through Corsham in Moses Pickwick's *coach* on his way to Bath; such as *Weller Road* and *Dickens Avenue*.

Some names on first presentation seem to make no sense at all, like *Goblins Pit Close* and *St Barbaras Road*. Where the origin is vague, I have listed more than one possible origin (such as *Sheppards*) and/or made a logical guess! In some entries, I have added additional references for interest; even though they may not be the exact origin of the name, they may be of interest to you.

But one thing is for certain - you don't have to walk very far to be reminded of Corsham Town's history or its landscape.

*[Author Julian Carosi]*

| PLACE NAME | ORIGIN |
| --- | --- |
| **ACADEMY DRIVE** | Named after the Bath' Academy' of Art which established itself at Corsham Court and at Beechfield House in Middlewick Lane from 1946 to 1983? |
| **ALBION CRESCENT** | On the old Royal Naval Stores Depot site opened as Copenacre in 1942, and named after the Navy 'Albion' Class landing, amphibious assault ships. |
| **ALEXANDER TERRACE** | Dr. Richard H. 'Alexander', was a 19th century Corsham doctor who lived in Alexander House in the High Sreet. |
| **ALLARD AVENUE** | Park Place estate road. Named after Lucas and 'Allard', the Corsham Quarrying Company (Bath Stone Merchants) who owned Ridge Quarry. William George Allard and Henry Lucas. |
| **ALLEN ROAD** | Colonel 'Allen' was the Commanding Ordnance Officer in the Corsham Ammunition Depot in Tunnel Quarry at Hudswell. Note: Fiona Allen was an Executive Head teacher at Corsham Primary School. |
| **ARNEY CLOSE** | The 'Arney' family once farmed at Pockeredge House. |
| **ARNOLDS MEAD** | William 'Arnold', member of the Corsham Wool Merchants Guild, late of Lacock (1700) at Arnolds Mill, was a clothier, and farmer. He became a success in the property market due to his wealth. |
| **ASHWOOD ROAD** | 'Ashwood' is derived from the Old English words 'æsc', meaning ash, and wood. May simply indicate its location near an 'ash wood'. |
| **ASTUTE PLACE** | On the old Royal Naval Stores Depot site opened as Copenacre in 1942, and named after the Navy's 'Astute' Class submarines. |

Chapter 2. Area Street and Place Name Origins.

| | |
|---|---|
| **ATWORTH LANE** | 'AEttas' worth or homestead: Atteworth Cotell, also known as Little Atworth, and now called Cottles, takes its name from the French family: it was held by Richard Cotel in 1242. Mechell or michel (from Old English michel) are synonyms for 'Great', used to distinguish the larger settlement. Locally known as Atford. Known in 1001 as Attenwrthe, 1249 de Attewurthe, 1402 Atteworth Cotell, 1404 Little Cotels, Cotels Atteward, 1427 Ateford, 1428 Parva Attworth, 1451 Mechell Attewarde, 1458 Great Atte Ward and in 1489 Atward. |
| **BAKERS CORNER** | A tithing of woodland where 'Mr Baker', a wood turner lived in the 19th century. Once called 'Street's Green' (common land). Once also known as 'Hales Corner', corrupted to 'Hell's Corner', then 'Paradise Square' before reverting back to 'Bakers Corner.' |
| **BANKWATERS ROAD** | Rudloe: Bank = sloping land (especially the slope beside a body of water). A body of water (such as an inlet or tributary) that is out of the main current of a larger body. |
| **BARN CLOSE** | See Purleigh Road. Purleigh Barn once stood here in this Corsham valley. |
| **BASIL HILL ROAD** | Basil Hill Road is named after the Army's 'Basil Hill' Barracks at Hudswell, now a Ministry of Defence establishment, Information Systems and Services (ISS). Note: A Mr 'Basil' Hankey was the Wiltshire County Director of the Red Cross Society during WWI. The War Office bought a section of the Pockeredge estate to provide space for the Basil Hill Barracks in 1936. |
| **BATH ROAD** | London to 'Bath' turnpike road route established in the 1600s. |
| **BATH STONE CRESCENT** | 'Bath Stone' quarried from under Corsham and Box for many years. |
| **BEECHFIELD ROAD** | Field name. Field with beech trees; i.e. a 'beech field'. |
| **BELLOTT DRIVE** | Richard 'Bellott', was a farmer of the Corsham Manor under the Abbess of Syon, who held it in lease for a term of years and left house-room in the Corsham Manor-house or Parsonage for his wife, Alice. |
| **BENCES LANE** | WWI Frederick James 'Bence' born in 1898 was reported missing on 23 March 1918, posted as dead July 1919. Lived in Pound Pill. Father (also Frederick) was a stonemasons' foreman with the Bath Stone Company. See also page 50. |
| **BETHEL ROAD** | Named after Charlie 'Bethel' the Town Crier for many years or possibly Richard 'Bethel', a scholar at the Mansion House School in Corsham. |
| **BLACK ACRE** | The 1816 Corsham Tithe Map shows Abraham Lloyd 'Edridge' as owning a plot of land called 'Black Acre' in Corsham (Ref:316). The term might originate with references to colours associated with certain crops (peas and beans are black). Or where the soil is 'brashy ' i.e. poor quality or dark brown. Or land covered by forest. |
| **BLUEBELL MEAD** | Hyacinthoides is a genus of flowering plants in the family Asparagaceae, known as 'bluebells'. When the Katherine Park estate designers ran out of Stone Quarry related street names, they simply named the remaining roads after flowers, shrubs or trees. |
| **BRADFORD ROAD** | The B3109 road that leads to 'Bradford'-on-Avon. |
| **BRAKSPEAR DRIVE** | Harold 'Brakspear' (1870–1934), was a restoration architect and an archaeologist, who lived at Pickwick Manor and Parkside in High Street. |
| **BREWER MEWS** | 'Mr Brewer' worked the quarry called Brewer's Yard at Rudloe Firs at the very top of Box Hill alongside the A4 in the 1880s. He also worked for Brunel on the Box Tunnel excavations. |

Chapter 2. Area Street and Place Name Origins.

| | |
|---|---|
| **BROADMEAD** | Derives its name partly from nearby 'Broadstone' under which flows a brook. It was said at midnight, that *'the devil comes and turns the stone over, but not if anyone could see of hear him'.* The name derives from a field named 'Brook Stone Mead' (Ref:1182) in the 1816 Corsham Tithe Map. Another field is called Broad Stone Ground (Ref:912). The Ladbrook stream flows nearby.<br>Possibly home to Thomas de Bradeston or Bradestan in 1340. |
| **BROADWOOD AVENUE** | Rudloe: Lieutenant General Robert George 'Broadwood', CB (1862 – 21 June 1917) was Commander of British Troops in South China.<br>Note: He was the grandson of John Broadwood the founder of the Broadwood Piano Company, founded in 1728. |
| **BROCKLEAZE** | Badgers Wood: Name derives from a field owned by William Dunsden named 'Brock Leaze' in the 1816 Corsham Tithe Map. Old English brocc, broc, of Celtic origin; related to Welsh and Cornish broch, Irish and Scottish Gaelic broc, and Breton broc'h = name for a badger.<br>Leaze = grassland or meadow. |
| **BROOK DRIVE** | The Ladbrook stream flows nearby. See also Broadmead above. |
| **BROWNS DRIVE** | Park Place estate road: Named after 'Browns Quarry' which is a small stone quarry to the north of Tunnel Quarry in Hudswell, once used as the underground WWII Headquarters of the RAF's No. 10 Group Fighter Command.<br>Browns Folly Mine is an average sized Bath Stone quarry which was originally part of the nearby Monkton Farleigh Quarry. In 1848 Colonel Wade 'Brown', who lived at the Manor House at Monkton Farleigh, built Brown's Folly overlooking Bath and the Avon Valley. The Bath House at Corsham Court was designed by Lancelot 'Brown' in about 1761-63. |
| **BRUNEL CLOSE** | Isambard Kingdom 'Brunel' who engineered Box Tunnel. |
| **BUCKTHORN ROW** | 'Buckthorn' is a large shrub or tall tree with glossy oval leaves. When the Katherine Park estate designers ran out of Stone Quarry related street names, they simply named the remaining roads after flowers, shrubs or trees.. |
| **BURLINGTON PLACE** | 'Burlington' was one of the many codenames for the WWII underground bunker built in Spring Quarry. Now derelict.<br>**BURLINGTON PLACE** |
| **BURN ROAD** | Royal Engineer's (RE) Colonel A. H. 'Burn', Commanding Officer of the Army Depot at Basil Hill Barracks, Hudswell. He wrote a two-page article in the Wiltshire Archaeological and Natural History Magazine ((No. CLXXX June 1944 Vol. L), concerning the Roman Skeleton find at Hudswell Barracks in 1942. |
| **BURROWS CLOSE** | Dr William Lewson 'Burrows' first came to Corsham in 1949 as a locum GP and never left, retiring from The Porch High Street Surgery after 36 years. |
| **BYDE MILL** | Old English 'byd' = hollow depression, i.e. a mill in the valley. Once known as 'Lydes'. Old English Lyd = torrent. Was Bidemille in 1273. Bydemel in 1300. Bidesknappe in 1341. Bydemylle in 1450. |
| **CATHEDRAL GROVE** | Park Place estate road: Named after the huge 'Cathedral' cavern in Box stone quarry. |
| **CHAPEL LANE** | The road that runs past the Neston Gospel 'Chapel'. |
| **CHAPEL KNAPP** | Chapel on a hill. Knap. Old English 'cnaepp' = top of hill. Chapel Knapp takes its name from a 15th century chapel to St. John built there some six centuries ago but long since gone. |
| **CHARLES STREET** | Used as a name to preserve the association with 'Charles' Dickens. |

Chapter 2. Area Street and Place Name Origins.

| | |
|---|---|
| **CHARLWOOD ROAD** | Name derives from a field named 'Charlwood Close' (Ref: 573) in the 1816 Corsham Tithe Map. Derived from the Olde English pre 7th Century word "ceorl", meaning "a free peasant", plus the second element the Olde English "wudu", a wood; i.e. freeman's wood.<br>CHIRL, CHIRLE, Churl, Churrel = wood cut small to kindle fire.<br>Charlwood is also the name of a small wood in Neston/Wadswick above Wormwood Park Farm. |
| **CHESTNUT GRANGE** | Named after the nearby Chestnut Trees alongside Park Lane, Corsham. |
| **CHURCH RISE** | The road to Neston's St. Philip's and St. James' 'church', just south of Neston primary school. |
| **CHURCH STREET** | The road from Corsham's High Street leading to St Bartholomew's 'Church'. |
| **CHURCHILL WAY** | The late C.W. 'Churchill', was Headmaster of Corsham County Primary School for many years. But more likely to refer to 'Churchill' the Prime Minister. |
| **CLEEVEDALE ROAD** | 'Cleeve' = steeply sloping area of ground; 'Dale' = an open valley. |
| **CLIFT CLOSE** | 'Clift' Quarry (halfway down Box Hill) was once a very productive quarry. It ceased working in 1968 and is now gated and locked. Two closes of Corsham pasture land called Hardam and Priors 'Clift 'sold in September 1803 at the Red Lion (now Methuen Arms). |
| **CLUBHOUSE PLACE** | Park Place estate road: Named after the old Neston 'Clubhouse' Quarry' near the old Neston Club in Pool Green. |
| **COPENACRE WAY** | On the old Royal Naval Stores Depot site opened as Copenacre in 1942. Name derives from a field owned by Henry Hall Joy named 'Coppenacre' (Ref:1368) in the 1816 Corsham Tithe Map. In the 1830s Henry Hall Joy became the owner of Hartham House as well as Hartham Park in a land swap arrangement and he chose to knock down Hartham House. Copenacre Quarry, later Royal Naval Stores Depot and then the Defence Communications Agency. Now a new housing estate. Old English 'copp' = pollard i.e. to cut back trees. Old English 'ac' = oak. |
| **COPPERSHELL** | Name derives from two field names owned by Robert Sadler named 'Little Coppershell' (Ref:866) and 'Copper Shells' (849) in the 1816 Corsham Tithe Map. |
| **COTTLE MEAD** | The 1816 Corsham Tithe Map shows Abraham Lloyd 'Edridge' as owning a plot of land called 'Cottles Field' in Corsham (Ref:316).<br>Name also shown on the 1816 Corsham Tithe Map.<br>Cottle = a band or wall typically of clay that encircles an object. Also a part of a mould used by pewterers in the formation of their wares.<br>There's a 'Cottles' Wood alongside the A365 just east of Atworth where the Roman Villa was. |
| **CORSHAM ROAD** | The road to Corsham from the Lacock Whitehall Garden Centre to the old Roebuck Inn (now a private residence). |
| **COULSTON ROAD** | Misspelling of 'Coulsden' Road. Coulsden Cross was the original name of the cross-roads at the Cross Keys on the A4. |
| **COWSLIP BANK** | Simply a sloping field of cowslips. When the Katherine Park estate designers ran out of Stone Quarry related street names, they simply named the remaining roads after flowers, shrubs or trees.. |
| **CRESSWELLS** | Name derives from a field owned by Walter Long named 'Cresswells' (Ref:1135) in the 1816 Corsham Tithe Map. Also a field name on the Tithe Award of 1838. In the 1930's 'The Porch' Corsham had a doctor named Dr. H.E. Cresswell who had been 'gassed' in WWI.<br>Possibly originally once the location of a well surrounded by cress (a plant of the cabbage family, typically having small white flowers and pungent leaves). |

Chapter 2. Area Street and Place Name Origins.

| | |
|---|---|
| **CROSS KEYS ROAD** | Cross Keys Inn (previously The Bell) on the A4 crossroads. Cross Keys are the sign for St Peter. |
| **CURLCROFT ROAD** | Name derives from a field owned by William Hulbert named 'Curlcroft' (Ref: 456) in the 1816 Corsham Tithe Map.<br>Croft = a fenced or enclosed area of land. |
| **DAIRY MEWS** | Site of the old Corsham Dairy at the top of Priory Street. Now new housing. |
| **DAMY GREEN** | In 1569 was a field name known as Damy croft.<br>Polish and Czech word 'damy' = lady or ladies. Ladies Green?<br>Danish Damme = to block up *[Pg.4 The Ways of Corsham: John Poulsom].* |
| **DANVERS ROAD** | Sir Henry 'Danvers', murderer of Henry Long in 1594. |
| **DEW CLOSE** | Albert Sydney 'Dew' was the first tenant on Pound Pill Farm which was owned by the Neston Estate. Mr Dew delivered milk in his pony and trap in 1940s/1950s. He died in December 1957 aged 77. |
| **DICKENS AVENUE** | Charles 'Dickens' who passed through Corsham in Samuel Pickwick's Coach. |
| **DICKETTS ROAD** | Name derives from a pasture owned by William Hulbert named 'Dicketts' (Ref:1172) in the 1816 Corsham Tithe Map. 'Dicketts' is also attributed to the 'Duckett' family, who held Hartham House from the late 16th century until approx 1830. |
| **DOVECOTE DRIVE** | Once the site of the Pickwick House 'Dovecote'. |
| **DOWDING AVENUE** | Air Chief Marshal Sir Hugh 'Dowding', Commander of the RAF Fighter Command during the Battle of Britain in 1940. Note also: Chippenham Brewery (C. J. Dowding & Son) became part of Pickwick Brewery in 1905. James Dowding was a local baker. |
| **DUKE CRESCENT** | On the old Royal Naval Stores Depot site opened as Copenacre in 1942, and named after the Type 23 ('Duke' Class) Frigates. |
| **DURLEY PARK** | Old English name 'dierna-leah' : Durley is a compound of Old English 'dierne', secret, hidden etc. and 'leah' a wood or clearing in a wood. This is *descriptive* of where this road is in Neston. In 1229 it was Durnley, 1235 Durle, 1264 Durnelyghe, 1278 Derley, 1279 Dorlegh, Dyerlegh, and 1360 Durlee. Durley is a family name that was carried to England in the great wave of migration from Normandy following the Norman Conquest of 1066. |
| **EASTON LANE** | Old English 'east-tun' = east farmstead. Lane leading to Easton, a tything in Corsham parish, 1 mile East of Corsham. |
| **ECHO CLOSE** | On the old Royal Naval Stores Depot site opened as Copenacre in 1942. Naval Radar equipment was once held in the Copenacre Naval Depot Quarry along with a large number of Bats in the underground! HMS Echo is the first of two multi-role hydrographic survey ships commissioned by the Royal Navy. |
| **EDINBURGH WAY** | At the time of his engagement to Princess Elizabeth in July 1947, the Duke of 'Edinburgh' was instructing cadets at the Petty Officer training school HMS Royal Arthur in Corsham. |
| **EDRIDGE PLACE** | The 1816 Corsham Tithe Map shows Abraham Lloyd 'Edridge' as owning lots of land in Corsham.<br>Captain Thomas Edridge Yockney who gave his life on 5 January 1901 in the Anglo-Boer War (1899-1902). The Yockney family lived at Pockeredge House c1830. |
| **ELDER COURT** | Elder is a small tree native to the UK. When the Katherine Park estate designers ran out of Stone Quarry related street names, they simply named the remaining roads after flowers, shrubs or trees.. |
| **ELLEY GREEN** | Old English haelig = 'holy', i.e. Holy Green. Previously known as Velly, and also Helley (see Rough Street map below). |
| **ELM GROVE** | Local field name. Elm = a tall deciduous tree. |

Chapter 2. Area Street and Place Name Origins.

| | |
|---|---|
| **ELM HAYES** | The 1816 Corsham Tithe Map shows John Fuller as owning a plot of land called 'Elm Hayes' in Corsham (Ref:1193a). Local field name. Elm = a tall deciduous tree. 'Heyes' is derived from a geographical locality. 'at the hey,' a hedge or enclosure. i.e. Elm trees surrounding the edge of a field. Mr G Hayes had a shop on the High Street in 1940 and was a member of Parish Council. |
| **ERNESTON CRESCENT** | Ernest Merrett local house builder. Named partly using his first name 'Ern' and partly with Neston 'eston' i.e. Erneston. |
| **ETHELRED PLACE** | King 'Ethelred' the Unready had a hunting lodge at Corsham. |
| **FLEETWOOD CLOSE** | Named after Neston's 'Fleetwood-Fuller' family, e.g. Robert 'Fleetwood' Fuller, Christopher Herbert 'Fleetwood' Fuller, John Gerard 'Fleetwood' Fuller, Gerard Henry 'Fleetwood' Fuller etc. |
| **FREESTONE WAY** | 'Freestone' was one of many names given to the local Bath Stone which has been quarried at Corsham from the 600s. |
| **FRONT HILL CLOSE** | Park Place estate road: Named after the 'Front Hill' series of 10 quarry entrances connected to the stone workings under Box Hill. Backdoor, Bridgegate, Clift Mine, Eastgate, Hazelbury, Lady Hamilton's Hole 1, Lady Hamilton's Hole 2, Jack's Workings, Northgate, and Westgate. |
| **FULLER AVENUE** | 'Fuller' family at Neston Park and Jaggards House. |
| **FURZEHILL** | Old English fyrs = gorse bramble.<br>The 1816 Corsham Tithe Map shows Abraham Lloyd Edridge as owning a plot of land called 'Furze Hill' in Corsham (Ref:308). |
| **GASTARD** | A tail of land where goats feed: Old English 'gat' = goat and 'steart' = goats tail or tongue of land. May be from Danish. 'gaas' = goose. Known as Gatesterta in 1154, Getestert 1167, Gateherst 1177, Gastard in 1428, Gadsteed in 1601. |
| **GIBBS COURT** | Jonathan 'Gibbs' was a horse dealer who lived at 115 (now No.3) High Street from the early 1700s. |
| **GLEBE WAY** | 'Glebe' is Church land and owned in order to provide income, to pay parochial clergy. Once part of a parish priest's ancient freehold, and passed on from vicar to vicar. |
| **GOBLINS PIT CLOSE** | Park Place estate road: Named after 'Goblins Pit' (previously Gobblers Pit) Quarry in Neston, now known as Brocklease Quarry currently used by Wansdyke Security for secure storage. (See Rough Street map below), a 'gobbling pit' is a place where there were 'gobbets' = lumps, especially of raw meat. Celtic 'gob' = mouthful. |
| **GOODES HILL** | Gastard: Named after Goodses Barn which is shown on the Andrews' and Dury's Map of Wiltshire 1810, in the field on the right halfway up the hill. |
| **GORNALL ROAD** | Services Cotswold Centre road: Probably associated with Lieutenant-Commander (S) Admiral's Personal Staff - Flag Lieutenant Commander J. P. 'Gornall'. WWII's HMS Orion's Captain J. P. 'Gornall' R.N. was awarded a DSO in 1945. |
| **GORSE PLACE** | Gorse is a yellow-flowered shrub of the pea family. When the Katherine Park estate designers ran out of Stone Quarry related street names, they simply named the remaining roads after flowers, shrubs or trees.. |
| **GREENHILL** | The 1816 Corsham Tithe Map shows a plot of land called 'Green Field' in Corsham (Ref:969a). Most likely to simply refer to a green and grassy hill. |
| **GREEN ROAD** | Road in Gastard, leading to Octavian: A green lane is a type of road, usually an un-metalled rural route, i.e. most likely to simply refer to a track through a green field. 'Green Lane' = a road along which cattle are driven. See also Greenhill above. |
| **GROUNDSTONE WAY** | Park Place estate road: 'Ground stone' was quarried in Hartham Park and is one of the stones that was used to build the beautiful ancient City of Bath. It weathers beautifully; especially when the stonework is detailed. |

Chapter 2. Area Street and Place Name Origins.

| | |
|---|---|
| **GROVE ROAD** | This road is at the rear of the 'Grove' House garden, which was the Methuen family's Dower House i.e. a moderately large house available for use by the widow of the previous owner of the estate. |
| **GUYERS LANE** | The 1816 Corsham Tithe Map shows Henry Hall Joy as owning a plot of land in that Corsham location named 'Great Guyers' (Ref:1344). <br> The lane leads to Guyers house, built in about 1670 by a Mr Snelling, who named it Snellings. A map of 1773 shows that John Bennett owned the property now called Guyers. Purchased in 1989 by Guy Hungerford. <br> The unusual surname Guyer is of Old French origin, and is a patronymic surname (i.e. derived from the name of a father or ancestor), from "Guyer", an occupational name for a guide, from the Old French 'guyour, guieor', a guide; with the patronymic ending "-s", son of (i.e. a Guide's son). |
| **HARDHAMS RISE** | The 1816 Corsham Tithe Map shows a plot of land called 'Hardhams' in Corsham (Ref:301). <br> Two closes of Corsham pasture land called Hardham and Priors Clift sold in September 1803 at the Red Lion (now Methuen Arms). |
| **HARTHAM LANE** | Home or enclosure of the 'hart' (a male red deer in its sixth year), stag or deer. Known as 'Heort-ham'. Anglo Saxon Heort = stag. <br> Old English word Ham = home. In 1086 it was known as Heortha, 1196 Hortham, 1202 Hertham, 1257 Hurtham. |
| **HASTINGS ROAD** | Named after Frederick 'Hastings' Goldney Lord of the Rector Manor of Corsham, born 26 May 1845 and 71 years a Freemason, (born at Beechfield in Pickwick, Corsham) High Sheriff of Wiltshire in 1908 and Mayor of Chippenham between 1875-1889; he died aged 94 on 21 February 1940. |
| **HATTON WAY** | Queen Elizabeth I retained the lordship of the manor in her own hands for some years, but in 1572 granted among other things the two parks, fish ponds, warrens, and patronage of the church, to her favourite, Sir Christopher Hatton. Shortly after Hatton became so impoverished that he was forced to sell Corsham and other estates. This sale resulted in the Corsham estate coming into the hands of Thomas Smyth and later into the hands of Paul Methuen, in 1745. <br> In the early 1900s the Fuller family also once had an extensive tea estate of 1,030 acres, in the town of 'Hatton', in the Dikoya region of Ceylon (now Sri Lanka), 200 acres of which was inhabited by monkeys, parrots and wild pigs. 'Hatton' is now a town in the Nuwara Eliya District of Central Province of Sri Lanka. |
| **HAZEL WAY** | The 'hazel' (Corylus) is a genus of deciduous trees and large shrubs. When the Katherine Park estate designers ran out of Stone Quarry related street names, they simply named the remaining roads after flowers, shrubs or trees. |
| **HEYWOOD HOUSE** | 'Heaga-wudu' = hedged or fenced woodland. In 1225 known as Heiwode, 1241 Heywud, 1268 Hewode. J Haywood was a tenant on adjacent land (part of the Rectory Manor) which was sold in 1856. |
| **HIGH STREET** | High Street is used to describe a substantial thoroughfare. In Old English, the word '*high*' meant something excellent of its type or of elevated rank or degree. |
| **HILLY FIELDS** | The 1816 Corsham Tithe Map shows a plot of land called 'Hilly Ground' (Ref:7779). Local name that was once given to these fields; now the Valley Road. |
| **HIGHLANDS CLOSE** | Being on top of the hill in Rudloe is very likely to simply mean high land. |
| **HITHERSPRING** | The 1816 Corsham Tithe Map shows Sir Harry Bernard Neale as owning a plot of land in that Corsham location named 'Hither Spring' (Ref:268). <br> Old English 'hider' = being on this or the closer side; nearer: the hither side of the meadow/hill. Spring is a place where groundwater flows out of the ground. John Taylor owned a separate plot called 'Hither Spring' (Ref:848). |
| **HOBBS WALK** | Arthur 'Hobbs'. Corsham saddler, news reporter and fireman for many years. |

Chapter 2. Area Street and Place Name Origins.

| | |
|---|---|
| **HOLLY CRESCENT** | Holly is an evergreen shrub with distinct spiked, glossy leaves. When the Katherine Park estate designers ran out of Stone Quarry related street names, they simply named the remaining roads after flowers, shrubs or trees.. Hollybush Quarry was an old small stone workings in Wadswick Lane, Neston. It closed on 11 December 1902. |
| **HOME MEAD** | There are many field names beginning with 'Home' on the Corsham Tithe Maps, including the 1816 Corsham Tithe Map which shows Abraham Lloyd Edridge as owning a plot of land called 'Home Mead' in Corsham (Ref:388). John Fuller owned a plot of land called 'Homestead'(Ref:686). And another plot was called 'Home Stead' (Ref: 7896). |
| **HORNES MEAD** | Katherine Park; 'Horne' is a Corsham family name. In the High Street in 1875, there was a James Davis 'Horne' who was a Baker and Maltster. |
| **HUDSWELL LANE** | In 1770 was known as Hoodswell. Possibly a well owned by Hudd? In the 1700/1800s there were several families called Hudd who lived near Sandpits. |

## HUDSWELL LANE

| | |
|---|---|
| **HULBERT CLOSE** | William Hulbert = A local cricketer, a local landowner and clothier. |
| **IVY FIELD** | Once a beautiful field used for grazing and no doubt full of ivy! |
| **JACKSON CLOSE** | Named after Arthur Stanley 'Roy' Jackson MBE. Roy chaired the North Wiltshire District Council for seven years (1991-1998) and became a Corsham Parish Councillor in 1967. He was also a Patrol Leader of the Corsham Scouts and helped to start the Over 18's Club. Roy died aged 82 on Monday, August 31 in 2009 at the Royal United Hospital in Bath. He was awarded an MBE for his services to the community in 2000. |
| **JAGGARDS LANE** | Henry 'Jagard' lived there in 1327: 'jaeger' Danish = hunter: May be associated with Flemish immigrant Joseph Marie Jacquard (1752-1834), French weaver and inventor of the Jacquard loom. |
| **JARGEAU COURT** | Corsham town twinned with the town of 'Jargeau' in France in1982. |
| **KATHERINE PARK.** | Believed to be named after 'Katherine' Parr the 6th wife of Henry VIII who would have inherited Corsham House (Court) on her marriage. This area was once known as West Park and was once part of the Corsham Estate. |
| **KIDSTON WAY** | Possibly named after Major George Jardine 'Kidstone' of Hazelbury Manor. b. 25 January 1873, d. 26 December 1954 aged 81. He was invested as a Companion, Order of St. Michael and St. George (C.M.G.) in 1918. |
| **KINGS AVENUE** | Corsham was known as Corsham Regis, and was a Manor in the Queen's Dower. |
| **KINGS LEA AVENUE** | The primary meaning of Lea or leah is 'wood' or clearing in a wood. King's wood-clearing Avenue. |
| **KINNEIR CLOSE** | Named after Septimus 'Kinneir', famous Corsham and England cricketer. |
| **KIRBY ROAD** | Richard 'Kirby', founder of Kirby's Corsham Charity on his death in 1672. |
| **LADBROOK LANE** | Probably derived from the Lud brook. 'Lud' was the Celtic river Gog. Previously called Squillers = Anglo Saxon land put to use by serfs. On parchment, t's often became l's and vice versa, hence also known once as Squitters. |
| **LACOCK ROAD** | The road that takes you from Corsham to Lacock! |
| **LANCEFIELD PLACE** | Jenkins & 'Lancefield', Pickwick, Corsham were specialists in Boat building and repairing. |
| **LANES END** | The west 'end' of the long Folly Lane, Wick Lane connection between the Lacock (A350 road) and Gastard. |
| **LEAFIELD WAY** | Wood field Way. The primary meaning of Lea or leah is 'wood' or clearing in a wood. |

Chapter 2. Area Street and Place Name Origins.

| | |
|---|---|
| **LEAFY LANE** | Woody or clear Way. In recognition of the many tall trees that line each side of this route. Lea or leah is a 'wood' or clearing in a wood. |
| **LEWIS CLOSE** | A stone-quarrying term for a three-pronged shackle. Sometimes called a Lewisson or 'Lewis' Bolt. A lifting device used by stonemasons to insert onto large blocks that enabled them to lift the stone with a crane. |
| **LEYLANDS ROAD** | John 'Leyland' (1506-1552). Known as 'Father of English Local History' who visited Corsham on his travels (1540-1546). He described Corsham as a 'good country town'. |
| **LIGHT CLOSE** | Parish Clerk and Chairman of North Wiltshire District Council William 'Light'. |
| **LIMESTONE DRIVE** | This road is near the old Hudswell 'Limestone' quarry. Bath Stone is an oolitic limestone comprising granular fragments of calcium carbonate. |

# LIMESTONE DRIVE

| | |
|---|---|
| **LOCKS CROSS** | Crossroads at the top of Neston. A 14th century document refers to John Lok who lived at this spot in 1345. The name indicates the place where Willelmus Clericus de Naston preached in the early part of the 15th century. From here, business would be transacted and public proclamations made. *[Ref: Ways of Corsham by John Poulson page 74].* |
| **LONG CLOSE AVENUE** | Possibly named after Henry 'Long' who was murdered 5 October 1594 by the Danvers brothers. The Long's were the first owners of Ridge Far, Neston. See also 'Long Ground' below. |
| **LONG GROUND** | 'Long' was a common field name in Corsham. For example, the 1816 Corsham Tithe Map shows Joseph Freeth as owning a plot of land called 'Long Mead' (Ref: 1116). 'Longlands' was owned by John Fuller (Ref: 366) along with 'Long Ley' (Ref: 578). |
| **LUCAS COURT** | Park Place estate road: Named after 'Lucas' and Allard, the Corsham Quarrying Company (Bath Stone Merchants) who owned Ridge Quarry. William George Allard and Henry Lucas. |
| **LUDMEAD ROAD** | 'Lud' was a Celtic river God. A 'mead' is a meadow. The Ladbrook stream flows nearby. |
| **LYPIATT ROAD** | The 1816 Corsham Tithe Map shows Charles Sheppard as owning a plot of land called 'Lipyeat Leaze' (Ref:285) and Lypiatt Farm is called Lipyeat Farm. Lypiatt is derived from Lepeyate, the "Leap Gate", a low gate in a fence that deer can leap over but not other animals. Leaze = pasture or meadow. |
| **LYPIATT MEAD** | Leapgate Meadow. See above. A 'mead' is a meadow. |
| **MACIE DRIVE** | Katherine Park: Named after Thomas 'Macie' Leir of Jaggards House. |
| **MANOR ROAD** | Corsham was known as Corsham Regis, and was a 'Manor' in the Queen's Dower. |
| **MANSION HOUSE MEWS** | A row of houses next to the 'Mansion House' in Pickwick Road. Mews = a row or street of houses or flats that have been converted from stables or built to look like former stables. |
| **MARSH GROVE** | Park Place estate road: Named after the 'Marsh' Son and Gibbs quarrying company (in Hartham - later Copenacre Quarry) who went bankrupt in 1910. R. J. Marsh Ltd. and Samuel Rowe Noble (along with others) amalgamated to form the Bath Stone Firms Ltd. |
| **MASONS WAY** | Stone 'Masons' - many who have worked in Corsham. |
| **MAYO CLOSE** | Rev. Charles T. 'Mayo' who lived at Ivy House and was a highly respected man in Corsham. He was the first Vice-Chairman of the Parish Council. |
| **MEADLAND** | The 1816 Corsham Tithe Map shows William Hulbert as owning a plot of land called 'Meadland Pasture' (Refs.1319 and 1320). 'Meadlands' was the field name where the Woodlands estate is now. |
| **MERITON AVENUE** | Named after Ernest 'Merrett', a local house builder, carpenter and undertaker. |

## Chapter 2. Area Street and Place Name Origins.

| | |
|---|---|
| **METHUEN WAY** | Named after the Methuen family of Corsham Court. |
| **MIDDLEWICK LANE** | The lane that runs west from the 'middle' of Pick'wick'. |
| **MONKS LANE** | The 'lane' that runs from the B43353 (Corsham to Melksham road) past 'Monks' Chapel. |
| **MONKS PARK GARDENS** | Road that arcs just behind the Monks Park House gardens. The name Monks originates from Henry Monke who married Agnes. She later handed Monkes Park estate to her son William in 1406. |
| **MOOR GREEN BARTON** | 'Mor '= marsh. 'Barton' = farm-yard or rick-yard. Old English 'beretun' = barley farm. This area adjoins Overmoor, previously known as Nethermore - Old English 'nither' = lower. |
| **MOOR PARK** | See Moor Green above. On the site of Moor Park Quarry which closed in 1949. |
| **MOXHAMS** | The 'Moxham' family were once large farmers in the area c1600s. In his will of 1621 William Moxham left £10 'to remain in stoke forever, in the hands of the churchwardens and overseers of the poor'. In 1611, the tenor bell was re-cast and the rest were re-hung on a new frame. Thomas Moxham, the smith, was paid 44s; from which it is not unreasonable to suppose that this bell was re-cast at Corsham by Moxham. In 1606, he lived in BOLTONS, the oldest house in Corsham, dating from the fifteenth century. The house is at the very beginning of the High Street's north end. |
| **NEALE COURT** | Robert 'Neale' built the Mansion House in Pickwick Road 1721-1724. |
| **NESTON** | Village on a hill or headland. A 'naess '= a ness headland. Standing isolated. |
| **NESTON CRESCENT** | A 'crescent' shaped road in Neston! |
| **NEWLANDS ROAD** | The 1816 Corsham Tithe Map shows Ezekiel Hanham as owning the plot of land called 'Newlands' in Corsham (Ref:772). <br> 'New Land' which Henry III gave to his brother Richard Earl of Cornwall. Newlands Road occupies part of this New Land. |
| **NINE ACRE DRIVE** | From an old field named Nine Acre. |
| **NOBLES PLACE** | Park Place estate road: Named after Samuel Rowe 'Noble' of Box who (along with others) amalgamated with Marsh Son and Gibbs to form the Bath Stone Firms Ltd. |
| **NORTHCROFT ROAD** | To the 'north' of Rudloe. 'Croft' = a fenced or enclosed area of land. |
| **NORTHLEAZE** | The 1816 Corsham Tithe Map shows Henry Hall Joy as owning the plot of land called 'North Leaze' in Corsham (Refs:246, 251 and 252). <br> A north field. A 'leaze' is a pasture, pasturage, meadow-land or a common. |
| **NURSERY GARDENS** | Once a 'nursery' garden for the Pritchard family who ran a groceries shop there on Station Road. |
| **OATHILLS** | The 1816 Corsham Tithe Map shows Abraham Lloyd Edridge as owning a plot of land called 'Oathills' in Corsham (Ref:308). Also a field name on the Tithe Award Map of 1838. Possibly where oats were sown on the hillside! |
| **OLD SCHOOL YARD** | Alongside the 'school playground' site of the old Corsham County Primary School, now the Pound Arts Centre on Pound Pill. |
| **OLIVER AVENUE** | Named after 'Oliver' Twist - Charles Dickens character. |
| **OMAR ROAD** | This MoD Services Cotswold Centre road is named after the 'Omar' Chalets made by Omar Park and Leisure Homes (https://www.omar.co.uk/), that replaced the original Hostel Site WWII bungalows in 1991. <br> Note: St Omer is also a French town lying 26 miles south east of Calais, which became the headquarters of the British Expeditionary Force from October 1914 until November 1915. St Omer Barracks is part of the Aldershot Garrison. |

## Chapter 2. Area Street and Place Name Origins.

| | |
|---|---|
| **ORCHARD ROAD** | Gets its name from Cherry 'Orchards' the old allotments site where Light Close is today. In 1944, the Cherry 'Orchards' site was earmarked for the Regis School playing field, but was ploughed up by the Parish Council into allotments to help the war effort. The Regis School playing fields were subsequently constructed on the opposite side of the road from the school. |
| **PADDOCK LANE** | Once the 'paddock' of nearby Hudswell House; i.e. a small enclosure for horses. |
| **PARK LANE** | On the site of Corsham's West 'Park'. |
| **PARTRIDGE CLOSE** | Corsham, particularly on the Hartham Estate, is synonymous for its 'Partridge' Shooting season which runs from 1st September to 1st February. |
| **PAUL STREET** | In honour of Field Marshal 'Paul' Sanford Methuen, 3rd Baron Methuen, GCB, GCMG, GCVO, DL (1 September 1845 – 30 October 1932). |
| **PEEL CIRCUS** | Styled in a circle like 'Peel Circus' in Kensington, London. 'Peel' is a type of *retreat* practiced by modern-day infantry. |
| **PENLEIGH CLOSE** | An enclosed pasture meadow. 'Pen' = to shut into a sty or pen. 'Leigh' = clearing in a wood i.e. a field. |
| **PICKED MEAD** | The 1816 Corsham Tithe Map shows Abraham Lloyd Edridge as owning a plot of land called 'Picked Mead' in Corsham (Ref:339). A 'picked' field is a harvested field. The 1816 Corsham Tithe Map also shows Ann Michell as owning another plot of land called 'Pickled Mead' in Corsham (Ref:344).<br>A 'mead' is a meadow or a fermented beverage traditionally made from honey, water and a yeast or bacterial culture. Sometimes called 'the drink of the gods'. |
| **PICKWICK** | Anglo-Saxon 'pic' = sharp point. Old English 'wic' = dairy farm on a hill (peak). |
| **PICKWICK ROAD** | Charles Dickens character Mr 'Pickwick'. Once known also as 'The Broadway'. |
| **PICTOR CLOSE** | The 'Pictors' came to Corsham in the 1870s and opened up the Monks Pictor Quarry. J Pictor and N M Pictor served on the Parish Council 1917-1922. |
| **PINE CLOSE** | Reference to the nearby Rudloe Firs Wood ('pine' trees) on the north side of the A4 at the top of Box Hill. |
| **PITTS CROFT** | Stothert and 'Pitt' were a British engineering company founded in 1785 in Bath who made quarry cranes and equipment that were used in Corsham. 'Croft' = a fenced or enclosed area of land. |
| **POCKEREDGE DRIVE** | Was the home of Henry de 'Poltrigge' in 1327. Was known in 1346 as Polkerugge. In 1363 as Pockeredge. Pockeredge House is shown on the 1839 Tithe map as Puckeridge House then owned by Abraham Lloyd Edridge. Now known as Pocker**e**dge Drive. |
| **POCKERIDGE ROAD** | See above. The 1816 Corsham Tithe Map shows this area as Puckeridge.<br>**POCKERIDGE ROAD** |
| **POOL GREEN** | There is a pond/pool in the fields south/east of the Pool Green road. |
| **PORTAL AVENUE** | Named after Major R.E. Portal's third son (see photo) Officer Commanding-in-Chief, Bomber Command, Air Marshal Sir Charles Frederick Algernon 'Portal', K.C.B., D.S.O., M.C., who was appointed Chief of Air Staff in 1940.<br><br>Sir Charles originally enlisted in the Royal Engineers as a despatch rider in 1914. On 8 February 1946 he was further honoured when he was made Viscount Portal of Hungerford.<br><br>*Camera portrait by Bertram Park.* |

17

Chapter 2. Area Street and Place Name Origins.

| | |
|---|---|
| **PORTERS MEAD** | Samuel 'Porter', a Corsham Carpenter, who appears in the 1783 Trade Directory. The Church Pew Records of 1786 shows a Deal Wainscot Seat allocated to Samuel Porter of the High Street.<br>Also a field name in the Tything Map of 1848. |
| **PORTLAND RISE** | Refers to the Bath and 'Portland' Stone Company who once employed many men in Corsham. |
| **POST OFFICE LANE** | Once the location of the second Corsham 'Post Office' 1859-1885. |
| **POTLEY LANE** | A path on a hill: Potley was once known as 'Podley' Hill and in 1579, Podley Lane. Also as Podley Herring. A 'herepath' is a military road (literally, an army path). Pod (Danish 'pad' = path). Leigh = clearing in a forest i.e. a field. |
| **POUND MEAD** | See Pound Pill below. |
| **POUND PILL** | A 'pound' is an animal enclosure. 'Pyll' comes from the Middle English word "pile," meaning 'stake,' or 'post'. A pound is where animals could be tied to a stake. Pound Pill was once pronounced locally as 'Pumpill' and 'Pound Pitt' 'pitt' denoted 'pond'. 'Pill' is the old name for a Willow tree. The old (animal) pound which was situated where the present Bowling Club is today. In 1570 the hill was known as 'Wimblesteed'. Wimble was a specific grass for sheep. 'stede' = 'place' in Old English. |
| **POYNDER ROAD** | Named after Sir William Dickson 'Poynder', later Lord Islington who lived in Hartham Park. |
| **PRESTLEY WOOD ROAD** | The 1816 Corsham Tithe Map shows Henry Hall Joy as owning a plot of land called 'Prestley' in Corsham (Ref:1406).<br>Priest's (Prest) clearing (ley). There is a copse called Prestley Wood in the Hartham Estate to the east of Weavern and near Pickwick Lodge Farm. The primary meaning of Ley, Lea or leah is 'wood' or clearing in a wood. |
| **PRIORY STREET** | It is thought that there was once a 'Prior's' Cell in the grounds of Heywood Preparatory School in Priory Street. Corsham 'Priory' was referred to in 1336 as having been given to Marmoutier Abbey during the time of Henry I (1068–1135) as an alien priory. Later a Georgian house was built on the site, which is now part of the Heywood School. |
| **PRIVET WAY** | Privet is a flowering plant in the genus Ligustrum and makes a good hedge! When the Katherine Park estate designers ran out of Stone Quarry related street names, they simply named the remaining roads after flowers, shrubs or trees.. |
| **PROSPECT** | 'Prospect' = a place where the distance can be viewed. |
| **PROVIDENCE LANE** | 'Providence' is the means by which God directs all things - animate and inanimate, seen and unseen, good and evil — toward a worthy purpose, which means His will must finally prevail. Or as the psalmist said, 'his kingdom ruleth over all' (Psalm 103:19). Could be a link to the Corsham Baptists. |
| **PURLEIGH ROAD** | 'Purley', purlieu denotes a copse or a piece of land on the edge of a fringe of a forest. Old French puralee = boundary, border land or land disafforested.<br>The 1816 Corsham Tithe Map shows Ann Michell as owning three plots of land called 'Purleigh Copse' (Ref:299), 'Purleigh Rails' a pasture (Ref:300) and 'Purleigh Barn Yard' (Ref:326) in Corsham.<br>Leigh = tract of land bordering a forest. There was once an ancient Purleigh Barn in the Valley Road area. Previously called Purly Brake on 1828 map. |
| **QUEENS AVENUE** | Corsham was known as Corsham Regis, and was a Manor in the Queen's Dower. |
| **RANDALL COURT** | Park Lane Quarry was opened by quarrymen, 'Randall' and Saunders in 1800. |
| **REA ROAD** | Services Cotswold Centre road. The Royal Engineers Association ('REA') is the Regimental Association of the Royal Engineers. |

Chapter 2. Area Street and Place Name Origins.

| | |
|---|---|
| **REGIS** | Corsham was once known as 'Corsham Regis' due to its reputed association with Anglo-Saxon Ethelred of Wessex. It was often called Corsham Regius (Royal Corsham) or Corsham Reginae (Queen's Corsham). |
| **RIDGE** | Old English 'hrycg' = ridge of the town, or ridgeway. Stands on a prominent Ridge Hill. |
| **ROUGH STREET** | The 1816 Corsham Tithe Map shows Audrey Harvey as owning a plot of land called 'Row Mead' (Ref:1133). William Hulbert is shown as owning 'Rough Street Orchard' (Ref:328).<br>Previously shown on 1810 Andrews' and Dury's Map of Wiltshire, as Row Street. Possibly Old English Rowan = Row. Rowan is a shrub or trees in the genus Sorbus of the rose family. Could be named after the two adjoining fields Great Rowland and Little Rowland adjoining to the west. 'Row' is Anglo-Saxon 'ruh' = rough, uncultivated. |
| **ROWAN LANE** | Rowan Lane travels through woods to Wadswick Green. 'Rowans' are shrubs or trees in the genus Sorbus of the rose family. In Celtic mythology it's known as the Tree of Life and symbolises courage, wisdom and protection. Likely to simply be named as a lane that travels through a wood that includes 'Rowan' trees. |
| **RUDLOE** | A compound of Old English 'hrycg' (ridge) and 'hlaw' (burial mound), i.e. a ridge burial mound or barrow.<br>It lies on a well marked ridge. In 1167 it was known as Riglega. 1249 Ryggelawe or Ridlawe. 1268 Riglawe. 1338 Rydlawe. 1409 Redelawe. 1476 Ridelawe. 1497 Ridlowe. 1713 Rudlow. 1767 Rudlowe otherwise Ridgelow.<br>Previously this area is shown as also being called 'Rudley' on an 1828 map. |
| **SANDOWN CRESCENT** | On the old Royal Naval Stores Depot site opened as Copenacre in 1942, and named after the Navy's 'Sandown' Class of Navy minesweepers. |
| **SANDY LEA AVENUE** | The 1816 Corsham Tithe Map shows William Hulbert as owning a plot of land called 'Sandy Mead' (Ref:1170).<br>Sandy Wood Avenue. The primary meaning of Lea or leah is 'wood' or clearing in a wood. Possibly could simply be 'Sandy wood' Avenue. |
| **SAUNDERS GROVE** | Park Lane Quarry was opened by quarrymen, Randall and 'Saunders' in 1800. |
| **SAVERNAKE ROAD** | Possibly from the Irish name 'sabhrann' = boundary; with a Celtic suffix '-aco'. In WWII, the Royal Army Ordnance Corps (RAOC) used 'Savernake' Forest as an ammunition storage location. Hudswell Tunnel Quarry in Corsham was also a huge ammunition storage facility in WWII. Savernake Road was used in WWII to carry ammunition from the Box Tunnel (Pockeredge Drive) entrance up to the Hudswell Laboratories for testing. |
| **SAWYERS CRESCENT** | A 'sawyer' (occupation) is someone who saws wood, an important job in Corsham's underground quarries. |
| **SHEARWATER WAY** | Near Potley. Anglo Saxon 'scir' or 'scire' and English 'sheer' water = Clear water. Shearwater Way, is close to Spring Lane in Westwells.<br>'Shearwater' is the name of a lake in Crockerton.<br>Shearwaters are also medium-sized long-winged seabirds.<br>In Canada, there is a Royal Canadian Naval Air Station called (RCNAS Shearwater). |

Chapter 2. Area Street and Place Name Origins.

| | |
|---|---|
| **SHEFFIELD LANE** | The Depot Commandant, of the Hudswell Corsham Ammunition Depot (CAD) in WWI was Colonel J. 'Sheffield', R.A.O.C., a former Olympic hurdler. |
| **SHEPPARDS** | Neston: 1835 Walter 'Sheppard', residing in Corsham (priest). Or c.1827-1835 Charles Sheppard part-owner of the Pickwick Brewery. Or Frank Sheppard who in the 1940s and 50s was building trolleys on which huge blocks of stone were transported at the Bath and Portland stone yard in Corsham. His obituary in 1955 said that he had worked for some 34 years as a valued employee of the Bath and Portland Stone Firms Ltd. He lived in Bay Cottage in Elley Green.<br>E.H. Sheppard, F.G. Sheppard and T.S. Sheppard were all members on the Corsham Parish Council at different times. |
| **SILMAN CLOSE** | Connection with the stone quarries. Named after Julias 'Silman', of Courtlands, Lacock Road who passed away 3 February 1998. Julius set up 'The Julius Silman Charitable Trust'. |
| **SILVER STREET** | Associated - 'Silver Street' rises over Beggars Hill, passes the 'Treasury' field and continues up 'Shilling' Lane to Lacock. |
| **SOUTH STREET** | Street to the 'south' of Corsham leading to the old Corsham Station. |
| **SKYNET DRIVE** | 'Skynet' is a family of commercially managed military communications satellites operated on behalf of the Ministry of Defence. Managed by Airbus Defence & Space establishment in Skynet Drive at the end of Park Lane. |
| **SMITHS YARD** | Named after the 'Smiths' who owned the land and had a Hardware shop that fronted the High Street. Now 'Previous Homewares of Corsham'. |
| **SOUTHCROFT ROAD** | A 'south croft'. Croft = a fenced or enclosed area of land. |
| **SOUTHERWICKS** | A southern dairy farm or dwelling place. Old English 'wick' or 'wic' = a dwelling place, grange or dairy farm. |
| **SPACKMAN LANE** | Named after the well-known local 'Spackman' family famous for postcard photos of Corsham and a grocery business in the High Street. |
| **SPRINGFIELD CENTRE** | In Beechfield Road: Probably once a 'field' with a 'spring'. |
| **SPRINGFIELD CLOSE** | In Rudloe: Presumably once another 'field' with a 'spring'. |
| **SPRING GARDENS** | Alongside Heywood House near the large back garden pond and old spring. |
| **SPRING LANE** | Westwells: An area with many 'springs and wells'. |
| **STATION ROAD** | Leading to the old Corsham Railway 'Station'. |
| **ST BARBARAS ROAD** | Near Basil Hill Barracks. 'St Barbaras' was an early Christian Greek saint and martyr. The road is possibly named after the St. Barbara Barracks, Army Land, Barracks, Mess, Accommodation, Stores, Amenities in Neidersachsen, in Germany. There is an Army Garrison Church called 'St Barbara', in Deepcut Bridge Road, Deepcut, Surrey. |
| **STOKES ROAD** | Known as Pound Pill Mead Lane in 1770. Named after builder William 'Stokes' who lived in South Street (listed in the 1881 census). There was once a Keary 'Stokes' and White Solicitors office at 36 High Street. |
| **STONE CLOSE** | Near Hartham Quarry where the quarried Bath Stone was stacked up high! |
| **STOWELL LANE** | Old English 'stow-welle' = a dwelling house near a spring or stream. |
| **SUMMERLEAZE** | The 1816 Corsham Tithe Map shows Abraham Lloyd Edridge as owning a plot of land called 'Summer Leaze' in Corsham (Ref:331).<br>A 'leaze' is a pasture, pasturage, meadow-land or a common. |
| **SUMSIONS DRIVE** | Monks park quarry started its life under the name of 'Sumsions' Monks or Monks North as it was started in 1886 by Sumsions as a Bath Stone quarry. |
| **SWAN ROAD** | A small Brewery and Ale House known as the 'Swan Inn' once stood at 'Greystones' opposite the 'Hare & Hounds' in Pickwick. |

## Chapter 2. Area Street and Place Name Origins.

| | |
|---|---|
| **SYON CLOSE** | Corsham Church once paid revenues and rent to the St. Saviour and St.Bridget of 'Syon' Abbey in Middlesex, founded by King Henry V; a demolished monastery of the Bridgettine Order founded in 1415 which stood until the 16th century on the north bank of the Thames. See also 'Bellott Drive'. |
| **TASKER CLOSE** | The Corsham Station Hotel was managed by several members of the Tasker family for a total of 44 years until its demise in 1962. *[George Tasker 1918-1938: Sydney Tasker 1938-1946: Mrs Winifred Tasker 1946-1952: Kenneth Tasker c.1952-1962].* |
| **TAWNEY CLOSE** | Neston: The 'Tawny' Owl is a species that favours woodland habitats, but it may also breed in larger rural and suburban gardens.<br>Tawney is a brownish-orange to light brown colour. The Bullfinch is sometimes called a Tawny. |
| **TEDDER AVENUE** | Rudloe: Marshal of the Royal Air Force Arthur William 'Tedder', 1st Baron Tedder, GCB (11 July 1890 – 3 June 1967) was a senior Royal Air Force Commander. |
| **TELLCROFT CLOSE** | The 1816 Corsham Tithe Map shows William Hulbert as owning a plot of land called 'Tell Croft' (Ref:372).<br>'Tillcroft was the name of a field on the Tithe Award Map of 1838.<br>Till = to prepare land. Croft = a fenced or enclosed area of land. |
| **THE CLEEVE** | Cleeve = a steeply sloping area of ground; a steep hillside. Previously known as 'Prior's Clift', and was part of the ancient Pilgrims' route from Glastonbury to Malmesbury, via the Ridge. |
| **THE CLOSE** | Simply a residential street in Gastard without through access. |
| **THE CRESCENT** | Small part-circle of houses on the junction of Dicketts Road and the B3353. |
| **THE KNOWLE** | On the Valley Road estate: The name 'Knowle' is derived from the Saxon 'Cnolle' which means a small hill. |
| **THE LAGGER** | The 1816 Corsham Tithe Map shows Paul Methuen as owning a plot of land called 'Stumps Laggar' (Ref:1315).<br>From the field name 'Leggan Ground' (High German 'Laggar', meaning enclosed paddock used for sheep). 'lag' = Anglo Saxon word for 'stave' for penning up sheep. |
| **THE LINLEYS** | Anglo Saxon 'lin' = flax, the fibres that are woven into linen. Leigh = field. |
| **THE PRECINCT** | Built in1973. 'Precinct' = a space enclosed by walls or other boundaries. |
| **THE TYNINGS** | Derived from the meaning to 'enclose with a hedge or fence; to fence, to hedge in' given for the verb 'tine' or 'tyne'. A field name: 'Tyning', Tyn (enclosure) +ing (Marshy).<br>There was once a beerhouse called the Tyning Inn associated with the nearby Mansion House. There is a copse called Tyning Wood in the Hartham Estate to the east of Weavern. |
| **THINGLEY** | An assembly clearing place. Old English 'Ting' = a place for 'assembly' . 'leah' = forest clearing. Maybe, once an early Saxon settlement. Known in 1275 as Thingele, in 1289 Tyngle, and in 1332 Thyngele. |
| **TOGHILL CRESCENT** | Rudloe: 'Toghill' is a common surname around Corsham.<br>From toga, 'cloack' or 'mantle'. It started being used by thieves and vagabonds with the noun togman, which was an old slang word for 'cloack'.<br>By the 1700s the noun 'tog' was used as a short form for 'togman', and it was being used for 'coat', and before 1800 the word started to mean 'clothing'. |
| **TRAFALGAR CLOSE** | On the old Royal Naval Stores Depot site opened as Copenacre in 1942, and named after the Navy's 'Trafalgar' Class of Navy submarines. |
| **TRAMWAYS** | Tram lines taking Bath Stone from various Corsham quarries to the Corsham Station stone wharf ran along this street. |

Chapter 2. Area Street and Place Name Origins.

| | |
|---|---|
| **TRENCHARD AVENUE** | Marshal of the Royal Air Force Hugh Montague 'Trenchard', 1st Viscount Trenchard, GCB, OM, GCVO, DSO (3 February 1873 – 10 February 1956) was a British officer who was instrumental in establishing the Royal Air Force. Following his funeral at Westminster Abbey on 21 February, his ashes were buried in the Battle of Britain Chapel he helped to create. Trenchard's viscountcy passed to his son Thomas. He has been described as the Father of the Royal Air Force. *Photo shows Trenchard in RAF full dress c.1930* |
| **TROPENELL CLOSE** | Thomas 'Tropenell' JP - built Great Chalfield Manor in c. 1480. The Lady Chapel at St. Bartholomew's church was rebuilt by Thomas Tropenell. |
| **TROUT LANE** | Major F.G. 'Trout' Royal Engineers, Springside, Strenic Corsham.<br>Under the ground nearby, approximately eighty feet below ground, there was a massive underground lake which once had huge 'trout' in at the time of the WWII Burlington Bunker. |
| **TUPMAN ROAD** | Charles Dickens character in Pickwick Papers - Mr Tracy 'Tupman'. |
| **VALLEY ROAD** | Before its existence, the fields there were known as Slippery Jims, or the Hilly Fields. An area also once popular with winter sledging! |
| **VELLEY HILL** | Was near a field named 'Velley Close'. 'Velley' House was named from it. On on the 1810 Andrews' and Dury's Map of Wiltshire it was called 'Baggers Hill'. |
| **WADSWICK LANE** | Waeddes-wic = 'Waedda's outlying farm or dairy'. 'Wick' = a town, hamlet, or small district, or a dairy farm. c1200 it was known as Wadeswica, 1288 Waddiswyke, 1310 Waddeswyk and in 1623 Wadsick. |
| **WANSDYKE** | 'Woden's dyke' or Grim's ditch. Associated with the god Woden, the Chief or King of the Anglo-Saxon gods. He also had the nickname of 'Grim'. Known in 903 as wodnes dic. 1073 wondesdich. 1259 Wodenesdiche. 1563 Wansdiche. 1670 Wensditch. 1819 Wansditch. |
| **WASTFIELD** | William 'Wastfield' lived in Pickwick Manor House in 1639. His family came to Corsham in the latter years of Queen Elizabeth and gradually acquired a considerable estate in the manor. From the 1500s to the end of the 1700s there had been 46 people with the surname Wastfield in Corsham. There were also several more families named Wasfield, Wasfill, Wastfeild, Wastfeld and Wasfild! |
| **WATERHOLE AVENUE** | Park Place estate road: Named after the 'Waterhole' quarry opened by Pictor and Sons in 1855-1856 just west of Spring Lane, Corsham. This was part of (east) Spring Quarry and was also known as 'No.7 Corsham'. It soon became known as Waterhole as it was wet and tended to flood. |
| **WEIR HEYES AVENUE** | A 'weir' is Old English 'wer' from 'werian', dam-up. An enclosure of stakes set in a stream as a trap for fish, or a barrier of sticks across a flow of water. 'Hayes' is a piece of ground enclosed with a live hedge. A 'hey', is a hedge or enclosure. Possibly originally the site of a weir by a hedge. |
| **WELLER ROAD** | Charles Dickens character in Pickwick Papers - Sam 'Weller'. |
| **WESTWELLS ROAD** | The 1816 Corsham Tithe Map shows this area to be called 'Westrells' (field No's 360-369). Elle = source of natural spring water. A spring in the west of Corsham. Possibly once the home of Walter de Westwell. |
| **WEST PARK ROAD** | The 1816 Corsham Tithe Map shows Ann Michell as owning a plot of land called 'West Park Barn Yard' (Ref:343).<br>This area was once known as West Park, part of the Corsham Estate. |
| **WESTROP** | A west hamlet: 'Thorp' is a Middle English word for a hamlet or small village, from Old English (Anglo-Saxon)/Old Norse þorp (also thorp). |

## Chapter 2. Area Street and Place Name Origins.

| | |
|---|---|
| **WHITE ENNOX LANE** | In Boxfields and named after 'Ennox' wood nearby to the west, that sits right on top of Box Tunnel. Once locally known as Hinocks. In 1258 was Innok, 1549 Innox, in 1623 a close called Innockes. In the 13th and 14th centuries, the name 'Innox' refers to fallow land temporarily brought into cultivation. 'Inhok' was a medieval process of 'in-hooking', i.e. hooking or bringing fallow land into cultivation. *[Ref: 'The Placenames of Wiltshire', 1939 by EB Gover, Allen Mawer, and FM Stenton pages 86 and 134].* The large wood on the left as you approach Box downhill on the A365 Devizes Road is called 'White' Wood. Whitewood is any of various trees having soft light-coloured wood, such as tulip trees or fir/spruce trees. |
| **WILLIAMS GROVE** | Named after Mrs Annie 'Williams' a Corsham Labour Parish Councillor post WWII. |
| **WILLOW CRESCENT** | A 'Willow' is a tree or shrub of temperate climates which typically has narrow leaves, bears catkins, and grows near water. When the Katherine Park estate designers ran out of Stone Quarry related street names, they simply named the remaining roads after flowers, shrubs or trees.. |
| **WOODBOROUGH ROAD** | The 1816 Corsham Tithe Map shows the Great Western Railway as owning a plot of land here called 'Woodboroughs' (Ref:927b). <br> Wudu-beorg = 'wooded hill, mound or barrow'. In 1208 the name Woodborough was known as Wideberghe, c1220 Wodeberg, 1241 Wudeberg, 1277 Wodebore, 1278 Wodebore, and 1596 Woodborough. Dr. Arthur George Wood of Corsham's The Porch surgery in the High Street was one of the medical officers in the Corsham WWI Town Hall Hospital in the early 1900s. |
| **WOODLANDS** | This area lies alongside the old fir-tree lined Beechfield House carriage-drive that led from opposite Pickwick House on the A4 up to Beechfield House. |
| **YEW WAY** | 'Yew' is an evergreen conifer native to the UK. When the Katherine Park estate designers ran out of Stone Quarry related street names, they simply named the remaining roads after flowers, shrubs or trees.. |
| **YOCKNEY CLOSE** | Augustus 'Yockney' was a stone merchant in Corsham. The Yockneys, together with Randall and Sunders, and Pictors, amalgamated to become the 'Bath Stone Firms'. Augustus YOCKNEY of Pockeredge died 23 April 1892. |
| **YORK CLOSE** | The small Close leading to the Regis School. Bath Stone is the limestone under Corsham, but there are other limestones such as Portland, 'York' and Cotswold etc. The 'York' class was the second and final class of 8-inch (203 mm)–gunned heavy cruisers built for the Royal Navy; linked to Corsham via Copenacre. |

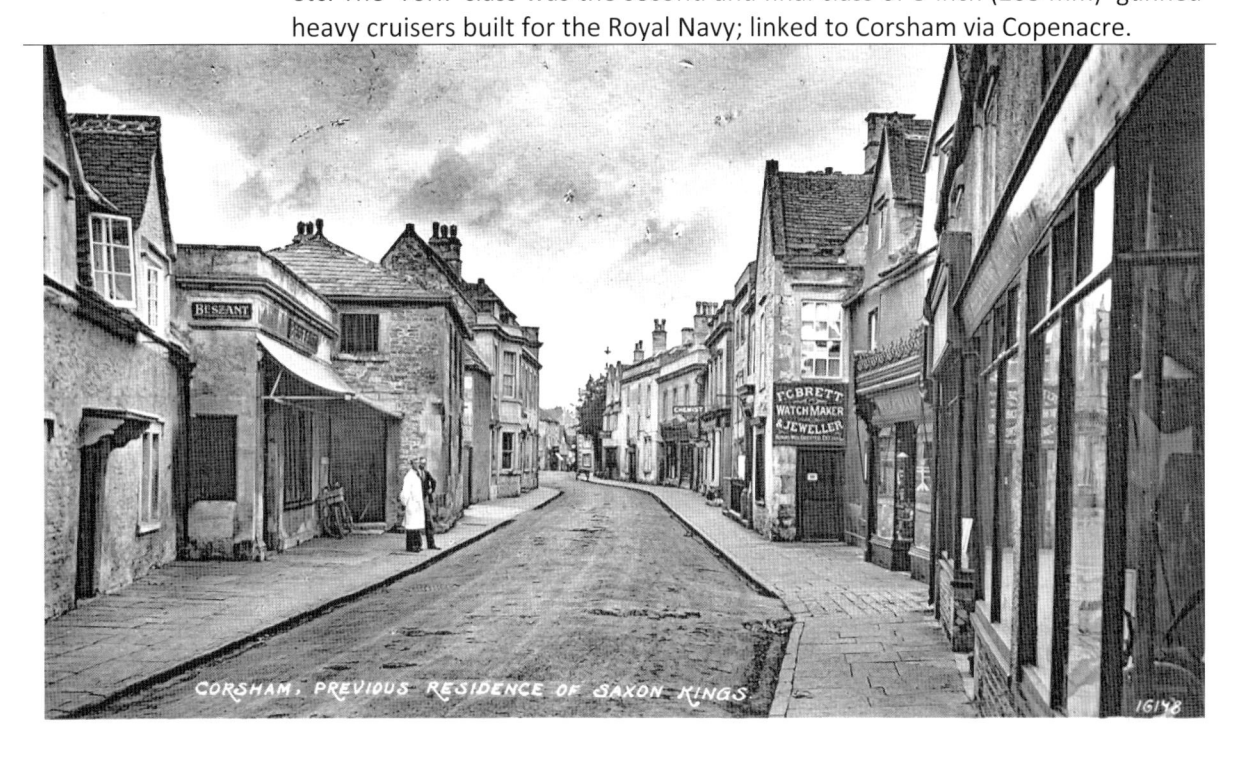

CORSHAM, PREVIOUS RESIDENCE OF SAXON KINGS

# Chapter 3. Around and About Corsham

The history of Corsham is a wonderful place to visit - but it must have been a terrible time to live in!

Below are a collection of mini-stories that were reported in the newspapers about Corsham in the hundred years between 1761-1861 when the very first news reports about Corsham appeared. This will give you an idea of what life was like in those far off days.

The first official census of 1801 showed Corsham as having 2,402 inhabitants. We were a very small town then, with very few houses compared to the number of houses today. Everybody knew everybody, so it was difficult for law-breakers to remain anonymous for long! *Enjoy:*

**1761: PEAL OF BOBS.** On Thursday 23 July, was rung at Corsham, in the County of Wilts, (by the young Ringers of this City) a complete Peal of 720 Plain Bobs, being the first Time of its being performed there.

**1762: MILK ASSES.**

Possibly the first Corsham advert to appear in a newspaper.

*Two fresh milk asses!*

> To be Sold,
> Two fresh MILCH ASSES,
> With FOALS about 3 Weeks old.
> Enquire at the Hare-and-Hounds at PICKWICK, near CORSHAM, Wilts.

**1769: BLOWS ON THE HEAD. Monday 3 July:** This could be one of the first Corsham crimes to be recorded in a newspaper………. 'A few days since the driver of a wagon belonging to Daniel Wyatt, of Corsham, near Bath, was attacked near the Turnpike at Walcot by two fellows, one of whom held the fore horse by the head, whilst the other knocked the driver down with a hedge-stake, and gave him several dangerous blows on the head, after which they robbed him of 25s *[approx £50 in today's money]* which was all the money he had.'

**1772: CHEAPER THAN THEY CAN BREW IT.** To be SOLD exceedingly Cheap, A Quantity of STRONG BEER, just fit to be moved. Any person willing to purchase the same, or any Part, by the Hogshead, may depend on having it cheaper than they can brew it. For Particulars, enquire of Mr Simon Collett, Distiller, in Horse-Street Bath; or of Jeffery Holliday, in Corsham.

**1777: CORSHAM GRAMMAR - SCHOOL. WANTED**, now or at Michaelmas next, a WRITING MASTER. Apply personally, or by specimen (post paid) to the Rev. Mr Page.

**1781: FIRST ADVERT.** Possibly the first Corsham Shop advert to appear in a newspaper. CORSHAM, Wilts. RICHARD HANCOCK, from Bristol, begs leave to acquaint his friends and the public, that he has just opened a large and commodious shop at Corsham, (near the centre of the town,) where he has laid in a fresh and valuable assortment of Linen-Drapery, Haberdashery, Hosiery, and Millinery Goods, of the newest and genteel patterns, which he is determined to sell wholesale and retail on the most reasonable terms. Fine Teas, Coffee, Chocolate, and all kinds of Grocery. Also a large and commodious Dining-Room with genteel Lodgings to let. No objection to a small family by the year.

## Chapter 3. Around and About Corsham

**1787: BELL INN CORSHAM.** CORSHAM, April 22. TO be LETT, and entered upon immediately, or at Midsummer next. A good-accustomed PUBLIC- HOUSE, called the BELL INN, situated in the Market-place in Corsham, now in the occupation of Edward Fricker, who intends quitting business. The stock and fixtures, with any part of the household furniture to be taken at a fair appraisement. For particulars, enquire of Edward Fricker, at the Bell Inn aforesaid.

**1801: ROBBERY ON THE BRADFORD ROAD.** On Saturday night 13 June, between 2 and 3 o-clock, a most daring robbery was attempted in the road between Bradford *[on-Avon]* and Corsham. One of the labourers has been generally dispatched every Saturday by the Surveyor of Mr Methuen's improvements, at Corsham, to the Bradford Bank, for money to pay the workmen. On this messenger's return, in a lane betwixt Wraxall and Atworth, he perceived a man sitting upon a gate, with his coat and waistcoat off, and his cravat tied all over his face, who on his approach jumped from the gate, and demanded his money. The labourer declared that he was a poor man, and had no money about him. The thief replied he knew better, and swore that he would have it, and immediately snapped a pistol at him, which luckily missed fired. This gave the trusty messenger courage, and thinking his breeches pocket not the best place of security for the bills he had about him, clenched them fast in his fist, and said, that he would lose his life sooner than would part with them. Being both well armed with sticks, in single opposition hand to hand they did contend for the best part of an hour; at last the robber, who was by far the stronger man, brought his opponent to the ground. Still the honest fellow held firm his treasure, and as a double security, placed his hand under his back, and whilst the villain was beating him unmercifully, with his other hand he tore the cravat from off his face, which was covered with blood; the inhuman rascal, fearing then he should be known, took to his heels, leaving his cravat and bludgeon behind him. Thus after a hard struggle the poor man got to Corsham where Mr Methuen gave him a guinea; and who, we understand, means to do something further for him as reward for his courage and fidelity.

**HOUSE TO LETT.** A Modern built HOUSE, in Church-Street, in the town CORSHAM, in the county WILTS, late in the occupation of Mr Stansfield Davis; consisting of two parlours in front, a china-closet, kitchen, and other useful offices, on the ground-floor; a good drawing-room, two bed-chambers, and light closet, on the first floor; four bed-chambers on the attic story, with garrets over them; and an-under-ground cellar; together with a coach-house, and stable for two horses. For particulars apply to Mr H Browne Corsham House. *[Ed. Very likely to be Ethelred House].*

**MANSION HOUSE SCHOOL.** A most eligible Situation for Young Gentlemen at School. THE Rev. RICHARD WEAVER, Master of the Boarding-School, Chippenham, Wilts, having taken a lease at that desirable Mansion-House at Corsham, in the same county, many years occupied as a Ladies' Boarding-School, and late in the possession of Mrs Evans, begs leave to inform his Friends and the Public, that he intends removing thither on about the July next, where he hopes to experience continuance of that patronage and support, which discerning people never withhold from persevering assiduity in, and unremitting attention to, so important a charge as the Care and Education of Youth. *[Ed: Let's hope he's not the one who teaches English lessons!].* Mr Weaver died 3 years later in July 1804.

**MURDER ON THE CHIPPENHAM ROAD.** Charles Rudman, one of the four felons executed on Tuesday night, in front of Fisherton Gaol *[in Devizes]* for sheep-stealing, confessed to Mr Waight, the keeper of the Gaol, that he had stolen great numbers sheep, calves, &c. and had been many years habituated to those evil acts. It should appear also that he had been concerned in deeds more enormously wicked; for he enquired of the Turnkey if he had heard of the murder of a servant girl, about two years since, between Chippenham and Corsham? (Such circumstance actually took place; the young woman alluded to was servant to a farmer at Corsham, had been at Chippenham market with butter, and was returning with the produce, about 18s. when she was robbed and murdered, supposed by men then working on the Canal, but every effort to discover the murderers was fruitless.) The Turnkey asked him if he wished to unburthen his mind; and Mr Waight, on learning what had passed, strenuously urged him to do so, and make all possible reparation to society for the act; but he said the murder was not committed by him, though *he knew who did it,* and he afterwards peremptorily declined saying anything further on the subject.

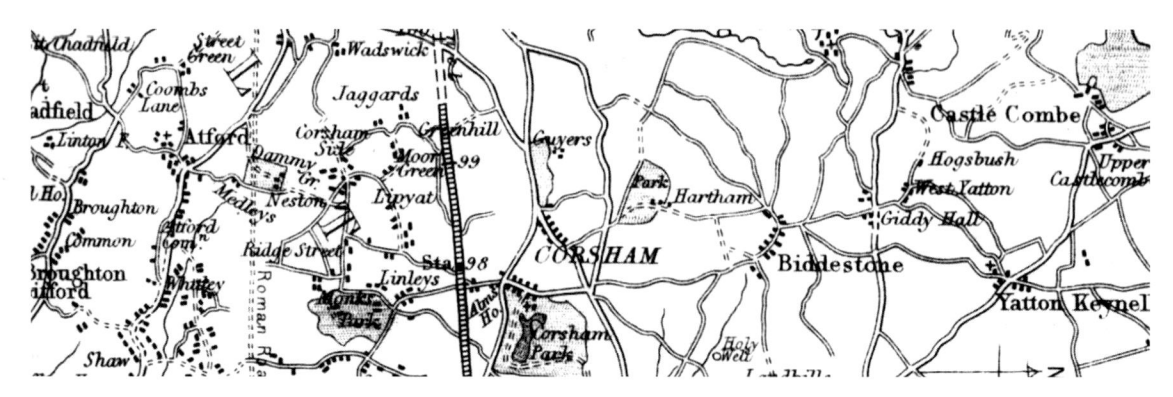

**NESTON PARK FARM SALE.** TO be SOLD by PRIVATE CONTRACT. - The above FARM, which is situated in the several parishes of Corsham and Atford *[Atworth - see 1860 map above]*, in the county Wilts, and consists of a remarkable good, strong, well-built, and roomy Farm-house, with extraordinary large Barns, Stables, and other convenient Out-houses, all in the most thorough repair with 153 acres Arable Land and 135 acres of Meadow and Pasture, and Right of Feeding on Atford Common without stint, all exonerated from Land-tax, and the whole Tithe-free (except about twelve acres thereof in Atford parish), and in the occupation of Farmer Joseph Taylor.

Note. There is an Aisle for burial, and a large Pew or Gallery in Corsham Church, belonging to this Estate, and nearly 140 acres of the land called the Park, may easily be made a Paddock for Deer, as it is already bounded by a high wall, and in about the centre of it is a most charming beautiful spot for a Mansion House, &c. to be built thereon, which would be well supplied with good water, and would command enchanting prospects of the near and distant country: the whole of the Land lies on an easy declivity *[a downward slope]* to the South, is within a ring fence, particularly dry and healthy, surrounded with most excellent good roads, and is in a very desirable and genteel neighbourhood. Plenty of Stone and Tile are to be found on part of the Premises for building, and the Estate is well stored with Timber. Neston is about eight miles East from Bath, five from Bradford [on-Avon], four from Melksham, and two from Corsham; all market-towns

**1804: WESTWELLS FARM SALE.** TO be LETT by AUCTION, Wednesday the 11th day of July next, at the Pack-Horse Inn, Corsham between the hours of three and five in the afternoon, by HARRY RUSS, free from Great Tythes (subject such conditions as will then be produced). - A most desirable ESTATE, called WEST-WELLS FARM, eligibly situated in the parish of Corsham; consisting of a very convenient Farm-house, with suitable barns, stables, and outhouses, and about 93 acres of arable land, and 64 acres of pasture. The Premises are now in the occupation of Henry Hopkins, who will permit the same to be viewed. - Possession may be had at Lady-day next *[25 March the feast of the Annunciation]*. Further particulars may be known on application to Mr Stump, Corsham, or Mr Merewether, Solicitor, Calne.

**1807: FAT COWS LOST!** CORSHAM, WILTS. LOST: Supposed to be STOLEN, on Saturday the 19th of September, from a field of Mr Taylor's, near Corsham,—Three FATTING COWS, of the Long Horned breed, one of them seven years, the other two older, of a White colour mixed with Brown spots, and Brown ears. Whoever will give information of the said cows, or bring the same to the said Mr Taylor, if strayed, shall be handsomely rewarded for their trouble: if stolen, whoever wilt detain the same, and give such information as may be the means of bringing the offender or offenders to justice, shall receive TEN GUINEAS on conviction *[£700 in today's money!]*, by applying to John Pritchard, of Corsham aforesaid.

**1808: SINGULAR ANIMAL.** Farmer Granger, of Westrip *[Westrop]* near Corsham, has a calf, now about six weeks old which has but three legs. The forelegs are perfect, but there is only one behind which, however serves him to walk with as much freedom as he had possessed the other!

**1810: LUNACY.** On Monday night, a young woman of the name of Elizabeth Davies put an end to her moral existence, by hanging herself in her friend's house at Biddestone St. Nicholas near Corsham. She was betrothed to a Corsham man in the neighbourhood, to whom she was to have been married on the following morning; but it is supposed that her affections being engaged to another, led her to commit the fatal act. An inquest was taken, and after a minute investigation, the Jury returned a verdict of Lunacy.

**STABBING.** On Wednesday 19 July, Mr Green, Coroner, held an inquest on the body of Thomas Morgan, who had that morning died, in fact of a liver complaint, - Verdict - *Died by the visitation of God*. Morgan was tried and convicted at the last Lent Assizes, under Lord Ellenborough's Act, for stabbing James Stewart, at Corsham, with a dirk, which had nearly deprived him of life. He had the sentence of death passed on him, but was respited during his Majesty's pleasure.

**BATH TO CHIPPENHAM COACH.** New COACH from BATH through CORSHAM to CHIPPENHAM, every Day. J. FOWLE respectfully informs his friends that on the 5th of December 1810, he began running a COACH every day from BATH through CORSHAM to CHIPPENHAM; which will set out every Afternoon, at Half past Four o'clock, from the SARACEN'S HEAD INN, BATH, and arrive at a Quarter before Seven every evening at the ROSE and CROWN INN, Chippenham; set out the next morning at Eight o'clock and arrive [back] at Bath at a quarter after ten. After the 1st March, it will not start from Bath before Half past five o'clock in the evening. Parcels taken in at the above places. J.FOWLE begs to say that every attention will be paid to the accommodation of those who may honour him with their support, and their favours will be most thankfully received. He also assures them that the utmost care and attention will be paid to the delivery of parcels, &c. FARE. - Inside, 4s: Outside, 2s 6p. *[Ed: Phew, and we still complain about the bus times now!]*

**1812: PACKHORSE INN, CORSHAM.** WHEREAS a BROWN Stallion HORSE was left in my stables some time in June by Mr John Millington; since which a very considerable expense has been incurred in the keep of the said horse, and attendance on him. Now I do duly give notice to the said John Millington, and all others whom it may concern, that if the said Horse is not taken from my stables, and all expenses paid on or before the 29th day January next I shall cause the said Horse to be Sold by public Auction, at the White Hart Inn, Chippenham, on Saturday the 30th day of January next, in order to pay all such expenses. REUBEN TANNER, Pack-Horse, Corsham Dated this 29th day of December 1812.

**1813: WHEAT WITHOUT SOWING!** The following statement has been handed to us by a Correspondent who pledges himself for its veracity: *"There is now growing in a field belonging to Mr Pocock, of Corsham side, as fine a crop of Wheat as can be seen, without either ploughing or sowing! The same piece of* *ground produced an abundant crop of wheat last year, and nothing has been done to the field since the crop was cut!! and there is a prospect as great a quantity to be had on the same ground this year!!! This productive seed was bought by Mr J. Edwards at the Moor farm, near Corsham, Wilts."*

.........................[Ed: Sounds like too much of a corny story to believe!]

**1814: PLUM PUDDING A PLENTY.** The poor inhabitants of Corsham to the number of nearly 1,800 were amply regaled in Mr Methuen's spacious avenue on the 4th July with roast beef, plum pudding, and strong beer, by a subscription raised amongst the gentlemen and other residents of the parish.

**1815: BODY IN POND.** An inquest was held at Corsham on 1 May on the body of Charity Richards, found drowned in a pond. Verdict: Insanity.

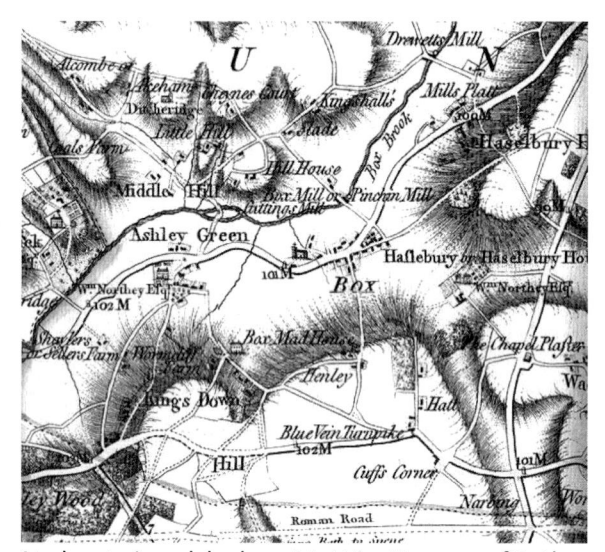

**SHOCKERWICK ROBBERY.** On the evening of Saturday the 21st October between seven and eight o'clock, as Mr John Wilton, junior was returning to Box from the city of Bath, he was stopped by three men, on the top of Shyler's-hill *[Shaylers Hill runs from Shockerwick to Ashley near Box]*, who dragged him from his horse, and after severely beating him, robbed him of £7 (over £400 in today's money).

The fellows then proceeded towards Bath, but afterwards turned into a lane leading to Shockerwick, where they had left some asses. In this lane they concealed themselves.

At about nine o'clock, as Mr Win. Hooper, of Bath, was returning from Shockerwick and passed the spot, one of the robbers knocked him down with a bludgeon; the other two then rifled his pockets, taking from him 4s. The villains were apprehended on Tuesday, and after an examination at the Guildhall *[in Bath]*, they were committed for trial. One of them has made a full confession. The names of the prisoners are Thomas and John Norris, from the vicinity of Corsham, and James Edwards, of Calne; they are well-known characters, who wander about the roads with asses, pretending to sell sand, &c. John Norris has been out of gaol scarcely three months. Great praise is due to Thomas Shell, a constable, of Box; Thomas Wilton (who was robbed), James Wilton, and Charles Webb, of Shockerwick; who went together on Sunday morning in pursuit of the fugitive offenders, whom they succeeded in apprehending, one at Calne, and the others in the vicinity of Corsham.

**1821: KILLED BY A ROD OF IRON.** On 28 Thursday at Hartham House, George, son of Mr Dunsden, plumber and glazier, of Corsham, being engaged in repairing the pipe at the bottom of a well about 140 feet deep, took down with him an iron rod 10 feet long; but finding in the descent, that he had the wrong end of it downwards, and the space not being sufficient to allow of turning it, he requested that it might be drawn up. On its being returned to him, the string slipped, and the rod fell a distance of 90 feet, and the point of it entered his shoulder, passed through the lungs, and came out at the kidneys. The sufferer uttering a heavy groan, cried *"Pull up!"* which was immediately done; and he had the presence of mind to hold the bar perpendicularly in his hand till he reached the top. Medical aid was immediately procured; but it was one hour and a half before the bar could be extricated, which it was found necessary to saw it at its entrance into the body, in order draw to it out at the side. The young man was then conveyed home and on Saturday evening he died.

## Chapter 3. Around and About Corsham

**1822: DOUBLE-SNAP.** On Thursday 21 February Mr John Truebody, returning to Corsham from Bath fair, fell from his horse, and broke his thigh. He was taken to the Casualty Hospital. It is a remarkable coincidence, that on that very day twelve months ago, he met with an exactly similar accident, on his return from the same fair.

**1823: POOR SHOT.** On the 5 September, Phebe Aust, of Corsham, was crossing a field near Pickwick, in order to glean some corn, she received the contents of a fowling-piece from a company of unskilful sportsmen Corsham, who were illegally sporting in the field, which passed through her right hand, left arm, and under her left eye, and wounded her in the breast. She was much maimed, that it will be a long time before she can recover.

**THE GREAT STORM OF 30 October.** The storm of Thursday night seems to have swept from north to south, the whole western coast of our island from Scotland to Cornwall, some parts laying entirely open to its fury. In Corsham, upwards of 200 trees were blown down, and chimney-stacks and out houses were much injured. In short, the whole tract of North Wiltshire, extending from Devizes to Cirencester, appears to have been the scene of the greatest violence and destruction. On Friday morning there was not a road that was passable; the whole country was blocked up.

**1824: TAKE YOUR COAT SIR?** A few days since a man called at the George Inn, Corsham for refreshment; at the same time a traveller was enquiring of the company how to extract some paint from his great coat, which was a valuable one; The person above alluded to offer his services, which were accepted; he then went out of the house to perform the operation, but immediately decamped with the coat, and without paying his bill.

**HAIL CORSHAM.** Corsham, Wilts, was on 11 April Sunday afternoon visited by a storm of hail, lightning, and thunder, which lasted nearly two hours. The hail covered the ground to the depth of six inches; some of the hail-stones were as large as plums. Considerable damage was done to the windows and trees in the neighbourhood.

**FROM THE CORSHAM CORRESPONDENT.**
When you told us last week of the Widow and Lot,
And that in his stead another she'd got,
You made a mistake, I really must say,
By writing of Knap without putting the K.
The husband's name is Knap.
*Your Corsham Correspondent's Reply*
When I received the gentle rap,
For leaving out the K in Knap,
A hearty laugh ensued the joke,
Nor did I feel the chast'ning stroke.
Without the K it sounds the same,
Then, Sir, why is not Nap the name?
I'm sure the woman's not belied,
She took a Nap, and K beside........

........Had K last week been kept at home,
She might have slept unknown by some,
But now all know, that ev'ry day,
She has a Nap behind a K.

*Postscript; or. Your Corsham Correspondent's Second Reply.*
When I'm again taught how to spell,
Let wiser wits the secret tell,
If from mistakes we would be free,
NAP lies between K and P,
She takes the soundest N A P, I find,
With K before and P behind,
The name of KNAPP is thus exprest,
Here let the woman take her rest.

# Chapter 3. Around and About Corsham

**1825: CLEANSED!** Bath Hospital - Patients that have been discharged, cured or relieved in the course of the last month. Mary Waite, Corsham Wilts. Leprosy cleansed!

**POACHERS CAUGHT.** On Wednesday night 21 September a gang of 16 poachers from Colerne were surprised at Hartham, near Corsham, by a party of keepers and tenants of Paul Methuen, esq; 19 in number, and after a sharp scuffle 11 were secured, and lodged in the Corsham blind-house. On the following morning they were taken before J. Fuller, esq; and committed to the Devizes house of correction for trial.

**HIGH PENALTY.** Two young gentlemen behaved in a disorderly manner at Corsham Chapel on 6 November Sunday evening that the Minister was obliged to close the service: they were pardoned, on acknowledging their fault. The penalty for this offence is £50 (over £3,000 in today's money), or 12 months imprisonment.

**1826: HALLELUJAH.** In the Independent School Corsham, there is a blind boy, 14 years old, who can correctly repeat upwards of 50 hymns and several chapters, which he has learnt by hearing them read.

**SPOT OF BOTHER.** Miss Stump, of Corsham, whose death we lately noticed, expired suddenly in the same room where her father suddenly died: her grandfather likewise died suddenly near the same spot.

**PULL THE OTHER ONE.** A mechanic of Corsham, the name of Tayler, has invented perpetual motion; and has written a letter to the King, informing him of the circumstance. It is a wheel set in motion by the help of magnets; and it had been going three days, when the letter was sent.

**1827: SHOCKING ACCIDENT.** An inquest was held on the 16th January, by Mr G. Archer, bailiff of Corsham, on the body of William Aust, quarrier, of Pickwick, aged 60, who was killed the preceding evening by the Company's coach, when crossing the road with a mug of beer, which he was taking home from the Hare and Hounds Inn, Pickwick. The coach was just starting out from that Inn at the instant, and the coachman could not stop the horses in time to save them from going over the unfortunate man, who was taken out from between the wheels after the fore-wheel had gone over his body, and crushed his ribs into his heart, which, of course, occasioned instantaneous death. He has left a widow, eight sons, one daughter, and 41 grand children, to lament their loss. Verdict - Accident Death.

**BROMLEY v. TREWMAN.** I was drinking with the plaintiff and defendant, and several others at the Pack Horse Inn, Corsham, on Monday the 20th Nov. A pastry cook came into the room, to whom Trewman said, *"How is your wife?"* The pastry-cook replied, *"Very well, thank'ee, how is your's?"* Bromley then said to Trewman, *"You don't ask after my wife?"* No, Trewman, replied, *"Because I am not in the habit of seeing you and your wife every day."* Bromley then taunted Trewman on his suspecting the charges of his tradesmen's bills; on which Trewman became irritated, and offered to fight Bromley for £5. Bromley refused to fight, observing, *"I suppose you are angry, because I have not asked after Mrs Trewman, but I did not know you were married, you are not married are you?"* Trewman (who, it was afterwards stated, had been married upwards of 20 years) became greatly enraged, and said to Bromley, *"Do you mean to say that I am not married?"* On the question being repeated 3 or 4 times, Bromley replied, *"Well, I do say so."* Trewman then gave him a violent blow on the nose, which produced two black eyes. Mr Sergeant Wylde, in an animated address to the Jury, said, that by law, the plaintiff, after receiving such provocation, should have put his hands quietly into his pockets, and have walked away, suffering all the discredit attached to his wife; but he appealed to the Jury as Englishmen, and to their feelings as husbands, how they would act toward the man who dared question the virtue of their wives, and then would ask them what compensation the plaintiff was entitled to in the present action. Mr Justice Burrough summed up, observing that the plaintiff must have a verdict, the defendant having put a justification on the record but the amount of damages he would entirely leave with them. The Jury retired for a few minutes, and returned a verdict for plaintiff. Damages 1s *[about £40 in today's money]*.

**GENTEEL VILLAGE.** The most genteel village in England is said to be Corsham, in Wiltshire, nine miles from Bath, in which, the newspapers tells us, forty-one families of independent fortune reside, of whom fourteen keep close carriages. It has within it four superb mansions and parks, and sixteen other gentlemen's villas.

**EAR LOSS.** William Townsend, labourer, was at work with a threshing machine, at Poundclose Farm, in the parish of Corsham, his smock frock caught a pin of the apparatus, whereby he became so entangled that his right ear was torn off, and his life was despaired of; but we are happy to state that the poor man now so far recovered be out of danger.

Pound Hill, Corsham.

**SHOCKING ACCIDENT.** On 13th June, a man named Parkes, in the employ of Mr Pearce, millwright, of Bristol, was repairing the cogs of the mill at Boydmill factory, in the parish of Corsham, owing to his propping the wheel in an insecure manner, the increasing pressure of the water upon the wheel at length crushed a stone in the wall against which the prop was fixed, when the works were set going, and Parkes, in pulling the boy (who was in danger) out of the way, got himself entangled between the cogs, so that his right arm from the wrist to the elbow was laid bare to the bone, and 5 of his ribs were crushed. His life was at first despaired of; but there are now some hopes of his recovery. This should operate as a caution to all millwrights either to well secure the wheel in such cases, or to throw the shaft out of gear.

**1829: HIGHWAY ROBBERY.** George Smith was indicted for assaulting and robbing Matthew Jenkins, on the road to Corsham, on the 2nd of January. The prosecutor stated, that after being at the Harp and Crown public house, which is on the road to Corsham, he was proceeding home, when the prisoner came up to him within about half a mile of his house, and gave him a violent blow under the left ear, which brought him to the ground; and when he was down robbed him of 14s. and a piece of cloth; he then began to feel for his watch, and said, "D—n thee, thee used to have a good watch, but thee has'nt it now," Jenkins is perfectly sure as to the person of the prisoner, for he had known him from a child.

## Chapter 3. Around and About Corsham

**LAST LAUGH.** On Saturday 2 May evening the ostler who attends to the horses of Mr Lawes' Calne coach, died at Corsham, consequence of the rupture of a blood-vessel, produced by violent laughter.

**CRUSHED.** Yesterday week [28 August], as Charles Dunsdon, of Semington, aged 29, was hauling timber from Jaggard's, in the parish of Corsham, for Mr Flower, of Melksham Park, in descending the narrow lane from Monks, near the old meeting-house in Corsham, the timber became loose, and having galled the backs of the horses, the animals became restive, and jammed the unfortunate man between the wheel and the wall; beating all his ribs on the right side, dislocating his shoulder, and dreadfully injuring his whole person. The poor sufferer was taken to the Asylum at Corsham, where he died on Sunday morning.

**LAST LAUGH.** An inquest was yesterday *[Friday 4 September]* held at Biddestone, before W. Adye, Esq. and a very respectable jury, on the body of John Gibbs, one of the gamekeepers of Paul Methuen, Esq. of Corsham House. From the evidence adduced, it appeared that Mr Methuen, accompanied by his son (a young gentleman about 17 or 18 years of age) and two of his gamekeepers, had, on the preceding day, been shooting in the parish of Biddestone; and that Mr Methuen, and one of the keepers, were a short distance before his son and the deceased, when they heard the report of a gun. Conceiving that some accident might have happened, Mr Methuen instantly turned round, and observing a smile on the countenance of the deceased, was impressed with the momentary idea that he was smiling or congratulating himself on his escape from danger. Immediately after, however, the poor fellow fell backward a corpse. Mr Methuen junior, it appeared, had given him his gun (having previously taken the precaution to uncock it), for the purpose of assisting him (Mr Methuen junior) over a hedge.

The deceased got upon the hedge, and gave the butt-end of the gun to his young master, holding the other end himself: in a moment, a branch in the hedge, by some means, forced back the cock, the gun went off, the contents passed into the heart of the keeper, and without uttering a word, he was a corpse. Upon hearing the facts, the jury, without the slightest hesitation, returned a verdict of Accidental Death; expressing their unanimous opinion that every possible precaution was used, and that not the slightest blame was attributable to any one. None can more deeply regret the sad accident than both Mr Methuen and his son; and Mr Methuen, we understand, has, in the most handsome and feeling manner, expressed his intention of providing for the wife and family of the deceased.

**FEMALE COURAGE.** A few days since *[Tuesday 3 November]* the widow of John Gibbs, gamekeeper to P. Methuen, Esq. of Corsham House, secured a man while in the act of poaching! This is the third poacher which this heroine has taken!

**1830: A DRUNKEN PIG.** A pig at the Harp and Crown in the parish of Corsham, was taught to drink beer out of a glass, and would run from his company in the court-yard into the tap-room, and jump up into any one's lap for glass of his favourite liquor. Last week being Whitsuntide, 'Jim,'(for that was his name, and which he would answer,) had 'quite bout of it' but not being satisfied in the tap-room, got into the cellar, and drank the beer droppings, till he died literally *'as drunk as a pig.'*

**1831: DEATH JUDGEMENT.** Thomas Day, was indicted for having broken open the house of Mr R. Lawrence, of Corsham, and stolen there from 9 yards of Irish cloth, calico sheet, and other articles of his property, was found guilty. Judgement of death recorded. *[Ed: Yikes!]*

**PRIMULA ELATIOR.** A cowslip was gathered last week in the garden of Mr Jeremiah Jaques, Corsham, containing the extraordinary number of 342 petals.

## Chapter 3. Around and About Corsham

**OAPs.** Of 586 persons who have died at Corsham since the year 1813, 215 have exceeded the age of 70; 124 aged 70; 83 aged 80 and 10 aged 90. And there are now living in the place persons nearly 100 years of age.

**FIRST UNIFORMS.** On Friday 29 May the Corsham troop of Yeomanry Cavalry appeared in their uniforms, for the first time, accompanied the band of music: their soldier-like appearance was much admired.

**1832: THANK YOUR LUCKY STARS.** At about half past six o'clock, a meteor illuminated the whole atmosphere for miles round Corsham. A spectator describes it about 10 degrees south of the planet Mars, and as a small circle of light, increasing brightness from the centre of the circumference, which gradually enlarged till it had the appearance of annular eclipse of the Sun; the north and south sides then stretched forth to the extent of 10 deg. each, forming a beautiful elliptic ring, extending from Mars to Menkar *[the second-brightest star in the constellation of Cetus]*, near the horizon. The luminous boundary of this ellipse appeared exquisitely beautiful and perfectly defined for several seconds, when it burst info innumerable fragments and disappeared.

**1833: SMALL SENTENCE.** Samuel Butler was indicted for feloniously killing and slaying one William Waite, at Corsham, in September last. It appeared from the evidence, that the deceased and prisoner met at a beer shop on the day in question where there were many other persons, that the deceased struck a woman, and that prisoner took her part and knocked the deceased down, a scuffle ensued, the deceased was dragged out of the house by the prisoner and a man named Aust - three blows were heard to be given; the deceased became insensible and died the next day from injuries caused by the blows or the fall. The prisoner was found guilty and sentenced to one month's imprisonment.

**1834: PRAYERS ARE ANSWERED.** On Sunday night 9 March, as Mr Smith, farmer of Pickwick, Wilts, was returning from his place of worship, between Corsham and Pickwick, he was attacked at about eight o'clock by two villains, who robbed him of his watch and appendages; they then made their escape across some fields. Smith followed them but the night being so dark, he lost sight of them. On Monday Mr S. came to the Guildhall, Bath, where he gave information of the robbery, describing the watch. One of the fellows was apprehended with the watch in his possession at about seven on Tuesday evening. **DISTRESSING SUICIDE.** In June, a person named Verrider, a tailor from Corsham and a member of the Corsham troop of Yeomanry Cavalry, *put a period* to his existence on Wednesday afternoon, by shooting himself. No cause can be assigned for the commission of the act. He has left a wife and three young children. A brother of the deceased terminated his life in similar manner a short time since.

**1835: HEADBANGER.** On 26 January, Mr Sweatman, of the Methuen Arms, Corsham, was thrown from his horse, as he was riding down Pickwick-street, and his head pitched on a stone, which must have occasioned his death, had it not been for the protection which his hat afforded him. By the prompt medical aid that he received, he is likely ultimately to recover, although at present he is very ill. **ALTERCATION.** On the evening of the l6th April as Francis Collinson and Richard Newman were returning towards their homes at Corsham, from the Plough Inn, situated at a little distance from the place, the former individual embraced that opportunity to revenge himself on the latter for an old grudge, which had been rankling in his mind for years past. The result of the altercation which ensued was that Collinson stabbed Newman with his knife in five different places, four about the head and one on the hip of a very serious nature. A warrant has been taken out for the apprehension of the offender, but the officers have not yet been able to take him.

## Chapter 3. Around and About Corsham

**UNNATURAL MOTHER.** On the evening of 22 April, a well-dressed female child, about a month old, was left on the upper step of the residence of F. Williams, Esq., of Corsham. It was conveyed to the Asylum and a reward has been offered for the discovery of its unnatural mother. There is every probability that the inhuman mother who left her infant child will be discovered and apprehended, as the Corsham parish authorities have been within the last day or two written to from Bath, informing them that a woman delivered of an infant some time since, which must now be of the age of that which had been left at Mr William's door, has been subsequently seen about Bath without her child, she has hitherto eluded the officers, who are in search of her, but there is every reason to hope that she will be secured.

**1836: CRIED ALL NIGHT.** Ann Whitcombe was indicted for wilfully deserting a female infant child in Corsham, the night of the 22 of April, 1835. It was proved in evidence, that the child had been left at the door of Mr Gilbert Williams that the prisoner had been delivered of a child at Bath, in March, which, from several peculiar marks upon its person, was identified by the medical attendant as the one which had been thus cruelly deserted. The prisoner in her defence said, that she went into the service of Mr Pegler, in Dec., and was afterwards in the family-way by him. She went to Bath by his wish; he took a lodging for her and he visited her there: he came to Bath on the 21st of April, and took her and the child back with him.

Mr Pegler desired her to go across towards his house, and he would come and meet her. He came to her, and wished her to put the child at some person's door, which she refused to do; he said, if she did not, he would never allow her one farthing, and as the law now stood, the magistrates could not compel him. He came again, and took the child away, and said he would put it under Mr Williams's door; he did so: she cried all night about it. The child was dressed; he said he knocked at the door, and saw a light. The Judge summed up in an affecting manner; the Jury returned a verdict of Not Guilty.

**HIGHWAY ROBBERY.** On 15 June Monday night last, Mr Joseph Pegler, butcher, of Corsham, was robbed on the highway, near John Wiltshire's, Esq. Shockerwick, of four £10 notes (£3,500 in today's money). A spaniel dog belonging to the thieves was captured by Mr Pegler and is still in his possession. The dog loitered behind to lick the wounds of the unfortunate victim, as he lay bleeding on the ground.

*Chequers Inn Corsham, 1890 image courtesy of Stephen Flavin.*

**INN CHILD.** A travelling Irish woman on her road to London, deserted a child about four years old at the door of the Chequers Inn, in the parish of Corsham, a few days since.

The parochial authorities, on receiving information of the circumstance, immediately pursued and came up with the inhuman mother at Beckhampton.

She was brought in custody to Corsham, and has since, with her child, been removed back to Ireland.

## Chapter 3. Around and About Corsham

**BOILING BEER.** On 17 August Monday night, an extensive fire took place at the brewery of Mr Charles Sheppard, of Corsham. The whole of the brewery and extensive stock of beer was destroyed, and nothing but the extreme stillness of the night prevented the fire from spreading to Mr Sheppard's dwelling-house as well as numerous other houses adjoining. From the prompt assistance rendered, the fire was fortunately got under control, but the loss to Mr Sheppard must be extremely heavy. The flames were visible for a considerable distance and excited great alarm.

**1837: FATAL LAST DRINKS.** On Friday 19 May the butler of Mr Fuller, of Neston, accompanied by an assistant, went into the woods for the purpose of clearing the shrubs, taking with them some bread and cheese and a bottle beer. After being at work a short time, the butler partook of the bread and cheese, and drank from the bottle. The assistant declined eating, but took some beer. Within a few minutes, both were taken violently ill; and before half an hour had elapsed, the assistant was a corpse. The effect of what he had drunk was not so rapid on the butler, consequence of his eating some of the bread and cheese; and he contrived to reach home, when Mr Morgan, surgeon of Corsham, attended, and, by the prompt use of the stomach-pump, saved his life. Every means were used also to restore his companion, but without effect. An inquest was held on Monday on the body, and from the evidence adduced, it appeared, that the fatal accident was occasioned by the beer having been put into a bottle, which had previously contained an embrocation, and had inadvertently been omitted to be cleansed. The Jury returned a verdict of 'Accidental Death'.

**WILLIAM IV DIES.** The 8 July day appointed for the interment of our late excellent deceased Monarch *[William IV died 20 June 1837],* was observed at Corsham with due solemnity. All the shops were wholly or partially closed. At three o'clock, the minute bell began to toll, and continued till a late hour, after which the ringers ascended the tower and rung three excellent muffled peals. On Sunday evening, the united choir sung, at the Independent Chapel, Handel's beautiful funeral anthem, 'How are the Mighty fallen' and the Rev. G. Slade delivered a most appropriate discourse.

**SHOCKING EXPLOSION:.** On Thursday 3 August the two sons of Mr Reeves, of Corsham, being left alone in the house, got a powder flask, and began playing with the gunpowder. Whilst thus employed the powder in the flask which was in the hands of the younger boy ignited, and both the child's hands were blown off by the explosion. The elder boy was also much injured.

**SHATTERING.** On Monday evening (November) some wanton person discharged a loaded gun in the then crowded street of Corsham near to the Methuen Arms, the contents of which lodged in the hand of the gamekeeper of E. Broome, Esq., which is much shattered, and another ball in the hip of a man named Shewring whose life is in consequence despaired of.

**1838: THE UNFORTUNATE GIRL.**

On Saturday 2 June, an accident of melancholy nature occurred, in consequence of loaded fire-arms being indiscreetly left within the reach of children, to a young woman of the name of Sarah Brooks, native of Farley, near Bradford, at the Chequers Inn, Box *(see photo right).*

## Chapter 3. Around and About Corsham

It seems that a boy of the name Henry Ashby *happening to go* into the kitchen of the Inn, took up from the table as he supposed, from what the unfortunate girl said, an unloaded gun, and after trying it with a ramrod, which misled him by not being of the proper length, he naturally enough pointed it at her, and intending to show how the fire flashed in the pan, he shot off. The poor woman instantly fell, with her right jaw nearly shattered into pieces, as several portions of the bone were afterwards picked up from the floor. Every assistance was instantly rendered which medical skill could devise. She is not yet dead, although there is little chance of her recovery. The poor lad is said to be so much alarmed at the accident, and what he anticipates will result to himself should she die, that he wanders about the adjacent fields in an inconsolable state.

**DOUBLE FRACTURE!** On the morning of the 23 July, a carter in the employ of James Hunt, esq., of Rowden Hill, near Chippenham, named Gardner, as he was proceeding up the Chequer Hill, in company with several other men, was knocked down by the horse, and one of the wheels passed over his leg. On perceiving this, his comrades prevented the animal from pursuing its course, when unfortunately, it ran back, and the wheel passed a second time over the unfortunate youth, exactly in the same place. The leg was broken. The weight of the cart and its load was nearly two tons. Mr Little [surgeon], of Corsham, was immediately sent for.

In the meantime, the sufferer was conveyed to the Chequer Inn, from which a messenger was despatched to his master, who sent a spring cart to convey the young man home, and has since requested his own surgeon to attend him; most kindly requesting that any expense attending the cure should be charged to him, although Gardner had not been in his employ a fortnight.

**HOPELESS FATAL AFFRAY.** At Corsham, on Monday 16 September an inquest was held before John Edwards, Esq., on the body of Henry Hope, aged about 40; it was adjourned until this day, in order to receive the medical evidence consequent upon a post mortem examination. It appears that the deceased had been drinking on Saturday last at a beer-house at Elly-Green [Neston] in this parish, with others, when a wager was made up for him to run with William Clark a certain distance, for a gallon of beer. The race was won by Clark. During the time the beer was being drunk, the deceased continued wrangling telling Clark that if he could not beat him in running he could beat him at fighting. After some time a fight took place in an adjoining field between Clark and the deceased when from the difference between the two men with regard to their state of sobriety, it was evident that the deceased had no chance, yet, although several persons were spectators, among whom was the deceased's own son, none attempted to interfere, even to act as seconds.

The deceased was knocked down every time and after twenty minutes was so beaten as to be unable to stand or speak. In that state, he was left from 7 o'clock on Saturday night until Sunday morning until some person passing the spot recognised him, and had him conveyed to his lodgings, where he died about one o'clock. The medical evidence given at the adjourned inquest proved that the excitement caused by the running, the drinking and the fighting, produced the fatal result, the immediate cause being considered to be the fighting. The jury returned a verdict of manslaughter against William Clark. The excitement produced here is considerable upon the occasion from the brutal manner in which the deceased was left in the field the whole of the night, and the delay in procuring medical attendance after he was discovered and conveyed home [to his lodgings], no one being sent for until twelve on Sunday. The deceased never spoke after the last round but one. Both parties were labourers on the works at the Box Tunnel. Clark is a native of Atworth; the deceased *[Henry Hope]* of Gloucester.

## Chapter 3. Around and About Corsham

**continued..........March 1839....** William Clark was indicted for killing and slaying Henry Hope, at Corsham on the 15th of September. Mr Cockburn conducted the case for the prosecution. The witness statements are as follows:-

William Oram: *"I lived at Corsham, close to the line of the railway. I saw the deceased at Austin's public house on the 15th of September he challenged the prisoner to run with him, and the prisoner won. The deceased then challenged him to run again, but the prisoner refused. The deceased then attempted to kick up a row. I went away, and returned about 6 o'clock, and the prisoner and the deceased were then fighting. The prisoner knocked him down, and the deceased appeared sulky and would not get up; his eyes were only partly open. He did not speak. I helped another man to put his shirt on, and then I left him."*

Evan Lidiard: *"I saw the prisoner and the deceased fighting; the fight continued for about 20 minutes. I persuaded Clark not to fight any more, as the deceased was drunk. Clark went up to him and told him he would not fight any more, but the deceased said he would, for he was not half beaten yet. They then fought four or five other rounds, and after the last round he appeared as if he could not get up again."*

Austin: *"As I was going along the field the next morning I saw the deceased lying by the ditch; he was alive, but did not appear to be sensible. I had him carried to his lodgings, and a doctor was sent for."*

Joseph Goldstone, a surgeon: *"I was sent for to see the deceased between 12 and 1 in the day: he was perfectly insensible; he lived about an hour. I afterwards examined the brain; there was an infusion of blood on the brain. I consider the death to have arisen from the blows and falls in the fighting."*

Mr Baron Gurney having summed up, the jury returned a verdict of Guilty. The learned Judge in sentencing the prisoner said, there was great inhumanity in this case; he had first fought with a man who was rendered incapable of standing up against him in consequence of being completely drunk, and then he and those who had been present at the fight had left the unfortunate man in a field all night without assistance or covering, and had acted in such a manner as he had never before heard of. He therefore sentenced him *[William Clark]* to be imprisoned and kept to hard labour for six months.

**THE SIX SISTERS.** There are six sisters in the parish Corsham, four of whom are living in the same house, whose united ages amount to 423 years. Their maiden name is Fairman.

**1839: JUGULARS at ATWORTH.** An Inquest was held on Monday last, by William Adye, esq., coroner, Bradford, on a man unknown. It appears that the deceased was booked at Bristol for London, by the Company's Coach, and on arriving at the White Hart, Atworth, where they changed horses, he got off the coach and asked for a small glass of brandy, at the same time complaining of the extreme cold, he had scarcely swallowed it when he fell on the floor in a fit. Every attention was paid him by the landlord, Mr William Newman, and the neighbours, but after two hours, finding that he did not get better, Mr Washborne of Corsham was sent for, who very promptly attended, and opened the jugular vein and temporal artery, but without effect; the poor fellow died in about four hours. Verdict - died by the Visitation of God. *[Ed: More like the visitation of the doctor!]*

**NOT A BAD SECOND PRIZE.** The second prize of 150 guineas *[over £10,000 in today's money]* has been awarded by the Corporation of Liverpool to George Alexander, esq., of Adam-street, Adelphi, son of R. H. Alexander esq., of Corsham, for his architectural design for the New Town-Hall, proposed to be built at Liverpool.

## Chapter 3. Around and About Corsham

**PICKPOCKET DEATH.** On the 23rd September, Mr John Osborne, of Monks [Gastard] near Corsham, dealer, was in the act of pursuing a pickpocket, at Kingsdown Fair, when the stirrup leather broke and he was precipitated on his head. He rode home without experiencing much inconvenience, but during the night he became alarmingly ill. Medical aid was procured, but we regret to say, proved to no effect: he died on Tuesday last, aged 41.

**A BRIDGE TOO FAR.** A fatal accident occurred at Pound Pill, on Friday last. The road under which the Railway is being excavated is unprotected on either side, where the depth is at least 20 feet. A Beer Housekeeper had, it seems on the evening alluded to, turned out a workman somewhat intoxicated, who, going towards Corsham, fell over the side of the road into the Excavation; he was supposed to have lain groaning and nearly suffocated for at least an hour, when his moans attracted a passer-by. He was found bruised and from lying in the water, much chilled, and although removed to a Public House in Corsham, where his case received every possible attention, he expired the next evening.

**OPEN GATE TO DEATH:** Thursday night 12 December, three Newfoundland dogs belonging to the Right Hon. Lord Methuen killed and mangled upwards of 40 sheep the property of Messrs. Plummer and Parker of Corsham.

Forty sheep have been killed, and it is feared that several more must be slaughtered, they being so dreadfully bitten.

No blame whatever imputed to any of Lord Methuen's servants, for not securing the dogs; but the occurrence must be attributed to two fellows [tramps] who came to the house to beg and in going out left the gate open.

**1840: A FAST LIE?** A line in the Bell's Life in London and Sporting Chronicle - of Sunday 9 February 1840 read, *'It is not true that, John West of Corsham ran a mile in 4 minutes and 26 seconds; and Mr May may as well tell his lies to the wind.'* [Ed: A hundred years later in 1954 Roger Bannister ran the first sub 4 minute mile in 3:59.4 minutes on 6 May 1954 at Oxford University's Iffley Road Track. John West's boast may well have been true!]

**FIRS FIND.** Friday morning 22 May, the body of a newly-born infant was discovered, enclosed in a linen cloth, in a plantation by the roadside, near the Half-Way Firs in the parish of Corsham. A diligent search is being made by the police and others to find out the parties concerned in the exposure, but as yet without success.

**HOUND'S FIGHT.** Peter Naylor, of Corsham, has two dogs, one 30lbs and one 28lbs in weight, and is ready to make a match with any person, from £5 to £10, to meet halfway from any place appointed. His money will be ready at Mr John May's Hare and Hounds Inn, Pickwick, near Corsham.

**OUTRAGES NEAR THE LINE OF THE GREAT WESTERN RAILWAY.** A short time since a young married woman, whose husband was working on the line near Corsham was passing not far from the place where he was employed when she was seized and used with brutal violence by several of the labourers.

## Chapter 3. Around and About Corsham

The husband, coming at her cries which were heard by others at a great distance, was shamefully beaten, and her brother attempted in vain to interfere. After some time a few men out of the hundreds within sight and bearing interfered to prevent the brutality of others, and the woman suffering much injury, was released in the deepest affliction. Some of those who assaulted her have gone away to another part of the line.

**1841: SCREWS LOOSE!** Thursday evening last on 8 July, two of the evening down trains of the Great Western Railway were detained for several hours in the deep cutting near the east entrance of Box Tunnel, in the parish of Corsham, consequence of one of the engines of the up-trains getting off the rails in the tunnel. This unfortunate affair is said to have happened through the carelessness of the workmen, who had taken up the rails during the interval of the passing of the trains, to raise them where they were a little sunk, and they were not screwed down before the before-named engine and train arrived. The train was going slowly, and no damage either to person or property was done.

**IN MEMORY.**

A neat mural tablet has been placed in Corsham Church, to perpetuate the memory of Dr. William Sainsbury.

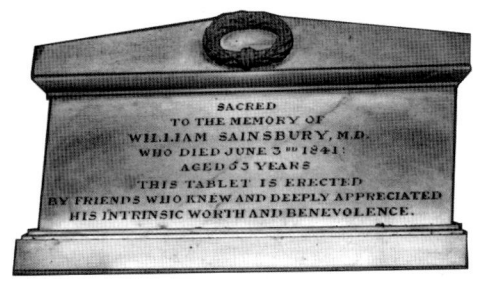

SACRED
TO THE MEMORY OF
WILLIAM SAINSBURY, M.D.
WHO DIED JUNE 3RD 1841;
AGED 53 YEARS
THIS TABLET IS ERECTED
BY FRIENDS WHO KNEW AND DEEPLY APPRECIATED
HIS INTRINSIC WORTH AND BENEVOLENCE.

**ON THE WRONG TRACK.** On 31 August a melancholy accident attended with loss of life occurred to a young man named Martin. The labourer employed on the Great Western Railway was accidentally killed on the line between Corsham and Chippenham, a short distance from the former place. To avoid the down train of the approach of which the poor fellow was aware, he got upon the up-rails. It so happened that a train from Bath was passing at the same time, which gave the proper signal by whistle &c but it appears to have been unobserved indeed, it is likely that the noise of the one drowned that of the other; the engine of the up-train went over the man, and as may be supposed, death was almost instantaneous. The poor fellow did not know the up train was close upon him, which knocked him down, smashed his head, and severed one or two of his limbs. No fault is attached to the engineer. The unfortunate man's remains were conveyed to the Roebuck public house, to await a Coroner's inquest. He was not native of the neighbourhood: was a remarkably steady character, and had by of industry saved money.

**VERDICT SAYS IT ALL.** On 28 October at Whitly [*Whitley*], in the parish of Melksham, Samuel Pocock, aged 25 years, who was sent by his own desire from Corsham to Whitly, in a state of illness. Being delirious, he arose from his bed during the night, and thrust his arm several times through the glass of the window, which produced such extensive haemorrhage as to the immediate cause of death. Verdict, 'Died from the effects of haemorrhage, caused by the thrusting of his arm through the glass window whilst in a state of delirium.'

**CAUTION, YEW BETTER LISTEN TO THIS.** In December, a valuable cow, belonging to Mr Plummet, of the Park Farm, Corsham, was killed in consequence of eating yew in a withered state, a great portion of which was found in the creature's stomach.

**1842: DARING HIGHWAY ROBBERY.** One of the most daring instances of highway robbery that has occurred for many years past was committed in the parish of Corsham, on Monday 31 January. It has excited very great surprise and spread much alarm in the neighbourhood, from the circumstance of its having been effected in open day, at about 11 o'clock in the morning, between the hamlet of Easton and Chippenham, and in a lane that from its frequent use cannot strictly be called a byway. A man of the name of Tylee, the waywarden of Corsham, was on his way at the above hour, to overlook the men in his employ, and to pay them their previous week's wages, when he was stopped by four men, having the appearance of railway labourers. Just before he met them he heard one of them say. *"Here comes Tylee"* They asked him whether he had any money. He replied *"No"*. But, remarked one of the gang, *"You have a watch"* and immediately knocked Tylee down, and otherwise ill-treated him, but not to any serious extent. They robbed him of his watch and £8 10s in money, consisting of a £5 note, two sovereigns, and thirty shillings in silver. Through the activity of the police, several men have been apprehended and taken before the magistrates at Chippenham, but Tylee was unable to swear to them.

**A CUT TOO FAR.** James Cole was indicted for cutting and maiming Robert Glasby, at Corsham, on the 8th of January. The prisoner's wife had abused the prosecutor on his return from market, for saying she had encouraged a girl whom he had lived with to come to her house: a quarrel ensued, the prosecutor struck the prisoner, and was getting the upper hand of him, when the prisoner rushed into his house and brought out a bill hook, with which he inflicted a severe cut on the prosecutor's shoulder, from which he is at present disabled from work. Verdict: Guilty. Fifteen years' transportation.

**AFFECTED WITH STUPOR.** An inquest was held on Wednesday 9 November, at the Duke of Cumberland Inn, by Mr Edwards, Coroner, on the body of Jane Cole, aged 74, wife of W. Cole, for many years a confidential servant on the Hartham Park estate, the residence of the late H. H. Joy, Esq. The unfortunate woman was sitting by the fire, and being drowsy, or affected with stupor or giddiness, of which she frequently complained, the under part of her dress caught fire, and gained considerable ascendancy before she discovered it; and in consequence of moving about the room in alarm, it raged so violently, that an opposite neighbour, on seeing an unusual light in the apartment, hastened to the house, but was unable to extinguish the flames. Before she could receive the assistance of another female in an adjoining house, Mr Kemm, the surgeon, passed by and succeeded in subduing them, and afterwards administered necessary cordials. She was sensible for some hours, and conversed, but afterwards lost her utterance, and died in 24 hours after the accident. Verdict: Accidental death from burning, in consequence of the clothes of the deceased taking fire.

**1844: DEATH SENTENCE.** At Salisbury assizes, on Saturday 16 March, George Smith, James Smith, and Stephen Roberts Common, were indicted for a burglary at the house of John Hulbert, Lypiatt, in the parish of Corsham, and stealing thereat certain articles enumerated in the indictment, and beating and wounding Elizabeth Hulbert, the wife of the prosecutor, with intent to murder, or do her some grievous bodily harm. The jury returned a verdict of Guilty against all the prisoners. Judgement of death recorded.

**A FISHY TALE.** On Sunday morning 14 April, as one of the men employed to overlook the park and water of Lord Methuen at Corsham House, was going about his rounds, he discovered what appeared to be a very large fish floating on the surface of the water on the great pond, and taking a boat, his suspicions were verified. He brought to land one of the great leviathans of those waters, an immense pike, which *[itself]* having lately captured *[in its mouth]* a carp of at least four pounds, was so mistaken in the size of his victim, which, by the dorsal fins, had stuck in the pike's throat about halfway, that the monster could neither effect a complete swallow nor disgorge his prey entirely, and which ultimately, hooked him for ever. The pike weighed twenty-eight pounds, measured three feet six inches from the two extremities, and was supposed to have been dead nearly a week.

## Chapter 3. Around and About Corsham

**FROM ASHES TO ASHES.** An inquest was held on Thursday 23 May at the Packhorse Inn, Corsham, before Mr Edwards, coroner, on the body of a male infant child, of premature birth. It appeared from the evidence before the jury, that on the same morning, between 7 and 8 o'clock, as the son of Mr White the cooper, a lad of about nine years old, was with his little wagon conveying some horse dung and road dust from the street into his father's yard, he saw something visible from under a few coal ashes, which had been placed there; and on removing it with a shovel he discovered the infant. His father, on being apprised of the circumstance, sent for Mr Little the surgeon. Mr Little said it was about a six months child, and from the state of the body, then bordering on decomposition, he thought must have been born *[alive for]* at least a week. No further evidence could be received beyond that of Mr White, and his son, and the surgeon, the Jury returned their verdict that the infant was found dead, and placed in the situation as discovered by some person or persons unknown. Up to the present time (Monday afternoon) no clue as to the mother, or any parties concerned, has yet been discovered. A correspondent, in allusion to the above, says, *'As it was proved at the inquest that the manure and ashes had been partly removed and disturbed the day previous, surprise has been excited that the Jury did not adjourn their enquiries into the cause of death, until time had afforded them an opportunity of ascertaining who the criminal parties were, especially as the crimes of abortion and concealment of birth are on the increase. Fortunately, however, the County Police are on the alert, and it is to be hoped that the unnatural mother may be brought to justice, and the parish obliged to prosecute.'*

**FIRE BANKS.** In consequence of the long continued drought this summer, the grass banks of the Great Western, near Corsham, had become so completely dried and withered, that some sparks from one of the *[train]* engines having fallen upon it, it immediately ignited, and was speedily a blaze to the extent nearly 40 yards. Fortunately, there was at the time but little wind and it was speedily extinguished; for within a very short distance from the spot, there was a thatched dwelling house and several ricks, which would otherwise most probably have been destroyed.

**THREE CHEERS.** The reception given to Paul Methuen and his bride at Corsham Court on Monday 14 October evening was most gratifying to the feelings of the youthful couple. The whole town was illuminated, and triumphal arches erected, under which they passed, amid the joyful acclamations of the assembled thousands from all parts of the country, who came to welcome back to the seat of his ancestors the heir of the house of Methuen; and many fervent prayers were offered up that he and his young bride might for very many long years enjoy uninterrupted happiness and prosperity. The bells rang out a merry peal, and nothing was wanting to testify the heartfelt joy of the tenantry *[tenants of the estate]* on this auspicious event. When his feelings permitted him to speak, and the cheering had somewhat subsided, Mr Methuen expressed his gratitude for the reception he had met on his return to the home of his childhood, and concluded by saying that he hoped they might find him the same sort of man as his father.

**1845: Devizes and Wiltshire Gazette.** A short time since, a labouring man named 'Acher' living at Westrop in this parish, had a considerable sum of money left him, and of which he was very proud, constantly exhibiting before his neighbours. It is reported that his large family derived not the least advantage from his good fortune: and one night last week *[in February]*, whilst he was spending a convivial evening with some friends, all his money, amounting to £68 in sovereigns *[over £6,000 in today's money]*, were stolen from his cottage, where he was simple enough to imagine it would be more secure than in a savings bank. No one as yet has been apprehended for the robbery; but strong suspicions are entertained that will probably lead to the discovery of the thief.

## Chapter 3. Around and About Corsham

***The following Wiltshire Independent report takes a slightly different view of the above robbery!***
**CORSHAM Daring House-Robbery.** On Monday last, January 27th, a dwelling-house of labouring man named 'Archer', of Westrop, near Corsham, was entered, during the temporary absence of his daughter, and £68 *[over £6,000 in today's money],* stolen from a box in the bed-room. The man had left home that evening to attend the wedding of his sister, who was that day married in Box church, and the thieves no doubt knowing he had saved some money, watched his daughter out of the house, and, though she was gone but a short time, succeeded in entering and making off with the cash.

The robbery was not discovered till the return of Archer and his wife from Box, late in the evening, when the disarrangement of the boxes excited their suspicions. We understand that the police have obtained some information respecting this mysterious affair, and it is hoped the thieves will speedily be brought to justice.

**VERY SAD.** On the afternoon of 13 February, an inquest was held by Mr Edwards, at Corsham Side, one of the little hamlets within the Manor and Liberty of Corsham, on the body of Sarah Bath, a fine healthy girl about 13 years of age, who was burnt to death under the following most heart-rending circumstances. It appeared from the evidence of her mother, who is such a cripple as to be utterly incapable of even feeding herself, that about one o'clock Monday she was sitting by the fire as usual, the deceased standing near it, and within the distance of a yard from her: that the girl's clothes suddenly took fire, and in an instant was a complete flame, the poor woman not being able from the disuse of her own hands to extinguish it, became also on fire.

The unfortunate girl got out of the house, and making an alarm, brought a neighbour to the spot, who found her on her knees in the snow near to the door, in a state of nudity, with the exception of her shoes and stockings, and dreadfully scorched and disfigured. The mother was also on fire within, and in a few minutes the furniture must have ignited, and all probability the house, which was thatched, would have been a prey to the flames.

The deceased died about 8 o'clock the same evening. What renders the case doubly distressing is, that the deceased was the chief manager of the whole family, consisting of her father, an industrious labourer, the crippled mother, younger brother, an idiot: other branches *[of the family]* being married and settled at a distance.

**DON'T DRINK TO THAT.** Died, at Corsham, on Thursday 8 May, Mr John Clack, aged 68. The deceased was the father of the Corsham Tee-Totallers; being the first who signed the pledge, which he kept inviolate for the last seven years. His remains were interred Monday last, in the burial ground adjoining the Ebenezer Chapel. The funeral was attended by forty of the leading members of the Corsham Temperance Society, the pail being borne by six juveniles. The funeral service was performed by Mr Pulling, agreeably to the desire of the deceased.

**POND DEATH.** On the afternoon of Monday 30 June an inquest was held before Mr Edwards, the coroner, and a respectable jury, at a beer-house kept by Mr Mark Rawlings, in Priory Lane, on the body of a new born male infant, found the same morning in a pond, at a short distance from the inquest room.

It appeared from the concurrent testimony of two youths (brothers), the eldest about 14 years of age, that between 11 and 12 o'clock in the forenoon they were returning from Pickwick to Corsham, and having a dog with them, one of them threw a stone into the pond, for the purpose of inducing the dog to fetch it out, when the dog dived to the bottom and brought up the body of the infant. Many persons were soon on the spot, and the body was taken to the premises of Mr Rawlings.

A post mortem examination was made by Aaron Little esq., (surgeon), who gave it his opinion that the child had been dead about a month. No external marks of violence presented themselves, although the blood vessels of the neck appeared dark and full, and the air vessels of the lungs denoted that the chid had been born alive; decomposition, however, had so far advanced as to preclude the possibility of Mr Little giving a more conclusive opinion.

A curious coincidence occurred the same morning, which appeared strongly connected with this affair, and tending to throw suspicion on a woman at present unknown. About five o'clock, the landlord of the Hare and Hounds at Pickwick, not far distant from the pond, had been attending some market gardeners and others who usually make early calls, and just as they left, a strange woman came in and called for a glass of liquor; and during her stay, (only a few minutes), she made the following uncalled for extraordinary remark to the landlord, *"They are giving me a pretty character - they say I have drowned my child in a pond."*

The landlord paid no particular attention to her, but merely replied, *"What is there they won't say?"* The woman then drank off her liquor, paid for it, and departed in the direction of Corsham. A look out is on foot for the supposed delinquent.

**MIRACULOUS ESCAPE.** A man named Richard Sheane, one of the Bath City police, took his place on Monday evening at the Bristol Station of the Great Western Railway to proceed to Bath on the mail train. Soon after the train started, both he and the boy who had accompanied him fell asleep, and were carried some distance beyond their destination before either awoke. The rushing noise of the engine in the Box tunnel aroused the man from his slumbers, and he then discovered that he had ridden some miles farther than he had wished. His first impression was that the train would stop at Corsham, but it was not so. Onwards he was carried at the rate of 40 or 50 miles an hour. He at last opened the door of the carriage, alighted on the step, made a spring, and fortunately he was not dashed to pieces.

On the arrival of the train at Chippenham, the circumstance was made known through the boy, and immediately a search was made for him, but be could at first no where be found. He states that he recollects nothing but coming in violent contact with something which he supposes to be a bridge; how long he lay there he does not know, but on recovering his senses he crawled to a house close at hand, where he was lodged for the night.

The next morning he was well enough to walk into Corsham, to see a medical man, when it was found that besides being much cut and bruised, his shoulder was dislocated. The man bears a very good character, and it does not appear that he was the least intoxicated at the time of the rash act. He had gone from Bath to Bristol in the morning to search for a man who had broken into Trinity Church *[Bristol]*, and the boy in company with him was taken to identify the thief.

**1846: A STEP TOO FAR.** On 8 February, a man named Norris was standing upon the platform at the Corsham Station waiting for the late uptrain, to proceed to Wootton Bassett, when in the most foolish manner, as the train was coming in, and before it had stopped, he attempted to get into one of the carriages containing some of his fellow workmen, slipped his footing, and fell between the carriages. Although he escaped with his life, he has sustained such severe injuries, that little hopes are entertained of his recovery.

# Chapter 3. Around and About Corsham

## *1890s GWR 4500 Class Steam Loco in Corsham Station*

**ACCIDENTAL DEATH AT THE MANOR OF CORSHAM.** On Tuesday afternoon 5 May an inquest was held by Mr Edwards, coroner, at the Spread Eagle, Pickwick, on view of the body of Daniel Marks, a lad aged about 11 years. It appeared by the evidence of his mother, who was the principal witness, that her husband (who is an itinerant razor grinder), herself, and four children had Saturday last come into the neighbourhood, from the village of Slaughterford, the deceased being unwell at the time and after staying about the whole of the afternoon out of doors, proceeded to a barn at some distance, where the family passed the night. On Sunday morning, they rose early to proceed to Trowbridge, and very soon after, the deceased was seized with strong convulsive fits. A doctor was sent for; and Mr Little, the surgeon, shortly arrived, and the necessary restoratives were given, but the deceased remained totally insensible until he died on Monday evening. The jury, after receiving the evidence of Mr Little, who attended the inquest, returned the following verdict, *'That the deceased died from neglect, and want of proper treatment in illness, wholly produced by lying in cold and damp places, when travelling the country.'*

**THUMBS OFF.** On Saturday 25 July, as a boy named Barnes of Corsham was holding a horse, which was teased with flies, the animal made a snap at his hand, and bit off the thumb, tearing out the tendon a considerable length. Medical aid was procured, and the boy is doing well.

**MELANCHOLY DUTY.** We have the melancholy duty of reporting the death of Mrs Edridge, wife of John Edridge, Esq., alderman, of this city *[Salisbury]*, and of Pockeredge, near Corsham. The unfortunate lady has for some time been labouring under aberration of mind; and on Monday afternoon, during a short absence from the family circle, she destroyed herself. Mrs Edridge had just received a visit from her brother (Mr Yockney) and his wife, and left the drawing-room soon after two o'clock, retiring to her bedroom. On her way thither, it is supposed that she entered the dressing-room of her husband, and provided herself with a razor, with which she inflicted the wounds of which she died. About ten minutes after Mrs Edridge had gone upstairs, the servants were alarmed by violent ringing of the bell, and one of them [*Mrs Edney*] proceeding to the room, Mrs Edridge was discovered standing with her throat cut. She exclaimed, "Oh, Mrs Edney!" These were the only words that escaped her. Another servant was immediately called for by Mrs Edney, and Mrs Edridge was again found in a standing position. Medical aid was at once sought; and Mr Kemm, surgeon, of Corsham, was speedily in attendance. On his arrival, every means which skill could devise was adopted; but in about ten minutes the unfortunate lady ceased to exist. Mrs Edridge has been in a desponding state of mind for some months past; and it was only on the day of this unhappy occurrence that her husband consulted Dr. Langworthy as to her mental condition. A Coroner's Inquest was held upon the body yesterday, at the residence of Mr Edridge, when the facts given above were detailed in evidence, and a verdict was returned, that the deceased committed suicide being of unsound mind at the time.

**1847: INTELLIGENT HEIFER.** A heifer in the possession of Mr E. Manley, of Pickwick, Corsham, has acquired the art of pumping water for itself. The method which it uses is to put its nose under the handle of the pump (which stands in the yard), to raise it up, then drawing it down with its teeth, and drinking at the stream. It is now three years old, and has been known to pump water for the last year.

**FATAL TRAP.** On Friday 1 May a fatal accident occurred at the Pickwick Brewery, Corsham, Wilts, to a youth aged 15 years, named Manley. It appears that the poor fellow was sent for grains, and having ascended to the second story of the brewery he found some men at work, who asked him to assist in carrying a shute, which he did, and, not perceiving a trap-door open in the floor, under which there was a corresponding one in a large store-piece, he unfortunately fell in. Prompt assistance was immediately rendered, but, before the unfortunate lad could be got out he was suffocated in the beer and grounds which lay at the bottom of the cask. An Inquest was held on the body. Verdict, Accidental Death. In order that no prejudice shall exist in the minds of the public, Mr Herbert has very judiciously caused the store-piece to be closed up and sealed immediately with the signet of a number of the most respectable inhabitants of the place who will shortly see its contents destroyed.

**A MALIGNANT TYPE.** We are sorry to hear that a fever of malignant type has for some months past prevailed in the singularly healthy parish of Corsham. Neat as the town is in general appearance, we understand that the drainage is most neglected, and that, in some parts, an unwholesome air is constantly brooding, which at certain seasons develops a pestilence. Already several persons have died of it, and others are now lingering under its depressing effects. It is remarkable that much indifference prevails in two places - so easily drained as Corsham and Colerne, from the latter of which a low fever is seldom absent. The approach of the cholera from the East, it might be thought, would direct the attention of the waywardens and others most anxiously which that plague delights to revel……………………………………………..

**Reported a few days later by a correspondent:** ………………To allay the fears of some of our readers, we insert the result of an enquiry relative to the fever prevailing in the town of Corsham :- Deaths during the 1st three months, 17 - the average being about 36 - 2 violent deaths, 4 infants who survived the birth for a short time, 3 above 80 years old (one being 90,) 1 in a lunatic asylum, 2 of pulmonary consumption, of long standing - , total 12 ; leaving only five from the ordinary chances of mortality. The fever (not of very malignant character) is confined to one spot, and the deaths (only two) occurred in debilitated subjects. That the drainage of the town is bad, there can be no doubt, and requires that some immediate steps be taken to improve it. *[Ed: It must have taken them a long time to improve it, as I can remember the drainage stream running through the Batters in Corsham being an open sewer in the 1960/1970s.]*

**ELECTRO-MAGNETIC TELEGRAPH.** We understand the electro-magnetic telegraph, Messrs. Gamble and Co.'s patent, has lately been put down on the Great Western Railway, from the Corsham station to the Box station, through the Box tunnel. It has completely answered the expectations of its most sanguine friends and admirers, and is at once to be adopted on all the Great Western lines of railway. The Admiralty are also about to adopt Messrs. Gamble and Co.'s telegraph on whatever lines they determine to have telegraphic communication. The wire also is nearly completed for crossing the channel to France.

**DIES IN THE DRINK.** On Tuesday 7 December an inquest was held by Mr Edwards, at the Cross Keys public house, within the Manor and liberty of Corsham, on view of the body of Shadrach Skuse, a young labouring man about 24 years age, who lost his life on the previous Saturday night under the following circumstances. It appeared that on the night in question the deceased had been with his brother and others drinking at public houses; that the two brothers and another person left for home about 12 o'clock, rather the worse for liquor; that on their way they had to cross a field with several paths, one path leading to the homes of two of the party, and another to that of the deceased, where they separated; and that the weather being boisterous, and a pond being situated between the direction of each, the deceased was believed to have missed his way and fallen in, the state of the weather and the direction of the wind at the time, precluding the possibility of hearing him. Sunday passed without creating any alarm, the parents of the deceased supposing he had gone to his brother's overnight. A hat was at length seen blown into a corner of the field close to the public foot path; and on its being recognised by his brother on Monday, at once created a suspicion. The pond was immediately dragged, and the body of the deceased was very soon found. Verdict: Found drowned!

> April 5, at the General Hospital, Bath, whither he went to have an operation performed, Mr George Ayliffe, saddler, of Corsham. The deceased was a cavalry soldier at the battle of Waterloo, and was one of those who assisted in capturing the Emperor Napoleon's traveling carriage after the retreat of the French troops. He was much respected.

**1848: NAPOLEON'S CAPTOR.** [*Wiltshire Independent - Thursday 13 April 1848*]: Mr George Saddler, of Corsham died at the General Hospital in Bath on 5 April. The deceased was a cavalry soldier at the battle of Waterloo, and was one of those who assisted in capturing the Emperor Napoleon's travelling carriage after the retreat of the French troops. He was much respected.

**1849: MUSICAL PRISON.** On Sunday 31 May, during the morning service at Corsham Church, a starling got into one of the large pipes of the organ, whence it could not extricate itself. When the organ was being played, especially the pipe which the bird was imprisoned, it expressed its alarm by cries. After the service, the pipe was taken out, and the captive released from its musical prison.

**DEATH OF LORD METHUEN.** His Lordship passed away at his house in London on Friday 14 September. Very soon after his Lordship had retired from the House of Commons, he was elevated to the Peerage on

## Chapter 3. Around and About Corsham

13 July 1938. The melancholy tidings of the decease of Lord Methuen reached Corsham on Friday evening. The intelligence at once spread a gloom over the entire town. The inhabitants, by partially closing their shutters and blinds, testified their respect and affection for the memory of the departed, as well their sympathy for the bereaved members of his Noble family. The deep tones of the great bell of the church were quite in unison with the general feeling. The works at Corsham Court were at once suspended. On Tuesday the body of the deceased Lord Methuen was brought to the Court (from his lordship's late residence in Park-street, by special train), where it lay in state the after part of that day, and throughout the whole of yesterday. The room which the coffin was placed was thrown open to the public, and upwards of 2000 persons were admitted to view it. The coffin was highly elegantly ornamented: on the breast-plate was inscribed. *'The right honourable Paul, Lord Methuen, born 21st June, 1779, died 14th Sept., 1849.'*

On a cushion at the head of the coffin the coronet was placed, and over it the hatchment, with plumes of feathers: eight large wax tapers were burning round the coffin. The whole of the beautiful new corridor, a portion of the picture gallery through which visitors had to pass, the ante-room which the corpse was placed, and the state bed-room, were hung with black cloth, and lighted with wax tapers. The remains of his Lordship were interred in the family vault at North Wraxall this morning *[20 Sept.]*.

The church bell at Corsham commenced tolling at an early hour; the shops were closed, and the blinds of all the private houses drawn down. The funeral procession left Corsham Court at 12 o'clock, in the order shown…………………………>

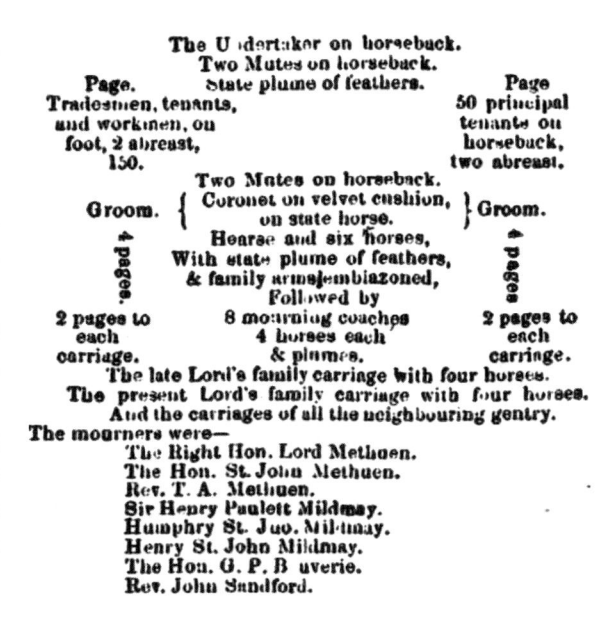

```
                The Undertaker on horseback.
                  Two Mutes on horseback.
    Page.           State plume of feathers.        Page
Tradesmen, tenants,                              50 principal
 and workmen, on                                  tenants on
 foot, 2 abreast,                                 horseback,
     150.                                        two abreast.
                Two Mutes on horseback.
   Groom.  { Coronet on velvet cushion, }  Groom.
              on state horse.
                Hearse and six horses,
                With state plume of feathers,
                & family arms emblazoned,
                    Followed by
 2 pages to        8 mourning coaches         2 pages to
   each             4 horses each               each
 carriage.          & plumes.                  carriage.
    The late Lord's family carriage with four horses.
    The present Lord's family carriage with four horses.
    And the carriages of all the neighbouring gentry.
The mourners were—
        The Right Hon. Lord Methuen.
        The Hon. St. John Methuen.
        Rev. T. A. Methuen.
        Sir Henry Paulett Mildmay.
        Humphry St. Jno. Mildmay.
        Henry St. John Mildmay.
        The Hon. G. P. Bouverie.
        Rev. John Sandford.
```

The funeral was conducted by Messrs Druce & Co., Baker Street, London, under the superintendence of Mr Flay, whom the greatest credit is due, for the admirable manner in which the whole arrangements were made.

**1851: SEVERE BURNS.** An Inquest was taken by Mr Kemm, on Saturday, the 14th September, at Corsham, on Maria Beezer, the wife of one of Lord Methuen's woodmen. She had partly lost the use of her limbs from an attack of paralysis, and was left alone when her husband was from home in charge of a little girl (Caroline Yeats), who, on Tuesday the 10th inst., on seeing her go into a neighbour's house, left for a short time. During her absence, the deceased returned to her own cottage, and put sticks on the fire to boil her kettle. In doing this, her clothes became ignited; her niece hearing a strange noise, opened the door, and saw her standing up with her clothes in flames. The fire was soon put out by the neighbours who ran to her assistance, but not before the poor woman was very severely burnt; she lived (to the surprise of Mr Washbourn the surgeon who attended her) for four days. Verdict, 'Died from the effects of severe burns.'

**CORSHAM LAKE REVEALS YET ANOTHER DEATH.** On Thursday 19 September a considerable sensation was created in this quiet little town *[of Corsham]*, by the discovery of the body of an infant child in the sheet water in the Park, commonly called the Park Pond, some suspicions were entertained, that a murder had been secretly committed. At six o'clock the same evening an inquest was held before Mr Kemm, Coroner, when the following appeared in evidence: Mr Chas. Southby stated that about 12

## Chapter 3. Around and About Corsham

o'clock on that day be was in Lord Methuen's Park, close to the edge of the water; he required a crutch, being lame, and with it was trying to ascertain the depth of the water; there were rushes four or five feet high growing near the spot where he was standing, and on pushing these aside saw, about six feet from him, what appeared to be a small white bundle; he could not quite reach it with his crutch, but called to his assistance men who happened to be near; he afterwards saw that in the bundle was a child.

Mr William King said he was in the employ of Lord Methuen, and was engaged in some iron work in the park, when a gentleman called his attention to a bundle the water. He got it out with a long stick, and his apprentice, a lad, took it up. He observed on its being squeezed the lad, that the outside was stained with blood; he thought it was a child, and on Charles Butler, another workman, tearing it open by breaking the stitches with which it had been sewn up, he then saw that it contained a dead female child. Butler then took it to the Pack Horse Inn. Mr Little, surgeon, said he had seen the infant, which was a seven months child. It had been [alive] born at least a week; the skin was some degree putrid; he could discover no marks of violence about the body or limbs; on the back part of the head was a large swelling; the umbilical cord had not been tied, but appeared, torn off about two inches from the body.

The state in which he found the child clearly proved that it had been entirely neglected at its birth. The inquest was then adjourned till Monday last, that a post mortem examination might take place, and that enquiries might be made by the police. Mr Little then stated that the body of the infant, which he had carefully examined, was quite healthy, the lungs were completely inflated with air, and floated when immersed in water; this would show that the child must have breathed. His attention was especially directed to the head; on dividing the scalp, he observed beneath it a quantity of extravagated blood, reaching from the crown of the head to the neck; the bones of the head were perfect, and nothing appeared unnatural on the inside of the skull. He found no indication of injury to other parts of the body. The appearance of injury beneath the scalp might be the result of protracted labour, or might be caused by an unskilful midwife. In answer to questions by the Coroner, Mr Little said Putrefaction had not commenced in the lungs; the surface of them when cut was of a pink colour. Crepitation took place on squeezing them. Extravasated blood under the scalp would not of itself cause death. The state of the back part of the head could not have been the effect of violence after death.

The jury returned the following verdicts; *'That the female infant was found dead in the Park Pond, concealed in a cloth, and they believe it to have been born alive, but grossly neglected at its birth; that there is not sufficient evidence before the jury to show in what way it came by its death.'* The unnatural mother has not yet been discovered.

**THE PROSECUTRIX.** An old lady said she was 64 years of age, and lived at Corsham About thirteen months ago she had separated from her husband and had lived in separate lodgings, maintaining herself by picking water-cresses which she sold in the town. On the 24th of August last she was on the road, when she met a young man who said he was *'a travelling painter.'* He asked her to have a glass of beer, and they went together into the *'New Inn,'* where she drank three glasses of beer. The prisoner [i.e. another man] then came into the house. After they had drank the beer, the painter, the prisoner, and herself left the house together, and walked the road some distance until they came to the crossroad. The two men asked her where she was going; and she told them she was out for the purpose of gathering water-cresses. At the crossroads the painter parted from them, and the prisoner said if she went with him he would show her where there were many fine cresses. She accordingly followed him down a long and lonely lane. When they had proceeded some distance, the prisoner threw her down on the ground with great violence, and gave her two black eyes and made her nose bleed. About half an

## Chapter 3. Around and About Corsham

hour after this, the prosecutrix *[i.e. female victim of a crime]* was found by a neighbour who was also following her stated occupation of picking water-cresses; but she immediately told this party that the prisoner had assaulted her, and her face was then bleeding. Mr Slade addressed the Jury in defence of the prisoner, and inferred that the prosecutrix herself was the party at fault, in drinking with strange men at a public house, and then accompanying one them alone down dark lane. The trial lasted upwards of two hours and half. The jury found the prisoner guilty, and he was sentenced to 12 month's imprisonment.

*[Ed: I've learned a new word now- 'prosecutrix'!]*

**TIMES UP.** On the evening of Tuesday 22 April at Corsham, Mr Bullock the watchmaker had been working in his garden, in apparent good health, only few hours previous to his death.

**A DRUNKEN FOLLY.** One of those revolting scenes which, unhappily, journalists are too often called upon to chronicle, and which result from an immoderate use of intoxicating drink, occurred a short time since at the village of Corsham and was well-nigh attended with fatal consequences. It appears that three tailors, zealous votaries at the shrine of Bacchus, sallied forth from their respective domiciles with the avowed purpose of quaffing a few *'jugs'* of mine host's XXX. After having imbibed no small quantity of the inebriating beverage, they were *'ripe for a spree,'* and were determined upon having one. The scheme they hit upon was nothing less than to enact, with all possible formality, the awful scene of an execution. For this purpose, one was to take upon himself the office of chaplain, another that of Calcraft *[a 19th-century English hangman, one of the most prolific of British executioners],* and the other that of the condemned culprit. The question as to who should personate the last was a difficult one to settle. At length, however, it was agreed that they should cast lots in order to decide it. Lots were accordingly cast; a handkerchief, having been fastened to a beam, was adjusted round the neck of the pseudo-victim, who stood upon a chair, and everything was in readiness for the *'culprit'* to be executed, when it was recollected that no burial service had been read, and neither of these tailors was in possession of a prayer-book.

This knotty dilemma was, however, set at rest by one being borrowed from the landlord, for the ostensible purpose of solving an argument which had been raised. This being procured, the door was locked, and the *'execution'* commenced with the soi-disant *[self-styled]* *'chaplain'* reading aloud the burial service! When this had been accomplished, the chair was kicked away from the feet of the condemned, *'and he was left suspended in the air'*. Fortunately, he was not a heavy man, or his neck would assuredly have been broken, and his recovery would have been utterly impossible. The struggles of the unfortunate man at length recalled his drunken companions to their senses, and they immediately released him from his perilous position. The tailor was in so weak a state that he was obliged to be carried home, where for a time his recovery seemed doubtful. He is now, however, perfectly convalescent.

**1852: LET THERE BE LIGHT.** The inhabitants of Corsham was last night (Monday 23 February), disappointed a second time in the lighting the town by gas, it was proposed to light it for the first time about a week ago, when by some accident, some part of the machinery became damaged, this being repaired, plans were arranged for a second time, to light it last night, several persons came from a distance of three or four miles, but were doomed to be disappointed, the gas was made, and all things ready, when it was discovered that from some defect in the apparatus it could not be lit till past midnight.

## Chapter 3. Around and About Corsham

**Corsham was last night** *[Thursday 26 February]* eventually lit with gas, for the first time. The Church bells rung a merry peal upon the occasion, a band of music paraded the streets.

**FOUND DEAD VERDICT!** On Wednesday 19 October, night, soon after eleven o'clock, a fatal accident occurred near the Cross Keys Inn, Corsham, to a poor man named Sidney Bence, a carter in the employ of Mr T Elliott, maltster of Biddestone. It appears that the poor fellow was returning from a coal-pit with a load of coals, and it is supposed that he was riding on the wagon asleep, and that some jerk caused him to fall, and the wheel passing over the back of his head caused instant death. The horses found their own way home with the cart and load, a distance of two miles, and the poor follow was discovered next morning by some men whom were proceeding to work; the deceased, who was a steady man, has left a widow and several children. An inquest was held on the body, and a verdict of 'Found Dead' was returned.

***1853:*** *[Devizes and Wiltshire Gazette Thursday 16 June 1853 and Sussex Advertiser, Tuesday 28 June 1853]:* At around 12 o'clock on Tuesday 21st June 1853 Maria Yoe of Puckeridge, Corsham spotted her 36 year old carpenter husband Henry's feet resting on the boards at the top of their garden well, with the rest of his body being head downwards under water. Maria called out to a young man (Barton) who was working in the garden at the same time, to come and help her lift her husband out. Maria and young Barton took hold of a leg each and started to raise up Henry's body, but in the act of doing so, Maria could not cope with the weight and let go of her husband's leg. The young man was not strong enough to hold onto the husband's body alone and was obliged to let go his hold and look for further assistance. In the meantime, Maria also now lay dead on the floor beside him. Thankfully, three or four men working in the nearby large stoneworks, heard young Barton's cry for help, and in a few minutes they helped to extract Henry's body from the well and managed to lay him down on his stomach with his head out of the water but still hanging over the well hole. One of the rescuers stated that Henry seemed to take a few last breaths after he was lifted out, but he was pronounced dead, along with his wife not long after the surgeon Mr Washborne had arrived to assist.

At the following inquest held by the Coroner Mr Kemm, the surgeon Mr Washborne sated that although he found a wound at the back part of the woman's head produced by her fall, it was his opinion that such a sudden death was caused by a ruptured vessel in the heart or brain (i.e. a fatal heart attack or stroke caused by the excitement and the physical and mental strain of the event). Barton and another witness stated that they had talked to Henry and his wife Maria together, about a quarter of an hour before he was found, and that Henry was then intoxicated. Another account stated that Henry had been seen by his wife a short time before attempting to throw himself in the water. Henry had threatened to destroy himself on a previous occasion and on Sunday last, he had attempted to hang himself. The Jury returned a verdict, *'That Henry Yoe was found drowned in a well, there being no evidence to show how he came there; and that Maria Yoe died suddenly from excitement and natural causes.'*

**LIGHT SERVICE.** In consequence of the additional service at Corsham church, gas has been introduced into the edifice, which has given much satisfaction to the congregation. The church was lighted for the first time on Sunday evening of 13 March.

**STAG HUNT ON THE GREAT WESTERN RAILWAY.** A singular circumstance happened on the Great Western line few days ago. A stag which had been uncarted *[released for hunting]* near Thingley got upon the railroad near Corsham station, and was making its way towards Box, just as the express train was emerging from the tunnel. The engine driver seeing the dogs coming, at once relaxed his speed, and

## Chapter 3. Around and About Corsham

sounded the whistle, and the pack divided to the right and left, and passed the train without one of them being hurt. The stag afterwards entered the tunnel and was secured there.

**THREE MEN KILLED.** A frightful accident occurred in Corsham, on Thursday morning 12 May, in which three men have been momentarily deprived of life. It appears that they were at work, with several others, in the extensive stone quarries of Messrs. Randell and Saunders, when a huge bed of stone gave way, and killed them upon the spot. Their names are Vowles, Mizen and Hulbert; each of whom has left a wife and family. The other men in the quarry escaped unhurt.

**DR W. B. SAINSBURY.** The little town of Corsham wore a more animated appearance than usual on Wednesday 14 December, which was the birth-day of W. B. Sainsbury, Esq., only son of the late much-beloved W. Sainsbury, Esq., M.D., who then attained his majority, and came into the possession of a good fortune. The bells of the parish church poured forth their merriest peals at intervals throughout the day; cannons were fired occasionally, and a brass band paraded the streets. The event will be remembered by many poor aged persons, who were not forgotten on this occasion. In the evening this young gentleman entertained a select party of friends at his residence, and the festivities closed with a brilliant display of fireworks.

**1854: STONE ME.** On Tuesday 21 June this neighbourhood was enlivened by the festivities attending the opening of a branch railway connecting the Box Hill Ground Stone Quarries of Messrs. Randell and Saunders with their Corsham Down Quarries, and through them with the Great Western Railway. The workmen and visitors assembled at the entrance to the Corsham Down Quarries about one o'clock, and after perambulating the works, which were brilliantly lighted for the occasion, they proceeded in carriages along the new railway to the Box Hill Quarries.

The first block of stone was then placed on the line, followed by the other carriages for the workmen and visitors. The train was conducted by Mr Saunders, who has throughout acted as engineer to the works, along the line of new railway to the Corsham quarries, and through them to the junction with the Great Western Railway at the east entrance of the Box Tunnel. After the business of the day, the workmen and visitors retired to a tent provided for the occasion, where about 300 sat down to a substantial repast.

**1855: FATAL RAILWAY ACCIDENT.** An inquest was held on Tuesday, the 17th September, at the Station Hotel, by the newly appointed coroner for Corsham, Thomas Gibbons, Esq., on the body of Evan Ellis, a railway watcher, who met with death on the day previous in the Box Tunnel, near the entrance. By the evidence it appeared the deceased was in the tunnel to keep the line clear, and that no workman or obstruction should be in the way of the passing trains, as the roof of the tunnel is being cased with arched brickwork to make all secure before winter. He had just directed *'all clear'* for the 3.40 down train, which was 17 minutes past due, when the train came suddenly upon him and threw him some distance upon the rails, fracturing his skull and thereby causing almost instant death. Verdict, *'Accidental death.'*

**1856: THUMB'S OFF.** On Tuesday evening 1 April, an accident occurred at Corsham to a boy about eleven years of age, named Thomas Rudman. It appears that he had been entrusted with a loaded gun to keep birds from the field, and while in the act of firing it, the gun burst, completely shattering his right hand. The thumb was quite blown off. Dr Smith of Corsham attended him but advised his removal to the Bath United Hospital. He is now progressing favourably.

## Chapter 3. Around and About Corsham

**RELIEVING OFFICER WANTED.** The Guardians require the Services of a competent person to perform the duties of a CHIPPENHAM UNION RELIEVING OFFICER in the THIRD DISTRICT of this Union. The District comprises the parishes of Box, Corsham, Ditteridge, and Lacock, with a population of 6931, and an area of 14887 acres. The person appointed will be required to find two sureties to join him in bond for the faithful performance of his duties. He must reside at Corsham, and be subject to the regulations of the Poor Law Board and the Board of Guardians. Salary £80 per *annum [£6,500 in today's money]*.

**HARD OF HEARING.** An inquest was held at the Station Hotel, Corsham, on the 18th December, before Thos. Gibbons, Esq , coroner for the manor and liberty of Corsham, and a very respectable jury, upon view of the body of William Little, an old man, who was killed on the day previous, by the express train which leaves Paddington at 9.40 a.m. It appeared in evidence that, the engine driver, John Thompson, saw the old man on the line about quarter of a mile from the Corsham station, and within 25 yards of the engine, which was going at the rate of 35 miles an hour; that he applied the brake whistle, and put on the drag, and did all in his power, but could not prevent the accident. The engine struck the deceased with such force on the head that death must have been instantaneous. Thompson stopped the train at the Corsham station, and gave information to the policeman, who went back with him and found the poor old man lying between the metals, quite dead. The jury returned a verdict of *'accidental death,'* at the same time expressing their conviction that the engine driver had done all in his power to prevent the accident, and that no blame whatever could be attached to him. The deceased was in his eighty-fourth year, and very hard of hearing, and this may account for the accident.

**1857: ABERCARNE MAN DROWNED.** On Friday 30 October, as some men, in the employ of Mr Firbanks, contractor, were crossing over the river on a plank, for the purpose of proceeding to their work at the ballast pit, near the coal works, one of them named George Jones, about 33 years of age, unfortunately fell in, and in consequence of the current of water being so strong, he was instantly carried out of sight. All possible efforts were made to recover the body, but were of no avail, until about 11 a. m. on the 31st, when it was discovered by P. C. James Jones, M.C. 36 lying on a gravel-bed, near Risca. An inquest was held at the Carpenter's Arms Inn, Pontywain, before W. H. Brewer, Esq., Deputy Coroner, and a respectable jury, on Tuesday, the 3rd of November. Verdict: *'Accidentally Drowned.'* He was a native of Corsham, Wiltshire, and has left a wife and one child.

**1858: HOLY SMOKE!** The vicarage of Corsham, Wiltshire, has become vacant, by the death of the Rev. W. C. Bennett, M.A. It is worth £150 a-year *[£13,000 in today's money]*, as the gift of Lord Methuen.

**FATAL ACCIDENT.** An inquest was held at the Station Hotel, by the coroner for Corsham, Thomas Gibbons, Esq., on the body of Charles Griffen, who met with his death at the Great Western Railway Thursday night Friday morning. On Friday morning, about two o'clock, the down goods train arrived at the station. The driver was surprised to find nobody on duty to arrange the signal, &c., as is always the case at Corsham Station.

## Chapter 3. Around and About Corsham

While the train stopped he endeavoured to ascertain the cause of absence of the man on duty there, and on looking about discovered his body laying across the rails, quite dead, the head being frightfully mangled, the back part of the skull being found some distance from the body. It is supposed that in the darkness of the night he was knocked down by the mail train, which passed about two hours before, the station being indifferently lighted with the old oil lamps, notwithstanding that the gas main is only a few yards from the rails. The verdict returned was *'Accidental Death.'*

**1859: DEATH TRAP.** Inquest held by W.B. Whitemarsh esq. at the Foss Farm, Nettleton, on the body of Mr Robert Granger, of Corsham, 41 years of age. Deceased had just left his father's residence, with his son, about 12 o'clock at night to return home, when the wheel of his trap ran upon the bank, soon after leaving, and he was thrown to the ground. He was taken back insensible, and died from a concussion of the brain. Verdict *'Accidentally killed.'*

**NOBLE CAUSES.** The noble owner of Corsham Court, although absent with his regiment at Dover, has remembered, with his usual liberality, the poor of this parish - beef, bread, coals, blankets, and stockings, having been distributed to about 130 families on Saturday last; and at Lady Methuen's school the children received their annual gift of bonnets, dresses, and warm cloaks. We may also mention that Thomas H.A. Poynder, Esq., Hartham Park, J. B. Fuller, Esq., of Neston Park, with M. Toghill, Esq., Mrs Alexander, and many other ladies and gentlemen, very kindly and liberally distributed of their abundance to the poor.

**1860: ARMLESS SHOT.** A very distressing accident occurred a few days ago at Corsham. A boy, named Smart, aged 12 years, was keeping the birds from a field belonging to his father, with a gun and powder, but no shot. Another boy named Bull, aged 8 years, came into the field, and was ordered out by Smart. On his refusing to go, Smart told him he would shoot him, and, having loaded the gun with small stones, he pointed it at him and fired, completely shattering Bull's right arm. Medical assistance was procured as soon as possible, but amputation was found necessary.

**SHAFTED.** A few days ago a very unfortunate accident occurred at the Quarry, near Pockeredge, in the occupation of Mr Pictor, of Box. Several men were employed in sinking a shaft hole, at which gunpowder was used for blasting the rock. Before the foul air which accompanies an explosion had escaped from the shaft, a man named Charles Cowley, hastened to descend. The foulness of the air took away his senses, and thus, being no longer able to keep his hold on the rope, he fell to the bottom. The back part of his head was smashed producing instantaneous death. Another man on the top, George Watson by name, anxious to know the fate of his companion, was also let down by the rope, but when about half way down he was also deprived of his senses and fell to the bottom. He lingered in a state of insensibility till the following Friday. Two or three men, having made themselves secure, *[also]* descended, but were pulled up as dead, from the action of the foul air, but remedies being applied they soon recovered. It is somewhat remarkable that the man *[Cowley]* who fell first was laying on the top of the other *[Watson]*, giving reason to suppose that a severe struggle for life took place. An inquest was held before W. Kemm, Esq., and a verdict of *'Accidental death, through neglect,'* was returned. Both men leave widows and family to deplore their loss.

**NO ROOM AT THE CHURCH.** The parish of Corsham, Wilts, which is four miles square, and contains 4,000 inhabitants, has only one church, and that not a very large one. The existence of 14 dissenting places of worship in the parish is a significant consequence.

# Chapter 3. Around and About Corsham

**1861: NOT SO COMFORTABLE.** On Thursday 11 April an inquest has been held at Corsham on the body of Mr Alfred James. The deceased was a very sober, steady, and well conducted man; and, from the opening of the railway from Bristol to London, was office porter at the Corsham station, in which situation he was faithful, obliging, and attentive, and was much respected. He was for a time promoted to the office of booking-clerk, but his abilities being not quite equal to this situation, he was obliged about 18 months ago to resign it. Reluctant to return to his old office of porter, he commenced the business of tea-dealer, and had a share of the trade of the neighbourhood; but he has lately been very gloomy and desponding in his religious views. On Thursday morning he left his house as usual, on business it was supposed, and wandered about a mile on the Lacock road, when he entered a field and cut his throat with a razor. He was soon found by some men who were at work near the spot; and medical and other assistance having been procured, he was conveyed home, where he lingered until the following Saturday. The verdict of the jury was *'Temporary Insanity.'* The deceased was in very comfortable circumstances, and has left a widow to mourn his loss.

**FRIGHTFUL AND FATAL ACCIDENT AT BATH.** Yesterday afternoon, an accident of a most frightful description, which resulted in the immediate death of one, and narrowly escaped, a like result to a second person, occurred in the above city. The deceased's name is William Hale, a carter in the employ of Mr William Gale, of Minety Farm, Corsham, near this city, and he, accompanied a lad named Francis Little, left his master's house yesterday morning with a wagon and three horses, and proceeded to Cox's lime kiln, at Weston, where they filled a load of lime.

On their return, they proceeded through Cottle's Lane and down Lansdown Road, which is a steep and difficult descent. The wagon was of a heavy description, and the weighty nature of the load appeared to be more than the shaft horse could keep back. The boy was stationed at the head of the horse, the unfortunate deceased guiding the *wheeler.* In passing over a crossing at the bottom of Belmont, which required a sharp pull, the impetus of the wagon at once became more than the hind horse could manage, although the skid had been properly placed under the front wheel. The *wheeler* coming on so suddenly forced the front horses together and the spreader of the fore traces falling out, the leaders commenced kicking.

The lad was knocked down by a kick in the mouth by the front horse, the others passing over him, together with the wagon, without inflicting further injury. Hale, seeing the danger in which the lad was placed, attempted to force the wagon out of the way, and endeavouring to do so, became jammed between the edge of the high pavement which adjoins the road and the vehicle, and was thrown down, the fore wheel passing over and breaking his legs. His head was then brought into contact with the dragged wheel, the shoe of which, from the terrific force with which it came against him, completely smashed in the fore part of the skull, and the unfortunate fellow was seen to roll over three or four times as the wagon progressed down the hill, being pushed forwards by the pressure of the shoe against his head. The bystanders immediately rushed to his rescue, but too late, for on being taken up his head was found to be so frightfully battered that a large portion of the brain was protruding and literally covered the face.

The blood from the head and body also ran down in a copious stream into the gutter of the road. The body was taken into the stable of Mr Dring, veterinary surgeon, to await the inquest, which was held last evening, before Mr A.H. English, Coroner, at the Lansdown Arms, when a verdict in accordance with the above facts was returned. He was about fifty years of age and bore a good character for industry and sobriety. He was a widower, and has left one son grown up.

## Chapter 4. Aircraft Bomber Flies over Corsham with Nobody Onboard!

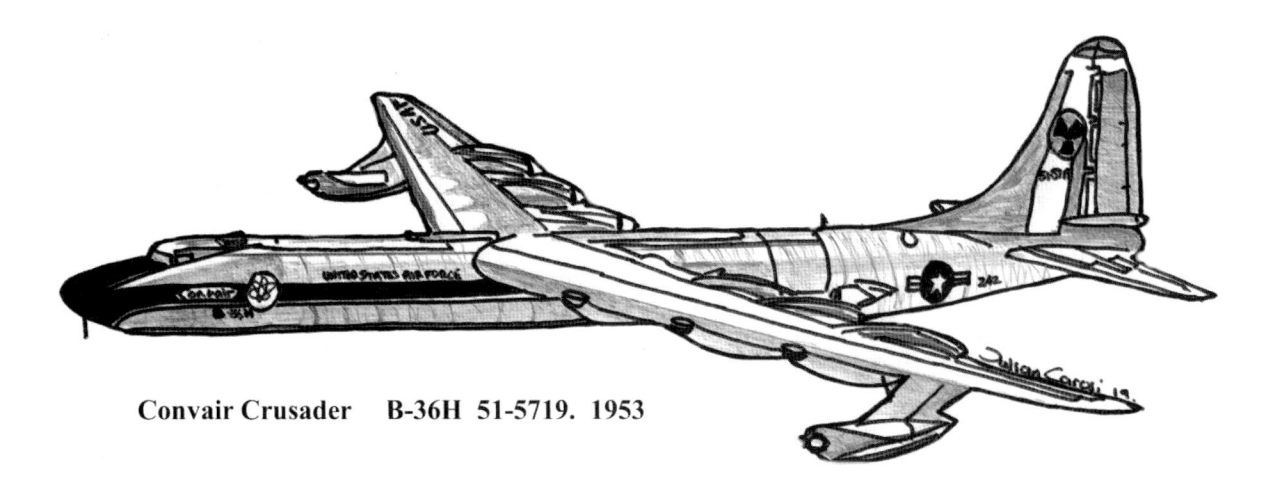

Convair Crusader    B-36H 51-5719. 1953

On the morning of 7 February 1953, local resident Charlie Ralph heard the roar of a very low-flying large aircraft. On looking up, Charlie spotted a huge Convair B-36H American Bomber cruising slowly and very low over Corsham............... without a pilot! A few moments later a muffled rumble could be heard in the distance as the aircraft crashed and exploded four miles away in Nethermore Wood just outside of Lacock. At the time, this was one of the world's largest aircraft.

Lt. Col Herman F. Gerick aged 34, of 700 Coates was the aeroplane Commander. He was commanding one of 18 bombers of the 492nd. Bomb Sq.(BS), 7th. Bombardment Wing. They had been deployed from Carswell Air Force Base (AFB) in Tarrant County, Texas, United States. They were heading to RAF Fairford via a refuelling stop at Goose AFB Canada as part of a unit simulated combat mission, codenamed "Operation Styleshow".

*Photo of Charlie Ralph taken by Becca Wilkin*
*www.beccawilkinphotography.com*

Six of the aircraft belonged to the 9th. Bomb Squadron (BS), six to the 436th. BS, and six belonged to the 492nd. The aircraft's registration number was 51-5719

On February 6th the aircraft took off from Canada, with one machine returning back to Carswell USA.
The remaining 17 set course for the UK. It seems like there were originally 17 men on the *ill-fated* plane; however, it is presumed that two of the crewmen either left the craft before it took off from Carswell USA or at Goose Bay, Labrador, where it landed en-route.
The aircraft flew over the Atlantic but weather conditions deteriorated and by the time the Squadron reached the English coast at dawn, they were running short of fuel.

## Chapter 4. Aircraft Bomber Flies over Corsham with Nobody Onboard!

As the pilot circled RAF Fairford in Gloucestershire (awaiting his turn to land as part of the formation), the weather started to deteriorate even more. Because of the inexperienced Ground-Controlled-Approach (GCA) personnel and his under-manned aircraft crew, the pilot missed two approaches which resulted in long periods of *holding* while the other seventeen NB-36s landed. This resulted in severe fuel starvation. It is not clear why the plane could not land while it had some fuel left.

Rather than risk the lives of his crew or the people on the ground, Commander Gerick ordered his crew to bail out 22 miles NE of Fairford. He then aimed the B-36 to crash in open country. All the crew members along with the pilot descended safely in their parachutes, except for the second pilot Capt. Newton Benham Jr., 37, of Dallas, who suffered a fractured ankle when he hit the ground. The crewmen from the stricken bomber parachuted into three southern counties - Oxfordshire, Berkshire, and Wiltshire.

The aircraft somehow remained airborne before breaking up and crashing in Wiltshire. Later indications show that frantic efforts had been made to put out a fire which had broken out just before the aeroplane commander ordered the crew to abandon ship.

Wreckage from the plane was spread over several miles of sparsely settled farmland near Lacock, but luckily nobody was hit. The plane could have easily crashed in Corsham or Chippenham with a heavy death toll but fortunately it came down in the isolated location at Nethermore Wood, near Pitters Farm, at Sandy Lane just east of Lacock. The site was cordoned off and US military officials soon arrived to remove top secret equipment.

The location of the crash is: Grid Ref: ST 9473 6892 : X/Y co-ords: 394735, 168921 : Lat/Long: 51.4193,-2.07711687.

Members of the crew included: William Minelli, Bill Plumb, George Morford (co-pilot), Royal Freeman, Edwin House and Doug Minor. In a cruel twist of fate, all except Minelli and Plumb were killed (along with Herman Gerick) in another B-36 crash near El Paso on 11 December, 1953.

The remaining 16 bombers all landed at the Fairford base without incident and remained in England for a week before returning home to their base in the United States.

The crippled B-36 had flown unmanned for over 30 miles before exploding and ploughing into the woods. The plane ripped through many trees before coming to a halt. The woods caught fire, but firemen were quickly on the scene to dowse the burning trees and to bring the blaze under control. Three of the engines were found about a mile away from the main wreckage.

J.P. Hollick, a local lawyer who lived near to the scene, told newspapermen at the time:
*"I heard the noise of a big plane obviously in difficulty. Looking out the window, I saw it going down in circles. It was all lit up inside. It might have been the electric lights or it could have been on fire. Bits were dropping off, so the impression I had was that the house was being bombed. I heard an explosion while the plane was in the air."*

Chippenham historian Paul Moran who compiled newspaper reports of the accident, also talked to witnesses at the time. He believed that the B-36 bomber was carrying top secret military equipment. *"We still don't know the full story,"* Moran said. *"Why on earth did the crew bail out, leaving the plane and the people on the ground to their fate, when they still had enough fuel to fly for 30 miles?"*

## Chapter 4. Aircraft Bomber Flies over Corsham with Nobody Onboard!

Mr Moran said details of the subsequent investigation were not made public and no facts have been released to shed light on the exact circumstances of the crash. It could be that there is some truth in the accident being caused by a combination of the lack of fuel and the fire that broke out onboard.

Malcolm Heath of Lacock still remembers the day well. He was with his father at home when they heard a strange throbbing noise. *"Suddenly there were two or three loud thumps. We later learnt that an aircraft had come down in Nethermore Wood,"* he said.

Following the crash, the site was cordoned off and USAF crews carried out a thorough cleanup of the area. Local civilians spoke of 'hush-hush' operations being carried out to recover items of sensitive equipment from the wreckage. Inevitably there was a certain amount of public outcry, but in the days following the crash the local Wiltshire Times newspaper carried no news stories of the accident except for one mention in its letters page No.2 from Mr W.A. Whittock of 18 Heathcote Rd, Melksham, in the 14th. February 1953 - edition:

*"Sir, I wish to express my horror, and I am sure that many hundreds of other people living in Chippenham, Melksham and the villages of Lacock and Sandy Lane at the crashing of one of the World's largest atom bombers. The machine flew for 30 miles or more over countryside with no one in it. We can be thankful that it did not carry any atom bombs, and we can also be thankful for a little place called Nethermore Wood, Lacock, where it came down without causing any loss of life.*

*Let us just try and think what would have happened if the machine had crashed in the middle of one of our towns and villages, which it quite easily could have done. I wonder what the pilot and crew were thinking when they bailed out over Oxfordshire - or was it Berkshire? Was it - to hell with everyone else - I'm all right?*

*I wonder whether any of our British boys would have done such a thing? Somehow, I don't think so. I am quite sure that Mr Pegg, the test pilot of the Brabazon, would not have left his machine quite like this if he had been in trouble in the air.*

*I also wonder what the people would say if I or any of their fellow workmates in the cause of our duty as public servants, were to jump from the cab of one of our buses with a full load of passengers on a skiddy road.*

*I sincerely hope that no secrets were taken from the plane before the American Air Force arrived, as we are told some of the plane's equipment is on the secret list. However, all's well that ends well, with no thanks to the American crew."*

It should be pointed out that this point of view was by far in the minority.

In November 1997, local Duncan Curtis managed to locate and speak with the present landowner of the crash site, and the latter said it would be OK for a survey of the site to take place with a metal detector, and to locate and dig up any wreckage (after the shooting season had finished - Feb 98). On 7 March 1998 Duncan managed to get to the site and started looking.

The first day's effort uncovered little; the search going by directions supplied by the landowner's neighbour. However, just as Duncan was leaving, the landowner himself (who was a schoolboy at the time of the crash, and remembered it well) turned up and stated that Duncan had been looking in the wrong place!

## Chapter 4. Aircraft Bomber Flies over Corsham with Nobody Onboard!

Therefore, Duncan returned with his sons Jay and Dale on 8th. March and immediately began to uncover pieces of aluminium on the correct site.

He managed to locate (mainly) brackets and a piece of electrical loom, with numbers visible on many pieces. Finally, he dug up about 3 feet of the port/LH wing aileron trim tab, which helped to surmise that all of the above was probably from the LH wing area.

On the following Saturday, 14 March 1998, Duncan returned to the site for the last time, and although he didn't turn up as much wreckage as the previous weekend, he did uncover a nice piece of rubber hose, which still had two immaculate stainless steel jubilee clips attached, and an aileron trim tab balance weight with a part number readily visible.

However, the real find was a massive section of wing; obviously a piece of stringer/rib, with aluminium skin attached, which seemed to go into the ground for some way - maybe as much as 6 ft. After digging for a good hour and still with no sign of it budging, Duncan gave up further excavation, and left this item at the site. It would probably need a crane to lift it out.

Maybe there's an engine on the end of it? It did seem to have a heat exchanger matrix attached, and considering the B-36's radials were air cooled, we can only think it was the supercharger intercooler, which sits beside the engine.

In addition, two portions of the LH Aileron trim tab were found. Balance weights are visible protruding from the leading edge, plus numerous unidentified aluminium brackets.

Also found was a length of rubber hose, approx. 4 inches long, with an aluminium pipe (approx. 1/4-inch o.d.) extending from one end, fastened by two 'Aeroseal' jubilee-type clips, pt. nos. AN-737-22 and AN-737-26. Both clips are marked '3/51'.

The recovered items were donated to the Jet Age Museum at Staverton Airport, Gloucestershire.

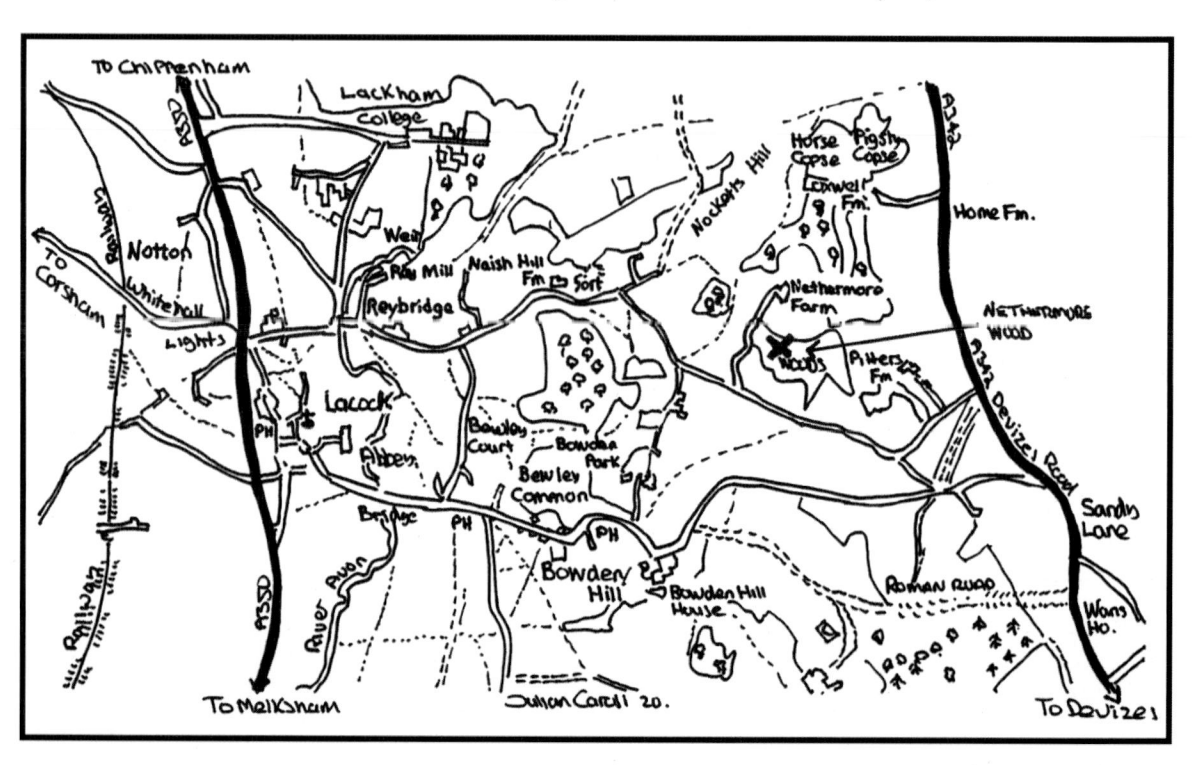

## Chapter 5. Arthur Hobbs, WWI Correspondent.

Here is a unique viewpoint from an ordinary shopkeeper who was whisked away from his peaceful job as a saddler in our little town of Corsham, Wiltshire, and sent into the hell of WWI. Born North Bradley 1880, he married his sweatheart Dorcas in 1902. In the early 1900s, Mr Arthur James Hobbs was a saddler and cycle shop owner by trade, working from his small shop at 38 High Street (now 'The Corsham Dental Practice') to the right of the Old Vicarage and opposite Alexander House.

Arthur was known as Mr Corsham, and was a member of the Corsham Fire Brigade and later went on to wear the silver helmet of Captain for 15 years (making a total of 36 years service).

He was also an archdeacon of the Baptist Church in Priory Street and a collector of local historical relics which included a set of Roman dice found by men digging a trench for a house water main; the dice are exhibited at Chippenham Museum.

Arthur James Hobbs 1880-1959 Corsham

His short portly figure was often seen leaning against the doorpost of his shop, watching the world go by along the Corsham High Street! When WWI beckoned, he enlisted in the Army and whilst on duty in the 5th Division of the 2nd Army Corps and later in the 10th Army, 3rd Arms Corps in France, Arthur continued his other role as a reporter for the Wiltshire Times and Trowbridge Advertiser, by sending periodic articles back from the war *Front*, a number of which are summarised below. He passed away in 1959 and is buried in the Corsham Baptist churchyard in Priory Street.

Arthur's newspaper reports, were often written in a factual and sometimes humorous way that belies what it must have really been like. Arthur's reports are a fascinating insight into his character.

It was as if Arthur Hobbs was trying to make the best of it by not sending too many worries back to those waiting for news back in Britain. His following reports sum up the pointlessness of war.

**"One thing I came across was a cemetery. I walked through it and at one place saw where English, French, and German soldiers had been buried side by side."**

**Saturday 10 April 1915 - Corsham Saddler at the Front:**

The former Wiltshire Times newspaper correspondent at Corsham is now Saddler A.J. Hobbs, No. 86848, with the 5th Division, 2nd Army Corps, France. He writes: 'Just a few lines to let you know that I am still all right and fairing very well. It has been beautiful weather until yesterday (April 3rd), when it set in wet, and I can tell you it is terrible getting about in the mud, and shall not be sorry when it settles down for fine again. We see plenty of life out here, and yesterday we marched to, and heard an address from the

Chapter 5. Arthur Hobbs, WWI Correspondent.

Bishop of London. It was fine to see so many men formed up in a square with the whole divisional staff and the special service held out in a plough-field. The Bishop, in his opening remarks, spoke of the valour of the troops in the field, and said as the men could not come to church they had decided to bring the church to them. The Bishop also said that England would not be satisfied until the Germans were driven out of Belgium and France and put back beyond the Rhine in their own country. "Rock of Ages" and "Jesu, Lover of my Soul" were heartily joined in by the men, the service lasting half an hour'. During the time, several of our flying machines were curling round [flying in circles above] us. The natives tell us here, that Von Kluck had a very narrow escape. He was staying in an Inn and the Allies dropped bombs, which just missed him, as he hurriedly left in his motor car, and our advanced lines were not far behind him in the retreat from Paris.' *Photo below shows Mr Hobbs' shop on the left of Corsham High Street.*

**In a letter to a friend at Corsham, Saddler Hobbs says:** 'I have had experiences that I never thought would fall to my lot, and as I write this, the guns are going great.

I met Gunner C. Allen (who was at the Red Cross Hospital at Corsham) and we had a fine chat. We had a visit from a German aeroplane which was chased by the Allies.

We got to our destination about dinner-time on Sunday. It was a barn, and we were handed over to a Sergeant who hails from Stafford and is a trump. In the afternoon I went to parade [church]. The speaker was the Rev. F.W. Gillingham, the old Essex cricketer. He was a very genial, bluff speaker - one that would go down [well] with the men. The food is very good here with the few extras we buy and the men are fairly comfortable, with the exception that they want to see the war finished and get back to old England.

A German aeroplane came not very far away and I had a good chance of watching the shell fire bursting all round it, and was very glad to hear that it had been brought down. I also watched one of ours doing a bit of scouting. I don't know who he was, but a more daring piece of work I never saw, though I must leave the telling of it till I see you. The big guns make a tremendous rattle. When they go off it seems as if you can hear the shells going through the air for quite a two minutes after you hear the sound of the guns.'

Mr Hobbs wishes to be remembered to all enquiring friends [back home in Corsham].

**14 August 1915 - Saddler A.J. Hobbs. No. 86848 D.A.C. R.F.A. 10th Army, 3rd Arms Corps, British Expeditionary Force, writing on August 5th says:**

At last I am writing to say that I am very well and trust it will find you the same. We have been having some very peculiar weather, some days so hot you did not know what to do, and then at night you shivered like anything, as our blankets have been taken away. We sleep in our clothes and do not get much chance to take them off, but must be thankful that we keep so well, as the wet which we have had

## Chapter 5. Arthur Hobbs, WWI Correspondent.

plenty of, has not caused much illness in the camp. We have all been inoculated and that caused more days rest in the camp than all the illness, beside I was very rough with it and shall want to be told a very good tale to have a second addition. All around, just in the part where we are staying, the corn and roots and hops have been in splendid condition. The sugar beet, which is about the greatest industry of the women of the country (if you can term it that way), is showing a very promising crop. Another cereal is maize: I have never seen so much growing before.

Well, our camp life has been very much varied. I had the opportunity of going right up into our lines and saw the damage done, fine farmhouses and humble cottages being one mass of ruins. I was told by some of your fellows who have come down since that an *estaminet*, which as you know takes the place of the English public-house that was at the corner of the road where I passed has been razed to the ground. A shell plonked into it from the German lines and blew it up. I shall not regret going up, as I saw some of the work our men were doing to stop the Kaiser and his Huns from breaking through *[Huns is a nickname based on a speech given in 1900 by Kaiser Wilhelm II to the German troops sent to help suppress the Boxer Rebellion]*.

Tommy Atkins *[often just Tommy, is slang for a common soldier in the British Army]* is never happier than when he has a pet to care for, and out here they are just the same. In our section we have two magpies and a pup, and of course, they go from bivouac to bivouac, and make friends with everyone and sometimes enemies. One of our sergeants had just written a good long letter home and Mrs Magpie paid a visit and seeing the letter, made a dive for it. When the sergeant returned to post the letter he found it torn to pieces. I am afraid the magpie would have had a rough time of it.

We also get plenty of fun from the pup, as it used to pay us a visit about four in the morning and lick our faces. If that did not move us, a bite of the nose or ear generally did the trick, which was very amusing to us, but not to those who participated in it. At breakfast one morning, fried eggs were on the menu. Of course, we use anything that comes to hand, and one in our bivouac, seeing a tin with holes in it, thought he would pepper his egg. On going to use it on the second one [egg], was asked what he was doing with the tin. "Putting some pepper on," was his reply."Why, that is Keating's powder in there [a long-standing insect powder for lice etc.]," was the reply, to his astonishment, whilst we could not help giving a laugh at the sight of his face.

Now, perhaps you have noticed that we have done a move and our troops for over a fortnight came out at night time. It was one of the thrilling episodes of the war, for here were men for the last nine months had held the Kaiser's hosts at bay, notwithstanding all the hellish inventions for the destruction of their lives, such as poisonous gases, fire and shell, as well as frost, snow and water. It was one of the proudest moments of one's life to feel you were part of them, and you felt proud you were a Britisher, as these men came out of the danger zone, and, raining hard as it was and mud nearly over their boots, passed our camp singing as if they were going on a picnic. Their band consisted of mouth organs and biscuit tins for drums, and doing their march almost as fresh as when they started.

We got out of bed and went down and had a chat with some of them, and one of them belonging to one of our best regiments told us the following story, and as there were a large number of his own chums there, I have no reason to disbelieve it.'

'There was a man' (he mentioned his name) 'whom we all looked upon as a coward: in fact, he was the funkiest *[frightened; panicky]* of the whole lot and was made the butt for all jokes, and a lot felt he was

## Chapter 5. Arthur Hobbs, WWI Correspondent.

beneath contempt. But there came a time when that was all changed. It was like this': he said, with a catch in his voice. 'The devils (the Germans) had bombarded our position. Then they gassed us, but we were pretty well prepared for them, but we lost our officers, and as they swarmed to our trenches; he whom they thought was a coward was the first man over the parapet. "Come on lads," he shouted, and led the way towards the German host. Our fellows rallied, and we charged and the enemy was driven back with the bayonet with heavy loss, and our position was saved. I am sorry to say that the one who led us, was amongst those who were killed, but he had nobly vindicated himself in our eyes and was worthy of any honour we could give him and nobly died a hero's death'.

Another story, although dating back to Mons *[The Battle of Mons was the first major action of the British Expeditionary Force (BEF)]* is equally true, if it seems a little far-fetched. That was on the retreat, and some of your artillery were told to hold on at any cost and they did until guns in some cases were smashed and the enemy was upon them and then they were told to retire with the guns, as ammunition was gone. The others were told to save themselves, every man for himself.

A gunner whose gun was gone was making a 'nip' for it, when he was pulled up by an officer, who was holding a pistol at him, and asked what he was running away for. 'Oh,' said the man, 'there is a terrible fight up there,' (pointing to where he had just come from) 'and I am after a policeman for him to stop it.' By this time the officer could see the other lot coming on and laughingly let him go. Before it came to our turn to move we had an inspection of the whole of our column by General Plumer, and at the close of it, he had the whole of us formed up and addressed us. He stated that the division that we belonged to had made such a name for themselves that it would go down in history and he complimented the men of the column on how they had carried out their part of the work. He said one of the important things of the war was the supply of ammunition and if they did not get it up when it was wanted, no matter how good the soldier was a fighter, if the supply of ammunition failed he *[the soldier]* failed also. He said that not once had we failed to bring it up [the ammunition] in quick time and personally he was very sorry we should not belong to him any more.

The first part of our column moved out on Sunday morning and this included two of our subsections. The other section, which I had to come on with, did not leave camp until 10 o'clock at night and in the meanwhile we had to clean up camp, burn all old sacks, paper etc., and bury tins, glass and wire and leave it tidy. This was done, and our officer who was in charge, told us to get it done as quick as we could as he did not want us to be at work all day, and when it was done we could have the rest of it to ourselves until we should be ready to move off. We had a fine night to move off, and we had to go about 8 kilometres by road until we reached the station where we had to entrain horses, wagons etc., and it was something after 2 o'clock before the train started. We were riding in cattle trucks, and were soon down to it so as to get an hour or two's sleep before daylight, as we were off and did not know how soon we should be out of it.

I woke up about five o'clock just as we were going through a big station and after this, we passed through some of France's historic towns and for a long time passed by the sea. Being Bank Holiday, I could almost fancy I was off for an excursion! After seeing some fine sights we reached our destination late in the afternoon, when we detrained and as I was one of the dismounted party I had a six mile walk to camp and was not sorry to get there, where a lot had already concentrated. Bivouacs were hastily rigged up and I was soon asleep. It came on to rain very heavily and two of my chums had to get up and seek other shelter but it did not wake me, and although wet through one side, I am none the worse for it. I might add that in one lot on the camp they had 600 mules, and the music they made (especially at

## Chapter 5. Arthur Hobbs, WWI Correspondent.

night) was anything but what would soothe anyone. Next evening we were further strengthened and amongst them was a young fellow who soon spotted me, as I knew him well, in the person of Driver Banks, of Lacock, who came out from Wilts the week before, and he was surprised to meet me.

The camp that we were in was a park, and in the grounds stood a chateaux dating back nearly 230 years, and the trees, instead of being allowed to grow anyhow, were planted in rows or avenues. I should think it was nearly a mile long. We were there only until Thursday, when we packed up and went between 16 or 18 kilometres, halting on the side of the road for dinner, and arrived here during the afternoon on the most peculiar bit of ground I was ever on. It was very marshy, almost like a bog, and when the horses pass over it, it looks as if they were walking in India-rubber, as it bounces and shakes everything round it.

We don't expect to be very long, as it has rained almost non-stop since we have been here and we shall not be able to move if we get much more. Not many have built bivouacs. My bed is made up underneath one of the wagons, with a ground sheet to lie upon and my great coat over me, and I can sleep well on it. We had an inspection in our last camp by our new commander, General Munro and he expressed himself how pleased he was at the appearance of the men, horses and kits. Flying high over our heads last night was what was thought to be a German captive balloon *[a lighter-than-air balloon secured by a rope to the ground, used to carry radar equipment or for parachute jumps]*, which had broken loose and passed nearly over our heads.

Some of or men have gone on furlough *[temporary leave]*. Bombardier Harvey, who was my bed chum, went and came back and another one is on leave now and another expecting to be in Devizes next week. The men would greatly appreciate the chance to go, as up to now it has only been N.C.Os *[Non Commissioned Officer's]*. Roll on the time when it is all over and we shall be back again!

**Saturday 5 August 1916. Keeping Fritz & Co. Busy. Saddler Hobbs writes from 'Somewhere in France'.**

'Just a few lines again to let you know I am well. Since I wrote to you last we have had some lively times. It started three weeks ago, when in the afternoon we had orders to be prepared to move. We started off about 10 o'clock to bring our guns out of action. This was done without much attention by the enemy except plenty of stray bullets falling round. It was nearly daybreak before we made a move and glad enough we were to get going and to reach camp, as we should have been an easy mark in the day-light. We passed Sergeant Fricker on the road with his Company; I gave him a passing shout.

Next day I was off into the barn for dinner, when looking across the yard, I saw Gunner George Fletcher, of Priory Street, who told me he was a temporary officer's mess cook. I have seen him several times since, as we are in the same Brigade. He is looking very well. The same day one of our bombardiers came to me and asked if I came from Corsham. I said 'Yes, that is where I was born.' He said, 'My name is Sparks, I used to live in Lake Cottage on Corsham Lake.' We stayed in this place a matter of ten or twelve days. Then the order came to pack up and in a short time we're off.'

Saddler Hobbs then describes the 'trek' and his meeting with Wilfred Baines, son of Mr Baines, of the High Street, Corsham from whom he heard that Ray Hiscocks was in the neighbourhood. They saw a number of guns, etc., that had been captured in the 'big push" also prisoners who were washing their clothes and some washing their legs and feet in a stream as well. Next morning they passed a gang of Huns who were repairing the road. It looked by their faces as if they received a bit of a shock to see a Brigade of Artillery march past. Further down on the road a General saw them go past. The scene later became very much like it was at Corsham years ago on manoeuvres.

# Chapter 5. Arthur Hobbs, WWI Correspondent.

Saddler Hobbs continues: 'Very soon we were in what for a long time had been 'No Man's land,' now held us. It was terrible to see the ravages of war - huge holes of every size, trees of every description blown about and what had been houses inhabited by peaceful farm folk razed to the ground, whilst implements of agriculture twisted and torn, with those of war, were scattered in endless confusion. Some enemy 'dud' shells were lying about and one big one had been decorated by a wag with the iron cross.

By the time we reached our position we had seen some gruesome sights. In one place was a dead German, next *[to]* a horse, then a boot with a leg in it, and parts of horses which had been blown up. A cross at the head of a body showed it to be an unknown hero, a British officer. A number of men were acting as salvage Corps and collecting German ammunition and other material, whilst from behind us came great shells. Another would come from the right, then from the left, till it seemed a perfect inferno. Evidently our men were trying to keep 'Fritz and Co' on the move, and it was not for the want of trying if they did not succeed.

The position which the Germans had been driven from was one of exceptional strength and great credit is due to our men who had turned them out. Our battery was soon in action and we have been kept busy ever since. Unfortunately, we have had several casualties and two of the young fellows who walked the biggest part of the way here with me are now no more.

We are sleeping in an old gun-pit for the present and can make ourselves fairly comfortable, but roll on the time when it is all over and we are all back again in our homes. We thought we were in for a lively time on Saturday night when the enemy started sending whizz-bangs over into the next field. Then at night our guns started and for hours the ground shook with the concussion, as our big shells were aimed at the enemy. One thing I came across was a cemetery. I walked through it and at one place saw where English, French, and German soldiers had been buried side by side.'

**Saturday 14 October 1916 - Saddler Hobbs's Experiences:**

Saddler Hobbs of Corsham, with the British Expeditionary Force 'somewhere in France,' writes that he is still well. He adds: 'I think when I wrote to you last I said that we were having a very warm time, and we were not sorry to hear that we were to be relieved and have a rest, but not before we had lost some of our best men, including our O.C. [Officer Commandeering]. Another wounded was one of the best sergeants it has been my lot to meet, always ready for a joke and a bit of fun. Two days before we came out his left hand was taken off by a piece of shell, but the first thing he said was, 'Don't bother about me, look to my men,' and they had a job to do anything for him until they could assure him his wounds were the worst. He was one of the bravest and coolest men that was ever with a detachment, and after two years it was very hard luck on him. It was only the day before it happened he told me that if he got through all right he was joining the Metropolitan Police.

The following Monday morning found us on the road, in ideal weather, going for our rest. We arrived during the morning close to a town about the size of Trowbridge, with factories, whistles, and all. As we passed, just as the lassies were going back from dinner, the boys were soon 'making eyes' and trying to talk to them. Next morning we had rather a shock, being awakened by the hooters going the first thing. I forgot to say we were billeted in the out-buildings of a farm-house, and had a very comfortable place to sleep and work in. Some of the buildings were occupied by other troops and in conversation with one he asked what part I came from. I said 'Wilts.' He then asked me if I knew Edington *[a village near*

## Chapter 5. Arthur Hobbs, WWI Correspondent.

*Westbury]* and I said 'Rather.' Visions of Sunday School outings passed through my mind. He then told me he had an uncle, mentioning the name of a well known farmer. There was a Y.M.C.A. hut across the road and going across for a cup of tea, I came face to face with Gunner J. Pullen (who came to see me just before I left home to join up, he having just come home from China) and he was very glad to meet me.

A night or two after I was out in the town when I passed a familiar face and found it was W. Holder, of Pickwick. We liked to take a walk down the town. You could get a large bunch of grapes for a half franc and you could buy almost anything, but fruit was especially plentiful, and as it was the first chance of getting some all the summer, we did not half go for it. Another fine thing was, we were marched down to town and had a fine hot shower bath. One felt wonderfully refreshed after it. Well, it was not all play even if we were on rest, as all of our gear had to be overhauled. We had all the harness to go over and it gave us plenty to do, but of course when the Battery sports *[sports competitions]* came off we had to have a holiday with the rest, and we were well away with them when down came a tremendous storm and ended the proceedings. I only went in for one event, the tug-of-war. We won the first heat in two pulls and in the final we were again successful in two pulls after a great struggle.

The next day it still rained hard, but the day after it being fine about eleven, and the sun coming out, the events were continued, causing any amount of fun. Some of the most interested spectators were a number of German prisoners who were repairing the road. I chanced to look across the field and was astonished to see them and their guards enjoying the fun as much as we were. The programme was concluded by an open-air smoking concert *[live performances, usually of music, before an audience of men only]*, at which the prizes were distributed. Some of our men were allowed *on pass* to a well-known city, and I was going to try and get one *[a leave pass]* myself, when the order came to get ready to move in the morning, back into action. Next morning at four o'clock reveille sounded; about 7 o'clock we were off. We had not gone very far before down came the rain and we were soon wet through. We stopped the night in a plough-field and stacked some sheaves of corn up to sleep under, but the rain came down and it was soon as bad as if you had no shelter. It was here that I heard the news of the loss of one of the first chums I made when I came out here. He was a provost-sergeant, one of County Sligo's best sons, and had been killed by a shell the day before, about a quarter-of-a-mile away, when moving his horse to safety. The next night I went to his graveside and coming back had a narrow escape myself, as 'Fritz' *[a name given to German troops]* started sending over some shells just behind, about twenty falling. A mounted man passed at the trot going in the opposite direction and a minute later, down *[back]* came his horse at breakneck speed. I thought the horse had been frightened and I just had time to spring back into the bank when it passed me by rider-less.

We were bivouacked in what was a cottage garden. A battery of heavy guns close beside us gave us a hard time of it. The ground shook beneath their roar and I could not help laughing at one of our lads "cribbing" [mimicking] at one of the gunners of the battery, because every time a certain gun fired it put his candle out and he had to use a match (and a match is a match out here). One of the things that was a source of wonder was watching the flight of the shell as it left the gun, looking just like a cricket ball hit by a mighty Jesse Smith *[famous Corsham Cricketer Jim Smith]* as it soared toward the German lines. We also had plenty of Germans passing, including officers. One little incident I should like to tell you about to illustrate how Tommy feels when it comes to a wounded enemy. Whenever we heard a party of Germans were coming we generally all had a look at them. One lot were nearly all slightly wounded cases, but it touched the heart of Tommy. One at the end shouted 'Stand back and give the poor devils a

## Chapter 5. Arthur Hobbs, WWI Correspondent.

chance.' They looked as if they had gone through the mill. Some were looking downcast as if they felt their position, others were laughing defiantly, whilst others again were looking as if they did not trouble what was going to happen to them, as if they were 'fed up' with it all. Dirty, unshaven, unwashed, they were anything but a pleasant sight. I forgot to mention that in the party that watched our sports was one with the same rank as our Sergeant-Majors. He could speak English and he would have it *[told us that]* our fleet was sunk. That was the reason they were kept in France and he expected to be back in Berlin in a month's time. Seeing a lot of mounted men close to us one day I walked across to see if they were from our county, and found they were.

A group of lads heard us speaking and one of them turned round and said, 'What are you doing here Mr Hobbs?' Looking at him I found it was a young fellow named Bean, from Biddestone. He was in a lot who were camping next to us. We found our county lads were just the other side of the road on the side of the hill, we being down in the valley. The first to jump off his horse was Sergeant Whiddett and I went up to their camp and saw faces I knew. Corporal Colley, who was close to me at Corsham, came down several times and told Trooper Fletcher his brother, who had been wounded, was back again in another unit and had left this part on that very day.

The following Monday rain set in, coming down in torrents, and of course we had orders to shift. I do not think I ever went through such mud. We were simply swamped and when I took my boots off and lifted them up, I could pour the water out of them. I managed to get under someone's big sheet for the night, but some would have been glad with a leaking tent. We have seen some sights up here. These have included the firing of a mine, the burning of an ammunition dump (one of the men from a sausage [Zeppelin] coming down in a parachute), and air-fights galore.

The first time we were here one of our Drivers won the Military Medal and a lieutenant the Military Cross. The other night we had a ration problem how to divide a loaf of bread between twenty two men. Some of them were out; it was put back until they were all there, but during the night the problem was easily solved by someone taking the lot! We have had glorious weather the last four days, a bit cold at night and in the morning, but grand during the day. I trust it *[the weather]* will last.'

**Saturday 3 May 1919 A.J. Hobbs, Saddler & Cycle Agent, High Street Corsham:** Having now been demobilized from the Army, wishes to thank all patrons for their kind support in the past and beg for a continuance of their favours in the future.

In June 1921, Hobb's daughter of 17 years and 11 months Gertrude sadly passed away after an operation to remove her appendix at the Bath Royal United Hospital.

She had hardly ever been ill throughout her short life. **R.I.P. Gertrude.**

## Chapter 6. Beechfield House (formerly Pickwick House) including the Goldney Family.

*The Tomkins & Barrett postcard above shows Beechfield House, Middlewick Lane, Corsham in 1915.*

**1538:** The Goldney family were the most notable owners of Beechfield House during its history and quite a few of them were christened as *Thomas*! Many of the Wiltshire based branch of the family are buried at St Bartholomew's Church, Corsham. The Goldney name can be traced back to a document entitled, 'The History of Parliament: The House of Commons 1509–1558', which shows that Henry Afternewell (born before 1517) was the son of a wealthy farmer and clothier named Nicholas Afternewell. The will of Nicholas Afternewell was apparently proved in 1538, but it did not specify the ages or seniority of his children, which seems to have caused a family rift – it resulted in Henry instituting legal proceedings against his mother and her new husband Thomas Scott in 1539 for the loss of some 240 acres of land at Chippenham and Langley, of which he had been named as his father's heir. When Henry sued his mother and his stepfather, he complained that they were, *'Of great substance and riches and also greatly friended and allied in the said county of Wiltshire'*, whereas he himself was but a poor man.

**1549:** From September 1549 Henry's surname was identified as being changed from 'Afternewell' to 'Goldney' and the new surname has been used by his descendants ever since. Initially, the Goldney family went on to make their fortune as weavers and clothiers in Chippenham in the sixteenth century.

**1553:** A number of the Goldney family still resided in Chippenham, where they had originally set up as clothiers and weavers in the town. Henry Goldney was a Member of Parliament for Chippenham and was appointed as the first 'Bailiff' of Chippenham. Goldney Avenue in Chippenham is named after him.

**1558:** Henry Goldney bought a forty-year lease on the Manor House at Rowde. The Goldney's were now established as a wealthy and powerful local family.

**1614: LEYCETERS.** The Beechfield site and the original house called 'Leyceters' were held by the family of Leyceter until 1614. It was later surrendered to the Sadlers who held it untill 1691.

Chapter 6. Beechfield House (formerly Pickwick House) including the Goldney Family.

**1620:** Some of the Goldney family are also known to have come from the Bristol area. Thomas Goldney 1st (1620–1694) was the first of three Bristol based generations each named Thomas, a popular name in the Goldney family. He became a very successful merchant and played a part in the activities of the newly formed 'Society of Friends', or Quakers, in Bristol. There is a Goldney House at Clifton, Bristol, a Goldney Avenue, a Goldney Road and even a Goldney Hall.

**1637:** Thomas Goldney 1st served as an apprentice for seven years in Bristol, this enabled him to become a Freeman. After almost nine years, on 22 June 1646, he paid his fee and became a Freeman of the City of Bristol. In the same year, he married Mary Clements and set himself up as a grocer. He died in 1694, his wife Mary died fifteen years later in 1709.

*Sketch of Leyceters in the 1927 Wiltshire Archaelogical Magazine Vol. 43 Plate IX by Edward Bayley in 1691.*

**1664:** Thomas Goldney I's son Thomas Goldney II married Hannah Speed in 1687.

**1688:** Thomas Goldney II took over the family grocery business, but also invested in other ventures, including: merchant ships; farmland at Elberton; as well as acting as an agent for the Collector of Customs for the Port of Bristol.

**1691:** The house came to a certain Edward Bayley in 1691 at whose death a survey was made of his property, whereon a primative sketch of the house was made *(see left)*. 'Leyceters' (a leasehold property) was renamed 'Pickwick House'. It was a substantial dwelling set in private grounds.

**1705:** Having invested in land at Clifton in Bristol, Thomas Goldney II leased an adjoining [Bristol] country estate complete with a manor house, which after purchasing for £100 he named Goldney Hall.

**1711:** Thomas II's son was Thomas Goldney III born in Goldney Hall in 1696. After a top-level education, he became apprenticed to his parents from 1711.

**1731:** After making several more lucrative investments and purchases, including a large investment in the Abraham Darby ironworks at Coalbrookdale, Shropshire, Thomas II began to retire in 1723, eight years before he passed away in 1731. He was succeeded by his son, Thomas Goldney III.

**1762-1775:** George Searle Bayliffe and Mary Merewether are in residence in Pickwick House *(now Beechfield House)*.
The blight on the family succession caused by premature death due to the smallpox and influenza epidemics of the time seemed to have lifted as they had two boys and three girls who were born between 1762 and 1775.

**1768:** Thomas Goldney III became involved as an investor in a number of businesses and bought shares in three ships. He died without an heir in 1768. He left his shares to his surviving family, who retained their interests until 1773.

*George Searle Bayliffe Esq., J.P., D.L., (1734-1813)*
*Pencil Drawing circa 1794 by his second wife Ann Banks.*

## Chapter 6. Beechfield House (formerly Pickwick House) including the Goldney Family.

**1778:** Any optimism in the Bayliffe family was shattered by the death of George Searle Bayliffe's wife Mary who was buried at Seagry *[5.5 miles northeast of Chippenham]* on 5 May 1779 aged 47 years. It was left to the eldest daughter Mary Susanna, baptised 30 May 1764 at St Andrew's Church (Chippenham), then 15 years of age, to help her father (George Searle Bayliffe) with the upbringing of her younger sisters Ann and Lucy who were 14 and 10 years old respectively.

**1779:** There is a document dated 14 September where George Searle Bayliffe signs as steward at Corsham which includes a good example of the seal he used at that time. The heraldic seal is of a Bayliffe impaling Merewether with the family motto 'Spe et Spiritu' [Hope and Spirit].

**1784:** George Searle Bayliffe's unmarried elder son, George 'Merewether' Bayliffe became an attorney in Chippenham but sadly he died on 9 February at Kingsdown near Bristol aged 22 years, only four years after his mother was buried at Seagry. His name joined those of his grandfather Charles, great-aunt Mary and his mother on the Bayliffe memorial in the nave at Seagry; 'Placida compostus morte quievit' *[i.e. Tranquil death rested]*.

**1787:** Mary Susanna Bayliffe married Thomas Crook of Tytherton Lucas, Wilts., Esq., on 3 July in the Church of St. Bartholomew's, Corsham. This was quite a society wedding, meriting an entry in the 'Marriages of Eminent Persons' section of the Gentleman's Magazine. By this time Mary's father George Searle Bayliffe was a widower of some 8 years, and had moved to Pickwick House. Mary's father George was then courting Ann Banks who was to become Mary's stepmother some 4 years later. Several sources show that the children of George's first marriage resented their father marrying for a second time.

**1791:** During the fifteen years or so as resident at Pickwick House, George Searle Bayliffe also had another property, a farm at Seagry. George was involved in a variety of work; including legal support to the Borough and Parish Councils, Manor Courts and the like and being an attorney which included dealing with criminal cases. He was a steward for the Manor of Monkton from 1758-1791 and for many years held the same position for the Manor of the Rectory of Corsham.

**1794:** The ownership of Pickwick House changed again before Thomas Bennett sold it to George Searle Bayliffe's landlord the Reverend John Law Willis, who in the early 1790s indicated that he wanted to rebuild the house. In due course George Searle Bayliffe gave up the lease, and the old house previously called 'Pickwick House' was demolished in 1794.

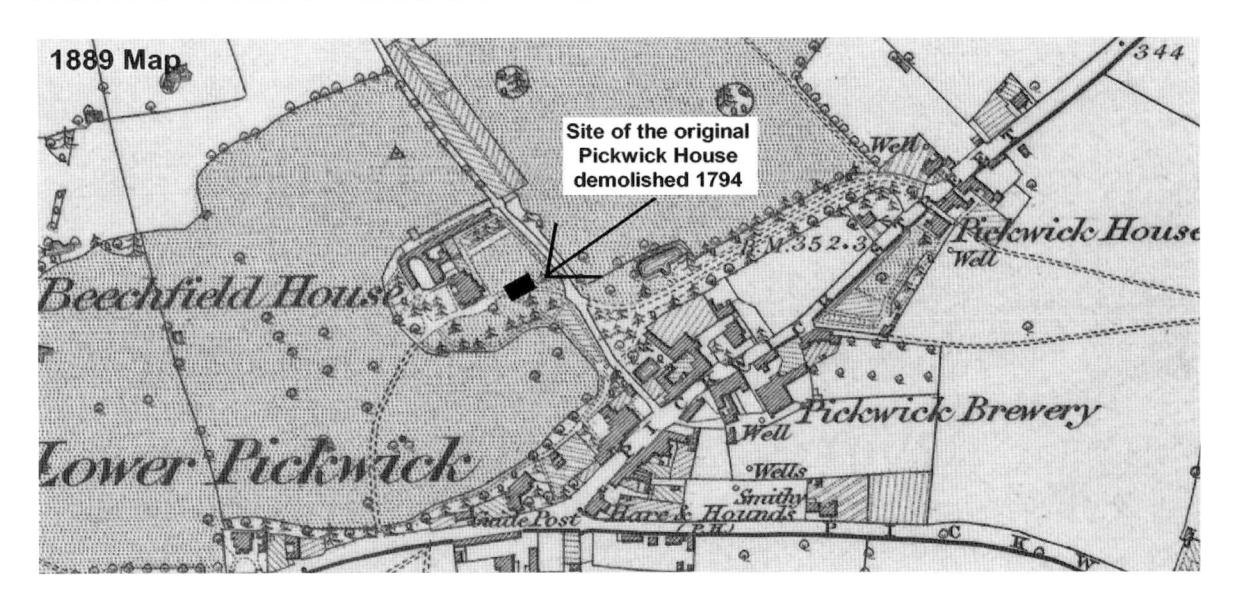

Chapter 6. Beechfield House (formerly Pickwick House) including the Goldney Family.

**1794-1799:** A splendid replacement house called Beechfield House was built immediately to the west of the old building during this period, with outbuildings and stabling to the rear.

The house has survived to the present time and is a Grade 2 Listed Building.

**1830s:** The approach of Brunel's Great Western Railway in the late 1830s caused Gabriel Goldney to move into Lowden, Chippenham to the west of the town and to start a practice with T.A. Fellows.

*Above are the ornate gates (now long gone) of the original long drive entrance to Beechfield House.*

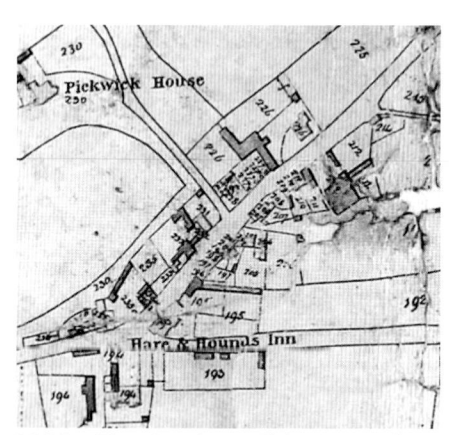

**1839:** Sir Gabriel Goldney (1813–1900) married Mary Anne Alexander of Corsham on 16 September and it is believed that he first acquired Pickwick House in Corsham around this time. There were four children:

- Mary Catherine Goldney (b.14 October 1841-1854).
- Gabriel Prior Goldney (b.4 August 1843-1925).
- Frederick Hastings Goldney (b.26 May 1845-1940).
- John Tankerville Goldney (b.15 June 1846-1920).

**1840s:** The Corsham Tithe Map of 1839 *(see photo above left)* shows the house without the Goldney additions, still named Pickwick House. Gabriel Goldney did not settle at Pickwick immediately after his purchase of Pickwick House. Nevertheless, he carried out major alterations to Pickwick House which included extending the house to north and east, whilst retaining the integrity of the Georgian elevations, adding more stabling in a 'U' shaped configuration, outbuildings and glasshouses. Gabriel Goldney was admitted to his freedom of the Borough of Chippenham on 19 May 1840.

The site of the old 17th century house now included a broad lawn extending from the house's bay windows on the east elevation to the edge of Middlewick Lane. More tree screening was added, and a new tree-lined drive directly from the Bath Road to the south west was now complemented by a large

Chapter 6. Beechfield House (formerly Pickwick House) including the Goldney Family.

extension of the old carriage drive to the east of Middlewick Lane for 150 yards before coming onto the main road then called Pickwick Street, giving a more impressive and commodious access through splendid entrance gates *[see photo top of page]*. It was during the rebuilding that Gabriel must have decided to rename the house from 'Pickwick House' to 'Beechfield House'.

Note: The house opposite the point where the eastern coach drive came out into Pickwick (on the A4 road) is now called 'Pickwick House' *(see photo below)* a cause of some confusion for researchers!

*Pickwick House photo courtesy and kind permission of 'On The Market.com'*

**1846:** Sir Gabriel Goldney's third son Sir John Tankerville Goldney, (1846–1920) who was baptised at Corsham on 14 July 1846 went on to became a barrister. He is also notable for introducing golf to Singapore in 1891. On 9 February 1875 he married Jane MacGregor Laird. In 1892, he was appointed Chief Justice of Trinidad and Tobago and was honoured as a Knight Bachelor in the following year. He resigned his office in 1899 and returned to England, where he was appointed High Sheriff of Wiltshire in 1910 and a Justice of the Peace for the same county. He died aged 74 on 11 April 1920 and was buried at St Bartholomew's Church, Corsham alongside other family members in the family vault.

**1853:** Sir Gabriel Goldney was Mayor of Chippenham.

**1854:** As a landowner, financier and banker, Sir Gabriel Goldney purchased Sheldon Manor in 1854 and Bradenstoke Abbey in 1863. He also owned land at Monks Park, which he leased for quarrying.

**1858:** The Pickwick District School (now St Patrick's Church) was built for Sir Gabriel Goldney, and its design was exhibited at the Royal Academy a year before in 1857.

**1860:** Gabriel Goldney appears to have moved from Chippenham into his Beechfield House at Pickwick, Corsham.

**1865:** Gabriel Goldney is elected as an MP for the first time for the Borough of Chippenham in 1865. He was still M.P. for Chippenham 20 years later in November 1885 when the Parliamentary Borough was disenfranchised.

Chapter 6. Beechfield House (formerly Pickwick House) including the Goldney Family.

**1869:** Gabriel Goldney becomes a Director of the North Wilts Bank and Deputy Lieutenant of Wiltshire. He was also a Freemason and Grand Warden of England.

**1878:** Alice Frances Holbrow Goldney was born in India – the daughter of Frederick Charles Napier Goldney who was a Major in the Indian Army.

**1880: GOLDNEY BARONETS:** The Goldney baronetcy, of Beechfield in the Parish of Corsham and Bradenstoke Abbey in the Parish of Lyneham, both in the County of Wiltshire, was a title in the Baronetage of the United Kingdom. It was created on 11 May 1880 for Gabriel Goldney, Conservative Member of Parliament for Chippenham. The title became extinct on the death of the fourth Baronet in 1984. A list of the four Goldney Baronets can be seen below:

- Sir Gabriel Goldney, 1st Baronet (1813–1900).
- Sir Gabriel Prior Goldney, 2nd Baronet (1843–1925)
- Sir Frederick Hastings Goldney, 3rd Baronet (1845–1940)
- Sir Henry Hastings Goldney, 4th Baronet (1886–1974)

**1885:** Sir Gabriel Goldney 1st Baronet resigned from his Chippenham Borough posts and privileges.

**1889:** Gabriel's son, Frederick Hastings Goldney, publishes the 'Records of Chippenham' in 1889.

**1900:** Sir Gabriel Goldney died aged 87 at Eaton Place, Belgravia, London on 8 May and the baronetcy passed to his first son, Gabriel Prior Goldney 2nd Baronet (1843–1925). Gabriel Prior studied at Exeter College, Oxford and qualified as a barrister of the Inner Temple.

**1908:** Frederick Hastings Goldney became Mayor of Chippenham, High Sheriff of Wiltshire and JP for Wiltshire and Surrey. One of Sir Frederick Goldney's daughters was a district nurse, visiting the houses of the poorer residents in the vicinity and taking presents at Christmas time. Miss Goldney rode a 'sit-up-and-beg' bicycle and could often be seen riding one-handed while holding an umbrella aloft.

**1912:** Frederick Hastings' daughter Eveline Margaret Hungerford Goldney, married Graham Dunsterville of Guyers House. The families had been close friends and attended Corsham Church together for Sunday services.

**1913:** In his later years, Sir John Tankerville Goldney married his second wife Miss Alice Frances Holbrow Goldney in Ealing on 15 Feb 1913. They lived in Monks House, Monks Park in Corsham. Lady Alice became Commandant of the Corsham Hospital at the Town Hall Red Cross hospital during the First World War. She remained as Commandant until the Red Cross Hospital in the Town Hall closed in 1919.

**1914:** Graham Dunsterville rejoined his regiment, the Devonshires and was killed in action in France in October. His son Hugh Dunsterville was born at Guyers House, Pickwick, in December of that year.

**1915:** At Hugh Dunsterville's christening in February 1915 the two families, Dunstervilles and Goldneys, planted an avenue of walnut saplings, six each side, running from the rear of Pickwick Village Street, into Middlewick Lane and the Beechfield estate. The site is now the Woodlands housing estate where most of the trees were felled during development, but two or three that have Tree Preservation Orders on have survived.

Chapter 6. Beechfield House (formerly Pickwick House) including the Goldney Family.

**1917:** Frederick Hastings Goldney served in the Royal Engineers, and as a Second Lieutenant was awarded the Military Cross on 26 January 1917 for *'conspicuous gallantry in action. He displayed great courage and skill in marking out assembly positions under very heavy fire, thereby materially assisting in the success of the operations.'*

**1920:** Sir John Tankerville Goldney died and Lady Alice Goldney is known to have sailed back to India soon after. She re-married in 1943 to Harold Robinson. She died in 1957 aged 79.

**1925:** Gabriel Prior Goldney 2nd Baronet (who lived at Derriads House in Chippenham) did not marry and on his death (by a cerebral haemorrhage) on 4 May 1925 the baronetcy passed to his younger brother Sir Frederick Hastings Goldney, 3rd Baronet (1845–1940). Among some of Gabriel Prior Goldney's achievements were as J.P. for Wiltshire and Deputy Lieutenant for the City of London in 1894. He was appointed High Sheriff of Wiltshire in 1906.

He also held the rank of Major in the Royal Wiltshire Yeomanry. He was an active Freemason and was also appointed a Companion of the Order of the Bath (CB) in July 1902 and a Commander of the Royal Victorian Order (CVO) in the 1904 New Year Honours.

*Sir John Tankerville Goldney's memorial at the old Ladbrook Cemetery gate.*

Sir Frederick Hastings Goldney 3rd Baronet was educated at Harrow School and became a landowner and Freemason, rising to become Grand Deacon of England. He also wrote, 'A History of Freemasonry in Wiltshire' (1880) and 'Records of Chippenham', privately published in 1889. He was Mayor of Chippenham in 1874 and 1888, High Sheriff of Wiltshire in 1908 and served as a Justice of the Peace for Wiltshire and Surrey. His residences were Beechfield House, Corsham, and Prior Place, Camberley, Surrey.

He married Ethel Julia Swayne, of Wilton, Wiltshire on 6 February 1875; they had five children:
- Katherine Long Goldney (b.1878).
- Mary Delarivière Goldney (b.1880).
- Eveline Margaret Hungerford Goldney (b.1882).
- Henry Hastings Goldney (b.1886).
- Lucy Hulbert Goldney (b.1889).

**1926:** Lady Ethel Julia Goldney (1855-1926) wife of Frederick Hastings Goldney 3rd Baronet died. Her body was conveyed in a hearse through Pickwick, down Pickwick Road and the High Street to St. Bartholomew's church, where she was interned in the vault (lined with moss and narcissi) alongside the remains of Sir Gabriel. The previous year, she had celebrated her Golden Wedding Anniversary with husband Frederick (married in 1875). Much of their early life had been spent in Rowden House Chippenham where Frederick was the town's Mayor with Lady Goldney fulfilling her duties as Mayoress. They had moved back to Beechfield House in Corsham on the death of Sir Gabriel in 1925.

**1940:** Sir Frederick Hastings Goldney 3rd Baronet aged 94 died on 21 February; his estate was valued at £127,000 (£5m in today's money). He was succeeded by his only son Sir Henry Hastings Goldney (1886–1974), 4th [and last] Baronet of Beechfield and Bradenstoke Abbey. Henry lived at Rowden House, Chippenham and became a Magistrate there in 1946. Sir Henry married Violetta Alyns Barnes (1886–1965), but they had no children.

Chapter 6. Beechfield House (formerly Pickwick House) including the Goldney Family.

**1940s:** The 'Beechfield' site was taken over by the military during the Second World War and the grounds were filled with timber huts.

**1946:** Mr Clifford Ellis Headmaster of Bath School of Art is appointed as the Principal of the Corsham Court Training College and School of Art, as from 1 July on an annual salary of £1,100 *(£32,000 in today's money)*. The new Training College and School at Corsham was named the Bath Academy of Art (located at Corsham Court and Beechfield). The Academy opened on 9 October with at least 56 students. The women students were housed (from December) at Monks Park House and the men in Corsham and Bath.

**1947: SCANDALOUS**: The Beechfield Camp used by the Army during the war, was to be converted into temporary housing accommodation, but the Army on leaving, had left the camp much damaged. The Royal Engineers had stripped out all the electric light fittings, switches, main switches, etc., which resulted in major damage to: electrical wiring, sanitary fittings, pans, sinks, cisterns, taps, etc., and to some of the water piping. The matter was taken up with the War Office, who informed the Ministry of Health. They replied that the equipment removed from the camp would remain available for the Council to use when the transfer was completed and that it was only being stored as a precautionary measure!

Mr W. J. Light from the Parish Council said that, *"It was a very naive statement and to expect them [the Corsham Parish Council] to swallow it was asking too much. Not tithe of the stuff that had been ruthlessly torn down would ever go back. It was perfectly scandalous. It just showed the complete lack of cooperation between the various Departments concerned"*.

Mrs K. D. Wilkinson said, *"Things needed desperately nowadays are destroyed right and left. They have given a charming answer but we [the Parish Council] ought to make a strong protest"*.

Beechfield House is recommended as a site for the Bath Academy of Art's hostel for men. The idea was that Corsham Court would be the centre of instruction and Monks Park and Beechfield as hostel sites. Behind Beechfield House was built a refectory, a modern single storey building that housed the canteen and also doubled as a venue for Student Union gigs and parties.

The catering staff kept many students alive by feeding them good wholesome and cheap meals; you could eat well on 30p and even better for 50p. Chips were on the menu to satisfy the *'chip buttie brigade'* who were mainly Northerners with dubious unhealthily eating habits. The horseshoe stable block housed the Academy's pottery and photographic darkroom/studio; it has now been re-designed into individual modern mews cottages.

**1948:** Three Ministry of Works Corsham hutments *[i.e. an encampment of huts]* and the N.A.A.F.I building were moved to Beechfield to accommodate the growing number of Bath Academy students.

Since the purchase of Beechfield House in c1840 by Sir Gabriel Goldney, the majority of Pickwick village was now owned by the Goldney family.

**PICKWICK SALE Many Tenants Buy Their Homes Whole Village Sold.**

Frederick Hastings Goldney's first child, daughter Katherine Long Goldney (b1878) and her brother Sir Henry Hastings Goldney 4th Baronet, undertook to sell at auction, a great deal of the Pickwick village estate as it stood at that time - it had been owned by the Goldney family since c1840. Most of the Pickwick village houses were tenanted, and some occupiers were able to buy their properties, but others

Chapter 6. Beechfield House (formerly Pickwick House) including the Goldney Family.

may have been transferred to a new landlord. This included 30 houses or cottages, plus the Old Malthouse, the village stores, the Old Brewery and Manor House Barn. The current annual Gross Rent Roll at the time was £407 10s 6p (£10,500 in today's money).

*[Saturday 3 April 1948 Wiltshire Times and Trowbridge Advertiser]:* The intimate and happy relationship between landlord and tenant which had prevailed and served the Pickwick village so well through the ages, comes to an end. At 6 p.m. Thursday 28 March, the majority of Pickwick village is auctioned by Messrs. Thompson, Noad and Phipp, in the Corsham Town Hall at a final total realised price of £17,460 (£450,000 in today's money). In the hope that many of the residents would be able to purchase their own homes, nominal reserves had been fixed.

All the 23 lots were sold. Many of the tenants bought their own houses. Some of the cottages were put in at £50 and sold at double the price (£100).

**Below are some of the final sale prices agreed:**

Three cottages, Nos 27, 29 and 31 Pickwick (£29 8s rent); sold for £325 to Mr R. J. Vowles, Corsham.

Manor Barn Farm, 19½ acres of land, with mediaeval barn and cattle shed, sold at £2,150 to E. H. Bradley & Sons, Swindon.

(Lot 14): The proprietress of the Village Stores *(see photo above)*, Mrs Cole, paid £1,200 for (Nos 30, 32 & 33) her place and the two cottages adjoining.

The early Georgian residence, 'Norway House' *also known as Ferndale*, Pickwick (£50 rent), sold for £1,850 to Messrs. C. W. B. Oatley and Co. of Corsham, along with 'The Old Malthouse', formerly the Beechfield House billiards room, but suitable for business offices, restaurant, tea rooms etc., offered with possession, at £1,525. *The postcard photo of 'Norway House' from Julian Carosi's collection.*

75

Chapter 6. Beechfield House (formerly Pickwick House) including the Goldney Family.

A small Brewery and Ale House known as the 'Swan Inn' once stood here at 'Greystones' opposite the 'Hare & Hounds'.

The detached Cotswold style residence, 'Greystones', 47 Pickwick, *(see photo above by Julian Carosi)* with possession, at a rateable value of £26, was sold for £3,650 to P. Hunter, Ltd. Curry Rival, Taunton.

The Pickwick sale generated great interest worldwide. A day or two before the sale, there arrived air mail from the little town of Hilvarenbeek in South Holland, a letter signed by members of Holland's *Mr Pickwick Club*. Inside was a picture of the Pickwick village street from a Dutch newspaper, the caption of which recorded the coming sale. They sent their mark of sympathy concerning the sale and asked if some photographs and a little description of Pickwick village could be sent to them!

Lot 1. Pair of detached cottages *(see photo below)*, Nos 17 and 19 Pickwick (current rent £23 9s per year), purchase price £875 (£22,000 in today's money) was bought by Mr E. Neate on behalf of the tenant of No. 17 Mrs Neate.

The 'Old Malthouse' on Pickwick (formerly the Beechfield House billiards room), once stood next to 12 Pickwick, on the east side. Part of its east wall can still be seen running up to the Bath Road frontage *(see the following photo)*. It was partially demolished in 1953 to allow greater access to the commercial yard behind. Number 12 Pickwick, was owned by Frederick Hastings Goldney until the sale of the property in 1948, when it was bought by Frederick John Smith the long-standing tenant of the house from the Goldney Estate for £450. The annual rent at the time was £18 4s.

Chapter 6. Beechfield House (formerly Pickwick House) including the Goldney Family.

**1949:** The Corsham Postmistress informed the Corsham Parish Council, that the postal authorities were experiencing considerable difficulty and confusion with the delivery of letters to the new *[prefab bungalows married quarters]* 'Beechfield Estate', as one of the main roads there was named Beechfield Avenue. It was decided to ask the Rural District Council to re-name the new prefabs bungalow estate to 'Pickwick Estate'.

**1953:** *[Wiltshire Times Saturday 5 September 1953]:* Serious proposals were submitted to build a 475 yard bypass through the middle of the Beechfield House gardens. Colonel R. W. Butler was appointed to conduct an inquiry.

The new route would start 140 yards west of the Hare and Hounds hostelry (near the roundhouse on the A4) and pass in a gentle curve through the Beechfield House gardens and come out further along Pickwick opposite the old Dairy and the Old Parsonage on the A4 at the top of Priory Street. A longer bypass extension had been considered but that would mean traversing valuable agricultural land. The proposal did not deal with the creation of two *blackspots* that would result at the top of Park Lane and Priory Street.

Another route east from the top of Box Hill to the Cross Keys had also been considered in the distant past. Ushers Wiltshire Breweries, owners of the Spread Eagle and Mr Fussell (for the owners) of the Hare and Hounds objected to the creation of a cul-de-sac near their properties. Thankfully, none of the above came into being and the tranquillity of the Beechfield gardens and Middlewick Lane landscapes were preserved.

**1957:** Lady Alice Robinson (was Goldney) passed away aged 79.

**1967:** *[By Pat Whalley Corsham Civic Society Article - 'The Goldney Family and Beechfield House']*. The Goldneys being a Quaker family, the men were heavily involved with Freemasonry and reaching high office in that organisation. It has long been thought locally that the Masonic Hall in Pickwick was once a Quaker meeting house. However, a letter has recently come to light written by Katherine Goldney, living in Camberley, dated 7 November 1967, to her brother Harry (i.e. Henry Hastings Goldney) ................

Chapter 6. Beechfield House (formerly Pickwick House) including the Goldney Family.

*'You are right ... Mr Fry's daughter married a Mr Matthews and they bought a house at the end of Pickwick village. It was a very appropriate place of abode, as Mrs Matthews was a Quaker, and as you know Pickwick was originally a Quaker village, built by Quakers who also built the Meeting House at the village end.*

*By the time our grandfather bought Beechfield and Pickwick, the Quaker inhabitants had died out, so as the Meeting House had not been consecrated he turned it into a club, for his male tenants in Pickwick, and paid for its gas and newspapers for the Club.*

*All went well for several years until two men arrived and said they were executors of the former Quakers, and had orders to pull the Meeting House down and sell its contents. Our Grandfather told them he had turned it into the village club, and offered to buy it from them, but they refused. So he bought two of the original benches, and put them in his billiard room. The Meeting House was duly demolished.'*

It has since been established, that the above Meeting House stood at 21 Pickwick, on the left-hand side at the entrance to the Woodlands estate, where new houses *(see photo above)* were erected in 2013. The plot had previously been the garden of the large house, the residence of the Eden Family, opposite the old Pickwick Brewery site.

**1960s:** The Academy of Art centre at Beechfield opened its doors to the local Corsham primary school children, giving them a weekly escape from normal lessons.

Making shadow puppets was just one of the skills taught that allowed the pupils to return to school and give rehearsed shadow puppet plays to their classmates with lots of brightly coloured crepe paper adorning the cardboard box stages.

Other skills required collecting sheep wool from the local hedgerows and then learning to make it into wool. And most memorable, was peddling frantically on a *wobbly* potters' wheel and making a mess of creating a misshaped ceramic bowl, which once fired, would be finished off with brightly coloured dabs of paint; to be kept as a fond childhood memory of the hours of fun spent there at Beechfield.

## Chapter 6. Beechfield House (formerly Pickwick House) including the Goldney Family.

**1974:** Sir Henry Hastings Goldney (1886-1974), 4th and final Baronet died and is buried at St Bartholomew's Church, Corsham, alongside other members of his family. He had married Violetta Alyns Barnes (1886–1965), but they had no children.

Above is an aerial shot of the Beechfield House site taken in 1980, showing all of the old Bath Academy of Art buildings, including the huge art studio middle edge left. Almost all of this area has been redeveloped, including the old Woodlands bungalow estate top right, the Wiltshire Council Depot bottom left and the whole of the Beechfield site which is now the beautiful Academy Drive private housing estate. Beechfield House itself (middle top centre), along with its stable block to its left, has been converted into luxury apartments.

The old wooden student's hut and canteen top middle, was purchased and removed by Corsham Town Football Club and used for a while as a changing room at their Southbank ground along Lacock Road. The large empty field to the left of the hut was used for many years by the successful Corsham Community Centre Sunday football team managed by Peter Ralph.

The land, approximately two hectares in size, was transferred to the Council's ownership in 2002 and is now a wild life sanctuary and dog walk. A wildlife pond was constructed at the western end of the site. Even the Pickwick Villas building bottom left, once a beautiful family home *(called Pictors House)* was converted into flats.

**1981:** There was a serious fire on 29th January when the old Bath Academy shop in Beechfield burnt down, causing £15,000 worth of damage.

**1986:** Bath Academy in Corsham was closed down in 1986. The buildings at Beechfield stood empty until 1996 before it was turned into a housing development when Gleeson Homes purchased the site to build Academy Drive as it is today. During those 10 years, the Beechfield site went through total disrepair, open to the weather and left crumbling and dilapidated as vandals destroyed what was accessible.

Chapter 6. Beechfield House (formerly Pickwick House) including the Goldney Family.

Beechfield House has been superbly restored into individual flats for those who want to (and can afford to) live in such a beautiful Georgian building. The Bath Academy of Art returned to its home in Bath.

The coach drive to the east of Middlewick Lane along with the splendid entrance gates have long since been replaced by the modern *up-market* Woodlands housing estate *(see photo above)*.

**2002:** Beechfield House was refurbished and the grounds landscaped into a beautiful park.

*Photo by Julian Carosi shows the modernised Beechfield House and stable block apartments in 2019.*

**Acknowledgements** in the making of this chapter include: Pat Whalley and the Corsham Civic Society, http://www.baacorsham.co.uk, Bryant G Bayli, Julian Rawes, en.wikipedia.org, The History of Paliament 1509–1558, ed. S. Bindoff, 1982. Wiltshire Times. Robert Currey. Miscellaneous papers held by Corsham Area Heritage - donors unknown.

Chapter 6. Beechfield House (formerly Pickwick House) including the Goldney Family.

*The beautiful Beechfield House in Academy Drive.*

*Photos by Julian Carosi 2019.*

**The End**

# Chapter 7. Claremont Ladies' College.

Claremont House (Linleys, Gastard, Corsham SN13 9PD) lies on the southern fringe of Corsham just before you get to the Linley's cottages where the road narrows on the B3353 Corsham to Melksham road, in an area of the town known as Broadstones. Claremont was built as a private house circa 1830/40 and converted in 1845 as a Private Girls School (Claremont College Corsham). In WWI, Claremont was used to house London evacuees and since 1946, it has been a care home for the elderly.

**A history of Claremont College Corsham:** *The photographs of the Claremont girls in this chapter belong to [Ed] Julian Carosi and are unique. They originally belonged to the Berry family - the Reverend C. H. Berry and his wife who managed the Claremont Ladies' College during 1914 - 1920.*

**1807:** The following appears in the *Salisbury and Winchester Journal - Monday 24 August 1807:* Boarding School for Young Ladies. - Corsham, Wilts. MRS ELLIS most respectfully informs her friends and the public, that she has taken a very commodious House in the healthy and salubrious town of Corsham, Wilts, for the reception of YOUNG LADIES, whom she purposes to board, and instruct in the English Language, with much regard to its grammatical construction and orthography; Geography, History; and every kind of Needle Work, for 14 Guineas per annum, and one Guinea Entrance. Vacations of a month each, Christmas and Midsummer.

Mrs Ellis pledges herself to exert her utmost endeavour to make the situation of the young Ladies entrusted to her both profitable and comfortable by using the plainest and most likely methods of instruction to insure the one, and by allowing every reasonable indulgence, accompanied by the kindest treatment, to effect the other.

She will likewise pay the strictest attention to the health of her Pupils, and carefully inculcate such principles of morality and religion as may best dispose the mind to future rectitude.

## Chapter 7. Claremont Ladies' College.

**1830:** The Kelly's Directory for 1830, under *Academies and Schools*, lists Ann Hemming in charge of the Ladies' Boarding School Corsham. The girls were often referred to by the locals as the *'Claremont Bulldogs'*.

**1866:** Together, Miss Lanham and Miss Turner now ran the Ladies' Boarding Seminary, Claremont House, Corsham. The demand for women to have equal political rights with men, started when a group of women organised a petition. Miss Lanham and Miss Turner were two of only three Wiltshire women to have signed the *'Votes for Women'* mass Suffrage petition in 1866. The third Wiltshire lady was Miss Cunnington from Devizes. Neither of the Corsham ladies Miss Lanham and Miss Turner, however, appears to be involved in the suffrage story in later years. The petition was presented to Parliament by John Stuart Mill MP on 7 June 1866.

**1875:** The Kelly's Directory for this year shows Sarah Butler as the Principal at Claremont College for Young Ladies, along with Governess Catherine Freeman.

**1880:** The Kelly's Directory for 1880 under 'Gastard' shows Principal Emma Butler at the Ladies' Boarding School Linleys.

**1881:** The following advertisement appeared in the Wiltshire Times and Trowbridge Advertiser - Saturday 19 March 1881:

**LADIES COLLEGE CORSHAM near BATH**

**A HIGH SCHOOL for YOUNG LADIES on Moderate Terms. Situation most healthy. Home comforts. Thorough Education Guaranteed. First-class resident teachers. Eminent professors visit for accomplishments. Preparation for the Locals, also for the Higher Examination for Women. For prospectus apply to Lady Principal, or to Mr C.H. Hulls. Term commences on Tuesday, May 3rd.**

**1883/1884:** Head Mistress at Claremont is Miss Shaw.

**1885-1889:** Mrs Clara Milne is Principal at Claremont for a short period.

**1891:** Misses Agnes Tennant aged 24 (English Teacher) and Laura Rigden (Music Teacher) are now the joint Principals of Claremont College. They held the post between them, with about 22 pupils aged between 11 and 19, for twenty-two years until 1913. These were ladies of substance, very well educated and enterprising women, who did a great deal for the town. During WWI Agnes Tennant ran the local Women's Land Army. She also became a Corsham Parish Councillor (1919-1941) during which time she served as Vice Chairman and Chairman and later became a Corsham Magistrate. Miss Rigden also served on the Parish Council from 1934-1937. Misses Tennant and Rigden lived in 'The Nutshell' Stokes Road.

**1913:** On Thursday 3 April 1913 - a farewell party took place at Claremont College, on the retirement of the Misses Agnes Tennant and Rigden after 22 years as Principals at the College. Miss Cockrom is the new Principal. On Friday 19 December the school *broke* for their Christmas holidays. Miss Cockrom distributed the prizes which had been gained during the past year. She congratulated the pupils who had been successful in gaining prizes and spoke words of encouragement and advice to those whose names did not appear on the prize list.

She referred to the good which would arise from their [the pupils] endeavours to keep *'The Golden Rule'*, and also urged them to uphold the school motto 'Veritas Vincit' [Truth Prevails].

Chapter 7. Claremont Ladies' College.

*Below is one of the Claremont dormitories of the time.*

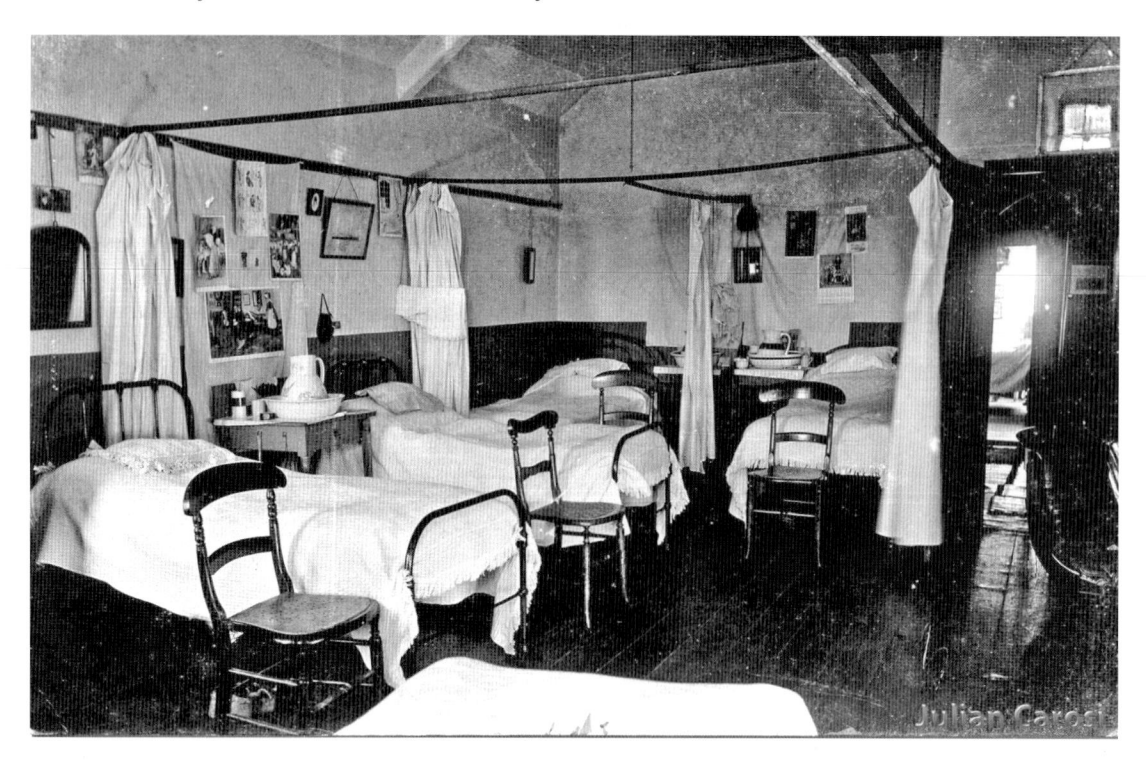

**1914:** The Reverend Cecil Huntley Berry *(first left back row)* and Principle Mrs Berry managed the Claremont Ladies Boarding School College between 1914 and 1920.

During the year, Claremont College pupils gave two performances of Shakespeare's 'Loves Labours Lost', in the Parish Rooms (Pound Pill) in aid of the Red Cross Hospital, (Town Hall) and the Red Cross Blanket Fund. They raised the princely sum of £11.10s.2d (nearly £1,000 in today's money).

## Chapter 7. Claremont Ladies' College.

On Saturday 3 July, at the annual prize giving ceremony at Claremont, Field Marshal Lord Methuen opened his speech with the following message,

*"Now the girls that went to school had the immense advantage of emulation, which they did not get out of the schoolroom. Then at school they got excellent chances of athletic pursuits, but for which, with all modern luxuries, there might be a tendency to become effeminate.*

*Girls of today were different to the women they read about in Dickens' novels. They were much stronger and healthier, indeed there was a danger of them becoming a little too masculine (laughter)."*

On Saturday 12 December the Claremont College Netball Team won their first match when they beat Tytherton Girl's School 7 to 1. The Claremont team consisted of Joan Little, Joyce Little, I. Adams, Miss Pearce, P. Fowler, K. Spackman and M. Adams.

**1915:** The Kelly's Directory for Gastard in this year, confirms that the Principal Mrs Berry and the Rev. Cecil Huntley Berry are still in charge of the Claremont College for young ladies.

The Claremont School's 1914/15 pamphlet information detailed below, gives you a good idea of what life was like for the girls who went to school there in the early 1900s.


**CLAREMONT CORSHAM**

**CLAREMONT (1915). Established 70 Years.**

A 'Recognised School' under the Board of Education. Registered by the Associated Board of the Royal Academy, and the Royal College of Music. Registered by Mr Ablett.

**PRINCIPAL** - Mrs BERRY.

CORSHAM is a village 250 ft. above the sea level *[Ed: it is actually 314 ft.]*, situated on the Wiltshire Downs, on the G. W. Main Line, 20 minutes from Bath, and two hours from London.

The College is out of the village, standing in its own grounds, with asphalt tennis court, playing fields, and a large fruit and vegetable garden.

CLAREMONT is a Home School, which provides careful Home-training with a thoroughly modern Education.

**SUBJECTS:** The Subjects studied are Scripture, Church History, Literature, History, Latin, French, Nature Study, Domestic Economy, Mathematics, Harmony, German, Drawing, Painting, Part-singing, all Musical subjects, Drilling and Swedish Drill, Gardening, Book-keeping, Poultry-keeping, Bee-keeping, and Miniature Rifle Range Shooting (a small charge is made for cartridges used).

The Food is unlimited in quantity, thoroughly good and constantly varied. No work is done before breakfast, nor after 8.30 p.m.

# Chapter 7. Claremont Ladies' College.

*Girls in the Arithmetic Class contemplating a very difficult looking calculation!* $3\frac{1}{16} \times 4\frac{5}{7} \times 1\frac{1}{5}$ *divided by* $1\frac{3}{9} + \frac{1}{5} = ?$

**TIMETABLE:**
7.00 Rise.
7.45 Breakfast.
9.00 Prayers.
Classes 9.15-1.15 (break at 10.45-11.00).
1.30 Dinner.
2.45 - 4.45 Preparation (Summer) or Games (Winter).
5.00 Tea.
5.45 Games (Summer) Preparation (Winter).
7.30 Supper.
8.00 Prayers.
Bed - Directly after Prayers.

**GAMES.** In the summer, cricket, croquet and tennis are played; in the winter, basket ball. Games subscription, 5/- per annum.

**LIBRARY.** There is a school library at the disposal of the Pupils; 2/6 per annum.

**EXAMS.** Children preparing for examinations might have to give a little more time to their preparation. Girls are prepared for the various Nursery and Horticultural Colleges, the Local Examinations, and all Music Examinations. The recommendations of the Board of Education are followed in the teaching in the School, so that the pupils are taught on the most approved modern lines.

Parts of Claremont Gardens are given up to the use of pupils desiring to learn practical gardening.

*Learning gardening skills.*

**INFECTIOUS ILLNESS.** 'The Cottage,' detached and separated from the School, is kept for use in case of infectious illness. The charge during illness requiring special nursing is £2 2/- per week; special foods, wine, etc., are extra. When, in the opinion of the Medical Officer, any special diet is required for a pupil, the parents will be communicated with.

**HEALTH.** Great attention is paid to the girls' health; in the fine weather in the summer the girls practically live out of doors, doing all their lessons and having some of their meals in the garden. Saturday is a whole holiday.

## Chapter 7. Claremont Ladies' College.

Frequent excursions to places of interest in the neighbourhood are taken and girls may bring their bicycles to use on these excursions.

At the beginning of each term a Certificate, signed by the parents or guardians, must be brought, stating that the pupil has not been exposed to any infectious disease during the holidays.

No pupil will be allowed to return to school on recovery from an infectious disease, or to attend the school from a house in which there is or recently has been such disease without a medical certificate of freedom from infection. Every new girl is examined by the School Doctor, and, if found necessary, special exercises and treatment are given to remedy any defects or tendencies. The heights and weights of the girls are also taken regularly, so that Mrs Berry can have a fairly safe guide as to the health and development of her pupils.

**SCHOOL YEAR.** The School year is divided into Three Terms of 12 weeks each, beginning about the last week in September, the middle of January and the first week in May.

**ATTENDANCE.** Punctuality of attendance is strictly enforced, and the parents of weekly boarders are requested to see that their daughters reach School not later than 8.45 on Monday mornings.

The Principal wishes to point out that unless there is some peculiarly important reason, weekly boarding is not conducive to the best all round development of girls.

**HOLIDAYS.**

The Holidays consist of 16 weeks in the year - 4 weeks at Christmas, 3 in April, and about 2 months in Summer.

**VISITING.**

Parents who desire to visit their daughters are invited to come on the first Saturday in the month; visits at other times may be arranged with the Head Mistress. Should friends desire to visit any pupil, the parent of that pupil must communicate with the Principal.

**LIST OF STAFF.**

Rev. Cecil Huntley BERRY, A.K.C.L.
Mrs BERRY, Higher Local Camb. (Hon. in Languages) London Matriculation; L.C.C. Cert, for Children's Care. Trained St. Stephen's, Windsor.
Miss SADD (sometime resident in Germany). Abletts Certificate. Trained Clapham High School.
FRAULEIN SCHROTER.
MISS RIGDEN, A.L.C.M. Music, Singing, Harmony.
R. W. PULLEIN, Esq., F.Gld.O. (Late Org. Lincoln Cathedral). Music, Singing, Harmony.
Violin. - Mr HEINRICH.
Guitar, Violin and 'Cello; Book-keeping.—Mr SPACKMAN.
Dancing. - Miss KENDALL.
Drill. - Sergeant. HAWTHORNE (Late Quarter-master Sergeant. Scots Guards).
*Swedish Drill. - Miss LALL (Regent Street Polytechnic).
Gardening (Theoretical and Practical) and Carpentry. - A. SMITH, Esq.
Medical Officer. DR. WOOD, The Porch, Corsham.

Chapter 7. Claremont Ladies' College.

*Photo: Broomstick drill with Sergeant HAWTHORNE (late Quarter-master Sergeant. Scots Guards).*

*Swedish Drill is a series of movements that students perform in response to the teacher's vocal instructions. The movements are performed slowly and gently (for the most part), with an emphasis on balance and complete muscle control. As students grow more proficient, the instructions progress to more complicated postures or movements.

**FEES.** Must be paid in advance and not later than the first week in each term.
Boarders (a) Termly.
Over 12 - £60 per annum. (approx £4,500 in today's money).
Under 12 - £50 per annum.
(b) Weekly - £45 per annum / £36 per annum.
(c) Daily - £15 per annum.
Day Pupils - £3 3s. per term.
Entire charge of children whose parents are abroad, £100 per annum. Inclusive of Laundry (but blouses and frocks, overalls, etc., are extra). Reduction for sisters, daughters of clergy and professional men.

**EXTRAS.**

Pianoforte - £2 2s. (Master) per term.
Pianoforte - £1 1s. per term.
Singing - £2 2s. (Master) per term.
Violin - £2 2s. per term.
Guitar - £2 2s. per term.
Swedish Drill - 7/6.
Dancing - £1 1s.
Book-keeping.
Elocution.
Carpentry.

*Fabulous photo showing the Claremont girls posing whilst demonstrating outdoors gymnastics!*

88

## Chapter 7. Claremont Ladies' College.

**STATIONERY AS INCURRED.** Boarders must be provided with 2 pillow cases, 2 pairs sheets, 2 bath and 2 face towels, 4 serviettes, 1 large and 1 small knife, 1 large and 1 small fork, 2 dessert spoons, and serviette ring. The Headmistress prefers all pupils to have their own text books; but copies belonging to the School may be borrowed, at 5/- per term. Girls should have for school-time blue tunics with white tops………..***End of the Claremont School's 1914/15 pamphlet***………………

**1918:** In May, Lord Islington decided to sell the whole of his Hartham Estate (including Claremont) only retaining the mansion and parklands. The Sale took place at the Picture Hall in Chippenham on Thursday 16 May. Claremont House is advertised 'For Sale' in the Wiltshire Times and Trowbridge Advertiser - Saturday 27 April. The sale is described as follows:

**Important Sale of a
PLEASANTLY-SITUATED COMMODIOUS FAMILY RESIDENCE (with possession).
containing: - 5 Reception Rooms. Domestic Offices. 7 principal Bedrooms. Dressing Room. fitted Bath Room with h. and c. supply : and having Lawn, Tennis Court, well laid-out Flower and Kitchen Gardens, Small Paddock, Poultry Run, et.,
known as "CLAREMONT HOUSE."**

The final Lot 75 was for the purchase of Claremont and it was bought for £1,050 (about £42,000 in today's money). In the following photographs c1915, you can see the girls taking part in gymnastics, dairy work, tennis, drawing, gardening, cookery classes, looking after animals, plasticine modelling, etc. There are photos of their dormitories, the dining room and buildings at that time.

# Chapter 7. Claremont Ladies' College.

*In the dairy churning milk etc.*

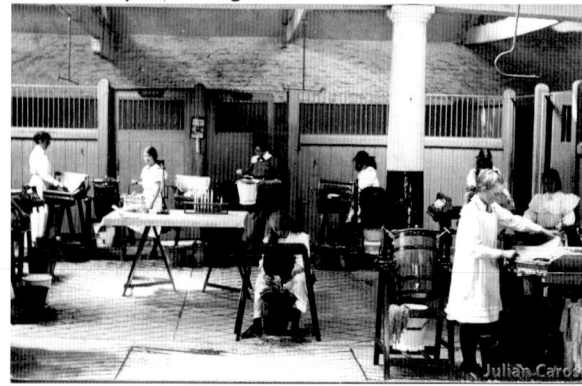

*In the dairy cheese making & how to milk cows.*

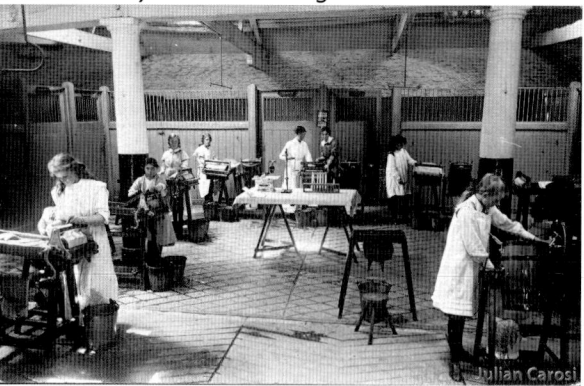

*Dining room.*

*One of the dormitories.*

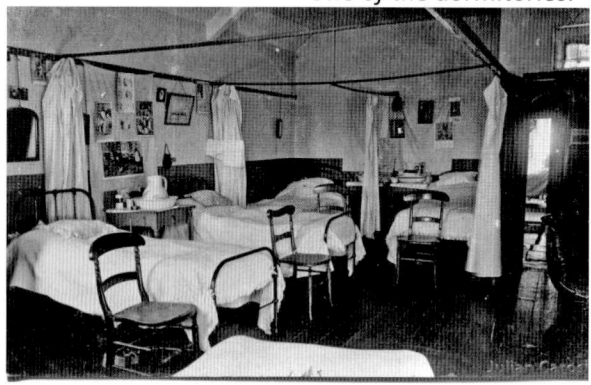

*Lessons in the garden*

*Tennis on the court.*

*Cookery lessons.*

*Make it yourself plasticine modelling.*

## Chapter 7. Claremont Ladies' College.

**1919:** On Thursday 5 June at the Auction Rooms Corsham, Charles W. Oatley auctioned off the furniture and effects from Claremont House. In August, a Mrs Taylor is in residence at Claremont. She provides apples from her orchard for the wounded soldiers in the Red Cross Hospital in Corsham Town Hall. Claremont is now the privately owned house of the Taylor family who remain there until 1939.

**1920:** Misses Agnes Tennant and Rigden set up the very first Corsham Women's Institute meeting in the Corsham Town Hall in January. Mrs G.P. Fuller of Neston Park is elected as President, Miss A. Tennant as Secretary and Miss Rigden as Treasurer, with a committee of ten.

**1923:** The Kelly's Directory for Gastard in this year, shows Mr J.R. Taylor at Claremont, Linleys.

**1925:** Mrs Taylor of Claremont House passes away in April aged 86. She was the widow of the late Mr W.H. Taylor of Higham, Malmesbury. Amongst the mourners were her sons, J.A., B. and J. Taylor.

**1935:** The remainder of the Taylor family, who are still living in Claremont House, advertise for a 'Girl' wanted as a general help for a family of three.

**1938:** The Taylor family who are still living in Claremont House, advertise again for a 'Girl' wanted as a general help for a family of three.

**1939:** In June, Claremont House is advertised for sale as a Freehold residence, stone built with slatted roof, containing on the ground floor a tiled hall, and 5 bedrooms etc. Included is a large walled garden, croquet lawn and paddock, and possessing a road frontage of 450 feet. The house lends itself for conversion of two maisonettes at a nominal cost with ample room for erection of further houses on the site. An auction by Messrs Tilley and Culverwell, took place in the Royal Oak on Thursday 13 July at 6pm. Having received instructions from Mr J.B. Taylor (who is quitting Claremont House), Messrs Tilley and Culverwell hold an auction of possessions on the premises at 2pm on 28 September. Amongst the usual paraphernalia, the auction included an invalid's wheel chair, a Bagatelle Board and 14 laying hens!

**1939:** WWII has now begun (1 September 1939 – 2 September 1945). From planning application papers held at the Wiltshire Record Office, the Claremont property is now owned by Osborne & Sons (Builders) of Osborne House, 1 Station Road, Corsham.

On Saturday 25 November, the following letter appealing for help from Grace Methuen and H.B. Coats (Billeting Officers for Corsham), appears in the Wiltshire Times and Trowbridge Advertiser newspaper on Saturday 25 November. The London County Council (LCC) who were the principal local government body for the County of London, are looking for places to evacuate London's children. Corsham was told to expect 650 children evacuees, plus 20 in Neston and 60 more for Gastard. In addition to these unaccompanied schoolchildren, there were 100 adults from Hastings and a considerable number of mothers and small families from elsewhere.

**LETTER TO THE EDITOR. AN APPEAL FROM CORSHAM.**

*Sir: May we beg the hospitality of your columns for this appeal, for it does seem to us to be effort worthy of support? In common with other places in the county we have had our due share of children from London and, like others, we have our difficulties. Now the L.C.C. have, we understand, authorised the renting of a house suitable to house that part of the Moberly Street School, Paddington, which we have here.*

## Chapter 7. Claremont Ladies' College.

*Miss Lodge, their head teacher, most anxious to help those concerned with the reception and care of the children here and has volunteered that she and some of her staff will live in 'Claremont' and that they will take to live with them some of the 'difficult' children. This seems to here to a truly public-spirited act the part the school-teachers and we in turn are anxious to help the effort on. But the L.C.C. will only provide the actual school equipment and we are writing, therefore, to appeal to your readers for help with the other things needed. Small sums in cash or, better, the offer to give or lend any of the articles mentioned below will be gratefully received either myself or by Miss Lodge, Claremont, Corsham. Trusting that you will support this effort in your columns and that the ever-generous Wiltshire folk will once more help a praiseworthy effort grapple with a very real and pressing trouble.*

*We are, Sir, yours faithfully, GRACE METHUEN, H. B. COATES, Billeting Officers for Corsham.*

**LIST OF ARTICLES REQUIRED:** Three chests of drawers, one wardrobe, six tables, 12 chairs, six mirrors, three washbowls, two slop-pails, eight chambers, ten pillows, ten pillowcases, one bolster, one double mattress, 24 single sheets and also strips carpets, mats, linoleum and mackintosh sheets for beds, mattress cases, straw, two table cloths, 16 towels, ironing irons, fire-irons, cutlery and crockery of all kinds, curtains or material for same, kettle, tray, teapot, jugs, cooking utensils, bread bin, two fenders, three fireguards, brooms, brushes, pails, coal scuttles.

**1940: FIRE ALARM:** A serious fire is averted at Claremont in June by the prompt action of a civilian Mr Fred Hughes and some soldiers who *just happened to be passing by*. The fire had started in an upstairs room and the smoke was so thick that the house could only be entered after wet handkerchiefs had been placed over the faces of the fire-fighters. Water was available from a tank in the bathroom. So efficient was the work of the amateur fire-fighters, that when Chippenham Fire Brigade arrived, the fire had been extinguished. Claremont was at that time occupied by Miss Lodge (London County Council Teacher) and her evacuee London school children.

**1945:** The Rev. Percy Warrington (who resided at Monkton Combe in Bath) secures the Claremont property as his own, and makes applications for extensions to the building to convert it into a *'Home for Aged People'* using Walter W Currie, an Architect at 25 High Street, Corsham.

**1946:** The establishment now an 'Old Peoples home' opens. Further applications to expand the building continue to be submitted in 1947.

*Submitted Claremont plan 1946*          *Submitted Claremont Plan 1947*

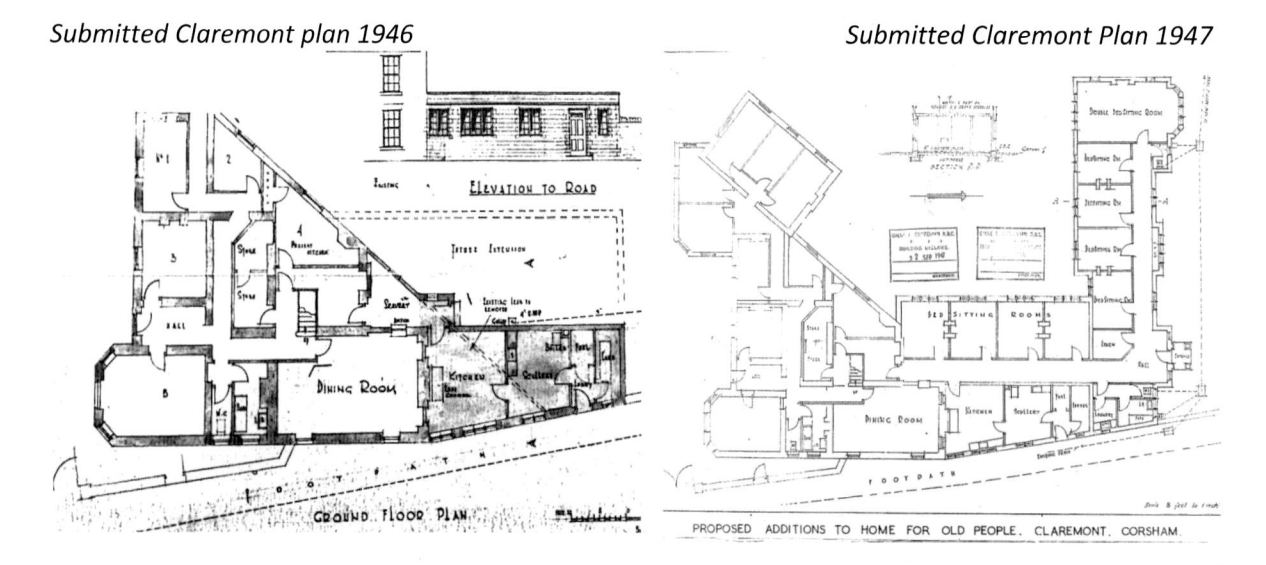

## Chapter 7. Claremont Ladies' College.

**1946 continued....** In the Wiltshire Times and Trowbridge Advertiser - Saturday 2 November, the following advertisement appeared: *TRAINED NURSE Required in Home for elderly gentle-folk; no chronic bed cases; night duty. - Apply Matron, Claremont.'*

Miss Agnes Tennant and Miss L. Rigden *(Claremont Principals 1891-1931)* bequeath to the Corsham Parish Council, the triangular piece of land at the bottom of Station Hill for the WWII Garden of Remembrance and agreed to pay for the Memorial which was opened by the Duke of Edinburgh on his first appearance at a public function.

*Photo: Prince Philip, Duke of Edinburgh opening the Garden of Remembrance on the 1 November 1946.*

**1950:** On 1 September Miss Agnes Tennant passes away aged 83. Miss Tennant was a native of Moffat, Scotland, and joined Miss Rigden at Claremont College, which they ran successfully for 22 years until they both retired in 1913.

[Ed: In the late 1950s early 1960s my father Francesco Carosi looked after the Claremont garden on a part time basis. My mother worked in the kitchens - which always smelled of boiled cabbage!]

**1961:** The Rev. Percy Warrington dies, and Warrington Homes (who own Claremont) becomes a Limited Company, run by Trustees.

**1985:** Claremont is sometimes referred to as 'The Claremont Home for Gentlefolk'.

**2019:** Today, Claremont is still a Residential Care Home. There have been many changes and additions to Claremont over the years and the building has been expanded several times.

It is now a 34 bed-roomed house of mixed age surrounded by scenic countryside and situated in large mature gardens, and one of two homes making up the Warrington Homes Limited organisation, recently managed by Mandy McCulloch and now Julie Lee (2019).

## Chapter 8. Famous and Notable Personalities of Corsham.

| | | |
|---|---|---|
| **AITKENHEAD** | Decca (b1971) | Decca is one of the country's top journalists who has specialised in interviewing significant public figures. She wrote for 'The Independent' newspaper from 1995 before joining The Guardian in 1997.<br><br>Her first book *'The Promised Land: Travels In Search Of The Perfect E'* appeared in early 2002. In 2009 she won the Interviewer of the Year at the British Press Awards and she is also a regular contributor to radio and TV programmes. Her book, *'All at Sea'* (2016) describes the tragic loss of her husband who drowned at sea in his native Caribbean in May 2014. |
| **ALFORD** | Dr. Sidney Christopher (b1935) | Sidney joined Leafield Engineering in Corsham for a while. He is considered the pioneer in water projecting disruptors driven by high explosive. These are used in bomb disposal. He also developed the renowned Dioplex linear cutting charge, and Vulcan shaped charge.<br>His explosive charges are some of the most highly regarded in the industry and are said to have saved many lives.<br>He was awarded the OBE (Officer of the Order of the British Empire) in the 2015 Queen's Birthday Honours List for his services to Explosive Ordnance Disposal Technology. He is the founder and chairman of Alford Technologies Ltd. of Corsham. |
| **ARNOLD** | William, (d1719) | The Arnold family originally came from Lacock - Arnolds Mill. William was a member of the Corsham Wool Merchants Guild and built Arnold House in the High Street.<br>He became a major landowner and one of the wealthiest people in Corsham. |
| **AYLMER** | Felix, (1889–1979) | Actor and President of Equity 1950–1969. Born in Corsham's Alexander House.<br><br>Appeared in many films and plays. Awarded an OBE in 1959 for his services to the stage and a knighthood in 1965.<br><br>Photo shows FELIX AYLMER in the 1956 Ken Annakin Drama LOSER TAKES ALL.<br>*Portrait by Ray Hearne.* |

Chapter 8. Famous and Notable Personalities of Corsham.

| | | |
|---|---|---|
| **BETHEL** | Richard, (1800-1863) | A scholar at the Mansion House School in Corsham. Later became Lord Chancellor and the first Lord Westbury. |
| **BEZAR** | Edwin, (1838–1936) | Born in Corsham. Edwin was an English soldier who fought in the Crimean War, counter-insurgency in the Aden Settlement and the New Zealand Wars.<br>At his death in 1936 aged 97 he was the last surviving soldier of the 57th Regiment that had fought in the New Zealand Wars.<br>He was a prolific correspondent who wrote of his experiences in the Wars. |
| **BIDDALL** | Jennifer (b. 1980) | Actress - trained at the Bristol Old Vic theatre school, and rose to fame as Jessica Harris in the Channel 4 serial drama 'Hollyoaks', which she left in 2008.<br>She has since starred in a number of West End musicals including 'Dreamboats and Petticoats', and television programmes such as 'Doctors' and 'Mount Pleasant'. |
| **BLACKMORE** | Richard, MD. (1654-1729) | Born 22 January 1654 in Corsham. Physician of some eminence and a prolific writer - but a dull one, whose poetry *'could put lawyers to sleep'*. Knighted in 1697 by William III who chose Richard as one of his physicians extraordinaire.<br>Despite his critics, his work was admired by Dr. Samuel Johnson. Richard died 9 October 1729 in Boxted Essex - and is buried in St. Peter's Churchyard, Boxted, Essex. |
| **BOYS-SMITH** | Winifred Lily, (1865-1939) | English science artist and lecturer, university professor at University of Otago New Zealand, school principal. She was born in Corsham on 7 November 1865.<br>She studied at the University of Cambridge between 1891 and 1895. She took the full honours course for natural sciences tripos *(i.e. the framework within which most of the sciences are taught in Cambridge)*, however, she was only given a certificate, as women were not granted degrees at the time. | *Photo shows Winifred at the Franz Josef Glacier.* |
| **BRAKSPEAR** | Sir Harold, (1870–1934) | Restoration architect and archaeologist, lived at Pickwick Manor and Parkside in Corsham High Street.<br>His son Oswald was also an architect. |
| **BRIAN** | Robert, (b1970) | Drummer and session musician, most notably for Siouxsie Sioux. Brian was introduced to drumming at an early age by his father, Ray Brian, who was a session drummer in the 1960s.<br>Robert has recorded with Goldfrapp, Simple Minds, Clara Ponty, Michel Polnareff, Loreena McKinnet, Modern English, David Rhodes, Herbie Flowers, Siouxsie Sioux, Hugh Cornwell, Charlie Jones, Jason Rebello, Derek Nash, Andy Sheppard, Coati Mundi, Alan Barnes, and Roger Cook. |

Chapter 8. Famous and Notable Personalities of Corsham.

| | | | |
|---|---|---|---|
| **CHAPPELL** | Miss Doris | Managed the Corsham Maternity Home on a voluntary basis for over thirty years between 1919-1951 for the benefit of the County of Wiltshire. She came from a famous family of music publishers and piano makers. | |
| **CLUTTERBUCK** | Lt. Daniel, Hugh (1828-1906) | The Clutterbucks were closely associated with Chippenham, Bradford on Avon and Corsham. Born 15 March 1828 at Bath, 2nd son of Thomas Clutterbuck, Royal Horse Guards. Daniel was wounded in the right foot by a shell fragment, in the Charge of the Light Brigade on 25 Oct. 1854. In December 1954 he was elevated to the rank of Captain. Received the Crimea Medal from Queen Victoria on 18 May 1885 then retired from the Army. He became a Justice of the Peace for Wiltshire and served as Chairman of the Corsham Petty Sessions Bench. | Daniel lived in Monks Park House and Middlewick House. He is buried at the rear of St Bartholomew's church.<br><br>*Lieutenant Daniel Hugh Clutterbuck.* |
| **CORNWELL** | Hugh Alan (b1949) | English musician and singer-songwriter, best known for being the vocalist and guitarist for the punk rock/new wave band the Stranglers from 1974 to 1990. Played bass in a band with Richard Thompson, later a member of Fairport Convention. In the late 1960s, after earning a bachelor's degree in biochemistry from Bristol University, he embarked on post-graduate research at Lund University in Sweden. Not long after, he formed the band Johnny Sox. Lives(ed) in Box but was often seen in Corsham. | *Photo by Theraven at English Wikipedia. H Cornwall in 2010.* |
| **COSA** | Cosa or Cossa | The meaning of Corsham is likely to have been the settlement, or ham *(home)*, of someone called Cosa or Cossa, i.e. Cosa'sHam. The 'r' is a later insertion, possibly caused by local pronunciation. | |
| **CROKER** | Nina | *Trooper* Nina Croker, who once worked on the till in Sainsbury's, became the first women to join the Queen's 359 year old Household Cavalry in 2019 as part of the Life Guards squadron. | |
| **CRUICKSHANK** | Flying Officer John (Jock) MBE (d2008) | Lived in Mayo Close for a time. A stone laid in memory at the National Memorial Arboretum in Alrewas, Staffordshire. | JOHN 'JOCK' CRUICKSHANK MBE CORSHAM BRANCH |

Chapter 8. Famous and Notable Personalities of Corsham.

| | | |
|---|---|---|
| **CURD** | Katy (b1989) | A fully qualified Cyclists' Touring Club (CTC) mountain bike instructor, Elite downhill racer and World Cup downhill star from Corsham. Katy's first race was at Churchill, near Weston-super-mare at the end of 2006. Her first National race was in 2007 at Rheola, South Wales. The CTC is a charitable membership organisation supporting cyclists and promoting bicycle use. |
| **DANVERS** | Sir Henry, (1573-1643) | Accompanied by his brother Charles, he murdered Henry Long in Corsham in 1594. Henry subsequently became Earl of Derby. |
| **EADIE** | Darren (b1975) | Played in the Premier League for Norwich City and Leicester City, for whom in December 1999 he became their record signing at three million pounds.<br>At international level, he earned seven England Under 21 caps, scoring twice. Now hosts a weekday evening television magazine show for Norwich based station Mustard TV. |
| **EASTWOOD** | David CBE MC (1919-2010) | A British Army officer and a veteran of Operation Market Garden, Arnhem with the 21st Independent Parachute Company (21 IPC) during the Second World War, for which he received the Military Cross for courage during Operation Market Garden and was one of the first to land at Arnhem as a pathfinder for the main drop. In their retirement, David and his wife Margaret bred Jacob sheep at Sandpits Farm, Gastard. David passed away aged 91 in 2010 and is interred in Gastard Church. |
| **ENRAGHT** | Revd Richard (1837–1898) | A religious controversialist Curate. He served as a Curate at St Bartholomew Church, (1861–1864), and was ordained into the priesthood in 1862.<br>His writings on Catholic Worship and Church-State relationships, led him into conflict with the Disraeli Government's Public Worship Regulation Act, for which he paid the maximum penalty under the Law, of prosecution, imprisonment and eviction with his family from the Holy Trinity Parish in Birmingham, for conscience sake. |
| **ETHELRED** | The Unready, (978-1017) | Corsham once belonged to the Kings of the day, and was therefore known as a Royal Manor, reputed to have been the seat of Ethelred the Unready. Surrounded by forests, the Saxon Kings came here to hunt deer. Ethelred had a hunting lodge in Corsham and the town is recorded as having a great 'Palace', and it was there that Ethelred the Unready once became ill, and had to return to London in 1015. |
| **EYRE** | William (1642-1675) | William from Neston, was a parliamentarian army officer and politician. He fought for the parliamentary cause in the English Civil War. On 29 November 1648 he was returned as the Member of Parliament for Chippenham. |
| **FORD** | Brian J. (b1939) | Born in Corsham. Independent research biologist, author, and lecturer, who publishes on scientific issues for the general public. He has also been a television personality for more than 40 years. |
| **FOWLDS** | Derek (b1937) | English actor, best known for playing Bernard Woolley in popular British television comedies 'Yes Minister' and 'Yes Prime Minister', and as Oscar Blaketon in the long-running ITV police drama 'Heartbeat', a role he played for 18 years.<br>He was known as 'MR DEREK', to those children brought up on the puppet show 'Basil Brush'. He's a Kingsdown resident in Box. |

Chapter 8. Famous and Notable Personalities of Corsham.

| | | |
|---|---|---|
| **FOWLER** | Robert (1828-1891) | Robert was born the only child of Thomas Fowler of Gastard, and attended Grove House School, Tottenham and London University where he was awarded a B.A. degree in 1848. He was a banker and M.P. for the Penryn and Falmouth Constituency, (1868–1874) and Conservative M.P. for the City of London Constituency (1880–1891) and elected Sheriff. He was created a baronet in 1885. Died of pneumonia in Harley Street, London 22 May 1891. |
| **FULLER** | Fuller baronets | George Pargiter Fuller, Liberal Politician - Born 8 January 1833 in Baynton - Died 2 April 1927 - Resident of Neston Park, Corsham and MP for Westbury 1885-1895.<br>**Fuller baronets, of the Inner Temple (1687):**<br>Sir James Chapman Fuller, 1st Baronet (died 1709).<br>**Baronets of Neston Park:**<br>Sir John Michael Fleetwood Fuller, 1st Baronet (1864–1915).<br>Sir (John) Gerard Henry Fleetwood Fuller, 2nd Baronet (1906–1981).<br>Sir John William Fleetwood Fuller, 3rd Baronet (1936–1998).<br>Sir James Henry Fleetwood Fuller, 4th Baronet (born 1970). |
| **GABRIEL** | Peter (b1950) | Original lead singer and flautist in Genesis. Musician & Record Producer. Long term resident of Corsham - Proprietor of the Real World recording studio in Box. |
| **GARRIHY** | Andrea (1948-2016) | Halifax-born, Andrea studied at Bath Academy of Art, at Corsham Court (1967-71) where she met painter John Garrihy and they married in 1969 and made their home in Corsham. After further study at Bristol University (1972-73) she taught in various educational establishments across the South West from Cheltenham to Newlyn Art Gallery, and continued to carve sculpture in stone, wood and plaster for commissions and exhibitions. For twenty years she had a studio in the Gatehouse of Corsham Court. John still lives in Corsham. |
| **GELL** | LT. COL. Rev. Edward Anthony Sydney (1875-1951) | Corsham vicar who fought in both the Boer and the Great War, winning a Distinguished Service Order (DSO) a Medal for Gallantry (MG). Involved in the selection of the *Unknown Warrior* after WWI. Lord Methuen, who lived at Corsham Court, provided Edward with a living and installed him in the new rectory at Corsham. He was Vicar at St Bartholomew's between 1902-1908. |
| **GOFF** | Max | A professional bassist and member of top rock star Tom Odell's band after beginning his musical career at Corsham School. Has performed on chart topping albums, touring the world's stadiums and appearing on prestigious TV shows. |
| **GOLDNEY** | Sir Gabriel (1813–1900) | Solicitor and MP for Chippenham (1880). Lived in Beechfield House. Sir John Tankerville Goldney resided at Monks Park - his youngest son Sir Frederick Hastings Goldney owned much of the Pickwick village along with Lady Margaret Goldney. |
| **HANNING-SPEKE** | Captain (1827-1841). | Discovered the source of the Nile and died accidentally after shooting himself in a Wadswick field; where in the far corner of the large field, near to the second Fiveways junction on the B3109 road to Bradford-on-Avon is a memorial dedicated to him. |
| **HATTON** | Sir Christopher, (1540-1591) | Queen Elizabeth I leased the Manor of Corsham to her favourite, Sir Christopher Hatton and in the 14th year of her reign granted the whole of the Royal Estates at Corsham to him, except the Lordship of the Manor. |

## Chapter 8. Famous and Notable Personalities of Corsham.

| | | |
|---|---|---|
| **HASTED** | Edward (1732–1812) | Historian and Master of Hungerford Almshouse, Corsham - born on 20 December 1732 in London. His indebtedness was legend, as was his time in prison, and his escapes to France.<br>It is not until 1807, when he was nearly 75 that his personal life finally settled down when his old patron and friend the Earl of Radnor arranged for him to spend his remaining years in modest comfort at Lady Hungerford's Almshouse at Corsham in Wiltshire. He died there on 14th January 1812. |
| **HODGKIN** | Sir Gordon Howard Eliot CH CBE (1932-2017) | Gordon studied at the Camberwell Art School and later at the Bath Academy of Art in Corsham and was a British painter and printmaker. His work is most often associated with abstraction. He became a prominent figure in British art in the 1970s for painting on wooden supports such as drawing boards and door frames instead of canvas. During the Second World War, he was an RAF Wing Commander. |
| **HUNGERFORD** | Edward (1596-1648) | Purchased Corsham Court in 1602. It remained with the Hungerford family until 1684 and then passed through the hands of at least six different owners before being bought by Paul Methuen of Bradford on Avon in 1746. |
| **HUNGERFORD** | Lady Margaret (1603-1672) | Founded the 17th Century Corsham Schoolroom and Corsham Almshouses and resided in the previously known Corsham House, now Corsham Court. Married to Edward above. |
| **HURLEY** | Elizabeth (Liz) Jane (b1965) | Actress who attended St Patrick's Primary School, 1973–74. Her best-known film roles have been as Vanessa Kensington in Mike Myers' hit spy comedy, Austin Powers; International Man of Mystery (1997) and as the Devil in Bedazzled (2000). |
| **KINNEIR** | Septimus Paul (1871-1928) | Born next to the Brewery in Pickwick on 13 May 1871. One of Corsham's best ever cricketers. He was named one of Wisden's cricketers of the year in 1912. He went on to play for Warwickshire and in an England Test match in 1911/1912 against Australia in Sydney, having turned forty. He passed away on 16 October 1928 when he was found draped over his motorcycle which he had carefully laid down on the verge. |
| **MACNEE** | Dorothea Mabel (1896-1984) | After World War II Dorothea was involved in the Women's Voluntary Service, receiving the British Empire Medal for her services. She had two sons, one of whom was Patrick Macnee, the actor (John Steed in the British television series, 'The Avengers'). She was a long-term resident paid for by her son Patrick at the Methuen Arms until 1976 when growing health problems led to her move to a nearby rest home. |
| **MALONEY** | John M (b1950) | John was Principal Archaeological Excavations Officer [City of London], Museum of London. He led the largest urban archaeological unit in the world in the 1980s; was an important contributor to the first urban archaeological manual that has been translated into more than 30 languages and played a leading role in developing the principle of developer funding for archaeology which was latterly adopted by government as a basis for Planning Policy Guidance 16: Archaeology and Planning [PPG 16, 1990]. In 1996 he was made a Freeman of the City of London for *'his contribution to professional archaeology in the City'*. |

Chapter 8. Famous and Notable Personalities of Corsham.

| | | |
|---|---|---|
| **MANTLE** | Clive (b1957) | Lived in Box but was very often seen in Corsham. Tall actor 6' 5½" (1.97 m), best known for playing the general surgeon Dr Mike Barratt in the BBC hospital drama series 'Casualty' and 'Holby City' in the 1990s; also noted for his role as Little John in the cult 1980s fantasy series Robin of Sherwood. He returned to Casualty in 2016 as Mike Barratt for the 30th anniversary. |
| **MARSHALL** | Kris, (b 1973) | Actor, best known for playing Nick Harper in 'My Family' and lead detective DI Humphrey Goodman in 'Death In Paradise'. His father was with the RAF in Canada. When Kris was about four they moved to Corsham, with his Dad flying Hercules planes out of RAF Lyneham for 3 years before moving to Hankerton, in Wiltshire when Kris was 7 years old. |
| **MARTIN** | Paul (b1959) | An antiques dealer and professional drummer, best known for being the presenter of various BBC antiques programmes including 'Flog It!', 'Trust Me', 'I'm a Dealer' and Paul Martin's 'Handmade Revolution'. Opened an antiques shop called 'The Table Gallery' in Corsham High Street in 2019. As a session musician drummer, Paul has worked with Average White Band, The Quireboys and Dogs D'Amour in the 1990s. He still plays with local jazz and blues bands around Wiltshire. |
| **MASON** | Nick (b1944) | Musician, Composer and Drummer with legendary band Pink Floyd - Born in Edgbaston, Birmingham - Resident of Middlewick House, Corsham since 1996. |
| **MAYO** | Charles (1834-1885) | Lived at Ivy House, Priory Street with his brother the Rev Robert Mayo and played an important part in developing Corsham. The High Street Mayo Fountain is in memory of him. |
| **METHUEN** | Baron Methuen(s) | The Methuen family seat is Corsham Court. The house was bought in 1745 by Sir Paul Methuen for his cousin, also named Paul Methuen, whose grandson became Baron Methuen. The current owner James Methuen-Campbell, is the eighth generation of the Methuens to live there. |
| **MOUNTBATTEN** | Lieutenant Philip (b1921) | Now Prince Philip and married to Queen Elizabeth II. His career in the Royal Navy continued after the war. In February 1947, Prince Philip became a naturalised British subject, renouncing his Greek Royal title and adopting his maternal grandfather's surname, Mountbatten. At the time of his engagement to Princess Elizabeth in July 1947, he was instructing cadets at the Petty Officer training school HMS Royal Arthur in Corsham. |
| **MILLWARD** | Stephanie (b1981) | British Paralympic swimmer born on 20 September 1981 in Jeddah, Saudi Arabia. During the 2012 summer Olympics she won 3 silver medals and a bronze. At the age of 17 she was diagnosed with multiple sclerosis (MS). She was awarded the Freedom of the Town of Corsham on 2 March 2013. |
| **NEALE** | Robert (1706-1776) | The Mansion House in Corsham was built by Robert Neale in the early 1720s and remained in the Neale family for almost 200 years. Robert, his eldest son became a clothier, who supplied to the British Army and become Commissioner of the Peace and MP for Wootton Bassett. |
| **NEWEY** | Andrew (b1958) | He has worked in both Formula One and IndyCar racing as a race engineer, aerodynamicist, designer and technical director and enjoyed success in both jobs. Considered one of the best engineers in Formula One. He once lived in Pickwick in 1983. |

Chapter 8. Famous and Notable Personalities of Corsham.

| | | |
|---|---|---|
| **PARKER BOWLES** | Andrew Henry (b1939) | Army Brigadier and former husband of the Duchess of Cornwall, Camilla Rosemary Shand. Lived in Middlewick House Corsham. |
| **PHILLIPS** | Conrad (1925-2016) | Conrad Philip Havord, better known as 'Conrad Philips' was an English television and film actor. He is best known for playing William Tell and splitting precariously placed apples in the adventure series 'The Adventures of William Tell' (1958–1959). *[From Pete Comber]* Following a long career he resided in Chippenham after a brief spell living in Corsham High Street, behind where Shergold's the greengrocer (including apples!) and fish shop was located to the right of the Royal Oak, *(see photo below courtesy of Corsham Civic Society archive).* The house in Corsham was too small, so they moved to Chippenham. |
| **PICKWICK** | Moses, (b1748?-d1837) | Moses was a foundling who was discovered in Pickwick. He went on to own a coach business in Bath based in 'The White Hart Inn' opposite the iconic Pump Rooms. It is widely believed that Charles Dickens wrote the 'Pickwick Papers' after visiting Bath, using the surname he had seen there on one of his visits. |
| **PICTOR** | Pictor family | Job Pictor (farmer, builder and quarryman) married Mary Fluester (from Biddestone) in 1827 and had twelve children. Job began quarrying in Boxfields in 1829. In 1877, 'Pictor & Sons Quarries' was established and they worked several quarries in and around Corsham for many years. |
| **POWER** | Admiral Sir Laurence Eliot (d1927) | Lived in the old vicarage at 40 High Street and died there aged 62 on Thursday 20 January 1927. In WWI, he was associated in the production of shipbuilding for the Royal Navy. He rendered valuable service to the country, especially at the time when the German submarine campaign was at its height. He was also responsible for supervising warship repairs during the war. |
| **POYNDER** | Sir John Dickson, (1866-1936) | John was first a Baron then he was given the title of 'Sir' in 1884. He was also a member of parliament for the Chippenham area of Wiltshire before becoming Lord Islington and Governor of New Zealand. The Poynder estates in Wiltshire included Hilmarton near Calne and Hartham near Corsham. |
| **SANSOM** | Arthur Ernest (1838-1907) | Born 13 May 1838 in Corsham. English physician, known for his pioneering research on anaesthesiology, the use of carbolic acid in medicine, and diagnosis of heart disease. President of the Medical Society of London for the year 1897. |

Chapter 8. Famous and Notable Personalities of Corsham.

| | | |
|---|---|---|
| **SCHEFFLER** | Alex (b1957) | Born in Hamburg, Germany, Axel is an award-winning, internationally-acclaimed illustrator of several well-loved children's books, published in many languages. His work has been exhibited all around the world. Studied Visual Communications at Bath Academy of Art in Corsham (1982-1984). His first book illustrations appeared in 'The Piemakers' by Helen Cresswell. |
| **SCHMIDT** | Dr. Gavin Andrew (b1963) | Educated at The Corsham School, earned a BA (Hons) in mathematics at Jesus College, Oxford, and a PhD in applied mathematics at University College London. A climatologist, climate modeller and Director of the NASA Goddard Institute for Space Studies (GISS) in New York, and co-founder of the award-winning climate science blog RealClimate. He is now the Director of Nasa's Goddard Institute for Space Studies. |
| **SHAND** | Camilla, Duchess of Cornwall (b. 1947) | Born Camilla Rosemary Shand, later married Andrew Parker Bowles (they divorced in 1995) and resided at Middlewick House Corsham. She is now the second wife of Charles, Prince of Wales, heir apparent to the British throne. She is now a member of the British Royal family. Instead of the title Princess of Wales, she uses 'Duchess of Cornwall', her husband's secondary designation. |
| **SMITH** | Edmund (1672-1710) | Author of 'Phaedra and Hippolytus a Tragedy' in 1707. He died at Hartham and is buried in St Nicholas's church at Biddestone. |
| **SMITH** | Jim, (1906–1979) | Jim's family lived in Corsham's Havelock Cottage at 72 Priory Street. He became an English cricketer who played in five Test matches for the England cricket team between 1935 and 1937. |
| **SMYTHE** | Thomas, (1522-1591) | Thomas was the son of a Corsham farmer and made his fortune in London as a Customs and Excise collector in the Ports of London. He caught the eye of Queen Elizabeth I and was given the Corsham Manor by her in 1575. He built the great house (Corsham Court) near the site of the old manor house which later *passed on* to his son Sir Henry Smythe. |
| **SOUTHEY** | Elizabeth (1801-1892) | Elizabeth was an artist; she painted Corsham's St Bartholomew's church after the removal of part of its original spire in 1816. The painting (see photo below) was given to Miss Catherine Beames on her wedding day 10 May 1864.<br>The Southey family lived in Corsham High Street in Arnold House. Elizabeth died aged 91 and is buried in St Bartholomew's. |
| **SPACKMAN** | Spackman Family | Musical family who originally lived in their grocery shop in the High Street. Herbert Spackman (photographer) captured many of the old iconic images of Corsham in the early 1900s. |

Chapter 8. Famous and Notable Personalities of Corsham.

| | | |
|---|---|---|
| **SUGG** | Joseph (Joe) Graham (b1991) | British YouTuber, vlogger, author and television personality. Best known for his YouTube channels, ThatcherJoe, ThatcherJoeVlogs and ThatcherJoeGames and as runner-up of the sixteenth series of Strictly Come Dancing TV show in 2018. |
| **SUGG** | Zoe aka Zoella (b1990) | 'Vlogger', author and fashion guru. Involved in the latest 'Band Aid' charity single, appearance on 'Celebrity Bake Off'. In 2015 arrived in wax form at Madame Tussauds. Her novel 'Girl Online' broke records for first week sales of a debut novel. The follow up, 'Girl Online – On Tour' has also been very successful. She now has her own line of cosmetics and the 'Zoella Book Club' launched through WH Smith in the summer of 2016. Her online blog became one the most successful of all time with (at last count) over 5 million followers. Sister of Joe Sugg above. |
| **SYLVESTER** | Albert James (1889-1989) | Lloyd George's Principal Private Secretary who spent his last years in Corsham. |
| **TANNER,** | Heather Muriel (1903-1993) | Writer and Peace, Environment and Social Justice Campaigner - Born 14 July 1903 in Corsham - Died 23 June 1993 in Kington St. Michael - Resident of Kington Langley - Wife of Robin Tanner and daughter of Herbert Spackman. |
| **TEMPLETON** | Lucille Corinne (1935–1986) | Artist, better known as Rini, studied at Bath Academy in Corsham c1956 and learnt sculpture under Bernard Meadows (where she briefly wed Scottish musician Alistair Graham) and later spent time busking on the streets of London. For 20 years, Rini made drawings of activists in the United States, Mexico and Central America while she joined them in their meetings, demonstrations, picket lines and other actions for social justice. She called her bold black-and-white images 'xerox art' because activists and organizers could copy them easily for use in their banners, signs, leaflets, newsletters, even T-shirts, whenever needed. |
| **TIPPETT** | Michael (1905–1998). | One of England's greatest contemporary composers. Michael lived at Parkside in the Corsham High Street, 1960–1970. Among his best-known works are the oratorio 'A Child of Our Time', the orchestral 'Fantasia Concertante' on a Theme of Corelli, and the opera 'The Midsummer Marriage'. *Image Rights ID No. 9863027939 via National Portrait Gallery. 2019-04-10 Sir Michael Kemp Tippett by Walter Bird.* |

Chapter 8. Famous and Notable Personalities of Corsham.

| | | |
|---|---|---|
| **TROPNELL** | Tropnell family | In the 15th century Thomas Tropnell (1405-1488) owned Great Chalfield Manor and many other pieces of land close to Corsham. He later purchased 150 acres of land to create Neston Park which was eventually sold to John Fuller in 1790. In the Lady Chapel of St Bartholomew's church you can see a monument to the last 'Thomas' Tropnell and his wife. |
| **VIZEY** | Pamela (1932-1992) | An English actress best known for her roles as Kath Brownlow in Crossroads and as the mother of Carol and Trisha Yates in the children's television series Grange Hill. *[Ed: She lived in Alexander Terrace a few doors along from me in the 1980s!]* |
| **WHITE** | Marco Pierre (b1961) | After leaving Allerton High School in Leeds without any qualifications, celebrity restaurateur Marco decided to train as a chef. At 33, he became the youngest chef to be awarded three Michelin stars. He added the Rudloe Hotel to his growing collection of restaurants and reopened it under the new name 'The Rudloe Arms'. |
| **WODEHOUSE** | Sir Pelham Grenville (1881-1975) | English author of the Jeeves and Wooster stories. Young Pelham *(PG Wodehouse)*, spent school holidays with a clergyman uncle nearby and was often taken to Corsham to skate on the lake. |
| **WOOD** | Colonel David James MBE, (1923 – 2009) | David was born in Corsham and educated at Monkton Combe School. Last surviving officer of the coup de main operation carried out by glider borne troops of the 2nd Oxfordshire and Buckinghamshire Light Infantry (the 52nd), on D Day, 6 June 1944, tasked with capturing Pegasus Bridge and Horsa Bridge before the main assault on the Normandy beaches began. |
| **YOCKNEY** | Captain Thomas Edridge (1870-1901) | This memorial, within the St Bartholomew's Church, Corsham commemorates Captain Thomas Edridge Yockney, of the Imperial Light Horse, youngest son of the late Augustus Yockney, of Pockeredge, Corsham, was killed in action at Nauwpoort, Transvaal, on January 5th, 1901, aged 31, He had taken part in the Battle of Elandslaagte and the siege of Ladysmith in the Anglo-Boer War (1899-1902).<br><br>IN MEMORY OF<br>THOMAS EDRIDGE YOCKNEY<br>CAPTAIN IMPERIAL LIGHT HORSE<br>WHO WAS KILLED IN ACTION<br>AT NAAUPOORT TRANSVAAL<br>ON 5TH JANUARY 1901<br>AGED 31 YEARS.<br><br>The Yockney family, together with Randall and Sunders, and Pictors, amalgamated in 1887 to become the 'Bath Stone Firms'. |
| **YOUNGHUSBAND** | Captain Reginald (1844-1879) | Born in Bath and went to school in the Mansion House, Corsham. In 1879 he was Captain of the 1/24tth (2nd Warwickshire Regiment) taking part in the Zulu Wars in South Africa. He died aged 35 at the battle of Isandlwala on 22 January 1879. There is a family memorial to him inscribed on a headstone at Melcombe Regis Cemetery in Weymouth. |

*[Ed - the names listed above are not meant to be a comprehensive list, as there may be others who perhaps should also appear here. Nevertheless, the intention is to promote our little town of Corsham as playing an important part in society. I can only apologise if I have missed anyone out.]*

## Chapter 9. Gastard - a history.

**Gastard House early 1900s**

*c1905 Postcard photo shows Gastard House, previously called Gastard Court and Elm Grove House*

*[No. CLXVI Wiltshire Archaeological and Natural History Magazine page 538, Vol. 43. June 1927 By Harold Brakspear F.S.A.]*

**Gastard Tithing. Gastard Court.** This house dates mostly from the seventeenth century, though it possibly retains portions of earlier work. It belonged to 1½ virgates of land, and was in the hands of the Jones family in 1560.

The house then passed with their heiress in 1605 to Richard Sherfield, and he and his wife surrendered it in 1631 to Tristam Colborne. It stayed with that family until 1744 when it was bought by Edward Mitchell in whose family it remained until 1876 when it was surrendered to a family name that we are more familiar with, Robert Fowler, of Elmgrove.

**Gastard - a comprehensive history.**

**Part 1: Memories of life in Gastard in the 1940s by Dr. John F. James of Kilcreggan.**
*[Ed. From Dr James' lovely story that was passed to me via Charlie Ralph on 7 December 2018.]*

**Part 2: Gastard News excerpts.** *[Ed. Courtesy of Max Salmon of Lane's End Farm and the staff and archives held at the Wiltshire and Swindon History Centre in Chippenham.]*

*[Ed. I have added the images and also some additional information into the narratives.*

*Note: Knap = the crest of a hill and place names were originally spelt with one 'p', but now Knapp.]*

# Chapter 9. Gastard - a history.

**Part 1: Memories of life in Gastard in the 1940s by Dr. John F. James of Kilcreggan.**

*Postcard photo shows 1 Lanes End cottage opposite Lanes End Farm in Gastard in the early 1900s.*

I arrived in the village of Gastard in 1938 following my mother's appointment as headmistress of Chapel Knap School ('Knap' spelt with one 'p' at that time). Whilst our semi-detached house, which my father named 'Soundings', was being built (halfway up on the right on Velley Hill) by builders Merritt's of Corsham, we lodged in Attwood Farm with farmer Bevan, a dairy farmer, a Welshman from Oxwich on the Gower peninsula. The field opposite the farm was regularly ploughed by a two-furrow plough drawn by a pair of large horses. The milk was collected daily and stored in churns placed outside the farm gate on a platform at the side of the road. The milk was taken by a lorry to the Nestle's milk factory located alongside the river in Chippenham. *Photo below shows the Harp and Crown Gastard in 1904.*

## Chapter 9. Gastard - a history.

The 'Harp & Crown' Inn *(see previous photo)* at the crossroads was kept by the landlord, Mr Scudamore. Further along Silver Street towards Corsham, was the Gastard Post Office and Bakery where Mr and Mrs Gale issued postal orders, baked the village bread and roasted the Christmas turkeys. Opposite the post office was a small Market Garden run by Fred Hand, whose daughter Rachel was a pupil at the Chapel Knapp School. The school-leaving age was 12, but rose about that time to 14. There were about 35 Children in the school, from all parts of Gastard, from Prospect and from Monk's Lane. Fred Hand sold his vegetables to the neighbourhood from a horse-and-cart which was often parked just outside 'Soundings' on Velley Hill. The road was wider there than on the rest of Velley Hill and there was no pavement; these days it would be called a lay-by.

We - the James family - moved into our house the 'Soundings' at some time in the Spring or Summer of 1939. I recall hearing Mr Chamberlain declare war on Germany on the wireless in the living room one Sunday morning *[at 11.15 a.m on 3 September, 1939]*. Opposite 'Soundings' lived the Merrett family. In the attached house to the right of them was a single man called - as I remember - Mr Hoddinot, who delivered religious tracts on a bicycle. Behind them - up the little side-lane - were the Jones family, Albert and Sadie and three girls, Myra, Menna and Pat and a son born in the early 40's. Albert Jones cycled to Melksham every day to work in the Avon tyre factory. I recall clearly their orchard which had several splendid russet-apple trees.

Below the Merrett's residence was the Baptist Chapel, and below that lived Mrs Hudd, a plump old lady who was the village's 'Wise Woman', who (among other things) supposedly charmed warts away. Below her lived the Fielding's. Along the lane below them lived the Coates family, including a daughter, Marion. Mr Coates, I recall, had a withered left arm and ran a saw-mill over in Westwells. His horse and cart, loaded with logs in sacks, came around the village on Saturday mornings to sell firewood during the war years, this adequately supplemented coal which was in short supply.

Below the lane was a sweet-shop in the front porch of the next house and a couple of houses below that lived a branch of the Webb family. I recall the old man Granfer Webb, who must have been about 80 years old in 1940. He was as thin as a rake, walked with a stick and had one eye, with an empty socket where the other would have been. One of the nearby houses was sold in the late 40's to a family from London, who brought with them the first television set in the village. As there was no transmitter nearby, it *did not work*.

My parents had the first *working* television in the village in 1953, (a Pye VT4 14" set *(see photo)* which cost £58, a considerable sum of money in 1953, when my salary at the English Electric Company was £550 p.a.) which received its signal from the Wenvoe transmitter situated close to the village of Wenvoe in the Vale of Glamorgan, Wales.

There was only one channel, BBC of course, and everything except the old Hollywood films was transmitted live: there was no video-recording in those days. It made for good television. Actors were on their mettle. There were occasional hilarious (and sometimes obscene) cock-ups!

## Chapter 9. Gastard - a history.

The ladies who lived in the ancient Gastard Village houses earned pin-money by 'gloving', sewing pieces of leather cut to glove-shape by a factory in Melksham and circulated by a van which called about once a week.

There were essentially only three families in the village, all heavily intermarried since mediaeval times probably: the Austs, the Webbs and the Gales, and I believe the Austs and the Webbs were related to each other. We got most of our groceries in the Gale's shop during the war years, with coupons from our ration books carefully clipped out with scissors.

Gastard House was then owned by Miss Jean Elizabeth Fowler. She died at Hale, Farnham, Surrey in 1944 and her funeral was held in Corsham on Thursday afternoon 20 April. The local Defence Volunteers (later the Home Guard) patrolled in the fields beyond Gastard House and stayed out all night occasionally. Incidentally, these were ex-first world war riflemen from the Flanders and Somme trenches, now in their mid-forties, and they would have been quite a formidable force if it had come to the point. They were far from the characters portrayed in the 'Dad's Army' comedy series.

My parents had the only car in the village, because previously my mother had kept the family going during the great depression by working as a supply-teacher in rural Devonshire, where a car was necessary. We moved to Gastard when the Devon school system was re-arranged and her school was closed.

There was a succession of family cars of which the best was the last one, a Morris 10 series M, one of the last to be made pre-war.

It was bought new, early in 1940, by my father for £175 *[£7,000 in today's money]*. It spent most of the war years standing in the garage. I passed my driving test in it in Bath in 1953.

Most of the Gastard residents either walked or cycled. There lived one or two old people in the village in those days that rarely went into Corsham, had only been to Chippenham a few times in their lives and had never been to Bath. People were simply not mobile and with a shop at the top of Velley Hill that supplied almost everything, saw no reason to travel outside of the village.

In those days, only a few cars each day passed up and down Velley Hill and a horse and cart was just as likely to pass. Steam-lorries and Morris 'bull-nose' touring cars occasionally passed by. Tribes of gypsies passed through once a year or so, with four or five horse-drawn caravans, selling clothes-pegs and stealing chickens. One remarkable traveller, though, was Sir (Freddy) Frederick Hastings Goldney [26 May 1845 – 21 February 1940], 3rd Baronet Of Beechfield House in Corsham, who from time to time was driven through the village by his chauffeur in a 1905 Daimler, a Sedan with a huge, black, single cylinder engine, and a circular motor-hood; with Sir Freddy inside all muffled-up warm and dry, and his chauffeur out in the cold rain; the whole vision proceeding with a steady and dignified chug-chug-chug at 15 mph

## Chapter 9. Gastard - a history.

along Velley Hill. Sir Freddy must have been nearly 100 years old. There was a daily bus service into Corsham that normally went via the Roebuck Inn and along the Lacock Road. Another bus paused at Gastard on its way from Lacock to Corsham on Wednesday afternoons and again on Saturday afternoons.

The return journey was in the evening. Otherwise we cycled or walked. On Saturday mornings I walked to the Pictures in Corsham at the 'Regal' cinema on Pickwick Road to see Flash Gordon.

In 1940 I sat the 'Eleven-Plus' exam in the village school and having passed, was admitted to Chippenham Secondary School, a recently-built grammar-school at Hardenhuish, with an intake of about 600 pupils from as far afield as Sutton Benger to the north, and Melksham, Corsham, Biddestone and Box in the south and west. I was the only pupil from Gastard for many years, although Tony Gale, son of Reg Gale who lived next door to us in the other half of our 'semi-detached house', passed the exam, but was not allowed to go to the Chippenham Secondary School by his parents.

My mother bought a bicycle for me; a new Coventry 'Eagle' costing £2-12-6d, and from September 1940 I cycled every day the 5 miles to the Chippenham Secondary School along Coppershell lane via Pandown brook. I was a daring, high-speed dive-bomber pedalling furiously downhill and turning dangerously to cross the bridge at the bottom.

I never came off, but never once made it to the top the other side without dismounting. I passed Easton Village (where a Beaufighter crashed in 1941 and I collected souvenirs from the wreckage), then past the brick-works and on to the A4, then under the big GWR railway arch and left through Lowden past the Sir Audley's Arms in Chippenham.

The roads (apart from the A4) were virtually empty and cycling was quite safe, although unpleasant in the rain. I generally left home at 8.20 a.m. to get to school by 8.55. Later, cycling in wet weather was considered too onerous and instead I cycled to Corsham and took the morning train to Chippenham (the Calne Bunk it was called - two ancient articulated coaches and a GWR 0-5-0 pannier tank-engine to push or pull them between Calne and Box). The fare was three-ha'pence and a three-month season ticket, an oblong orange-coloured piece of important-looking cardboard, was 7/6d.

The homeward leg was on the 4.38 p.m., *("Corsham, Box, Bath and Bristowl"*, as called out loudly by the station porter as it arrived) a 14-coach express from Paddington pulled usually by a 'Castle' or a 'Hall' engine and once, famously by the 'Corsham Court' engine *(see photo).*

Throughout the whole war, even at the height of the blitz, the trains that took me to and fro to school never once failed to appear and were rarely late.

In winter, it always seemed to snow and we skated or slid (we kids had no skates) on the lake in the Corsham Court estate. In summer, those of us with bikes cycled off to Lacock, left our bikes at the side of

109

## Chapter 9. Gastard - a history.

the road which goes on to Bowden Hill, and walked across the water-meadows alongside Lacock Abbey to the S-bend in the river where there was a swimming place. It was not necessary to lock the parked bikes. One bank of the river was high enough for diving off, and the other was a shallow sort of muddy beach for beginners. The water was quite clean, with abundant coarse fish which tasted earthy when gutted, fried and eaten. The Fox-Talbots were still in residence at Lacock Abbey in those days.

After a severe frost, people in Gastard turned out on *'wooding'* expeditions. We went, adults as well as children, armed with sledges, axes and bow-saws, towing them across-country to a field where perhaps after the frost, a bough had fallen from a tree, and we chopped and sawed it up for fuel; it appeared to be a village tradition, and no farmer ever complained that I knew about. But they were dubious about sawing up boughs from Elm trees. *"Thurt spirits in elms"* was a remark I remember hearing. These days, most of the large Elm trees have disappeared as a result of Dutch Elm disease. Most of the fields around Gastard had ponds for the cattle to drink from, since nearly all the farming in the area was dairy-farming. I used to collect methane in a jam-jar (by poking a stick into the muddy bottom and catching the bubbles) from the ponds in fields behind our house. These days, most of the ponds around Gastard have been filled-in and have long since disappeared.

I remember the Gastard Village Hall being built, it was used for a variety of purposes; the Women's Institute met there (and discussed jam-making no doubt), the village cub-pack met there once a week, under the auspices of Akela *[the Lone Wolf or Big Wolf, a fictional character in Rudyard Kipling's stories]* Miss Finch-Noyes, known predictably as 'Tweet', who cycled out from Corsham.

On Saturdays in the Village Hall, there was a Whist-Drive-and-Social and an occasional dance with a live band or a pianist or more often than not - gramophone records producing the music. The gramophone was an old acoustic, wind-up machine of which sometimes I took charge of. There was no village policeman, but there was a local bobby, Mr Sparks, from Corsham, who appeared occasionally on a bicycle. He wore a peaked cap, not a helmet.

There was no serious crime that I can recall. The most serious crimes were the theft of apples (done for the sake of adventure, not because there was a shortage of apples). Occasionally, PC Sparks would be needed to search for a missing child. A few of the 1940 WWII London evacuees who arrived in Gastard, swiftly found their own way back home to Walthamstow by stealing our bicycles or hitching lifts. One 10-year-old in particular had made it all the way back to London by bicycle 48 hours after arriving in Gastard!

In Gastard, most folk when conversing together, spoke with a Wiltshire lilt. I am a fluent speaker, possibly one of the last of the local Wiltshire patois. For example: *"Wurr bist thee goin' then, with thickee gurt 'effer? Bist goin' tun market? Ah, thee'se goi thee new glasses then. Cast see I? No? Thee casn't see as well as thee could 'st, then, cast?"* But this was only when I was out playing with the other village children.

I dared not use the Wiltshire lingo indoors - not when my mother was the village schoolmistress! In university years later, I shared lodgings with a student reading English. As part of his course he had to learn Anglo-Saxon, or 'Middle English' as it is now known. Looking over his shoulder one evening as he was doing a translation exercise, I found I could read whole sentences of the Anglo-Saxon part. It was pure Wilshurr!

## Chapter 9. Gastard - a history.

**Part 2: Gastard News excerpts.**

The Fowlers were a well connected Quaker family and inter-married with other Quaker dynasties throughout England. By the 1790s Robert Fowler (1755-1825), a wealthy wine merchant of Melksham and a Society of Friends (Quaker) minister had purchased land in the parishes of Melksham and Corsham.

**1889 Map.** [*Order ID: maps215686*]

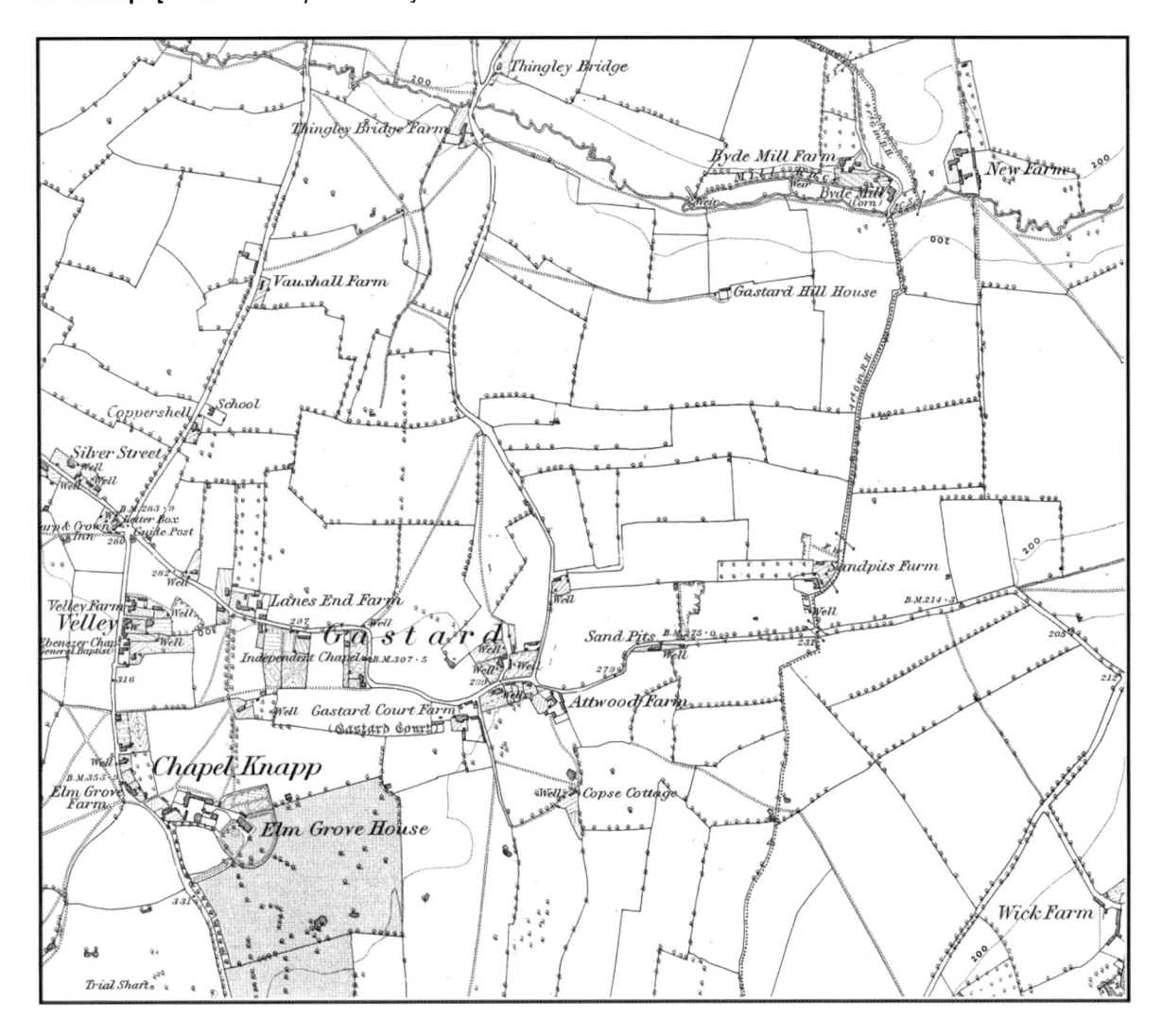

**Elm Grove:** In 1800 Elm Grove (named by Robert Fowler's children) was just a little shooting box of four rooms at the back of which was a farmhouse. In his will of 1825 he left estates and other property, to his wife, Rachel, and upon her death to his children Robert, Thomas, John, Rachel and Mary, including 'messuages *[a dwelling house with outbuildings and land assigned to its use]* and tenements' in Chapel Knapp and Gastard. The Salisbury and Winchester Journal of Monday 26 November 1832 reported that after a short illness, Robert Fowler of Melksham died at Avignon in the South of France aged 25.

Part of the estate was Elm Grove (Gastard House) and adjacent properties that were later consolidated into Elm Grove Farm, later known as Chapel Knapp Farm. His tenants included John Helps, Thomas Little, James Jeffries, Isaac Wait, John Banks, Richard & Harriet Biggs and Margaret Wootton. Other land included field-names we are familiar with today, such as Timber Leaze, Velley Close and Copper Shell.

## Chapter 9. Gastard - a history.

On the 1837 tithe map and apportionment, Elm Grove and an adjacent house and garden is listed as owned and occupied by John Fowler. Thomas Fowler (d.1851) became a London banker (Drewett and Fowler). It was his son, Sir Robert Nicholas Fowler MP (1828-91), who inherited Elm Grove in the 1860s through the terms set out in his grandfather's will.

John Fowler was certainly running the estate until his death in 1861 and is listed as the occupier of Elm Grove House and as a principal landowner in Gastard in Kelly's directories of 1848 and 1855.

He was married to Rebecca Hull (1799 -1842) and they had at least five children, named Henry (1823-1880), Robert (1825-1888), John Jnr. (1826 -1864), William (1828-1905) and Barnard (1833-1882).

John Fowler Jnr. was a notable agricultural engineer. Concerned with the large amount of land that remained uncultivated due to poor drainage, he decided the solution lay in a mechanical plough called the mole, which dug drainage ditches into which drainage pipes could be laid. In 1852 he also invented a steam driven plough, and set up a manufacturing business in Leeds.

There were only eight full-size ploughing engines built and these were for the Italian Government to reclaim the Pontine Marches, a large area of Rome.

According to John Poulsom in his 1989 book 'The Ways of Corsham', John Fowler junior (1826-1864), tried his first mowing machine to cut hay on Little Sands field in Gastard.

He cites reminiscences of Edward Aust who in 1894 recalled a story that Fowler's horses *'did not like the machine and were restive'* and recounts the following conversation between father and son, John Fowler senior and junior:

*"Ah John"* said his father, *"thee'll never get it go."* John replied, *"Well then father, I'll make it go and what's more, if I could get rid of thee and my mother for a year, I'd have the old house down and put up a new one.'*

John's work continued until World War Two when his engine was capable of developing 276 indicated horsepower. Robert, William and Barnard were partners in their brother's business, and later they were joined by their nephew Robert Henry Fowler (1851-1919), son of older brother, Henry. William Fowler was also a financier and became a Member of Parliament for Cambridge.

Elm Grove Farm can be seen clearly on Ordnance Survey maps between 1890 and 1925 adjacent to Elm Grove House in Chapel Knapp *(see map on previous page).* By 1867 it was occupied by a tenant farmer named Walter Hayward, but in 1889 he had moved to Boyds Farm.

# Chapter 9. Gastard - a history.

**Velley Farm.**

At the bottom of Velley Hill was Velley Farm. On the 1837 tithe map it is listed as a Homestead (a farmhouse) and the adjacent land, where Gastard Church is now, was called Home Orchard. Both were owned by Robert Sadler and occupied by Thomas Poulsom. Robert Sadler (d.1839) was a draper, novelist and poet living in Chippenham. He was involved in several land transactions with Robert Fowler in Gastard and enclosed land at Moore Green Common, south west of Corsham.

In 1855, Joseph Poulsom was the farmer at Velley Farm and in 1867 he is listed as a 'farmer, butcher and shopkeeper.' By the late 1880s the land behind the farm building became a quarry, stretching across to Lanes End, which was worked by Edward Aust; after 1890 the farm disappears.

In 1837 Robert Sadler also owned and leased land from Lanes End crossroads, to the east and west of Coppershell, up to Pandown Bridge. This was also occupied by Thomas Poulsom and probably part of Velley Farm. A map of 1773 calls the area on the east side of the lane 'Faxhall' and there were only two buildings here in 1837. To the east was a cottage and garden owned by John Fowler and inhabited by John Little and a field called 'Foxholes,' owned by Sir Paul Methuen and occupied by William Plummer; and on the west side of the lane was a yard and a barn owned by Robert Sadler and occupied by Thomas Poulsom. This area became known as Vauxhall.

About 1850 the Fowler family purchased around 100 acres of Velley Farm, leaving 14 acres in Velley Hill. This included the land from the crossroads at Lanes End to Pandown Bridge, with one small field at Thingley Cottage Farm. When Sir Robert Nicholas Fowler inherited Elm Grove in 1862, he set about purchasing all the farms in the Tything of Gastard, from the Roman Road at the bottom of Goodes Hill to Pandown. It was the family's intention to build a house for their only son, Sir Thomas Fowler, on the top of the hill towards Pandown, by the barn. Two wells were dug, with new stables and sheds for his hunters and polo ponies, on the opposite side of the lane. The family rebuilt two cottages for grooms, now Pandown Farm House. The foundations for the main house were also dug out, but never finished as Sir Thomas died in the Boer War on 20 April 1902.

On a 1890 OS map Vauxhall Farm is shown on the east side of the road, but in 1901 and 1925 it is very clearly depicted on the west side. In trade directories it is listed as Pandown Farm. By 1907 it was occupied by Andrew George Slade, who farmed it until about 1920 when it was taken over by William Jackson. Slade moved on to Monks Lane Farm. Jackson was still running the farm in the 1930s, when it was purchased by Mr Hutton Snr. By then it had reverted to its former name of Vauxhall. Mr Hutton continued to farm the land until 1976.

**Thingley Bridge and Thingley Cottage Farms.**

The Ladbrook stream formed the northern boundary of Gastard Tything in the parish of Corsham. It flows through Pockeredge around the south side of Corsham and past the sewage works at Pandown. From Pandown in Gastard it continues through fields to Thingley Bridge Farm, where it joins a tributary formed by two springs at Lanes End (Hither and Lower spring). At this point is becomes the Byde Brook which meanders to Lacock where it joins the Avon.

The Domesday Book notes two mills in Corsham parish and this is confirmed by an inquisition post mortem following the death of Edmund, Earl of Cornwall in 1300, who held the Manor of Corsham during the reign of Edward 1, which states that there were two mills worth 106s 8d a year. The first mill

## Chapter 9. Gastard - a history.

was supposed to be at Thingley Court Farm. In the early eighteenth century, Robert Neale the elder wrote that evidence of the second mill, a dam, could still be seen and was located on the Ladbrook near to the site of Thingley Bridge Farm. It seems to have been known as Byde Mill. A reference is found in the Crown Pleas of the Wiltshire Eyre, 1268. The Eyre was an occasional visitation by royal justices. An entry from the court proceeding says:

*'The inner wheel of Byde Mill in Corsham accidentally killed Gilbert son of Gilbert of Melksham. Judgement misadventure. The value of the wheel 18d. deodand, the sheriff to answer.'*

Deodand was a system under English common law whereby an object or animal that accidentally caused the death of somebody was forfeited to the crown. The property could then be sold and the profits used for charitable, often religious, purposes. However, this was seldom practical and jurors instead, assessed the value of the object, which was translated into a fine.

It is thought that the original Byde Mill was pulled down by a person called Bettering of Thingley around 1327, who rebuilt it a little further downstream, where it stood until it ceased as a working mill in the early twentieth century. The main purpose of the relocation was to generate more power by enabling a change from an undershot to an overshot wheel, and evidence of a weir and a mill race can still be seen.

During the eighteenth and nineteenth centuries, land around Thingley Bridge was owned by the Neale family, a late eighteenth century map calls it Dingley Bridge. Robert Neale the elder was a clothier or woolstapler, who lived in the Mansion House in Corsham. He had moved from Yate in Gloucestershire and married Sarah, the daughter of William Arnold, who owned Arnold's Mill in Lacock. Neale's business made the cloth for the scarlet tunics worn by soldiers who fought at the Battle of Blenheim, during the War of the Spanish Succession in 1704. When he died in 1733 his estate was worth around £40,000. One of his sons, Robert Neale the younger, was born in 1706 and in 1735 married Elizabeth, daughter of Thomas Smith of Shaw House, Melksham. By 1741 he was elected as a Whig MP for Wootton Bassett, which at that time was one of the most corrupt electoral boroughs in England. Neale was re-elected in 1747, but defeated in 1754 despite some heavy expenditure and bribery! He died in 1776.

By 1837 at Thingley Bridge there were two houses with gardens owned by Sir Harry Burrard Neale and occupied by James Wootten and Sarah Wait, with adjacent fields farmed by John Thompson. Admiral Sir Harry Burrard, 2nd Baronet, had a distinguished naval career and was Member of Parliament for Lymington between 1790 -1835. He married Grace Elizabeth Neale, daughter of Robert Neale the younger of Shaw House, Melksham. Burrard took the surname Neale on his marriage to Grace in 1795 and acquired land at Thingley Bridge through a marriage settlement; Grace having originally inherited the property from her grandfather, Robert Neale the elder of Corsham. Burrard Neale died in 1840 without issue.

There is a monument to him in Wallhampton, near Lymington. By 1900 the electoral register notes that the principal owner of land at Thingley Bridge, was another relative of the Neale family, John Alexander Neale (1849-1930) of Yate and Corsham. He was an author of books on Free Trade and Land Reform, and there is a portrait of him in Queens College, Oxford University, where he had been a fellow and a benefactor. It is not until sometime after 1837 that Thingley Bridge Farm was established. It is noted on the 1890 -1925 ordnance survey maps, but not listed in trade directories. In more recent times F & L Goodway farmed about 80 acres here, until the farm was sold in 1985.

# Chapter 9. Gastard - a history.

At the junction of Thingley Bottom on the right fork to Thingley Firs, stood Thingley Cottage Farm. In 1837 the first building on the right was a cottage and garden owned by William Hulbert with two further Cottages owned by George John Archer, who also held a field on the opposite side of the lane. A paddock behind the cottages, called Thingley Bridge Ground, was owned by Robert Sadler and occupied by Thomas Poulsom.

It is difficult to establish occupation of the houses here as the census does not provide enough detail. However, by the 1901 census those living at Thingley Bridge include the Whitfield, Carter, Hand and May families. However, by the 1920s some of the land appears to have been consolidated into a farm of 38 acres by the Methuen estate and leased by a Mr Fielding, who farmed there until the early 1980's.

**Byde Mill and Byde Mill Farm**

The original Byde Mill stood on a site near to where the Ladbrook becomes the Bydebrook, between Pandown Bridge and Thingley Bridge Farm. It is thought that around the 1320s the mill was moved further downstream by someone known as Bettering of Thingley, near to where Byde Mill Farm now stands.

The mill was stone built and no doubt enlarged over the following centuries. The Bydebrook weirs can still be seen, but the mill pond has gone.

The leat from the weir that fed the watermill was lined with clay from Lanes End quarry. Part of the original course of the leat can still be made out from aerial photographs. However, the buildings that remain today, which form Byde Mill Farm and adjacent cottages, appear to date to the late eighteenth century.

The history of this second Byde Mill can be pieced together through extracts from royal and manorial court records. In 1327 (Edward III) Bettering was *'seized of two messuages and two yard lands in Thingley in the Tything of Gastard with a mill'* by the king, who owned the manor of Corsham, and it then came into the possession of a man called Whetman.

His daughter Isabel appears to have married someone with the same surname (a cousin maybe), John Whetman, and they had a son called Walter. However, John Whetman was indicted for a felony and fled Wiltshire in 1378 during the reign of Richard II. The king seized the mill and placed it under the control of the powerful Lord John Lovell VII, who was Lord Farmer of Corsham Manor and had built Wardour Castle in South Wiltshire.

The mill was occupied successively by William Acton and William & Nicholas Salway until the death of John Whetman in 1423, when his son Walter attempted to reclaim it. Unfortunately for Walter Whetman, he only succeeded in retrieving the adjacent land and Byde Mill remained the property of the crown until it was sold by James I to Edward Stevens, a London mercer and Francis Phelps, gentleman, in 1610.

During the seventeenth century John Danvers (1638) and later William Hulbert owned Byde Mill. Hulbert was bailiff of Corsham Manor in 1682 and died at Byde Mill, leaving a widow Eleanor and a son William. Other owners included William Apprice, who sold the mill to William Wells of Hazelbury, Box, for £711 8s 5d in 1697.

## Chapter 9. Gastard - a history.

The mill appeared to be used for milling corn until sometime into the seventeenth century, as several records note attempts by the crown to claim 'millsuite' (the custom of paying one tenth of the corn to the king) and that the tenants *'did grinde there or elsewhere at their pleasures.'*

At some point during the late seventeenth or eighteenth century Byde Mill became a fulling mill, one of several mills supplying the increasingly important local cloth trade.

After the cloth was made by the looms, the *fulling* process cleaned and thickened it by adding fullers earth (a type of soapy clay) and water, and then by beating the cloth with hammers driven by a waterwheel. The cloth was then dyed in stone vats, such as those in the Mansion House, Corsham, owned by the clothier Robert Neale senior.

As one of the most important clothiers in the area, Neale would have been influential in establishing and farming out some of the manufacturing processes of cloth to local mills, such as Byde Mill.

On the right side of the Mansion House main door you can still see the height marks made by Robert Neale's children as they grew up.

During the eighteenth century, Byde Mill was worked by the Wells and Mitchell families, who also occupied adjacent farm land called Over (or Upper) and Lower Hams, the mill closes and an orchard. In 1747 Edward Mitchell of Byde Mill also inherited Gastard Court Farm. By 1800 a Thomas Mitchell sold the mill to a clothier called John Moore, who in 1807 is noted as owning a cloth and cotton manufactory or dye house and stone waterwheel house. Further evidence of the mill's use for fulling and dying is found through the history of the Simmons family. David Simmons was born in Chalford, Glos., in 1798, but moved to Corsham and worked as a manufacturer's clothier at Byde Mill. A direct descendant, Jack Simmons, helped to found K & S Builders of Lanes End, Gastard, and now lives in Corsham.

On the 1837 tithe map the mill is clearly shown with a leat north of the Bydebrook and named as 'Boydes Mill,' most likely a misspelling, although descendants of the early mill-owners, the Whetmans, did occupy Boydes Farm to the south of Gastard and the two place-names may be linked. It was listed as a 'House, Garden and Mill' owned and occupied by James Ray.

There were also three cottages adjacent to the mill, also owned by James Ray and occupied by D Simmons, James Robins and James Ray himself. These buildings were also known locally as Whetman's Cottages, again possibly alluding to the earlier mill-owner. The fields above the mill were called Home Ground and Walnut Tree, while the lower fields are named as Lower Hams and Upper Hams, all owned and occupied by James Ray. Two further fields south of the 'Bydebrooke' were noted as Lower and Upper Ryde (Byde?) Mill Grounds occupied by James Dunsden of Court Farm.

By 1837 Byde Mill had reverted back to a corn mill. In the 1848 and 1855 Kelly's Directories James Ray is listed as a Miller at Byde Mill. No mention of the mill is made in other trade directories until 1880, when Amaza Gale is noted as a *'farmer, Byde Mill,'* but both Joseph Brown in 1889 and William Cook in 1895 were recorded as 'miller (water and steam).' The 1890 Ordnance Survey Map shows the mill as a corn mill and also depicts Byde Mill Farm. Thereafter there is no further mention of the mill until the farm is

## Chapter 9. Gastard - a history.

noted on further maps of 1901 and 1925. Amaza Gale makes a few appearances in the newspapers of the day: In September of 1875, he is fined 15s for letting three of his cows stray onto the highway. In June of 1879 he was summoned by PC Cowdry and subsequently fined £2 for allowing thirty sheep and twenty-five lambs to stay onto the public highway.

In his memoirs called 'Where the Ladbrook Flows', Bob Hayward recounts his childhood in 1912 when his family was temporarily relocated to one of a pair of cottages at Byde Mill. He notes that the mill had recently been vacated - *'the tenant had been made bankrupt'* - and the mill worker who lived in the cottage had left. Hayward also remembers playing in the unlocked, disused mill, and the wagon house underneath the mill, where the local farmer Mr Pickford kept his farm machinery.

In the early 1920s the mill was purchased for £90 by Mr Pocock of New Farm, which was a short distance downstream in the parish of Lacock. After the mill was demolished he sold the remains to his cousin's husband together with 45 acres of land to build the house called Courtlands. This gentleman was Sir Seymour Howard, who was chairman of the London Rubber Company and became Lord Mayor of London in 1954. He also owned Thingley Farm. The mill stones along with the stones that held the housing for the wheel at Byde Mill formed part of the rose garden at Courtlands. By 1935 Courtlands had been acquired by Captain (later Squadron Leader) Claude Cecil Brill. His son David Brill was killed during the Second World War in 1943, aged just 22, and he is named on the Lacock War Memorial. The house was later owned by Sir William Breecher.

**Sandpits and Gastard Hill Farms.**

As previously mentioned, Robert Fowler senior had purchased Elm Grove in the 1790s and his son, Sir Robert Nicholas Fowler MP (1828-91) sought to consolidate and extend the estate. It was his ambition to purchase all of the land in the tything of Gastard to form an estate for his only son, Sir Thomas Fowler (although he also had 9 daughters). By the 1880s the only land he had not managed to obtain was Lanes End Farm, which was the land east of Gastard Lane owned by William Taylor, a yeoman farmer at Easton Farm; but Fowler did acquire some of the fields adjacent to the lane, which were part of Lanes End and Court Farms. The estate now included land between Gastard Lane, which leads from Attwood Farm to Thingley Bridge, and a by-way known locally as Sandpits Lane that adjoins the road between Gastard and Lacock and heads north to Byde Mill farm. This area included Byde Mill Farm, Gastard Hill Farm and Sandpits.

On the west side of Sandpits Lane is Sandpits Farm, depicted on the 1773 Andrews' and Dury's map as a cluster of buildings called Sand Pitt. The 1837 tithe map shows a field called Sandpits, owned by the Trustees of William Spackman, named as William Wilmot and Thomas Alexander, and occupied by James Hudd. Slightly further along the lane was a house, gardens, stables, and an orchard also owned by the Trustees and occupied by James Hudd. Adjacent to these buildings were four Cottages with gardens and once again they were owned by the Trustees and occupied by George Hudd, George Duck and Frances Jones.

In his will of 1834, William Spackman, a tallow chandler of Chippenham, had left property and money to his wife Mary and their sons Flower, William and Robert; daughter Hester and grand children Robert and William (by another son John Spackman). A tallow chandler made and sold candles (and sometimes soap) using fat or suet. This was an important job in the days before paraffin, gas and electricity. Spackman held land in Melksham and Corsham including *'hereditatments [any kind of property that can*

## Chapter 9. Gastard - a history.

*be inherited] situate lying and being at Sandpitts in the parish and parcels of the manor of Corsham.'* His trustees were charged with selling the property for the best price 'as soon as conveniently may be,' with the proceeds to be given to his son Flower Spackman. Presumably the trustees had decided to rent the property until a good price could be obtained for the farm.

By 1901 and during its ownership by the Fowlers, Sandpits Farm was occupied by Amy Perryman, who was aged 29, single and a *'farmer on her own account at home.'* The adjacent cottages seem mainly to be lived in by people working in stone quarries, such as Job Elmes and his family. In his memoirs called 'Where the Ladbrook Flows' Bob Hayward recounts his childhood in the early 1900s and suggests that 'Mrs Elmes at Sandpits' was one of the few people in Gastard to own their house, most being tenanted.

In 1911 Edward Parfitt is listed as the farmer, but by 1915 occupation of the farm had transferred to Cyrus Gilson who is recorded in the Wiltshire Gazette, March 1916, aged 35 and a smallholder farming 16 acres with 4 cows, 3 breeding sows and 1 horse; and also a pig dealer. He was still at the farm in 1931. By 1939 Sandpits Farm was purchased by Mr Higgins. Together with his two sons, Stan and Tom, he had moved to Gastard when his farm near Lyneham was purchased by the government to build the RAF airfield. He later purchased a farm in Devon. After the Second World War the farm had passed to Major Walter Skrine. During the war he had been in command of Corsham "C" Company of the Home Guard, around 270 men, including the Gastard Division that totalled 44 men under Capt. Harris and Lt. W Gale.

Major Skrine's son, Richard, farmed Sandpits as a small dairy farm until the mid-1960s, when he became a clergyman in the Anglican Church. When Richard's sister Margaret, was working at the military hospital in Kuala Lumpur, she met a district officer (Herbert) David Eastwood (born at Bangor, north Wales, on January 27 1919). There was a serious problem there with aggressive crocodiles and a cull was organised by David; he gave Margaret a wallet made from the skin of one he had shot and she kept it all her life. They married in 1948 and later in their retirement, they took on Sandpits Farm in the 1970s where they bred Jacob sheep. David Eastwood MBE was a veteran of WWII and he passed away aged 91 on 29 October 2010. His obituary appeared a week later in the Telegraph on 9 December 2010. His wife Margaret had predeceased him and he was survived by their son.

The Military Cross was awarded to David for his courage at Arnhem when fighting in Operation Market Garden with the 21st Independent Parachute Company (21 IPC). The Parachute Company landed on September 17 1944 and was responsible for securing and protecting drop zones (DZs) in preparation for the arrival of the 1st Parachute Brigade. On the next evening David, a platoon commander, was detailed to put out navigational aids for a supply drop. Finding Germans in occupation of the zone in some strength, he attacked, killing some and capturing the rest. On September 19 he returned to the DZ to assist in the landing of the first wave of Polish gliders. As soon as these appeared, the Germans attacked. David and his men drove them off until all the gliders had been unloaded. Cut off, however, he led his platoon through enemy positions under cover of darkness and reached Ommershof on the north-western outskirts of Arnhem. They dug in there and remained for two days before reinforcing the defensive perimeter around the nearby Hartenstein Hotel. For the next four days they held the crucial area near the Schoonord crossroads, which was constantly exposed to heavy enemy fire. Regardless of personal danger, David constantly moved between his sections encouraging his men. In spite of numerous attacks and heavy casualties, their morale was such that they remained in position until ordered to withdraw back across the Rhine on September 25. David Eastwood was awarded an immediate Military Cross.

# Chapter 9. Gastard - a history.

**Gastard Hill Farm.**

North of Sandpits Farm and below the Byde Brook, about halfway between Gastard Lane and Sandpits Lane, stood Gastard Hill Farm. It is clearly shown on an eighteenth century map, accessed by a track from Gastard Lane. It originally consisted of three fields. However, on the 1837 tithe map, it is simply listed as a cottage and garden owned by Sir Harry Burrard Neale and occupied by Robert Lawrence. The surrounding fields known as Pump House Ground, Beggars Hill, Inner Ground and Backward Hill, were also owned by Sir H B Neale. On the 1841 census it was known as Gastard Hill, its inhabitants being 6 members of the Lawrence family. By the time of the 1871 census there are no occupants listed and it is simply noted that Gastard Hill had *'2 houses dilapidated.'* The 1890 ordnance survey map referred to the buildings as Gastard Hill House, but it is absent on subsequent maps.

By 1890 three fields surrounding Gastard Hill Farm, which had been purchased by the Fowler family, were made into one by removing the hedges. This made one big level playing field for polo, created for Sir Thomas Fowler. The house and some of the farm buildings were demolished. The only building left standing was the skilling (an open fronted cow shed), which was used for stabling the polo ponies on match days. But its use was *short lived* as Sir Thomas Fowler sadly died in the Boer War in 1902. The stone from the demolished farm buildings of Hill Farm was used to build Willgarrupp Farm.

Sir Thomas Fowler had served with distinction throughout the greater part of the Anglo-Boer War, including mainly in the Brandwater Basin and the Hammonia, Wittebergen, Witnek and Thaba 'Nchu areas, and was promoted to the rank of Captain in January 1901. In September 1901, the Brigade had its headquarters established at Brindisi in the Brandwater Basin near Fouriesburg from which the Yeomanry operated for some time.

In October 1901, he wrote in one of his letters back home, that *'the men were in a most deplorable condition, half of them being dismounted and in rags, and that rations were getting short again consisting only of the bare necessities'*. The Wiltshire Yeomanry were having difficulty in obtaining remounts, and the Arab mare that Fowler had bought early in the War was the only fit horse he had.

Sir Thomas Fowler died at Moolman's Spruit on 20 April 1902. A force of about one hundred Yeomanry and forty Mounted Infantry (South Staffords) was despatched by night to attack an isolated farm in which a small body of Boers was supposed to be sleeping. Colonel Perceval was in command. The farm was reached after a difficult march, but the enemy were found to have been forewarned, and to be in much greater strength than was anticipated.

A furious fire was opened on the advancing troops, who were clearly visible in the light of a full moon. By morning the small British force had extricated itself, from its perilous position with a total loss of six killed (including Sir Thomas Fowler), nineteen wounded, and six missing. The whole affair was undoubtedly a cleverly planned Boer ambush.

**Gastard Lane and Willgarrup Farm**

The following concerns the fields and settlements adjoining that part of Gastard Lane which runs south from Thingley Bridge to just before the junction and green near Attwood Farm. Before 1877 the fields adjacent to the Thingley Bridge end of the lane and those along the east side of the lane were owned by at least five different people, but mainly farmed by John Thompson and James Dunsden, who was a tenant at Court Farm.

## Chapter 9. Gastard - a history.

In 1877 the farms of Thingley Bridge and Byde Mill and surrounding fields were sold by auction, including those fields surrounding what was Gastard Hill Farm. The owner is not named, but it was most likely the Methuen or Neale Estates. The occupier of both farms was a Mr Comley. The purchaser was probably Sir Robert Fowler of Gastard House, as the same properties were sold by his daughter, Miss Jean Fowler, in 1915.

Moving south from Thingley Bridge to the top of Gastard Hill the second gateway on the left was the main track to Gastard Hill Farm. Further along on the right, to the west of the lane, is the site of an opencast stone quarry. The stone was mainly used to build field walls. Included in that same sale of 1915 was Willgarrup Farm. The farm stood about two thirds of the way along Gastard Lane, on the east side of the lane, heading south from Thingley Bridge. It is not shown on eighteenth century maps or on the 1837 tithe. The fields in this location were known as the Lydes. They were purchased in around 1883 from the estate of the deceased William Taylor of Lanes End Farm. These and other adjacent fields were formed into Willgarrup Farm by the Fowler family sometime after the death of the last male heir, Sir Thomas Fowler, in 1902.

The name Willgarrup is unusual. It was sometimes referred to as Will Garrup's or Will Garry's Farm, but these names are probably misspellings or local derivations. There is no evidence so far of anyone with those or similar names in the area at least dating back to the eighteenth century. The only other reference to a place-name Willgarrup is a river and area in Western Australia.

This is quite speculative, but there was a fashion in Victorian times and later, to name farms after countries and areas around the British empire and the UK, for example 'New Zealand', 'Ireland' and 'Scotland' (a few field names called Scotland may also refer to a medieval tax on inhabitants called the Scot). Sir Robert Fowler MP toured America, New Zealand and Australia in 1886, which was reported widely in the Australian press at the time. He was accompanied by his son, Sir Thomas, and possibly some of his other of his children who often went with him on his travels. It might be possible that this or another family connection inspired the farm name. In 1920, the Prince of Wales' train was derailed near Willgarrup in Western Australia but nobody was injured.

The first farmer noted at Willgarrup was a Mr Guy in about 1905. During the first decade of the twentieth century the government encouraged people to move into small scale dairy farming, while the demand for liquid milk had also increased. Consequently, many small dairy farms sprang up in Wiltshire at this time. The sale particulars for Willgarrup Farm in 1915 notes that it was *'a compact little dairy farm'* 37 acres in size of which 27 acres *was 'capital dairying land.'* The tenant was a Mr Dicks who paid a rent of £18 per annum. It records that the building was a 'modern stone-built farmhouse' that included a parlour, kitchen, wash-house, dairy and three bedrooms. There was also a stone and tiled cow shed for eight and a calf pen, two-stall stables and two piggeries. The farm was purchased by Mr Benjamin Charles Hill of Home Farm, South Wraxall, though the sale was not completed until February 1918.

Before the completion of the sale there had been a change in tenancy. A reference to 'Will Garry's Farm' in the Wiltshire Gazette, March 1916, mentions Thomas Bird, farmer, and his son Arthur Bird. It notes that the farm contained 41 acres, including 10 arable, 6 cows, 4 young stock and 1 horse. Later, the farm was purchased during the inter-war depression by a Mr Bowles of Winsley, grandfather of Catherine Richards, now of Court Farm. The Bird family, however, continued as tenants of Willgarrup until around 1945 when George Lloyd took on the tenancy and then purchased it in about 1950. Mr Lloyd was still farming here in 1970.

# Chapter 9. Gastard - a history.

Between the First and Second World War, two fields on the other side of the road were purchased by Mr Bird for his sons Arthur and Frank. Arthur had the larger field called Long Ham and rented it out; Frank had the smaller field, Little Ham. Frank was married and lived with his wife and six children above the Chapel in Velley Hill. He became a wheelwright and started a sawmill in Little Ham field, making items for local farmers. He built a large timber and tin shed on the right of the field to house the saw mill until his steam engine failed. He and his son Colin then concentrated on converting horse machinery for use with tractors. One notable feature of the field was a fence made of 200 discarded wooden aeroplane propellers that Frank had purchased after the war.

**Brockleaze.**

Opposite the sawmill and after Willgarrup was the track and field called Brockleaze, which led to a stable block and some old buildings, probably an entrance to the old stone quarry in a field called *the 'Treasury'*. The track then became a footpath that led to Gastard Hill Farm and Byde Mill.

Adjacent to the lane and immediately after the entrance to Brockleaze is a cottage and garden, which was owned by William Hulbert and occupied by William Hillier in 1837. William Hulbert, Gentleman, of Corsham was descended from Yeoman Farmers. He owned considerable land in the area that included estates in Lypiatt and Woodlands in Corsham. In his will of 1844 he devised that his other estates were to be sold and the money to be divided between his sons Thomas and William, and his nephew Walter Spencer. The Hulbert family had been associated with Corsham and its surrounds since at least 1579, when Thomas Hulbert, John Hulbert of Thingley and John Hulbert of Goods Farm were recorded as farmers grazing sheep on common land. Thomas Hulbert (1756) and Robert Hulbert, Gentleman (1784), were listed as Tythingmen in Gastard. Branches of the Hulbert family were clothiers and trades people in Corsham and also brewers at Pickwick. Later, the cottage was known as 19 Gastard and appears to have been part of Sandpits Farm.

**The old hamlet of Gastard and Shilling Lane.**

Today we think of the centre of the village as the area near Gastard Church and the Harp and Crown. However, before the church was erected in 1912 the hamlet of Gastard was centred further to the east around Court Farm, Attwood Farm (also known as Gastard Farm) and the cluster of cottages around the small green opposite; with smaller settlements at Chapel Knapp, Velley, Silver Street, Coppershell, Thingley Bridge, Sandpits and Byde Mill forming the rest of the tything.

The hamlet of Gastard dates back to at least the 1500's, with its main house being Court Farm, a building of medieval origins located in the centre of the Gastard tything. The hamlet began at Lanes End, which in 1900 consisted of one farm and eleven dwellings. Heading eastwards at the first right hand bend is Chapel Hill and it is here that the houses started to be numbered; with only the farms, Timberleaze Cottages and Copse Cottage being named. The names of the lanes were rarely used; instead they were simply referred to as Gastard on the nineteenth century census returns. The lane names appear to have changed over time and can be confusing - for example Chapel Hill has also been known as Baggers Hill, Luzzells Hill and Gastard Hill, yet we also know that an area between Byde Mill and Thingley Bridge was called Gastard Hill. Gastard Lane used to run from Thingley Bridge to the junction by Attwood Farm, but now includes the road up to Chapel Hill. East of Attwood Farm the road is now known as Sandpits Lane, but previously was part of Shilling Lane (spelt Shitting Lane on eighteenth century maps) that went to Lacock, with the old Sandpits Lane being the track between Sandpits Farm and Byde Mill.

## Chapter 9. Gastard - a history.

Numbers 1 to 3 Gastard were at the top of Chapel Hill, 4 to 6 were Timberleaze and Number 4 was probably the oldest cottage in Gastard. On the right hand side of the lane after Court Farm the first track led across a field to Copse Cottage and after this track, down towards Sandpits, continuing on the right were numbers 8 to 17. The building after the track is now named Court House. This was once a house and stable built in the late-seventeenth and eighteenth centuries, but by the early 1900s it became a village shop, changing hands several times. In 1901 John and Mary Jones were listed as grocers, while other names associated with the shop were Silcocks and Edwards, with a Mrs Wootten being the last shopkeeper. It was converted back to a house in the 1940s. Further along on the right hand side, before Attwood Farm is a row of three cottages known as *'Conquest'*, which are made of rubble stone and date to the eighteenth century.

On the left hand side opposite Court House is a track that bisects two cottages, as it leads to a field beyond, and a small green. This was called 'The Drung,' where there was a cluster of mainly estate cottages, 20 to 27 Gastard, again made of rubble stone and mainly dating to the seventeenth and eighteenth centuries. In 1837 most of the cottages in this part of the hamlet were owned by William Dunsden / Dunsdon. William owned Linleys Farm, but died in 1848. His executors John Dunsdon (his brother) and Henry Spackman held all his estates in trust for his wife Mary Anne and their children. Later, the cottages seem to have been acquired by the Fowler family. Number 19 Gastard was in the old Gastard Lane, while number 18 was probably at Sandpits.

Census returns for 1841-1901 show the families who lived in the cottages, but as no precise address is given, it is not possible to identify a specific cottage. In 1851 most of the inhabitants were associated with agriculture and occupations included agricultural labourers, dairy maids, farm servants, wheelwrights, blacksmiths, wood and hedge cutters. However, by 1901 most of the men worked in the local quarries, mainly as 'freestone quarrymen' in the mines at the Ridge, Monks Park and later at Elm Park, rather than the smaller open cast quarries. Unfortunately, very few women's occupations are named on the census so it is difficult to say what work they undertook. Family names included Turner, Cleverly, Merrett, Hudd, Hayward, Pearce, Barnett, Shewring, Maslin and Freeguard. Some of the Fowler estate cottages were later sold to the tenants for around £200, plus solicitors fees.

**Treasury Field.**

Just beyond Attwood Farm the road to Lacock becomes Sandpits Lane. On the left hand side are three fields. The first two were once a single field called the 'Treasury', the other is called Sand Pits. The field-name Treasury probably owes its origins as a place where coins were minted, perhaps dating back to Roman times. This may also relate to other place-names in or near Gastard, such as Shilling Lane, Silver Street, Pandown and Gold Hill. By 1837 the field was owned by 'William Dunsden and others' and occupied by James Dunsden, and seems to have been be worked as a surface quarry and sandpits. In the late nineteenth century it was owned and run by Chippenham Rural District Council for quarrying hard stone for paving and kerbstones. The council put it up for sale in 1898. Prior to its purchase by Alfie Hopkins of Lacock in 1950, it was owned by a Mr White of Chippenham. Alfie bought the land with money he received on leaving the army and he built a bungalow on it when he got married. He kept pigs in the field while maintaining a milk round in Lacock.

There are also two cottages on the S-bend opposite the Treasury, numbers 16 and 17 Gastard. In 1837-1851 number 17 was occupied by a Baker called Mary Jones. She was a widow and lived in the cottage with her family. James and Elizabeth Jones (relatives of Mary?) lived at 16. James Jones was an

# Chapter 9. Gastard - a history.

agricultural labourer. By 1861 Mary, now listed as a 'former shop keeper', still lived at number 17 with her granddaughter, but the cottage next door was now occupied by a thatcher called James Elms and his wife Harriet.

**Romany Gypsies.**

The lane from Sandpits to Black Bridge, Lacock, was a staying place for local Romany Gypsies, such as the Smith family, since at least the 1920s. They had two traditional horse-drawn caravans, a horse-drawn trailer and about 5 horses or ponies. Jessie Smith senior also had the use of a tin building by Black Bridge. The families mainly stayed over winter harvesting holly and mistletoe to sell for Christmas and purchased logs from local farmers and woodsman to resell. In the early spring they would travel to find work for the whole family, including the children. The men always walked, with the women and children riding on the caravans. The families worked in the fields hoeing; then headed to the Vale of Evesham for employment with vegetable growers and in the fruit orchards; and later to the east of England for hop picking, before returning to Gastard.

Just prior to 1960 Jessie Smith junior broke with tradition that had lasted for generations and purchased the cottages number 16 and 17 Gastard, letting number 17 to Cecil Aust (a sitting tenant) while retaining 16 as the family home. The horses and traditional caravans were replaced by a lorry and a modern touring caravan. Most of the children lived in number 16, but Jessie never did, preferring to sleep in the caravan that was parked in the garden. The family left the village when Jessie died in about 1970, though they still live quite locally.

**Numbers 1-5 Lanes End**

Lanes End starts at the Harp and Crown crossroads and heads east towards Lacock. The Church was built in 1912 by Miss Jean Fowler as a memorial to her father Sir Robert N Fowler and her brother Sir Thomas Fowler who was killed in South Africa in 1902 during the second Boer War. It was built on a field called Home Orchard, which in 1837 was owned by Robert Sadler and occupied by Thomas Poulson. Sadler had owned it since at least 1810. The church probably got its name from the old chapel at the top of Velley Hill, this was known as the Chapel of St John the Baptist, which had been in existence in some form since the 1300s.

Further along was Velley Quarry, on land that had seen quarrying since at least the 1550s. It was a sandstone open cast quarry. It is not known who worked the early quarry, some remains can be seen in Tythemere Cottage garden, but it is likely that the original closed in the early 1800s and a new one opened up on the left side of Velley Hill. It was worked by Edward Aust in 1889, who was succeeded by Arthur Aust by 1903. According to Ted Aust, it was necessary to dig down to about 20 feet before you reached some hard brash stone that could be used for yards and tracks. The next layer was formed of blue clay, which was used as puddling for farm ponds and the mill pond and leat at Byde Mill. At a depth of around 40 feet was sandstone (Cotswold stone) then forest marble (hard limestone) both used in the local buildings.

**Elm Park Quarry.**

About 1900 four trial shafts were sunk between Lanes End and Goodes Hill to see if it was feasible to open-up a shaft to quarry freestone (Bath Stone). The land was now owned by the Fowler family who leased or licensed the quarry and extraction rights. It opened first in Lanes End (on land that had also

## Chapter 9. Gastard - a history.

been part of Home Orchard in 1837) with a new name, Elm Park. The trial shafts were reused for ventilation as quarrying began in 1912. It soon became apparent that the accessible stone was only suitable for kerbstones due to its hardness and the County Council became the main customer for it. However, in 1920 Sheppard & Son of Bath took over Elm Park quarry and using new machines to cut stone blocks they could now supply the building trade. The company also owned two quarries in Neston, but by the 1930s they were in difficulty. It passed to a conglomerate of quarries known as the Bath Portland and Stone Firms Ltd. The superintendent was a Mr Chaffey. In his memoirs, local quarry man Frank 'Tanky' Elms recalled of Chaffey: *"He was a Chapel man and he always wore a bowler hat, gaiters and polished boots. He would be immaculately dressed with a white collar, black tie and a black suit."* He would come from Bath by train to Corsham where he was met by local stone masons.

Around 1938 the quarry was taken over by the Air Ministry as a store for aviation oil, with Frank Bryant of Neston as winchman. The Admiralty later used it to keep ammunition. An unsuccessful attempt was made to reopen the quarry in the 1980's, but it was finally re established in 2000 as the Elm Park Stone Company.

**No.1 Lanes End (Lanes End Cottage).**

Opposite the quarry on the north side of the road was No. 1. Lanes End, sometimes known as Lanes End Cottage. In 1837 it was owned by Robert Sadler and occupied by James Merrit the Younger and later purchased by the Taylor family, who owned Lanes End Farm. By 1871 the tenants were William Bryant, railway plate layer, his wife Elizabeth and their family. In 1881 occupancy had passed to the Gibbons family, who were mainly farm labourers, including John and Mary and later James Gibbons. At one point the land contained a bakehouse, barn and orchard. By 1909 on the death of John Alfred Taylor the cottage passed to William Frederick Taylor and around that time the tenancy had passed to the Sheppard Family. Albert Edward Sheppard, born in 1864, was the village postman. In his childhood memoirs, Bob Hayward recalls that Mr Sheppard delivered the post two times a day Monday to Saturday and once on a Sunday, he was *'so reliable in his time-keeping that clocks could safely be set by his appearance.'* In 1942 the cottage was sold to Edward (Ted) Aust for £500.

**No.2 Lanes End (Stonecroft) and Lanes End School.**

Further along on the same side, before Lanes End Farm, was No. 2 Lanes End, known as Stonecroft. This had been the original farm house at Lanes End and some of the building dates back to 1604 as evidenced by an inscription in plaster to the north face of the initial house. It was altered in about 1630. A date stone was found with the initials TR when the current windows were inserted around 1720-40. By the early nineteenth century it was in the ownership of Joseph Taylor of Corsham and is noted in various deeds and wills. It seems to have been abandoned as a farm house when a new one was built behind it utilising old farm buildings (this is No. 4 Lanes End).

By the 1830s No. 2 had been passed to John Taylor and was a cottage and garden occupied by a Sarah Pearce. In 1870 it was occupied by Pamela Taylor. However, in the 1871 census it was referred to as Lanes End School and the residence for the head master of the school, James Harris and his wife Lucy. If it had ever been a school it was for temporary use while the public elementary Chapel Knapp National School was being erected by Sir Robert Fowler and Lord Methuen at Coppershell in 1873. This may have been partly in response to the Elementary Education Act 1870 that provided for the establishment of local school boards and new schools to educate children aged 5 -13, where there was a shortfall.

## Chapter 9. Gastard - a history.

A survey of schools in Wiltshire, 1859, noted that 'at present the Corshamside [Neston] and Gastard children attend in a school-room formed out of two cottage rooms, in which divine service is held, at the back of Monks Park.' Furthermore, it stated Lord Methuen claimed 'many persons wished new schools ... to be erected at Corshamside' and with the cooperation of landowners was about to "set on foot a school in that place." Interestingly, Kelly's Directory for 1867 has an entry for Chapel Knapp Church of England School, though it does not say where the children were being educated. The new school at Coppershell was built to accommodate 130 pupils and had an average of 103. In 1875 Miss Eva Woodward is recorded as school mistress.

By 1880 No. 2 Lanes End had become the established residence of the local school master and mistress, James and Mary Anstis. Mr Anstis was from Devon and stayed until sometime after 1891. In 1895 the new school master and mistress was William and Alice Forward, they also resided in the cottage.

They were replaced by William Tessyman Dent around 1904-07, who came from Lancashire. He was a churchwarden as well as a school master. In 1920 The Taylor's sold the property to the Dents, passing to Celia Augusta Dent in 1938 on the death of her husband William, and it remained in their family until they in turn sold it in 2007.

**No.3 Lanes End (Yew Tree Cottage a.k.a the Old Coffee Tavern).** *See also page 130.*

Opposite No. 2 is Yew Tree Cottage (No. 3 Lanes End - sometimes referred to as the '*old* coffee tavern'), which in 1837 was owned and occupied by William Moody and later the dwelling of Frederick and Emily Banyon; followed by George and Harriet Hillier; Alfred Archer, packer for Great Western Railway company and his wife Maria; and by 1901 William and Sarah Merritt and family. William Merritt was a carpenter. It was later occupied by a Mr Merrett, a builder, who was no relation to the former.

The Gastard Coffee Tavern would have been a meeting place for the locals as well as a place where social activities were held (similar to a village hall). The Coffee Tavern served non alcoholic beverages and it was open both during the day and in the evening. It contained a reading room with a library and newspapers, and a smoking room with games such as bagatelle; and provided activities such as wood carving for boys and men. Members paid a subscription of 2s per year. In view of the following newspaper reports, it seems as though Gastard also had some form of *parish committee that served the inhabitants.

On page 3 of the Thursday 8 November 1888 Bristol Mercury newspaper, the following was reported: *'GASTARD (CORSHAM). The annual tea and social gathering of the *members was held on Tuesday evening, at the Yew Tree Coffee Tavern, the Rev L.A. Lyne presiding. The financial report showed a deficit of about £8* [over £700 in today's money], *which Sir R. Fowler, M.P., has undertaken to defray.'*

On page 6 of the Thursday 11 April 1889 Devizes and Wiltshire Gazette the following was reported:

*'GASTARD. Wood carving. - During the past winter, the Misses Fowler (of Elm Grove) have held a class for teaching wood carving, at the Yew Tree Coffee Tavern, and the season's work was brought to a termination by the presentation of prizes by Miss Mary Fowler to the most successful wood carvers: Mr William Bryant securing the first class-prize, and Mr Lodge the second-class prize. The Rev. G. Linton (vicar) made a few appropriate remarks as to the value of classes of this description, and the evening was pleasantly spent in singing &c.'*

# Chapter 9. Gastard - a history.

In the Saturday 21 December 1895 Wiltshire Times and Trowbridge Advertiser, the following was reported: *'GASTARD. - The 17th anniversary of the Yew Tree Coffee Tavern, Gastard, was held on Friday evening, when the members were invited, by the kindness of Sir T. Fowler, to supper at Gastard House. After ample justice had been done, a meeting was held to appoint a committee for the ensuing year, and to transact other business, Sir Thomas being chairman. - At the conclusion of the business, Mr C. Poulsom proposed a vote of thanks to Sir T. Fowler and the Misses Fowler for their great kindness, not only in giving those present such a splendid supper, but on superintending and keeping up the institution, which is of so much help and good. - Mr F. Aust seconded the vote of thanks. - Sir T. Fowler, in thanking those present, spoke of the pleasure it gave him to further their interest, and said with the advance of education, lads after leaving school would find such places as reading rooms of especial value to them. - The rest of the evening was spent in various games, Sir Thomas being untiring in his efforts to please everyone.'*

Just past No. 3 is a gateway, which opened into a private drive to Timberleaze and Gastard House. The drive was once formed by an avenue of fine elm trees, the last ones being felled in 1976 with the onset of Dutch Elm Disease. Local legend suggests that the junction of the gateway and road formed a ring where quarrymen would settle arguments, after they had been in the Harp and Crown. They mainly argued over gangers' piece work or with rival gangs. This possibly inspired the creation of the Coffee Tavern, as a social meeting place.

Coffee Taverns became especially popular across the country between 1875 -1900 as part of a temperance movement. In Gastard the tavern was most likely established in the 1870s. The original tavern was located in Yew Tree Cottage, presumably between tenancies. However, a new tavern was later built further along Lanes End, now No. 5, opposite Lanes End Farm c1900. Miss Mary Fowler became secretary of the Coffee Tavern followed by her sister Jean in around 1903. In addition to the Harp and Crown, the Coffee Tavern formed the centre of the village's social life. Between 1881 - 1891 the Coffee Tavern caretaker was Mrs Elizabeth Bryant, a widow, with her son William, a mason, who continued living in No.5 with his family until at least 1901. It seems to have finished by 1907.

## No.4 Lanes End: Lanes End Farm and the Taylor family.

Joseph Taylor was born in 1735 and died on 24 March 1828 aged 93, although there is some confusion, as his tombstone in Corsham Churchyard says he died as *'Bailiff of this town in his 87th year.'* Paul Methuen purchased the manor of Corsham in 1777 and around this time Joseph Taylor became his bailiff of the manor. He is listed as a tythingman *[tythings were under the leadership of a tythingman]* for Gastard in 1784 and may have already purchased Lanes End Farm by then, possibly from John Strawbridge, a Bradford-on-Avon cloth worker, who had bought the land from Thomas Stephens of Corsham in 1749. The Taylor family became associated with the farm for the next 200 years.

The original Lanes End farmhouse was No. 2 Lanes End, Stonecroft, which dates back to 1604. Sometime in the late 1700s or early 1800s it appears that Joseph Taylor wanted to separate the old farmhouse from the rest of the farm and a new farm house (No. 4 Lanes End) was built out of rubble stone behind the original house by remodelling some of the associated farm buildings that also dated back to the 1600s. The date 20 June 1814 is carved in a stone on the first floor, indicating that the roof was raised or the building was extended at that time. It appears that the building was extended at both ends - the east end was used as a cheese store and also for malting barley to supply the local beer brewing industries. This was one of two maltings in the village.

## Chapter 9. Gastard - a history.

By the early 1800s Joseph Taylor styled himself as a 'gentleman of Corsham.' He seems to have been an ambitious man, buying up land and properties around Melksham and Corsham, including Gastard, and mortgaging them to his sons and other family while still holding the property in trust. This was a device to work within the restrictions of copyhold (the way land subject to the customs and rights of the lord of the manor was transferred or bequeathed). His property included cottages or tenements with gardens at Chapel Knapp and a cottage and garden near the Harp and Crown. He also acquired cottages and about 20 acres called Lydes, near to where Willgarrup Farm was located, and three fields of about 30 acres south of Copse Cottage, near Court Farm. These two blocks of land were eventually purchased by Sir R.N. Fowler in 1883 and are now part of Attwood and Court Farms.

In 1801, Joseph Taylor was also farming at Neston Park Farm when it was put up for sale in June 1881 *[page 4 of Salisbury and Winchester Journal - Monday 1 June 1801].*

By 1822 Joseph Taylor appears to have overreached himself and had fallen into debt. He had taken out a loan with Thomas Heath and William Hawkins Heath, bankers in Andover, and owed them £5,000. The bankers pursued Taylor at the Court of the Kings Bench, where they received a judgement in their favour and Taylor had to remortgage his property to them as indemnity bonds. Interestingly, the judgement notes that the bankers complained that Taylor *had 'put himself under the Lord Marshalsea.'* This is a term that refers to the famous debtor's prison the Marshalsea, which at that time was located in Southwark, London.

The prison was divided into two parts, one side for Admiralty prisoners and the other side for debtors. The debtor's side was a curious mix of poor prisoners with small debts unable to find a way of escaping their predicament and the better-off who had put themselves in the prison, usually by asking business partners to arrest them, to escape creditors. Inside it was run by a prisoners committee, debtors could receive family and friends, and some could come and go during the day. But it was also notorious for promiscuous behaviour and extortion. Famously, Charles Dickens' father had been sent to the debtor's prison in 1824 and this experience led him to write about it, notably in his novel Little Dorrit. It is possible therefore, that Taylor had voluntarily put himself under the jurisdiction of the prison as a way of temporarily escaping his creditors and buying time to raise the money elsewhere. It is also not clear whether by doing so he even had to enter prison at all. Certainly it was an action that had annoyed Taylor's plaintiffs, the Heath bankers.

As a consequence of the court judgement, Joseph Taylor had to redraw all his property transactions in favour of the Heaths, including those of his son Richard, who was a joint mortgage owner with a relative, Thomas Home, including property at Chapel Knapp. Sadly, by this time Richard was recorded as being of 'unsound mind' and seems to have been incarcerated in a private asylum. This further complicated the re-mortgaging of property to the Heaths. But whatever the predicament a few years later Taylor was able to recover his property and in his will of 1826, proven in 1828, he left it to his sons Thomas and John and his grand children by them, with a provision of an annuity and rent free accommodation for Richard should he ever be well enough to return home.

In March 1829, a year after Joseph Taylor's death on 24 March 1828, the eldest son heir-at-law Thomas, sought to recover the copyhold estate held under the manor of Corsham, comprising a messuage and about 100 acres of land, inherited by his younger brother John Taylor in accordance with their late father's will. In the court case, it was stated that their late father Joseph Taylor, had done substantial justice to all his children. During his lifetime, Joseph Taylor had been called upon to make heavy

## Chapter 9. Gastard - a history.

advances for his eldest son Thomas, and did not feel justified in leaving him so large a portion of property under this will. Therefore, the property had been left to the younger son John. Thomas sought to show the court that either his father was too old and infirm to know what he was about, when he signed the will, or that John (his younger son) had exercised an undue influence over their father. There was not the slightest ground, however, for either of those imputations.

John Ladd who knew Joseph Taylor for 15 or 16 years previous to his death said that Joseph was as clear and sensible as ever he was in his life when the fair copy of his will was made. Three witnesses wrote their names in the margin of each sheet, and afterwards at the bottom of the attestation in John Ladd's presence as he sealed the will.

By Joseph Taylor's request John Ladd took the will home, and kept it until Joseph Taylor's death. The learned Judge at the hearing said that he had never known a more clearly proved will and he had certainly never seen one better drawn. The property subsequently remained in Joseph Taylor's younger son's (John Taylor) hands.

However, this did not end the family's encounter with the Court of the Kings Bench. In 1829, Thomas Taylor defended a claim made by a gentleman named Harris. This was probably Charles Harris or his heirs, who had been a servant to Joseph Taylor. In his original will, Joseph Taylor had left a copyhold cottage and tenement with a garden at Chapel Knapp to Harris, but later altered it in favour of his grandson William Taylor, son of John Taylor, who would receive the property after the decease of Harris. The court dismissed the claim on the basis that an earlier case brought by 'other parties who held other premises' *[see paragraphs immediately above]* had also been dismissed.

In his will of 1843, John Taylor said he was a yeoman farmer at Lanes End Farm. He also owned a farm at Somerford Keynes [Gloucestershire]. He had a wife Catherine, sons William, Thomas, Joseph and John, and three daughters Eliza, Sarah and Pamela.

The will made his son William and friend William Stockman trustees, with provisions at Lanes End to *'carry on the business for a period they shall think proper during the lifetime of my son Joseph with full power to cultivate, sell and diffuse any part of the stock and produce etc., purchase cattle, employ bailiffs and labourers'* and to *'permit and suffer my wife and three daughters to reside at the farm and take part in the management of the farm as the trustees may deem advisable ... [and] apply income and profits for the maintenance of my wife and daughters ... [and] after the decease of my son the trustees to sell or dispose of household furniture, farming stock etc. and invest the produce in stocks or funds or real securities to pay an annual income to my wife for her life and after her decease pay, transfer or divide the money or stocks or securities equally between my youngest son John and three daughters as tenants in common.'*

By 1871 the farm was occupied by George Gingell Taylor, his wife Jane and their children. George was the son of William Taylor and grandson of John. He had three brothers William Henry Taylor, Thomas Elborough Taylor, Joseph Elborough Taylor and a sister, Elizabeth Gingell Birch (nee Taylor).

Their father William Taylor was a farmer at Easton, but he also owned properties at Velley, No. 2 Lanes End and to the north of the county at Sherston. Another William Taylor occupied the farm in 1899, followed by John Alfred Taylor who farmed the land from around 1923 -1932 and was the last of the Taylor family to occupy Lanes End. Between and after these dates it was also occupied by a succession of tenants, until it was sold by William Hiller Taylor and his sister Mabel Hester Taylor in 1954.

# Chapter 9. Gastard - a history.

**Postscript:**

Within the archives at the Wiltshire and Swindon History Centre there is a curious letter. It is undated, but has a watermark for George III and probably dates to around the mid - late 1700s. It is addressed to Richard Taylor Junior of Chapel Knapp near Corsham and is a proposal of marriage from *'an admirer at Melksham.'* It seems that Richard was socialising in fashionable society in Bath and his admirer wrote:

*'Sir,*

*Departing as I do from the rules of decorum prescribed by my sex, I must trust to your good sense and politeness to excuse the seeming impropriety of my behaviour, and while I declare more than is customary for a Woman to do, I must hope that there is one man who possesses more humanity than to affront a woman merely because she has partiality in his favour. I will tell you sir, (though blushing), I tell you that I have enjoyed little repose since I saw you at Bath races, and if you are not absolutely engaged I shall hope for the honour of seeing you at Bath on Sunday next at the Pack Horse, as I shall be there waiting to see you, so don't disappoint me.*

*It is superfluous for me to mention matters of fortune as I believe you will not have any dislike of my person or fortune. If you have any previous engagement, or an unconquerable objection to my person, I will immediately decline all pretensions to your favour. If I am so happy as to obtain your permission, I will submit my proposals to the consideration of my friends and endeavour to obtain their concurrence to our union, and I shall now conclude with a solemn promise that to contribute toward your happiness shall ever be the principal care of her who now presumes to describe herself,*

*Sir your most respectful Admirer.'*

Unfortunately, a note scribbled on the letter by Richard suggests his response was less than complimentary, he writes:

*'A very polite address indeed. Who can have any objection in either request? P.S. I am afraid your appearance has a different countenance in other respects.'*

By the early 1800s the Taylor family were in possession of No. 4 Lanes End (i.e. Lanes End Farm), but what of the farm itself? The new farm house was extended at the east end about 1814 to form a cheese store for the curing of cheeses.

At this time North Wiltshire was still an important cheese making area, although by the middle of the 1800s and with the coming of the railways many farmers were able to start producing liquid milk for markets further afield. Lanes End farm continued to produce cheese, however, and in 1866 Mr Taylor took his horse and wagon to sell cheese at Reading Market, which became available because of the impact of an outbreak of foot and mouth disease in the south east of England.

The cheese room was also used for malting barley for the local breweries, according to information handed down by old farm workers. This connection is perhaps through the tenant of Lanes End Farm in 1848 - c1860s, Robert Manning, whose family were brewers.

The Taylor family took only a sporadic interest in farming at Lanes End, with the farm occupied by a succession of tenants including John Tanner in 1881 and Walter Lewis during the 1880's and 1890's, whose tenancy was terminated around 1895 because he kept turkeys in the end room of the farmhouse.

# Chapter 9. Gastard - a history.

William Taylor took on the farm for around five years. He had two daughters, Cynthia and Peggy, who married Frank White of Thingley Farm.

Thomas Greenland was tenant in the early 1900s and by 1911 the tenant was Horace T Watkins until the Taylor Family, through John Alfred Taylor, returned to the farm between around 1923 -1932. However, the farm was rented again around 1932, when Stanley Salter became the last tenant and he stayed until 1954.

Before mains water came to Lanes End Farm it had to rely on three spring-fed ponds and four wells. The ponds had sufficient water for the farms needs. Virtually all the farms in the village were dairy farms and when drought came, other local farmer's used the springs for their cattle.

During the Second World War the Francis family, evacuees from London, lodged in the attic of Lanes End Farm. After the war they stayed in the area and opened a newsagent shop in High Street, Corsham. Also towards the end of the war, a number of Italian prisoners of war were designated to work on the farm to dig out drainage ditches.

About 1936 the war office purchased both the Ridge and Eastlays Quarry, this became the Central Ammunition Depot Corsham (C.A.D.) or Corsham 'Dump.' With other quarries following, this became one of the largest ammunition depots in the country. With war fast approaching, railway sidings were built at Thingley and Lacock providing transportation for the depot. However, to get to the Thingley sidings by road, vehicles had to travel via Corsham, Pickwick and Chequers Hill, which was thought to be too long. A new direct road was proposed to go from the junction at the Harp and Crown, heading north east across Lanes End Farm (behind Coppershell). It was marked out with stakes, but was never built. However, telephone lines were erected along the proposed route, using Elm trees to support the wires. They remained until 1976, when the trees were felled, having caught Dutch Elm disease.

Also during the Second World War soldiers came along Lanes End to remove topping stones that would provide construction material for a Home Guard look-out site that was built in the front garden of number 9 Lanes End, near Chapel Hill. This position had a clear view to Thingley. Ted Aust, who lived at number 9, was the Air-Raid Warden for the village and his son Donald was in the Home Guard. On the 8th May 1945, Francis and Les Goodway, also of the Home Guard, cut out a wooden 'V and attached it to the barn door of Lanes End Farm to commemorate V.E. Day. It can still be seen today.

**No.5 Lanes End (the new Coffee Tavern).** *See also page 125.*

Opposite Lanes End Farm was the *new* Coffee Tavern, number 5 Lanes End. It was built by the Liberty Movement, inspired by Florence Nightingale during the Crimean War, who had written to Lord Herbert of Wilton House, who was Minister of War, suggesting that reading rooms should be privided in every village for injured servicemen, an idea extended after the First World War. The tavern was established by Jean Fowler of Gastard House; but later, when it ceased to be used for its original purpose, it became a house. By the early 1950s it was purchased by Mr and Mrs Fowler (no relation to Jean Fowler), who previously kept the village shop on Velley Hill.

**Nos. 6, 7, and 8 Lands End.**

Beyond the new Coffee Tavern, heading toward Chapel Hill, are numbers 6, 7 and 8 Lanes End. No. 6 had originally been some kind of out building, converted to a cottage by the mid 1800s, while No. 7 and No. 8 are a pair of cottages that date to the mid 18th century. These were owned by the Hayward family,

## Chapter 9. Gastard - a history.

who had been tythingmen in Gastard in the eighteenth century. In 1837 the properties were owned by Hezekiah Hayward and then Reuben Hayward. On Reuben's death in 1856 he passed the cottages to his two daughters, Mary Anne and Catherine Anne Hayward. Mary Anne married Edward Gane Flook and they had a daughter Mary, who married Arthur Herbert Manning, a draper, outfitter and wine merchant in Melksham. The Mannings were a notable local family, with Joseph Manning acting as Home Steward to Lord Methuen in the 1840s.

The Manning family were also connected to the Pickwick Brewery, which probably took the malt from Lanes End Farm. The Pickwick Brewery was established by William Hulbert, common brewer, of Pickwick. In 1804 he leased a newly erected brewery building to William Hulbert of Westrop and Robert Hulbert of Roundway for 21 years. It included a brewery, malt house, furnaces, coppers, boilers, grates, kilns and other fixtures. It then passed to Henry Hulbert in around 1840 and between 1865-1870 it was owned by Thomas Hulbert and Henry Padbury Manning. They were listed as beer brewers, wine merchants and dealers in malt and hops at the Pickwick Brewery in the Kelly's Directory 1867.

The cottages (Nos. 6, 7, and 8 Lands End) remained in the ownership of the Manning Family until 1962. When Mary Manning (nee Flook) died in 1947, she left the three cottages to Phyllis Manning of Shaw, in trust until the death of her father Arthur Herbert Manning (who died in 1952). As Phyllis never married, the ownership of the properties passed to her brother Kenneth, who in turn gifted them to the tenants.

In 1871 No. 6 was occupied by James and Jane Beams and then, by 1881, Francis and Ann Weston. They were agricultural labourers. In 1963 the cottage was given to Frederick Freegard, who had been a tenant since 1923. It was sold in 1977 to Ceri Davies and then purchased in 1985 by Rae and Patricia Marshman, who are still the owners today.

The tenants at No. 7 included John Russ the younger; agricultural labourer James Gibbons and his wife Christian Gibbons; James and Ann Oram and family. James was a railway labourer and son Frank a coal miner. In 1963 No. 7 was also given to a tenant, Mr P. S. 'Sam' Maslin, by the Manning family, who was succeeded by his son Ted. Sam Maslin was a farm worker for John Taylor at Lanes End Farm.

In 1837 the tenant at No. 8 Lanes End was John Russ senior. The Russ family worked Elm Grove Farm, now Chapel Knapp, adjacent to Gastard House. No. 8 was later occupied by William and Elizabeth Hayward; John and Harriet Cook; and Frank Webb and family in 1891. They were quarrymen and agricultural labourers. However, the most notable family associated with No. 8 were the Freegard family. William Freegard was a gardener and the head of the household around 1900.

Together with his wife Emma, he had five sons and four daughters. Two of the son's later associated with Lanes End were Frank, who married Edith Hand; and Frederick. Both Frank and Frederick enlisted in the army during the First World War, as did their father William, who joined the Royal Flying Corps. Frederick enlisted with the Royal Field Artillery, while Frank joined the Life Guards and ended up as a prisoner of war in Germany. Frank and Edith had two children, Daphne (born in 1920) and Jack (1924), and the family went to live in No. 8 in the mid 1920s; while his brother Frederick took on the tenancy of No. 6. Frank worked for the GWR and Frederick was employed as a groom at Guyers House in Pickwick.

Jack Freegard, son of Frank, continued the family connection with No.8. He worked in the GWR ticket office at Chippenham railway station for 44 years, interrupted only by his military service during the Second World War, when he served with the Royal Engineers and saw action in North Africa, Sicily and the Italian mainland.

## Chapter 9. Gastard - a history.

He married his wife Marie in 1954. Jack was also a renowned gardener and took on the land that had previously been allotments, which was situated behind the row of cottages.

One interesting feature of No.8 is the hole in the wall of the front garden, now filled in. This was a goose hole, created by the occupants to allow them to take their geese for a walk.

**Luzzells Well.**

The only recorded public well in Gastard was Luzzells Well. It was situated opposite No. 9 Lanes End in the corner of the field by the stile. The field was first called Shewell or Luzwell Mead, but when the walling stone was taken away from the top corner opposite Timberleaze Track, the field-name changed to Quarry Ground.

To access Luzzells Well, local people had to open a wicket gate from the road and walk down five steps to reach the spring water, which could be collected by dipping a bucket into the water. A stone wall was erected around the steps to keep the cattle out. About 1930, the local authority filled-in the well and topped it with rubble.

**Chapel Hill (Baggers Hill).**

Originally, Chapel Hill was called Baggers Hill. Its name changed with the erection of the Independent Chapel in the 1830s. At the bottom of the hill is No. 9 Lanes End, which was once the site of two cottages - Number 9 originally, called Well-Keepers cottage, and 10 Lanes End), but is now one dwelling. Two further cottages (11 and 12 Lanes End) were located above no. 9, but were demolished around 1930.

The garden to these can still be seen as you look up towards Timberleaze Track. In the 1830s two of the cottages were owned by John Horn and tenanted by the Lawrence and Merrit families and at least one owned and occupied by Joseph Banks. Other families associated with the cottages in the mid nineteenth century were the Hiscock, Dyke, Jones and Manley families, again all quarrymen or labourers.

Later, by the 1930s, the original cottages numbers 9 and 10 had been made into one house (called No. 9) and was owned by Edward 'Ted' Aust, with his wife and three children. Descendants of the Aust family had lived in and around Corsham since the early 1600s and by the late 1800s they were a well-known Gastard family. A relation, William Aust was established as a shoemaker at Velley Hill by 1851. Also in 1851, Ted's grandfather, Edward Aust senior, was a quarryman and later a Stone quarry master at Velley. He lived with his wife Sarah, sons Arthur, Frank, Sidney, Thomas (Ted's father), John and Albert, and daughters Fanny and Elizabeth.

During various times Edward employed his sons at the quarry, although Frank became a gardener and Sidney a baker. The eldest son, Arthur, seems to have taken over running the quarry around 1911. A possible relation, Frederick Aust, a coal merchant, lived and worked with his wife Fanny and their children in Coppershell since at least 1907.

## Chapter 9. Gastard - a history.

In 1911 Edward senior's son Thomas Aust, his wife Ann and six children - Edward junior (Ted), Arthur, Ernest, Oliver, Lewin and Cecil - were living in Coppershell (they also had a daughter called Fanny who was not listed on the census). By that time Thomas and Ann had been married for 24 years, with Thomas listed on the census as a rock quarryman, while 23 year old son Ted was a stone dresser.

Thomas had originally run a coal business, but gave this up to work for his brother Arthur at Velley Quarry. By 1927 Ted had taken on Velley Quarry from his uncle Arthur. Living at No. 9 Lanes End during the Second World War, Ted was the village Air Raid Warden and kept his A.R.W. helmet in the front porch. When Ted died, son Donald and his wife Molly moved in and they were the last of the Aust family to live there. The cottage later fell into disrepair and is today replaced by a new build.

In his book 'The Ways of Corsham', John Poulsom suggests that there was at one time a beer house or Inn called the Olive Branch located near to Luzzells Well and Baggers Hill. Beer houses were often quickly established and then closed just as speedily during the 1600s - 1800s and earlier, so it may possibly have existed, but there is not any evidence to support this theory.

Heading up the hill beyond Bonds Knapp (site of the former Congregational Chapel) the top of Chapel Hill becomes numbers 1, 2 and 3 Gastard. These were country cottages and by 1837 they were occupied by the Macey, Francis and Thomas families. By the late nineteenth century families included Simon and Eleanor Jones, John and Lucy Ferris, Valentine and Mary Elms; and later George and Eliza Harris; and James and Mary Hiscock. All the families were, again, either quarrymen or agricultural labourers. Descendants of the Harris and Hiscock families had been tythingmen in Gastard in the late 1700s.

In around 1900 a Mr Bartlett lived in number 1. His main trade was stone walling and building stone drocks that carried water from pond to pond. Later, it was occupied by Mr and Mrs White and their daughter Irene, who later married Mr Bill Brown. Mr White worked at Avon Tyres in Melksham. A Mr and Mrs Pearce (nee A'Court) later lived at number 2.

**Gastard Independent Chapel.**

Heading up Chapel Hill, there was an orchard adjacent to No. 1 Gastard called Bonds Knapp. This parcel of land now mainly forms the front lawn of No. 9 Lanes End and a plot of land that was the site of the Independent Chapel, which later evolved into a Congregational Chapel. There were steep stone steps that led from the road to the chapel. A history of the Congregational Church suggests that a chapel was built in Gastard in 1831, but it does not seem to appear on the 1837 tithe map (perhaps because no tithe payment was due).

In 1837 the land was shown as a single plot, being a house and garden owned and occupied by Naomi Davies. By the early 1850s it had been acquired by George Slade, a Dissenting Minister of Corsham, and William Wilmot a Gentleman of Chippenham and who was Town Clerk of Chippenham. George Slade had been the Minister at Monks Lane Chapel since 1819 and resigned in 1858, on consideration that he should be paid £100. In the event he was given between £130 - £150. Monks Lane Chapel had a congregation of 48, though 1 person had left and 7 recently died. Slade had also been connected with an Independent Meeting House at Biddestone in 1821.

In 1853 Slade and Wilmot sold the Gastard Chapel and adjoining land for £2 to Daniel Head Marler, a Gentleman of Corsham and John Freeth a Yeoman of Corsham. It contained *'two perches and a quarter situate at Bonds Nap in the tything of Gastard ... part and parcel of the garden and orchard attached to a*

## Chapter 9. Gastard - a history.

*cottage or tenement now late in the occupation of Eden Phillips ... together with the Meeting House now lately erected therein.'* It was for the use of Daniel Head Marler and John Freeth, and the rest of the gentlemen of the congregation - George Freeth, yeoman; George Henly, yeoman; Thomas Henly, yeoman; John Stantial, chemist, John Dunsden, Gentleman; George Hancock, shoemaker; James Phipps Taylor, confectioner; William Ring, blacksmith; George Helps, carpenter; William Bryant, labourer; all of the parish of Corsham. They also included Jacob Jones, a Dissenting Minister of Melksham, and John Thomas, a schoolmaster from Chippenham. It is probable that this was a breakaway or additional congregation from the Chapel at Monks Lane or the one in Pickwick in Corsham.

Prior to the erection of the Chapel, some local people met in worshipper's homes in Gastard. Meeting House certificates note in 1821 a building occupied by George Frankling and including Thomas Gay, James Dunsdon and John More; and in 1803 a large room *'now in the occupation of and belonging to Thomas Osbourne, labourer, Methodist.'* Also named were Benjamin Bishop, John Moore, James and Thomas Marrett, Matthew Shepherd and James Roadway. The other and more popular chapel to be built in Gastard (and attended, for example, by the Aust family), was the Ebenezer Baptist Chapel, at Velley.

The new Congregational Chapel was still noted on an Ordnance Survey map of 1924 and in Kelly's Directory for 1939. It probably closed around this time as many small chapels struggled to survive. When the chapel ceased to be used as a place of worship, it became dilapidated and was used as a carpentry workshop by George Phillips, who lived in the cottage by Black Bridge in Lacock parish.

Albert Sylvester, Lloyd George's *Principal* Private Secretary *(see Chapter 23)*, who owned the site and several others in Gastard, sold it to Mr Jack Simmons, who built a new dwelling called 'Bonds Knapp' in the 1960s. The adjacent land or paddock was used by Ted Aust for pigs and poultry and looked after by his son Donald.

**Timberleaze.**

Turning back west from the top of Chapel Hill is the track, running alongside a field that was called Home (or house) Ground, leading to one detached and two semi detached cottages, numbers 4-6 Gastard. Number 4, now called Timberleaze, is the oldest of the cottages and perhaps one of the earliest in Gastard. It stood on land owned by the Fowler family.

Robert Fowler senior's will of 1825 mentions an orchard and three adjacent fields *'house (home) ground and timber leaze containing thirty acres, one rood [unit of area, equal to one quarter of an acre] and twenty two perches [perch = unit of length exactly equal to 5½ yards], Little Sands four acres and three perches.'* 'Little Sands' was on the cottage's northern boundary and 'Timber Leaze,' the large field on the southern boundary. The cottage itself was also known as Little Sands. It was surrounded by a garden and had an orchard on its eastern boundary. In 1837 the cottage seems to have been two semi-detached dwellings, owned by John Fowler. By the 1880s the two cottages appear to have been made into one. The early census returns do not give numbers or names of the cottages so it is difficult to say who lived in Little Sands, but from later returns it is clear that the Fowlers used the building as accommodation for some of their domestic servants.

In addition to the Timberleaze track, the cottage could also be accessed by a track that led north from the Fowler's home Elm Grove (now Gastard House) to Lanes End, near Yew Tree Cottage and Lanes End Farm.

## Chapter 9. Gastard - a history.

**Little Sands.**

In 1871 it seems that Little Sands was inhabited by Frederick Banyer, a butler who was born in Kent, his wife Emily, who originated from Essex, and their three children all born in Middlesex. This suggests that the family had moved around, perhaps being in service to Sir Robert Fowler junior in his London residence. By 1891 the cottage was occupied by William Maslin, his wife Sarah and their three children. William Maslin was a coachman for Sir Robert Fowler, Sarah was a British Subject who had been born in Barbados. One of William's sons, Samuel Maslin, worked on Lanes End Farm.

By 1901 it appears that the cottage was occupied by William Hazell, another coachman to the Fowler's, his wife Ann and their family. Meanwhile, the Maslin family had moved to another cottage in Gastard, probably number 7 Lanes End, where William Maslin is listed as *'living on his own means'*.

By this time Little Sands Cottage had become known as Timberleaze.

In 1953 Timberleaze cottage was sold to Mr A. J. Adby, who used the garden and adjacent orchard as a poultry unit, providing hatching eggs, with a large poultry house covering the ground right up to number 6 Gastard. About 1960 the poultry house caught fire and following this the Adby family moved away. Timberleaze was then purchased by Nancy Varley in 1961.

On the other side of the orchard, built between 1890 and 1900, were the semi detached cottages, numbers 5 and 6 Gastard. Oliver Aust lived in number 5 sometime before the Second World War and by the 1950s it was occupied by Ted Maslin (grandson of William and son of Samuel). Frank Bollen lived in number 6.

In the 1920's the Chapel Knapp Football Club was founded. They played on the field called Timberleaze, between the Timberleaze Track and Gastard House.

**Court Farm**

The place-name Gastard most likely originates from the Old English words 'Gate', meaning Goat, and 'steart', which was a strip of land; so it refers to a piece of land where goats were kept. In 1155 it was written as Gatesterta and by 1193 Robert of Tregoze held the farm of Gastard in Corsham. We know this because the arrears Tregoze had accumulated in the farm were cleared by the Earl of Salisbury in return for Tregoze giving up the castle at Old Sarum (Salisbury). In 1401 it was recorded that Robert de Gateshurd holds 3 virgates of land (90 acres).

It is probable that this was the location of Court Farm and the centre of the hamlet of Gastard. The Court Farm farmhouse, also known as Gastard Court and Gastard Court Farm, has mainly seventeenth century features, but parts of it are late medieval. The barn dates to the eighteenth century. The farmhouse probably gets its name from being the place in the village where the local Manorial Court of Corsham met to receive payments such as fines or fees; settle disputes; and undertake other court functions and customs. In the 1500s it seems to have been occupied by the Jones family. However, from the late 1560s things get a little confusing. In 1569 Henry Capper demanded part of the messuage (house and grounds) called 'Court of Gastard' from Phillip Brown and Christopher Colborne, suggesting the latter two gentlemen had an interest in the farm. But the local antiquarian Harold Brakspear suggested that the farm passed from the Jones family through marriage to Richard Sherfield in 1605 and he and his wife surrendered it via the lord of the manor of Corsham to Tristram Colborne in 1631. Certainly it remained in the hands of the Colborne family for the next 100 years.

## Chapter 9. Gastard - a history.

The Colbornes seem mainly to be centred around Lacock and were involved in the cloth trade. In 1639 Isaac Colborne, the son of the late Henry Colborne, had surrendered the copyhold in the farm to his mother Grace, which was a way of getting around manorial customs to enable Grace to inherit the farm from her late husband, Henry. By 1677 Thomas Colborne, a dyer, occupied Court Farm, followed by his son Thomas junior, who in 1694 also inherited the family cloth mark called the 'Golden Cross.'

We know much about the building and contents of Court Farm at this time through an inventory of property taken on the 28th December 1677 after the death of Thomas Colborne senior. The farm house included on the ground floor a hall, kitchen, parlour, buttery, pantry, cheese loft and *'the white house'* (a dairy); on the first floor 6 chambers, including 'the best chamber,' a maids chamber and four other bedrooms. There is a detailed list of contents, which include:

In the kitchen - 3 kettles, 2 brass pans, 2 bell metal pots, 1 skillet, 1 warming pan, a brass chafing dish and 1 dripping pan, all worth £4; 2 racks and spit valued at 5 shillings; and 1 cheese press. In the hall -1 table and frame with 6 'joyne' stools worth £1-1 shilling. Nearby in the entrance to the hall was 1 table board, 2 'joyne' stools, 4 chairs, 1 cupboard, 2 spits and a bacon rack, 1 hangle (an iron hook and chain for pots) and 1 stool, and 1 pair of andirons, all valued at £2 -10 shillings. In the parlour -1 table board and frame, 3 chairs and little stools, 1 cupboard, 1 little table board and side board, 2 carpets, 5 cushions and 3 pictures.

In the chamber over the entry - 2 bedsteads, 3 flock (wool) beds, 3 bolsters, 3 coverlets (bedspreads), 1 chest and sideboard valued at £4; 1 pewter flagon with other dishes of pewter £1; the clothes of the deceased £6. Debts owed to the deceased £7.

Other chambers contained bedsteads, flock beds, feather beds, brass and pewter candlesticks, chests and cases, several coffers and an old box; and 'slumber stuff' in the white house.

The farm itself included 2 cows, 2 heifers, 1 yearling bull and the hay valued at £41; 2 pigs £1-4 shillings; 'all sort of grain' £6; and 'the wheat upon the ground' £4 -14 shillings. In the cheese loft there was cheese valued at £10.

We know from the will how some of the contents were divided up. Thomas Colborne senior left most of the household goods to his wife Joan; a feather bed, a bedstead and all the furniture in the bed chamber to his son Thomas Colborne junior; and 'my four other best beds' to daughters Mary and Alice Colborne 'to be equally divided between them.' The whole estate was worth £136 -16 shillings - 2 pence.

In 1747 the farm passed to a relative of the Colborne family, Edward Mitchell of Byde Mill. It then seems to stay in the Mitchell family until the middle of the 1800s. By 1837, tithe map and *apportionment [i.e. distribution or allotment in proper shares]* records that the farm was owned by Richard Higgs and occupied by James Dunsdon, who farmed several adjacent fields or closes in the tithing of Gastard. However, Harold Brakspear suggests that the farm remained in the ownership of the Mitchell family until 1876, when it was sold to Sir Robert Fowler.

It is possible that Richard Higgs simply leased the farm and sub-let it, as happened elsewhere in the village. But in 1842 there are sales particulars and a plan for 'Gastard Court Estate and Lands' to be sold at an auction held at the Methuen Arms in Corsham. It describes the estate as *'an excellent dairy and grazing farm with substantial and convenient dwelling-house, yard, garden, barton, barn, stables, and skillings and several closes of excellent and highly improvable arable and pasture land'* in the occupation of Mr James Dunsdon, a yearly tenant. This included land to the south of the farm and also Sand-pits ground, upper and lower Byde Mill grounds to the north. In total the estate comprised of over 100 acres of land to be sold off in 7 lots. Unfortunately, the particulars do not give the owner or whether it was actually sold at auction.

We do know, however, that the Dunsdons continued to work the farm, with James Dunsdon's widow Sarah, listed on census returns as 'manager of farm,' taking on the running of the business in the 1860s until 1899, when it was occupied by two people called Jones and Ferris. They were followed in 1903 by William Bradford and then William Marsh from 1907 to 1915. In 1911 the tiles were taken off the roof for use on St John's Church and exchanged for Bridgewater tiles. As mentioned previously, in 1922 Miss Jean Fowler sold the farm to Mr Albert James Sylvester. Between 1920 and 1935 it was occupied and farmed by Edwin John Dowling, followed by Norman Reakes in 1935.

The farm was purchased by brothers-in-law John Jefferis and Hue Ferguson in the 1940s and they in turn sold it to Mr Sam Yeatman in 1957. It was then put up for sale again in 1974 and was acquired at auction by Mr B. Richards. It was advertised as a residential or grazing farm of 107 acres, including a desirable seventeenth century period house. The farm comprised of the same fields to the south as those listed back in 1842, with a couple of additions; the fields to the north having been consolidated with other nearby farms in the late 1800s by the Fowler family. The land, the sales catalogue suggests, was ideally suited to mixed farming.

**Attwood Farm.**

The Attwood Farm that we know today was not consolidated into its present form until the 1920s. There had certainly been a farm house or homestead since the 1600s and parts of the existing building dates back to that time. John Poulsom in 'The Ways of Corsham' believed that it had been the home of the Kington Family. This family were living in Gastard since at least the 1590s. Several properties in Gastard also date to the 1600s, plus others that did not survive or were rebuilt, and it is difficult to associate the family with a particular property unless it is specifically named in documents such as wills or manorial records.

If the farm house was occupied by the Kingtons their connection starts with John Kington, husbandman in the late 1500s and then Robert Kington, also a husbandman, and his wife Agnes. In his will dated 1606, Robert left his estate to his son Robert junior and four daughters Agnes, Elizabeth, Jane and Susan. His wife Agnes was presumably still alive as the will also made provision for 'my unborn child.' In 1669 John Kington, a Mason of Gastard, is recorded, while in 1677 there is a further will and inventory, this time for Robert Kington, Broadweaver. His widow Ann Kington was the administrator of the will and the inventory shows that the building contained a hall, buttery, an inner room that contained *'one kiver (a shallow wooden vessel), a spinning turn (wheel) and old lumber (wood);'* a chamber room, a chamber over the hall and an inner chamber; a shop with *'broad cloth and other appurtenances (accessories)* and a back room with the deceased's *'wearing apparel'*. In 1756 a Laurence Kington was recorded as a tithingman in Gastard.

Previously, we have noted other Gastard families in the 1600s, including the Colbornes at Court Farm, the Taylors at Lanes End and the Hulberts. Other's included husbandmen and yeomen such as the Pinchin, Fifield, Hales, Woodman and Wisdome families; and broad weavers including Butler, Feltham and Heyward. Families in other occupations at this time were a tailor called Mark Hulbert, Thomas

## Chapter 9. Gastard - a history.

Hawkins the plowright (a maker of plows), Thomas Lewis a chapman (a general dealer), John Woodman a wheeler and Robert Alden the Baker. Women who were recorded include widows Susana Kington, Elizabeth Wisdome and Mary Hancock.

It is not until 1837 that we are able to identify people with the farm house and adjacent fields. The tithe apportionment records show that there was a homestead and a close owned by an Ann Attwood and occupied by Isaac Dark. 'Farmer Dark' is recorded as a tithing man in 1822 and worked the fields directly to the south of the farm down to the southern end of the parish boundary, also owned by Ann Attwood. It is this family name that most likely led to the name of the farm in the 1920s. The Attwoods had been in the Corsham area since at least 1366, where a Henry Atewode and Willy Atewode were recorded as free tenants on land rented from the Rector of Corsham. A previous tenant had been John Atewode. By the 1700s and 1800s the Attwoods were mainly living and working in Lacock, notably Home Farm, and in Bremhill. Interestingly, Isaac Dark seems to have moved to Bremhill by the 1840s.

**Catridge Farm.**

After this time it becomes more difficult once again to identify the farm house as census returns do not always name it. In 1851 it seems to have been referred to as Gastard Farm, occupied by Henry Gibbons, a farmer of 60 acres, and his wife Eliza. They were employing two labourers. In 1891 it appears to be called Lower Farm, but was occupied by George Mizen a cowman on the farm and Mary his wife. By then it seems to have been owned by the Fowler family and their ownership most likely originated from the purchase of land associated with a much larger farm to the south east, Catridge Farm. The history of both Attwood Farm and Catridge Farm is intertwined.

Catridge Farm straddled the parishes of Lacock and Corsham (Gastard tithing). Fields within Lacock were in the ownership of the Talbot / Davenport families of Lacock Abbey in the 1700s. The rest of the farm, including the part within Corsham, was owned by the Montagu family of Lackham and later by James Burgess, and in 1837 the tenant was Anne Taylor. Burgess also had acquired Moxham's Ground and Gastard (or Guffins) Mead, adjacent to the lane to Lacock and opposite Sandpits. In 1852 Burgess put the farm up for sale, which naturally was of interest to the now owner of Lacock Abbey, William Henry Fox Talbot, who asked his agent West Awdry to bid for some of the land 'on the other side of the railway tracks' at auction in Melksham.

It appears that Fox Talbot acquired most of the lots that also included the rights to the tithes. Subsequently, most of those fields within the Gastard tithing were acquired by Sir Robert Fowler, presumably purchasing them from Fox Talbot, as the Fowlers continued to make tithe payments to Fox Talbot on their 'Gastard Estate.'

By the 1890s Sir Robert Fowler's son and heir, Sir Thomas Fowler, was struggling to maintain the estate during a period of agricultural depression. In 1894 he re-mortgaged the land associated with Catridge Farm, occupied by the Minty family, and the yet unnamed Attwood Farm house for £7,000 in return to J W and W H Awdry.

The Awdrys were among a number of local legal firms and land agents who prospered through such deals during this period. By now this estate also included the building behind Attwood Farm, Copse Cottages, and two further fields. In 1883 Sir Robert Fowler had purchased the cottages and four fields, Lower Copse, Upper Copse, Scotland and Figure from William Taylor for £1,200.

## Chapter 9. Gastard - a history.

When Sir Thomas died in 1902 his will left provision for his unmarried sisters to have the option to purchase Gastard House and any other part of his estate within 6 months of his death. This was undertaken by Miss Jean Fowler with the consent of her sisters. She paid off the mortgage for 'Catridge Farm Land' for £7,000 plus £190 interest.

She also purchased Copse Cottages and an adjoining field for £809 and Gastard Court for £3,320. By this time the Attwood Farm House was occupied by Phinian Dick, his wife Ann, daughter Ellen and son George, who took on the tenancy from his father Phinian sometime between 1915 and 1920.

In 1920, to help recover funds she had spent erecting St John the Baptist Church in Gastard, Miss Fowler sold a consolidated holding to Horace T Walter, which included the Attwood Farm House and fields immediately to the south down to the parish boundary called Summer Leaze, Rush Meadow, Middle Grounds, Dry Hill and Scotland; and Gastard Mead and Moxhams Ground to the east. This became the Attwood Farm we know today.

*Water tower that stood at the top of Velley Hill in Gastard until it was pulled down c1960s.*

### Scotland Field.

One interesting field name is Scotland. In previous articles we noted the fashion to name farms and fields after places, but the origin of this field is entirely different. In medieval times the Scot was a tax levied on inhabitants of a village or town in proportion to the size of their land. It was usually raised to pay for improvements to ditches and streams. Those people who had land or property in unfavourable places such as unworkable land or fields prone to flooding could avoid paying the tax, hence they were described as *scot free*, a term that today describes people who avoid fines or punishment in circumstances where they would normally have to pay.

Rent from the field Scotland (also known sometimes as Southcroft) was most likely used to pay the Scot tax. Later, by the 1700s, rents from the field continued to be used for the common good, where it was given over to a trust for the maintenance of bridges over the Bydebrook.

In 1931 Mr Walter sold Attwood Farm and later Copse Cottages to Frederick Bevan, who originated from Glamorgan in Wales. He continued farming through the Second World War and into the 1950s. His daughter Helen Bevan married John Jefferies of Court Farm and they lived in Copse Cottage for four years. However, Mr Bevan sold the farm and the cottage to Mr and Mrs Rose in 1955.

## Chapter 10. Ian Logan - a Corsham Lad Done Good.

*1942 Underground Factory at Corsham by Olga Lehmann (1912–2001). Bristol Aircraft Company: Image below © the artist's estate, courtesy of Olga Lehmann's son Paul Huson.*

**1939-1941:** My parents Nell and John Logan moved from Salford in Manchester, to the small village of Pilning, Gloucestershire. I was born there on 12 July 1939. My father worked as an engineer at the nearby Bristol Aeroplane Factory, my mother had been a spinner in the mills. Because of the bombing of Bristol and the temporary relocation (into the Corsham underground) of the Bristol Aeroplane Factory, we moved to Corsham two years later in the summer of 1941. The Aeroplane Factory was supposed to be an alternative bomb-proof factory for the Bristol Aeroplane Company's works at Filton. My father worked there in the Corsham underground at Spring Quarry, building Beaufighter Centaurus engines for the Bristol Aircraft Company until the end of WWII. At the time, Spring Quarry was probably the largest underground factory in the world and at its peak it employed upwards of 20,000 people.

**1941-1945:** The pianist Dame Myra Hess often entertained the workers in those underground canteens during dinner breaks. She was a war pianist who boosted London's morale during the Blitz. During WWII, she conducted 1,860 showcases throughout Britain. Her aim was *'To give spiritual solace to those who are giving all to combat the evil'*. Listening to the piano echoing around 100 feet below in the Corsham tunnels must have been a surreal experience for the underground workers. When the factory closed in April 1945, it was deemed overall to have been a flop. It produced nothing of significance, except for a small number of Centaurus engines, many of which failed at first testing, due to the damp and dusty underground conditions in which they were built.

Our Corsham bungalow at 19 Brakspear Road skirted the rim of Hilly Fields (now the Valley Road). My earliest memory there was sitting in a toy car and driving down the front path. Because my father was in

Chapter 10. Ian Logan - a Corsham Lad Done Good.

a reserved occupation (i.e. employed in work of national importance), he was not conscripted. Father became a member of the local Home Guard and for some reason he always stored his *Sten gun* in my tiny bedroom. My pre-school was located in Hartham Park at the end of Middlewick Lane (I was there with Dave Barry). I remember the lady who looked after us had a most wonderful Native American feather head dress! Dave's mother told him that *he wasn't to go near Ian Logan!*

When I reached 5, I attended the Corsham Regis School where my first teacher was Miss Smith who lived on Pound Pill. (Her sister taught me later at Bath Art Secondary school). Regis School opened in May 1943 especially for the children of war workers who were brought into the Corsham area. I was proud to be one of them!

*Original Regis buildings c1960s.*

The Regis School has many happy memories for me and some pretty dreadful ones too! When I was 7/8 years old, the boys in my class had small allotments on the left hand side of the school opposite the Domestic Science classroom.

The allotments were very competitive and early every morning boys would be weeding and hoeing their plots to perfection. The headmaster at the Regis School was Mr Hull and the geography teacher was Jack Laurence. I don't think that I was very bright at school and I was always getting in trouble. I failed the eleven plus, which in those days made you into a second class citizen which I remember very well.

*[Ed - I've always had that feeling, as I failed it too. But we didn't do too badly in the end Ian!]*

We always had a feature film around Christmas in the Regis School Hall. I remember watching 'Great Expectations' with John Mills as 'Pip'. When Magwich jumped out from behind the gravestone, the whole school jumped out of their shoes! *[Ed - and me also!]*

It was a treat to have school lunches in the School Hall; spotted dick, sticky and roly-poly pudding being some of my favourite desserts.

Some of my friends at school during that time were: Dave Barry, Alan (Arty) Shaw, Bill Nyman, David Beavan, Mike and John Nash and Gary Bartlett. Other names seem to have vanished into the ether!

## Chapter 10. Ian Logan - a Corsham Lad Done Good.

One of the things we would do as 6/7 year olds was to climb into the The Royal Army Ordnance Corps (RAOC) camp in the Basil Hill Barracks complex at Hudswell in the early morning and ask to have breakfast with the soldiers. We always got a bacon sandwich! Some United States (US) soldiers were billeted in Academy Drive in Corsham at the time. They would supply us with tins of Barley Sugar and sticks of chewing gum at the Community Centre, where every Friday we had a film show; mostly Gene Autry and Hopalong Cassidy. I remember one Sunday in particular, my parents took me to Lacock Abbey. While we were there, a bunch of US Army officers were also visiting the building. I went over to them and asked the usual question, *"Got any gum chum?"* They said. *"No, but we've got some of these".* I had no idea what they had just placed in my hand. They asked my father if there was anything wrong with me and my gaping mouth - and my father replied, *"He has never seen an orange before!"* Of course they gave us all they had.

**1947:** The winter of 1947 was amazing, with a huge big freeze. Our house backed onto the Hilly Fields a.k.a 'Slippery Jim' [now the Valley Road] where sledging took place for about two months. Brakspear Road was two inches deep in solid ice and it continued to snow until early April. The roads and paths remained covered in snow and ice for many weeks. The local boys who lived in the road started to dig and clear the ice away, as everyone was so fed up with it hanging around.

***1949:** Photo shows the Regis School May Day Celebrations.*

**1948/1949:** My father became a schoolteacher, first at Chippenham Secondary Modern and then as headmaster at Biddestone School. My mother Nellie became well-known in Corsham for being a staunch socialist – she took part in the Aldermaston 'Ban the Bomb' marches and joined the protests at Greenham Common.

**1950s:** I remember old Mrs Barnett delivering 'The Daily Express' newspaper through our letter box every day. One day, she delivered my first 'Eagle' comic. In comparison to today's technical world, it was like getting your first iPad! I was always getting into some sort of trouble or other. In those early days, we were given more freedom than the children of today. We would explore the miles and miles of underground tunnels via the separate small entrance to the right-hand side of Box Tunnel near Potley.

## Chapter 10. Ian Logan - a Corsham Lad Done Good.

**1954:** By this time we had been moved out of our bungalow at 19 Brakspear Road and into a proper house with an upstairs at 60 Arnolds Mead. Very posh it was too in those days! Around 1954, we moved into the Flemish Building at 92 High Street. It had 6 bedrooms; some which we let out to students. I also joined the Corsham Town Band to learn trumpet playing. They practised behind the Town Hall and I think a Mr Beveridge from Gastard taught us, but soon after I joined, the band disbanded. Then I bought myself a guitar from Duck, Son and Pinkers alongside Milsoms in Bridge Street, Bath. I learned to play three chords, which allowed me to become part of 'The Moonrakers Skiffle Group' which started in the Corsham Community Centre's 'Eighteens Group Gang Show'. We subsequently became West of England Champions! The other bands must have been terrible! The prize was to record a record which subsequently turned out not to be very good!

'The Moonrakers Skiffle Group' 1956 at a May Day gig at Corsham Regis School.
Band members left to right are: Sitting, John Abbotts from Boxfields, then Ian Logan with his 3-chord guitar, Doug Hudd from Pound Pill on banjo, Bill Beavan on guitar, and lastly Ken Oatley on his home-made double-bass.
Always looking for something new to do, I tried joining the Boy Scouts; their Headquarters were near to the Corsham Railway Station.
They wouldn't let me in, so I joined the 'Boys Brigade' based in the Baptist Church Hall in Priory Street.

Before going into the many entrances of the Box Woods quarries at the top of Boxfields in Rudloe, we would buy packs of 5 Turf or Player's Weights cigarettes from Rossiters, the grocery shop in Priory Street. We often purloined carrots from the many allotments that Corsham seemed to be blessed with in those days. And occasionally, if we were not quick enough or vigilant enough, we would be caught and dragged before PC Jones to receive the obligatory punishment of those days, a sharp slap around the ear - followed by something very similar when we got home!

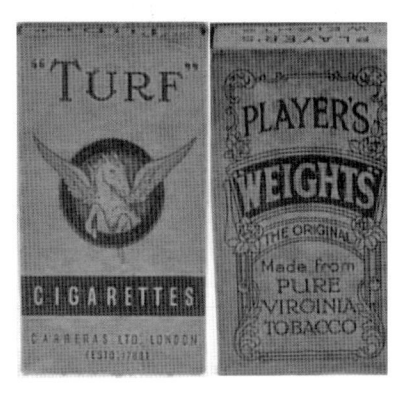

**1950-1955:** After failing the 11 Plus exam, I was placed into Mr Jones' Class. The 11 Plus was an examination administered to pupils in England and Northern Ireland in their last year of primary education which governed admission into grammar schools and elite secondary schools. As it turned out, failing the exam was the best thing that could have happened to me. Mr Jones was a talented music and geography teacher and he could see something in me that others could not. I was 12 when he got me a place in the Bath Art Secondary School where I stayed until I was 16 years old. To make myself a few pennies, I became a *paper boy* at Francis the newsagent in the High Street. If my memory serves me right, the pay was around 12 shillings and sixpence a week (about £12 in today's money).

## Chapter 10. Ian Logan - a Corsham Lad Done Good.

In addition to this, once a month I would make my way down to the Corsham Station at around 4.30 a.m. in the very early morning and collect the bundle of papers from the Station Master, return with them to the shop and then sort them out for the other paper boys.

*[Ed - I had that same job at Francis the Newsagent too Ian, some 10 or so years after you did!]*

On Saturdays, I worked at Honeychurch's hardware shop (now Hong Kong House) on Pickwick Road *(see photo left)* serving Esso Blue and Aladdin pink paraffin all day long in the winter months.

*Photo: Honeychuch Hardware Shop in Pickwick Road - now the Hong Kong House Chinese Takeaway.*

John Honeychurch became a great friend of mine, as was David Marsh of Marsh's greengrocers a few shops down (previously 'Il Gusto' now the 2019 'Prime Cut' restaurant). I always wondered what became of that fish above the shop? *[Ed: Below is the Marsh & Son's fish resurrected!]*

During WWII and for a time after, Corsham was one huge ammunition dump. It was inevitable that we (the ever inquisitive children of Corsham) would eventually find an ammunition dump, which we did after the Americans had left Academy Drive. One of my friends found a grenade and threw it at a raft causing a huge explosion. We also found some live bullet belts, one of which I proudly hung over my shoulders and wore into school as a proud trophy the following morning. I was promptly made to stand in the furthest corner of the playground on my own for a long period of time whilst the Police were urgently called to 'gingerly' remove my prized possession.

## Chapter 10. Ian Logan - a Corsham Lad Done Good.

After leaving the Bath Art Secondary School, I became an apprentice draughtsman at Westinghouse Brake and Signal Co. in Chippenham. My boss there was the famous railway writer (Oswald Stevens) O. S. Nock. He was nicknamed Ossie and was a British Rail signal engineer and senior manager at the Westinghouse Company; he is well known for his prodigious output of popular publications on railway subjects, including over 100 books, as well as a large number of more technical works on locomotive performance. I really hated it there at Westinghouse and was eventually called up for National Service, by which time conscription (compulsory enlistment into a national service, often a military service) had almost ended. I remember at the time, a friend of mine came home one weekend from the Army and said to me, *"Whatever you do Ian, try and get out, as I have spent the last two weeks cutting the barrack room lawn with a pair of scissors!"* So I took my friend's advice and as soon as I could, I applied to the West of England School of Art and managed to get a place there for two years; which was perfect for me, as my conscription into the Army had just come to an end.

**1958/59:** I applied for a place at the Central School in London (now Central St Martins) on a three-year textile design course which was most enjoyable. This was my introduction to a rather dirty and yet wonderful London. My digs were in Holland Park with another student for £1.50 a week (£25 in today's money) between us! Those were the days and I am still here in London, but sadly not at £1.50 a week!

After leaving the Central School I spent a year in Sweden on a scholarship in their top art school 'Konstfack'. Then I returned to London to help form a small textile print studio with ex Central School students. This was the 1960s and we became very successful (see http://www.ian-logan.co.uk/)

**1965:** The following is a newspaper article that appeared when I was 26.

**YOUNG MEN'S COMPANY FLOURISHES: FOREIGN CUSTOMERS LIKE THEIR DESIGNS:** P.V.C. coats for Mary Quant wallpaper for a stately home and textile fabrics for a luxury hotel, are among the design projects already carried out by 26-year-old Mr Ian Logan, a former Bath art student, who is now a director of a thriving design company with a flourishing export trade.

Mr Logan is the son of Mrs N. Logan, of the Flemish Houses, Corsham, and the late Mr John Logan, who for many years was Headmaster of Biddestone School. After attending local schools at Corsham, he went to the Bath Art School and from there to the West of England College of Art at Bristol and the Central School of Arts and Crafts in London. His qualifications include the Central School and National Diplomas in Design and membership of the Society of Industrial Designers.

**STARTED COMPANY:** Mr Logan and three or four of his fellow students, started their own company, J.R.M. Designs Ltd., when they found it nearly impossible to sell modern designs to the large manufacturing companies.

*"They were only interested in conventional bread and butter stuff and would not look at our work as they thought it non-commercial,"* he said. *"We formed our company to produce our own stuff and to convince people it would sell,"* he said, adding that after some success with work for Mary Quant and other 'with it' designers, they decided to produce and market their own textile goods.

Mr Logan designed traditional wallpaper, incorporating the coat of arms of Lord Lichfield for Shrugmoor Hall, Staffordshire and 3,000 yards of his textiles were used in connection with the interior decorations of the Grosvenor House Hotel in London.

Chapter 10. Ian Logan - a Corsham Lad Done Good.

**TEXTILE EXPORTS:** The most encouraging success of the new company however, has been in exports to America and to France, Sweden and other continental countries. Orders for large quantities of textile goods such as table and tray cloths and for colourful tin trays have been fulfilled. At present the printing of the designs is being sub-contracted, but, with business expanding, the young Directors are now looking for a factory of their own. In the New Year they hope to be in full control of their products, from design, to production and marketing.

This Christmas [1965], Mr Logan has brought his goods, which enjoy a wide international market to his home town of Corsham.

A surprise window in Corsham's shopping centre is in the ironmonger's shop of Mr John Honeychurch, which is devoted to a display of colourful and attractive linens, cottons and trays………………………

*End of newspaper article:*

**1966/67:** This is the very first tin tray that I designed. It was a deep purple colour with yellow and pink flowers. I had two designs at the time; the other was called 'Salome'. Both designs were inspired by Turkish textiles. Our company J.R.M. only produced one item of this design i.e. the tray. I think at the time they cost about 10p each (£1.30 in today's money) and our first order was for 2000. It was extremely successful. A store called, 'GEAR' in Carnaby Street was selling around 200 a week in the 1960s. This particular tray recently appeared for sale on eBay for £10!
[Ed - I know, and I bought it Ian!]

'Salome' became one of the most successful designs and products of the late 60s and early 70s. It was produced on almost all surfaces including tin-ware, fabrics, enamelware, saucepans, cushions, tea towels etc. etc. Copies of most of my tins are held in the archives, with textiles and carpets, at Central St Martins. www.csm.arts.ac.uk. I went on to became a consultant designer for Parker Textiles, Midwinter Potteries and for Whiteheads of South Africa. I taught at Hornsea College of Art, Middlesex Polytechnic and at Worthing College of Art, as well as becoming an assessor to many colleges and art schools around the country. I have produced two books, one on the graphics of the US railroads called 'Lost Glory', and the other 'Classy Chassy' about the pinups on WWII US aircraft!

**2001:** I merged my business with the two-year-old brand design consultancy 'The Nest'. I had been in business since the mid-1960s and was looking for a company to tie up with. By now, I felt pigeonholed by clients and teaming up with 'The Nest' was an opportunity to broaden my offer again. I had been winding down my business over the past two months from ten to three people, through redundancies and not renewing freelance contracts. I had an empathy with the people at 'The Nest', which was 18-strong and based in London's Farringdon.

Chapter 10. Ian Logan - a Corsham Lad Done Good.

I spent one or two days a week at 'The Nest', working with my own clients, such as Tesco and Boots the Chemists and Fast-Moving Consumer Goods (FMCG) projects in The Netherlands, Turkey and Germany. I also acted as a new business consultant for 'The Nest' clients including the Roald Dahl Estate, Concorde, LancÃ´me, The Conran Shop, Banana Republic, Cadbury's, Tonka and First Great Western. I spent the rest of my time at my design-led accessories shop in London's Charterhouse Square.

**2015:** I have a great nostalgia for my home town of Corsham and am quite often there landing my aeroplane at the Wadswick airstrip on the edge of Corsham to visit friends.

Right is a photo of Ian taken in August 2015 on one of his many flights into Corsham; just about to take off from the little Wadswick airstrip, with local photographer Graham Peaple sitting behind.

[Ed - On page 80 of the book, '50 GREAT SECRETS OF DESIGN PACKAGING' by Stafford Cliff, first published in the US in 1999, is the following testament to Ian; another *Corshamite* to be proud of.]

*'Ian Logan is the graphic designer who, with his passion for antique packaging forms, almost single-handedly revitalized the U.K. can container industry in the 1970s. Not only did he design packs for clients in the traditional material but, with his own company, reproduced original designs and lovingly rekindled the genre with money-boxes and toffee cans shaped as London buses, country cottages and even Harrods the department store. At the same time, his blend of historic references and contemporary techniques won him many design awards.'*

Ed: Ian was asked to design a range of 12 packs for the Boaters Coffee Company during their first foray into the flavoured coffee market. During his first meeting with them, Ian recalls; *"I had the solution right there in the meeting while the managing director of Boaters, Richard Affleck, was briefing me. Of course, I didn't tell him what it was, but everything I've ever done has been intuitive, my gut reaction has always paid off'.*

It certainly did pay off, as the Boaters Coffee Company sales leapt by 60 percent in two months.

Ian is happily married to Gail and they have two children, Harriet, who was a photo journalist and Barnaby who is a corporate film maker.

*You can read more about Ian Logan's life in Pat Whalley's book 'Corsham Memories 2. The Prefab Years'.*

## Chapter 11. Mallie Etherds. The Wise Woman of Easton

Throughout the ancient and medieval periods, ordinary people in Europe who could not afford the services of a university-trained physician turned to popular healers. These were often so-called 'Wise Women' who possessed knowledge, passed down through generations, of traditional or folk medicine.

They dealt with all kinds of illnesses and medical conditions, including childbirth and in some cases, abortion - though their knowledge and skills were by no means restricted to women's health.

*The Fortune Teller, by Adèle Kindt 1835.*

However, Wise Women also used many practical herbal remedies, drawing on plants and the rest of the natural environment, which they knew well.

Wise Women and their medicines were often scoffed at by professionally trained doctors, who were nearly always male and were anxious to protect their professional status.

In the past, most rural communities had, what they termed, a 'Wise Woman'. She was usually the local midwife, able to dispense herbal medicines and in some cases was reputed to have occult powers. Corsham was no exception and had its own *'Wise Woman'* called Mallie Etherds who was quite famous at the time, and lived in the small hamlet of Easton on the edge of Corsham.

Here is an excerpt published in 1828 by a 21 year old local author concerning Corsham's Wise Woman.

**Poetical Buds 1828: SONGS AND OTHER POEMS, by John Tayler (born 1807) of Corsham.**

It is but seven years since auld Mallie Etherds, (alias Mary Edwards) the noted fortune-teller died, whose fame for her skill and the art, has rung in every county in England.

> *'To whom the fates of men,*
> *And pretty maids were known,*
> *She read them o'er and o'er again,*
> *But could not read her own.'*

She lived not a mile from hence; and now let me tell a *tale* respecting her, which many in Corsham may not know, and it is more likely to be true, than some of the idle tales in circulation, viz, that she could command the spirit of the storm; make *little imps* dance on her table; and be revenged, from her knowledge of the *magic* art.

A certain butcher of Corsham, who is now dead, was about 20 years ago, overtaken by a farmer, between Bathford and Box, who asked him, *"How far to Corsham?"* *"Five miles,"* was the answer, *"I am going thither."*

## Chapter 11. Mallie Etherds. The Wise Woman of Easton

**Farmer.** *"Then we will go together."*
**Butcher.** *"With all my heart, sir."*
**Farmer.** *"Is not there a cunning woman near that town, by the name of Edwards."*
**Butcher.** *"Yes, sir, I know her well: are you going to her, make so bold?"*
**Farmer.** *"Yes, sir, I am; I have walked almost from Bristol today, for some person has stolen a horse of mine worth £20, and I am told she can tell me who had it."*
**Butcher.** *"Yes, that she can; do you suspect any person?"*
**Farmer.** *"The gipsies, who have been in our neighbourhood."*
**Butcher**. *"Never mind, sir; she will tell who had it, I'll venture to say, for auld Mallie's pretty deep."*

So they walked and talked till they came to the Roe Buck *[Roebuck Inn Lacock Road],* about a mile from Corsham, and near the cunning woman's house. *"Now,"* said the butcher, who wanted a joke, *"Go and take a glass while I do a little business, and then I will go with you to auld Mallie's."* *"With all my heart,"* said the farmer; but while he was drinking the contents of his glass, the butcher made it his *little business* to go and tell auld Mallie all about the *farmer and his horse*, and he added *"Dang me, if thee doesn't stick a good story into him, and charge him a crown, just for the fun o' the thing, I'll never help thee to another job !!".*

*"Be off an' vetch un,"* says Mallie, *"and I'll do't as thees tell me"*

The *little business* being finished, the butcher went to call the farmer, and both went to the house together: as soon as they opened the door, the old woman cried out, "Ah zur! then you be come a-foot now your 'orse is gone, ben't ye?"

The poor farmer was astonished; however he proceeded with his questions and her answers were highly satisfactory. She told him some gipsies had taken it away, and in a few days he would find it *upon* them; so she had the *crown,* and the butcher a treat for his trouble, but whether the farmer found his horse does not appear, nor does it much signify, for he walked about with a *light* heart afterwards, hoping to find the horse *upon* the Gipsies, instead of the gipsies *upon* the horse!! - Now, generous reader, be pleased to forgive any impropriety that may be seen in this book, and I hope my next publication will be better.

**John TAYLER**

**The above was written by John Tayler as a 21 year old in Corsham, Wilts, on May 5, 1828.**

**Note: 1832 February 23:** John Tayler author of Poetical Buds and Sabbath Minstrel etc. died in Corsham aged 25.

**Notes by Joe James :** The Roebuck Inn is now a private house. It is a prominent building in Lacock Road alongside the first railway bridge on the road to Lacock.
Mary Edward's cottage? There are about six 18th century cottages in the immediate vicinity. Take your pick.
Research into Parish records reveals: Martha and Mary Edwards (born 1735), daughters of Samuel and Martha Edwards. Mary died 8 January 1820 aged 85.
These dates fit in well; I have little doubt that Mary Edwards was our 'auld Mallie'. She would have been about 70 at the time of the above story.

# Chapter 12. Maternity Hospital, Alexander House.

In September 2014, nearly 100 people aged between 60-90 who were born in the Corsham Maternity Home between 1928 and its closure in 1951, held a reunion organised by Dominic Campbell. Most of them can be seen in the photo above, taken in front of Corsham, High Street's Alexander House, the old Maternity Home *(courtesy of the Gazette and Herald 4 October 2014)*. Afterwards, everyone met at the Springfield Community Campus to share photos and memories. People from the Midlands to Cornwall turned up. The old maternity home is now a block of flats. Alexander House (Post Code SN13 0HQ) is a Grade II listed house in the High Street, Corsham, Wiltshire, England. It dates from the early eighteenth century.

**1808:** On Monday 20 June, Mr Alexander, Surgeon of Corsham marries Miss Prior, daughter George Prior, Esq. Sydenham, Kent.

**1809:** Mr Alexander of Corsham subscribes to the Royal College of Surgeons @ £1. 1s (£60 in today's money). In those days, *'anyone with a medical degree or without one, or with a licence from Royal College of Surgeons or without, could practise physic in England at a greater distance than 7 miles from London, whether he be fit or not. Otherwise than that by the common law of England; if a person is guilty of mala praxis, whether it be for curiosity and experiment or by neglect, he could be indicted.'*

**c1830:** Kelly's Directory lists Corsham surgeons as William Colborne and 'Alexander and Morgan'.

**1832:** Pigot's directory of Chippenham – 1842 (which also includes information from Corsham) lists George William Dyke, MD is the Corsham Surgeon.

**1836:** The Lancet Volume 2 lists Mr Alexander as Corsham's doctor. Alexander House was the home of Corsham's Dr. Alexander.

## Chapter 12. Maternity Hospital, Alexander House.

In the early 19th century, and before the Maternity Hospital existed, Corsham had a very simple welfare state of its own. Mrs Kitty Wootton and Mrs Eliza Hayward were the two nurses and mid-wives, always on call, wearing a big white apron. The expectant mothers had to put down their names at Mrs Mayo's, Ivy House at the bottom of Priory Street. When the baby arrived, the mother was entitled to the Mayo Maternity Bundle which had everything for the baby to wear and all that mother needed whilst in bed.

**1830:** The 1830 Kelly's Directory shows Alexander and Morgan, William Sainsbury M.D., Thomas Washbourn and William Beard Newman as the surgeons in Corsham.

**1870:** John Sainsbury was in residence at Alexander House.

**1880:** Kelly's Directory lists Martin Folkes Bush as the Corsham Surgeon in the High Street.

**1885:** A sale on the 14/15 April takes place in Alexander House of the household furniture and silver, the property of the late James Popham Sainsbury, previously of the Bristol Road in Bath in 1832.

**1887:** Captain Thomas Edward Aylmer Jones and his wife are in residence at Alexander House. On 19 December their son is born there. Sadly, the infant son dies 10 months later in October 1888.

**1889:** Felix Edward, the second son of Major, later Lieutenant Colonel Thomas Edward Aylmer Jones of the Royal Engineers, is born in Alexander House on 21 February. Felix went on to become a famous actor, appearing in many Bernard Shaw and Shakespearian plays. During WWI he served in the Royal Naval Volunteer Reserve and resumed his stage career after the war ended. He also appeared in several films; he played Merlin in 'The Knights of the Round Table' (1953). On TV, he appeared with Hugh Griffiths in the comedy series 'The Walrus and the Carpenter' (1963-1965) and appeared in all the 19 episodes as Father Anselm in 'O Brother' (1968-1970) starring Patrick McAlinney (as Brother Patrick) and Derek Nimmo (as Brother Dominic). In 1959 he received an OBE for his services to the stage and a Knighthood in 1965 as Sir Felix Aylmer OBE. He passed away in Pryford, Surrey on 2 December 1979.

**1915:** Kelly's Directory lists Dr. James Ellis Crisp M.R.C.S Eng. of Alexander House as the Corsham Surgeon and Medical Officer.

**1923:** Kelly's Directory lists Dr Arthur George Woods as the Corsham Doctor.

## Chapter 12. Maternity Hospital, Alexander House.

**1919:** Miss Doris P. Chappell (of Hatts House in Box), who came from a famous family of music publishers and piano makers, adapts the residential property Alexander House to become a Maternity Home. It was also known as the Corsham Nursing Home. Miss Doris Chappell was the secretary of the local Nursing Association. The Corsham Maternity Home originally had three beds, one of which was reserved for Wiltshire County Council cases. There was only one other Maternity Hospital (Swindon) in the County of Wiltshire at that time. The Swindon hospital is initially staffed by Corsham Nurses.

**[Ed: It's staggering to think that the Corsham Maternity Home functioned entirely on a voluntary basis for over thirty years between 1919-1951 for the benefit of the County under the auspices of Miss Doris Chappell. She was also the President of the Women's Institute in the nearby village of Box.]**

**1920:** Dr Arthur George Woods' son, Peter Wood (Dr Crisp's grandson) is born in the Alexander Maternity Home. His father Dr Arthur George Woods lived and worked a few doors away, along the High Street in Corsham 'The Porch' Doctors' Surgery.

*[Note taken from Corsham WI history]:* Dr. Wood was a regular visitor to the Corsham Maternity Hospital and was loved and respected by all. For half a century he was the medical practitioner in Corsham High Street. A friend to all; he often wrote the wills of his patients. He made notes on his shirt cuffs, and gave one and all this kindly advice, *"Take plenty of slopes, keep yourself warm and you will soon be better"*. When they were able to go out, he told his patients to walk down the Lacock Road, *"Where the air was as good as the South of France"*. One of his patients, a Mrs Cole of Church Street, invited him to a birthday party, and after he had told her how well she looked and what good his medicine had done her, she opened a cupboard door and showed him a great number of bottles of medicine she had not taken. The doctor thoroughly enjoyed the joke. He thought nothing of walking to Box and Colerne to do a surgery for another doctor if they were ill. In the latter years he did his rounds driven in a carriage drawn by a nice fat pony. People in Corsham often talked of that wonderful little man, in his grey top hat and his Cape-Ulster coat *[a Victorian working daytime overcoat, with a **cape** and sleeves]*, a typical country doctor.

**Late 1920s:** Dr Crisp's son James Ellis Crisp, shot and killed some of Dr Woods' pigeons resulting in loggerheads between the two families, until...............daughter Kathleen Crisp met Dr Woods' son Cyril Wood skating on Corsham Lake - and in due course married him! Dr Arthur George Woods later retired c1930 to Bath and passed away just after the end of WW II.

**1923:** Matron of the Maternity Home is Miss E.A. Davis. Dr Crisp passes away.

**1924:** Tom and Florence Jackson of 34 Priory Street were one of many Wiltshire parents who made good use of the local Corsham Maternity Hospital.

Florence, who everyone called Ciss, gave birth to daughter Greta on 24 October 1924 only 5 years after the hospital had been opened in 1919.

*Photo: Florence (Ciss) Jackson 1896-1989*

Chapter 12. Maternity Hospital, Alexander House.

Greta was born *bottom first* in what is known as a breech birth. Most babies in the breech position these days are born by a caesarean section because it is seen as safer than being born normally. During the birth, the labour was so bad, that Florence didn't quite know what she was doing and grabbed hold of the Doctor's tie in her anguish.

Thankfully, Greta was born safely, but the following day, mum Florence was made to apologise to the Doctor by the Matron.

After the birth, Florence was kept in bed to recuperate in a darkened room for two weeks and only fed Milk Sop, which is bread soaked in milk with a little nutmeg added to give it some taste.

*Photo shows Tom and Florence (Ciss) Jackson in their retirement.*

Because of the way Greta had laid in Florence's womb, her legs had been so squashed up, that by the time she was 2 years old, she could only crawl. Not long after, a gypsy selling pegs came to the door of 34 Priory Street and asked Florence (Ciss) what the problem was with her baby (Greta).

Florence explained that the breech birth had somehow effected baby Greta's ability to walk. The gipsy told Florence to go into the garden and collect a handful of snails and then to rub the snails and their slime into baby Greta's legs every night and she should be fine. As Greta's parents Ciss and Tom had tried all other remedies in vain, they were willing to try anything new.

Tom collected as many snails as he could find and every night for several months he rubbed baby Greta's legs with the snails and the slime

*Photo: Florence (Ciss) Jackson 1896-1989.*

Eventually, the *snail-rub* seemed to do the trick, as it was not long after, that she took her first steps. Nobody knows if the Gypsy's slimy medicine worked or she might have walked eventually anyway. It is more likely, that the application of the cure was so disgusting each night, that baby Greta's only escape was to start walking - and quick!

*[Ed: In fact, the land helix, or snail, has been used in medicine since antiquity and prepared according to several formulations.]*

## Chapter 12. Maternity Hospital, Alexander House.

Greta, who later married George Harris, followed her mum's footsteps and gave birth to her own daughter Wendy in the Corsham Maternity Hospital on 27 February 1948.

Just prior to the birth, the letter below was received by Greta in July 1947, confirming her application to attend the Corsham Maternity Hospital for the birth.

The costs to be paid to the Matron, in addition to the Maternity Benefit shown in the letter below, was £1. 13s 6p (£40 in today's money). The 1946 National Insurance Act gave each mother a maternity grant which was paid for each baby of £4 (£100 in today's money).

In case of multiples, the grant was multiplied by the number of children born. The act also introduced a 13-week maternity allowance for female insurance contributors. In order to receive the allowance, women had to abstain from gainful employment during that period.

Most recipients started to receive the maternity allowance at around six weeks before confinement.

*Above are George and Greta Harris.*

If there was an unexpected delay in the confinement, the allowances were paid until six weeks after birth. In 1948, the weekly rate was £1.80 (£50 in today's money).

In order to qualify for the maternity allowance and maternity grant, women had to have been employed or self-employed for at least 26 weeks, and to have made contributions to National Insurance for at least 50 weeks in the year prior to the 13th week before confinement.

*(The Institute for Fiscal Studies, 2011).*

---

**WILTSHIRE COUNTY COUNCIL.**

J. BURMAN LOWE, M.B., Ch.B., D.P.H.,
County Medical Officer of Health.
County School Medical Officer.

AGNES L. SEMPLE, M.B., Ch.B., D.P.H.,
Deputy County Medical Officer of Health.

Telephone No. Trowbridge 777.

Please Quote MCW/ba.

Public Health Department,
County Hall,
TROWBRIDGE, Wilts.

17th July 1947

Dear Madam,

Your application for admission to the Corsham Maternity Home has been considered and approved. The contribution promised by you (Maternity Benefit (double) and £1.13.6 per week), should be paid to the Matron in due course.

The Matron will make the necessary arrangements with you for ante-natal examination and for your admission when necessary.

Yours faithfully,

Mrs G.D. Harris,
34, Priory St.,
Corsham, Wilts

Deputy County Medical Officer.

---

Many thanks to Wendy Kent (nee Harris), for her stories, memories, photos and for the letter which make up the great little story above.

Wendy Kent (nee Harris) can be seen in the 2014 Corsham Maternity Hospital reunion photo at the beginning of this chapter, standing immediately behind the front row's seated lady second from the right.

Chapter 12. Maternity Hospital, Alexander House.

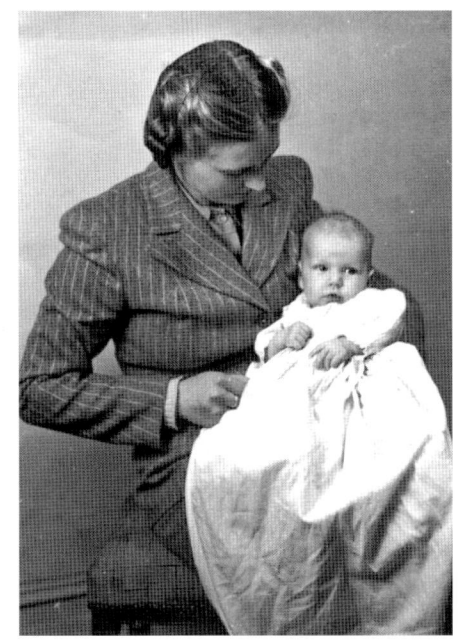

*Above: Wendy Kent (nee Harris) born 27 February 1948.*

*Left: Greta Harris and baby Wendy.*

**1926:** The results of the Corsham Maternity Home Baby show, held at the July Corsham Fund Raising Fete in Corsham Court was as follows: 'Drs. Lawrence and Lowe had a very difficult job to decide who should have the prizes kindly given by Miss Doris Chappell. It was only regretted that prizes were not available for all who entered.

The winners were declared as follows: **1 to 6 months** - Frederick Romaine (Corsham) consolation, Gordon Cooper (3 weeks), Linleys, Corsham. **4 to 13 months** - Jean Batley, Corsham. **Open class, 1 to 6 months** - Joan Tucker. **6 to 12 months** - Hilda Palmer, 9 months (Corsham). **1 to 2 years** - **1** Doreen Clifford, 1 year 11 months (Moor Green). **2** Frederick Wootten (Corsham).

On the afternoon of Tuesday 12 October, the Minister of Health, Mr Neville Chamberlain, visited Corsham Maternity Home for half an hour. He was received by Lady Hobhouse, the Hon. Mrs Anthony Methuen (hon. treasurer), and Miss Doris Chappell (Hon. Secretary).

The inspection lasted half an hour, and Chamberlain expressed himself quite pleased with all he saw. [Note: When Stanley Baldwin retired in May 1937, Neville Chamberlain took his place as Prime Minister.]

**1930:** *News Flash:* On 15 April, a baby was born in a taxi whilst the mother was being conveyed to the Corsham Maternity Home from Devizes. Both mother and child are doing well. This is the second time such an event has happened. A few years ago, whilst a patient was coming from Melksham, a similar incident occurred.

**1931:** The Corsham Maternity Hospital, still functioning on a voluntary basis, is kept busy, but now has a fund deficit of £400 (£19,000 in today's money). Regular fund raising events continue to take place locally to raise money for the Hospital, with Field Marshal Lord Methuen and Lady Methuen (Hon. Treasurer) taking a leading role.

During the year ending March 1931 the nurses attended 823 patients, 256 midwifery and 587 general cases, whilst health visits and school visits were into four figures, and maternity and child welfare clinic attendances numbered 382; this shows the magnitude of the work undertaken by the hospital staff.

The hospital now incorporated an orthopaedic unit which dealt with 113 cases in the same period.

## Chapter 12. Maternity Hospital, Alexander House.

**1932:** Corsham Nursing Association fundraising events over the past year, including Fetes and a car competition, managed to accumulate a staggering total of £515. 10s 3d (£25,000 in today's money), more than enough to clear the £400 debt of the previous year.

One of the Fetes held to help the Nursing Association's Maternity Home, took place at Corsham Court on 1 September, to celebrate Field Marshal Lord Methuen's 87th birthday. There were 74 entries for the 'Baby Competition'.

The winners who were born at the Corsham Maternity Hospital were: **Up to six months**. 1st Josephine Bolland, Corsham; 2nd Cynthia Holbrow, Chippenham.

**Six to 12 months old.** 1st Wallace Slocombe, Lacock; equal 2nd Brian Mace, Corsham and Patricia Whittle, Neston. **One to two years old**. 1st Philip Daniels, Quemerford, Calne; 2nd Valorie Harris, Corsham.

**1934:** In November, a young married woman living only a short distance from the Corsham Maternity Home was on her way there with her husband at 4 a.m. when she collapsed not 100 yards away from it. Before she could be moved, she had given birth to her child in the street.

Nurses from the Home were hurriedly summoned, and mother and child were speedily moved into the Home, where they recovered well and little the worse for this strange happening!

**1936:** The Matron is Miss Walker. Seventy children were born to Chippenham parents this year in the Corsham Maternity Home.

**1939:** *The Wiltshire Times and Trowbridge Advertiser - of Saturday 22 April 1939* reported the following. **'FATHER AT 75:**

At the age of 75, Mr Caleb Slade, of Shrub Cottage, Hardenhuish, in Chippenham, became the proud father of a daughter, born to his 29-year-old wife in Corsham Maternity Home on Thursday of last week.

The announcement recalls the romance between the couple last year, when Mrs Slade (then Miss Gladys Humber, of Dorchester) came to keep house for Mr Slade.

She took the position on trial, but shortly after her arrival it was announced that they had decided to get married. Mr Slade is the father of two sons and two daughters from a previous marriage.

It is interesting to note that Mr Slade already has six great-grandchildren, the new-born baby is great aunt to six and probably the youngest great-aunt in the world.'

**BORN CORSHAM MATERNITY HOME, May 1948 – by Pat Whalley** from the Arnold's News: 'The Newsletter of Corsham Area Heritage' (No.17 and 18) Winter 2014-2015.

Mrs Joan Leighfield (b1929) from Chippenham was admitted to the 'Maternity Home' in 1948. Although she and her husband Bertie lived at Castle Combe, everyone in the area had to attend Corsham, as it was the only local Maternity Hospital available at the time.

Joan's experience was a little different from the norm. She was only 7 months pregnant when she was rushed to Corsham. She was attended to by a gentle Welsh nurse, SRN Price. Adrian weighed in at 2lbs.7oz.

## Chapter 12. Maternity Hospital, Alexander House.

Mother and baby had to remain at the hospital for three months until baby weighed 5lbs. This gave Joan ample opportunity to get to know the building and the nurses very well. Joan remembers a long ward, probably on the first floor, where the mothers slept, and a nursery downstairs.

*Photo: Mrs Joan Leighfield, baby and Matron.*

The nursery contained a large coal fire with a screen around it, and a notice which forbade moving too close.

Matron Green was a special favourite of Joan.

Matron Green was a lady of mature years who married late in life, and is known to have transferred to Greenways Maternity Hospital when the Corsham Maternity Hospital closed.

Once Joan had recovered from her labour, she had to remain at the hospital, in order to feed baby Adrian, initially using a 'fountain pen' filler.

But she also had some spare time, and was able to help the nurses in their general duties and by assisting the kitchen staff to prepare meals, etc.

Matron Green seemed particularly fond of Joan and baby Adrian.

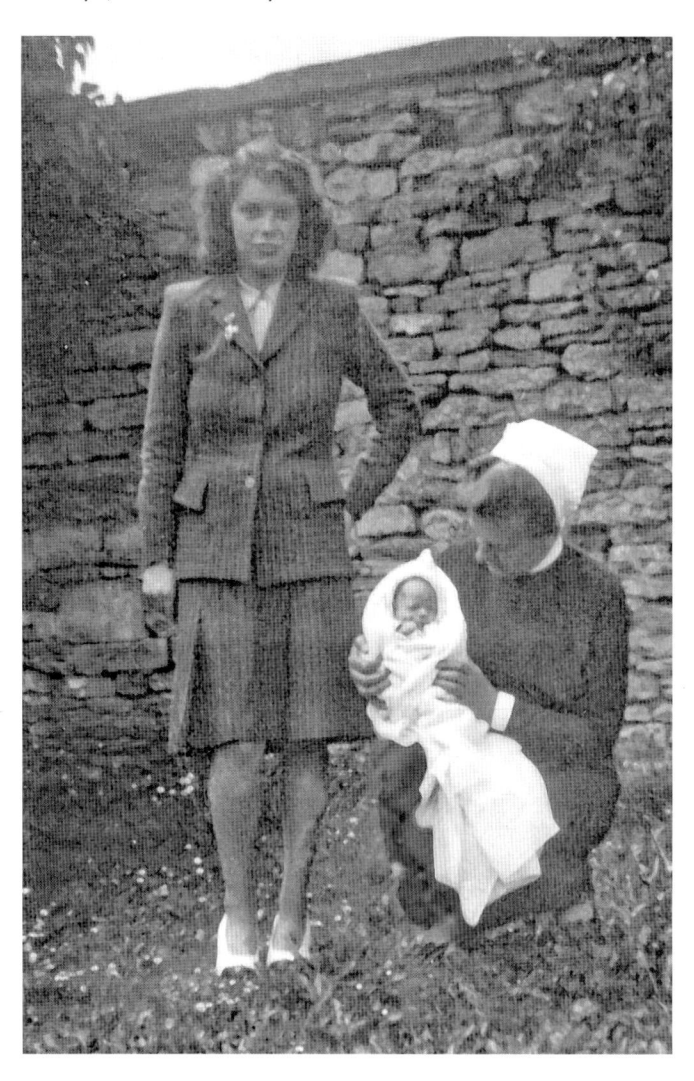

Once, when Matron was away on holiday, she sent a postcard to Joan, which was addressed, *'To Joan and Tom Thumb, from Matron'*, recalls Joan. There was a strict regime of timekeeping, but Joan managed to find time to sneak out one evening, to meet a couple of friends and her husband, and go to the Corsham Fair.

A late return was observed by a nurse, but thankfully, no recriminations followed. This was a particularly happy period of Joan's life, the nurses went out of their way to be helpful and friendly and made everyone's stay at the hospital really enjoyable.

When it was time to go home, Joan found that the fashions were changing. She had gone into the Maternity Home in a costume (suit) with a skirt demurely sitting at the knee. When she returned home, skirts were moving to calf length.

Travel was also something of a problem. To go shopping in Chippenham, Joan had to set Adrian in the pram, and walk 6 miles to Chippenham, and 6 miles back to Castle Combe just to fill the larder!

Sadly, Joan's husband, Bertie, died in 1999, and their son Adrian died in 2003, aged 55.

## Chapter 12. Maternity Hospital, Alexander House.

*Photo shows four uniformed members of staff and baby Adrian, taken in the rear garden of the Maternity Home.*

[Ed: Joan lived alone for a while and was visited regularly by her other son Alan who lived nearby and visited her daily.

Sadly, Joan passed away in 2017 - **R.I.P Joan and Adrian**]

**CORSHAM MATERNITY HOME TWINS HELEN and JOHN.**

Miss Helen Black who has lived and worked in Aldershot, Hants since 1974, where she has pursued a career as a secretary in a Forces Charity was born in Corsham.

Helen was born, with her twin brother John *(see 1947 photo left)* at the Corsham Maternity Home on 21 December 1946.

This was in the bad winter of 1946/1947 when heavy snow fell. As it was so cold when the twins were born, the nurse wrapped them both in cotton wool and put them in a box in the airing cupboard! Being premature babies, mother and the twins had to remain at the hospital until February 1947, when they were considered strong enough to leave. Helen's father, Ian Black, was a Police Constable. Because there were so many troops in Corsham, the constabulary needed more officers and in 1943/4 he was transferred there. It was here in Corsham that he met his wife to be, Patty Jenkins, in 1945. Born in 1913, Patty had attended the Methuen School and the Council School (where the Pound Arts Centre is today). She later trained to become a nurse.

The little family settled in one of the prefab bungalows at Ethelred Avenue, remaining there until 1949/50, when Ian was posted to Swindon. The family came back to Corsham regularly to visit Helen's grandfather who lived in Station Road.

## Chapter 12. Maternity Hospital, Alexander House.

Helen's grandparents were David John and Ada *Jenkins (see photo)*. David had been a wheelwright in London and came to Corsham to open a new business. David bought the house and premises at 28 Station Road. At the time, this consisted of an end of terrace house and a large barn at the rear of the property, now converted into a house. It was Mr Maynard who sold the business to Mr Jenkins in 1923. This remained the Jenkins family home until David died in 1953.

……………………End of the Arnold's News 'The Newsletter of Corsham Area Heritage'………………………..

At the side of the Station Road terrace you can still see the painted sign on the wall declaring *'Maynard - Carriage Builder & Wheelwright'*.

A little adjunct to this story is of interest………. David Jenkins had an uncle, Robert George Jenkins, who was a Crimean War veteran, and came to live in Corsham with David and his wife in his later years. He died in April 1928, aged 95, and was given a Military Funeral in Corsham.

The Rev. W. E. Bryant, Congregational minister, officiated. A gun team from 'D' Battery, Royal Horse Artillery (R.H.A) at Trowbridge, under the charge of Sergeant W. Mantle, conveyed Robert to his last resting place. Robert's old battalion was represented by Sergeant J. Denholm, who carried a wreath from the battalion. Bugler Warren sounded the *'Last Post and Reveille.'* Admiral G. Bullard. C.B., and Capt, the Hon. Anthony Methuen were also present.

After his discharge from the army, on April 4th, 1857, Uncle Robert George Jenkins was a keeper at York Gate, Regent's Park for 36 years, and whilst there some exciting incidents happened. He caught a man wanted for a Regent's Park murder case, and was one of the valiant band who went to the rescue, when on 15 January 1867, the ice broke when crowded with skaters and 200 people were immersed in the icy depths of the lake, 39 being drowned, and one died while undergoing medical treatment. He was also there when the *'Monkey Boat'* the Tilbury blew up, laden with powder, at 3 am on 2 October 1874. It was carrying gunpowder to a quarry in the Midlands and exploded, demolishing the Regent's Canal's Macclesfield bridge by London Zoo and killing three people.

*[Ed: Thankfully, Uncle Robert's final few years in sleepy old Corsham were peaceful.]* **R.I.P Robert.**

## Chapter 12. Maternity Hospital, Alexander House.

**1944:** The County Council, at the 23 February Wednesday's meeting at County Hall Trowbridge, adopted the recommendation of the Public Health Committee, that the County Council take over, as from 1 April, 1944, the existing lease from Miss Doris P. Chappell, of the Corsham Nursing Home premises, and to administer the Home as a *County* Maternity Home, and pay to the Corsham Nursing Association the sum of £1,257 (£40,000 in today's money), the agreed value of the furniture and equipment to be taken over by the County Council. Miss Stephenson, chairman of the Committee, said this was a thing the County ought to have done a great many years ago. The Corsham Maternity Home had hitherto been carried out entirely on a voluntary basis for the benefit of the County, and really the work had fallen to one person - Miss Doris Chappell, of Box - who had carried out wonderful work for something like thirty years, entirely voluntarily. It was quite obvious that these things could not go on for ever, and she thought this was the only Home of its size in the whole Country which was run quite like this. She would like to say publicly how grateful that the Council and the County were to Miss Chappell and her Committee and to all the old residents for the very good work done there over many years.

**1945:** Matron Walker retires after 14 years in charge. *(pg 79. 100 Years in Corsham Parish).*

**1946:** Matron Miss M Green takes over the Matron's role in January. Miss M. Green was trained at the Bristol General and had held appointments at Torquay and Leicester Infirmary. She was also a Ward Sister at the North Middlesex Hospital.
**From David Gordon-Farleigh:** *"I made my entry into the world on 1 September. My mum walked across the road from The Wine Lodge in the morning and I arrived in time for lunch!"*

**1947:** The Corsham Maternity Hospital was still running on a voluntary basis. The foundation of the NHS later in 1948 marked a turning point in the history of maternity services and sparked renewed interest in maternal health.

**1950:** Two babies were born in the Corsham Maternity Hospital on New Years day, the first being born at 1.15a.m. In April, Mrs D Sartain of 185 London Road, Chippenham, celebrated her 21st birthday in the Corsham Nursing Home, a week after she had given birth to twin daughters. To mark the first ever *coming of age* of a patient to be celebrated in the Home, the patients and staff presented Mrs Sartain with a necklace of pearls as a birthday gift.

For some weeks now, ever since the Matron Miss M. Green at the Corsham Maternity Home was appointed to take charge of the new Maternity Hospital at Greenways, Chippenham, rumour had been rife in Corsham that the local Maternity Home which has served the area so well, is to be closed. On Thursday 8 November the closure is officially announced. The Mid-Wiltshire Hospital Management Committee announced that the Corsham Maternity Home is to be closed from 31 December next. The Committee's statement continued: *'The two new Maternity Hospitals, Greenways Chippenham (17 beds) and the first section of the Devizes Maternity Hospital (13 beds) will provide a total of 30 beds from 1 January in the area covered by the Mid Wiltshire Hospital Management Committee in place of the existing beds in Corsham.'*

The Corsham Parish Council was not happy; they were not consulted prior to the decision being taken and the views of the residents of the area were not obtained. It was decided to organise a petition against the proposal throughout the town, with the help of the Women's Institutes, and to ask Mr D. Eccles, M.P. to take the matter up and to invite a member of the South Western Hospital Board to meet the Parish Council.

## Chapter 12. Maternity Hospital, Alexander House.

There was a lot of anger circulating about the decision - not least from the Council Chairman Mr A.R. Gough who said, *"The Home had done much valuable voluntary work under Miss Chappell for many years and this was [like] throwing water in the faces of those who had worked so hard for years in connection with the Home and in raising funds for it."*

By October, the conversion of Chippenham Greenways Maternity Hospital has been completed and the first patient will shortly be admitted. Miss M Green. S.R.N S.CM. formerly the Matron of the Corsham Maternity Home, will be in charge.

**1951:** By March, it was clear that the Maternity Home would definitely close. The authorities stated that it was so below standard, including the equipment and the situation, and that it ought to be closed on those grounds. The Minister involved had apologised for not consulting the representatives of Corsham before the decision was taken, but by now, it was too late. There followed a suggestion that the building could be used for a new Corsham Post Office, but this did not materialise and the Post Office remained in situ where it is today. Alexander House was sold by Charles W. Oatley at the end of March and was no longer a Maternity Hospital. The Housing Committee reported to the Calne and Chippenham Rural District Council, that having been informed by the architects that from preliminary survey, it appeared the former Corsham Maternity Home was suitable for conversion into four flats.

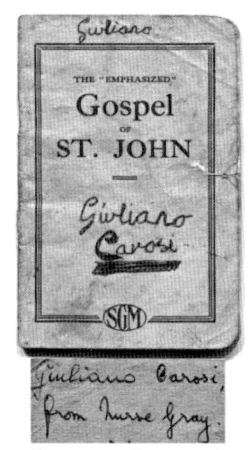

They instructed the architects to prepare detailed plans and estimates of the cost of conversion and to ask the owners details of the purchase price. The proposals would then be submitted informally to the Ministry to ascertain whether approval to purchase was likely to be given.

[Ed: I was one of the first to be born in the new Greenways Hospital in Chippenham in 1952. We were given the small Gospel of St. John pamphlet by our midwife *(see image above)*, mine being Nurse Gray; and she even spelt my name right!]

**1952:** In July, the following advertisement appears in the Wiltshire Times and Trowbridge Advertiser on Saturday 05 July 1952. The property did not reach the reserve and was sold by private treaty.

*Sale of the Valuable **FREEHOLD PROPERTY**, known as **'ALEXANDER HOUSE,' HIGH STREET**,*
*immediately adjoining the Street frontage and containing; Spacious Entrance Hall, Reception rooms, Bedrooms, 3 Bathrooms, well-appointed Domestic Offices, and Secluded Pleasure and Kitchen Gardens. The Property has a frontage to the High Street of 38 feet, a depth of about 210 feet, with frontage to Post Office Lane 50 feet and a total Site Area of over 18,000 square feet, having All Main Services connected.*

**1954:** Alexander House had by now been converted into Council Housing flats. The rent charged was between 9s and 13s per week, exclusive of rates at between 6s and 7s per week. This meant that the flats were being subsidised to the extent of £340 per year. The original intention was to make these flats available to those who could afford to pay economic rents which would be 37s 6p to £2 per week.
The Wiltshire Times and Trowbridge Advertiser - Saturday 23 January lists the following eight people who were selected in January to be housed in eight of the Alexander House flats: Mr W. D. Foan, 61 Clutterbuck Road, Corsham; Mr J. P. Butcher, 33 Fuller Avenue, Corsham; Mr F. E. Featherstone, 27 Brakspear Road, Corsham; Mrs W. Simpkins, 2 Ashe Cottages, Box Hill; Mr S. G. Earl, 24 Corsham Road, Lacock; Mr J. Carolan, Thornypits Hostel; Mr H. G. Davis, 29 Corsham Road, Lacock; Mrs B. Light, 7 Corsham Road, Lacock.

## Chapter 12. Maternity Hospital, Alexander House.

**1955**: Plans are put in place to build 20 new flats for old people behind Alexander House at a total cost of £25,000 (£1,250 per flat). Rents would be from 8s 6p to 15s per week, at an estimated annual deficiency of £342.

**1956:** In November the Corsham Parish Council were told by the Calne and Chippenham District Rural Council that the new flats behind Alexander House would be called 'Alexander Gardens' but in the end it was called 'Holton House'. In the photo below right, you can see how several extensions to the back of the original building have increased the overall size and capacity of Alexander House.

*Alexander House High Street view today.*   *Side-view showing expansion to the rear over the years.*

*Left is the three story Alexander House in the early 1900s with the iron railings outside before it became a Maternity Hospital.*

*[Vera Romain Gulliford]* I was born there in 1931.

My mother had seven babies there, and said it was the only holidays she ever had.

Vera stayed there for two weeks each time. I remember as a child, if we had cuts and bruises, we were sent there from school for treatment, as the Doctor's surgery in 'The Porch' did not have a Nurse.

*[Jean Howarth]* I was born in the Maternity Hospital on 15 November 1945. During the war, radio announcers had to give their name before reading the news. One famous newsreader was called Stuart Hibberd, so apparently the nurses called me Stuart, even though I was a girl. I was the biggest baby girl there at the time and the biggest baby boy was Miles Ward. We were put end to end in a large cot. Both Miles and I grew up being told this by our respective mothers.

## Chapter 13. Mushrooms and Counterfeit Coins.

**A NEW INDUSTRY - Mushroom Culture at Corsham 1914.**

During the early years of the nineteenth century, mushroom growers in France had discovered that the relatively stable ambient temperatures and high humidity found underground in the disused limestone mines in and around Paris provided ideal conditions for the cultivation of mushrooms on an industrial scale. The French system proved successful and spread across the Channel to England shortly after the First World War. The Agaric Company established itself at Bradford-on-Avon and at Corsham where large areas of the disused Tunnel Quarry at Hudswell were used for mushroom cultivation.

In 1914, Messrs. Agaric and Co. Ltd. leased a disused portion of the underground quarries of Yockney and Hartham Park Stone Ltd. in Hudswell Corsham for the purpose of cultivating mushrooms after the French method mentioned above. The area consisted of 25 acres, each section comprising of three acres. It came under the local management of Mr W. Pepler, assisted by Mr Chibleur, and was supervised by Mr Durbec, one of the Directors of the above firm. Large Towns such as Liverpool, Edinburgh, Glasgow, London's Covent Garden, and large cruise-liners were supplied direct. A large amount of local Corsham labour was employed to prepare and cultivate the underground mushroom beds. The difficulty in the initial stages of the industry was in getting a sufficient supply of manure from the local farmers and other sources, down into the underground.

The Agaric Company's operation at Corsham was on a scale sufficient to warrant the construction of an extensive narrow-gauge railway system in the warren of underground chambers. At the same time a rudimentary ventilation system was installed consisting of a brazier of hot coals positioned at the bottom of a ventilation shaft in order to encourage the circulation of air movement by convection.

**Bad Smells at Corsham from Manure and a Plague of Flies!**

In September/October of 1915, a petition was signed by the residents of Corsham and presented to the Parish Council, complaining of bad smells arising from the removal of manure through the town. This also resulted in a plague of flies. The manure was carted from Corsham Railway Station, up Station Hill, then along Pickwick Road to the underground mushroom beds at the Hudswell Quarry along Park Lane. The smell was so bad that it lingered about for hours. Motorists would not travel along Pickwick Road if a manure cart was approaching! The stench along Park Lane 'was something dreadful'.

Following ten years of successful mushroom production, in 1926, the mushroom beds at Hudswell Corsham eventually became infected with *'plaster'*, an ineradicable virus. Within a year however, the company had taken possession of a greater part of the old Godwin's workings at Westwood (near Bradford-on-Avon) and was able to resume production there on a somewhat reduced scale. The Agaric Company eventually moved out of the underground workings in Corsham in 1928, following 10 years of mushroom production underground.

Aware of the risk of transferring the virus to their new site in Bradford-on-Avon, the Company abandoned the railway system used in Corsham. Initially at least, Agaric employed the same hot-air convection system to ventilate Westwood Quarry; the curious, square stone structure capping a quarry ventilation shaft in the garden of the large semi-detached house beside the lane, halfway between Westwood and Lye Green is a relic of that system. Agaric's tenure of Westwood Quarry was fraught with difficulties and was brought to an end by the Second World War.

Chapter 13. Mushrooms and Counterfeit Coins.

In 1935 the go-ahead was given for the construction of three ammunition sub-depots – one at Tunnel Quarry Hudswell, and the others at neighbouring Monkton Farleigh and Eastlays Ridge. Collectively, they were known as the Central Ammunition Depot (CAD). Much of Agaric's underground mushroom-growing plant/equipment at Tunnel Quarry Hudswell Corsham remained rotting away, until 1936 when it was swept away during the major refurbishment works undertaken by the War Office.

Officers supervising the work in the old underground mushroom area were surprised to find that concealed in a corner of the workings, one local entrepreneur had made clandestine use of the area to make counterfeit half-crowns. A die-press was discovered with a considerable stock of counterfeit half-crowns nearby. Arrests were subsequently made and a successful prosecution was brought against the perpetrators. But the affair was not widely publicised at the time, as it would have prejudiced the security of the project to prepare the quarries for World War II use for the storage of ammunition.

It would not take much imagination to link the counterfeit half-crown die-press mentioned above, to the following story. In fact, it's almost certain that George Gilmore Long would have known of the illegal die-press, and it is most likely to have been the source of his seemingly stash of dud half-crowns, as he lived in *Seven Shaft Cottages* 'bang on top' of the location of the underground counterfeit half-crown die-press mentioned above.

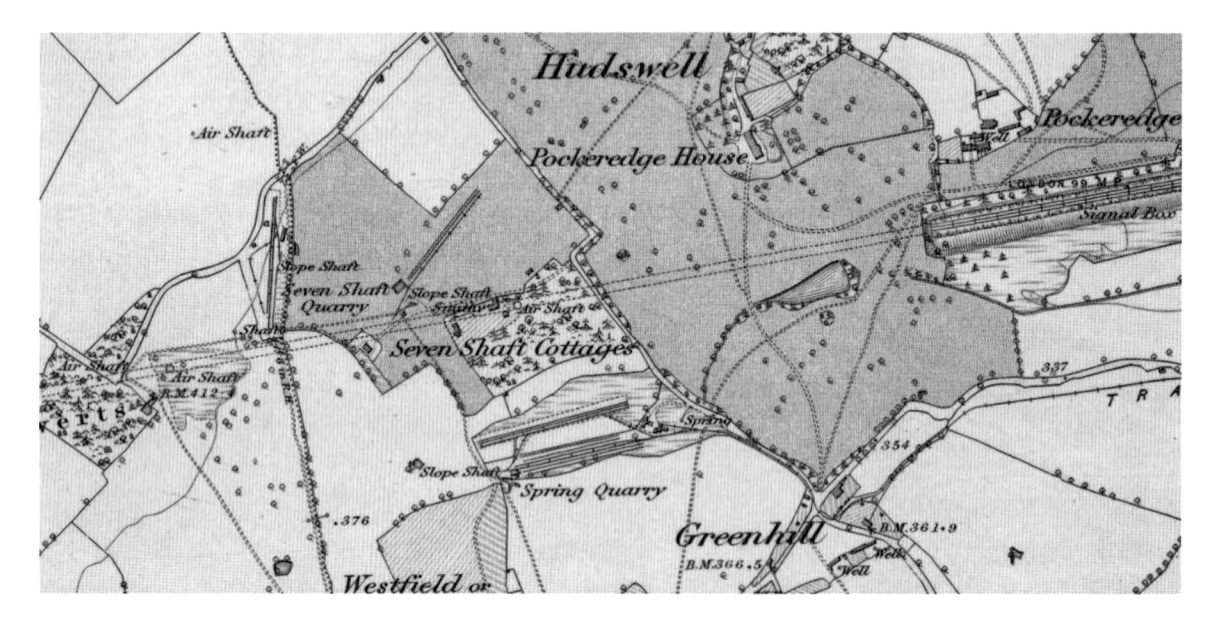

On 9 January in 1937, three Corsham people, George Gilmore Long (30) described as a salesman and dealer, Kate Long (66) his mother and Mary Long (44) his wife, all formally living in Newbridge Road, Bath three years ago but now residing in *Seven Shaft Cottages* Corsham, were arrested in Bromsgrove just south of Birmingham, for issuing counterfeit half-crowns. The *Seven Shaft Cottages* were on the Basil Hill site to the rear of the new main building, roughly where the new man-made drainage lake is these days on the rebuilt Ministry of Defence (MoD) site.

George Gilmore Long , Kate Long and Mary Long were arrested on Saturday night 2 January 1937 and remanded in custody at Bromsgrove Police Station on a charge of using counterfeit coins with intent to cheat and defraud (amongst others) Mrs Lawrence of the Midland Café Bromsgrove. They were remanded in custody until Tuesday January 12th. It was stated by PC Griffin, that the women went to the Midland Café and tendered a half-a-crown which was found to be bad. The proprietress Mrs Lawrence made a complaint to the Police and the three miscreants were arrested.

## Chapter 13. Mushrooms and Counterfeit Coins.

The three had journeyed from Corsham to Bromsgrove in a hired motorcar on 2 January, apparently for the purpose of *passing on* the bad coins and receiving genuine coins in change. It was largely due to the alertness of Mrs Lawrence of the Midland Café, that they were arrested.

The three were each sentenced at the Bromsgrove Police Court to six months imprisonment for being concerned in issuing counterfeit coins. The two women had visited the Café and tendered a counterfeit half-crown in payment for chocolates.

Mrs Lawrence had detected the bad coin and watched them go from shop to shop tendering more bad coins before informing the Police, who quickly arrested the two ladies. Later that night, George Gilmore Long who was driving his hire car around the streets looking for his two missing accomplices, stopped his car and asked a Policeman if he had seen two women shopping for him.

A Detective came up at the same time and Long was arrested and taken to the Police Station. Long stated that he had obtained £5 worth of 'dud' half-crowns from a man on the Bristol Bridge in Bristol whom he knew as 'Taffy' (and whom he had previously met at Weston-super-Mare), and got his mother and his wife to pass them on for him in various shops.

He paid £1 for forty half-crown coins and drove straight to Bromsgrove. He said he had a lot of bad luck recently and was *'up to his neck in debt'* and would not have accepted the coins if he had not been in distress.

In possession of the two women, were found considerable amounts of money, including a large proportion of two-shilling pieces, which suggested that they had been given in exchange for bad half-crowns. In the car were also many articles, including chocolate, tea, sweets, etc., denoting that a lot of small purchases had been made. Kate Long said that £3 of the money found on her was rent money.

The Bench at the Worcester Police Court made an order for a refund out of the money found on them, to be reimbursed to the shopkeepers who had been the victims. Mrs Lawrence of the Midland Café was publicly thanked for her help in bringing the three prisoners to justice.

After completing his 6-month prison sentence, George Gilmore Long, was once again in trouble in September 1937, on a charge of being drunk and disorderly in Lansdown Road, Bath.

He had been seen following a Mr Murphy on the footpath of Fountain Buildings and adopted an aggressive attitude towards Murphy - looking for a fight.

In evidence, Long admitted having drunk six pints of beer, but denied he was drunk. He declared that Murphy had insulted him. On dismissing the case, the chairman E. Shewring told Long to be more careful in the future and not to look for trouble.

But the Law eventually did catch up with George Gilmore Long when ten years later in March 1948 he was sentenced to four years servitude for being in possession of counterfeit one-shilling coins. His wife Mary was bound over and required to refrain from certain activities for a stipulated period, and to be of good behaviour.

**Acknowledgements: Kevin Gaskin and Nick McCamley for their contribution in this chapter.**

## Chapter 14. Neston - Aeroplane Crash 1941.

**Neston Glove Factory Plane Crash on Friday 7 November 1941.**

On Friday 7 November 1941 the greatest air armada of giant bombers ever sent out from Britain dropped tremendous bomb loads on Berlin and other German cities. On that same busy night, Pilot Officer Joseph Hugh Jolliffe (101070) was out on a non-operational exercise flying a Hawker Hurricane Mk IIC Serial No BD939 of 247 Squadron based in Colerne. He was engaged in a Turbinlite Exercise paired with a Douglas Havoc Night Fighter, when he crashed south of Corsham village at 20.08 hrs. The cause of the crash was thought to have been due to Pilot Officer Jolliffe's aircraft being caught in the Douglas Havoc's slipstream and stalling.

**Frederick Brixey** aged 24 of 3 Elley Green, Neston, Corsham, and **Albert James Compton** aged 40 years who lived opposite Fred at 30 Elley Green were involved in a daring rescue to try and save the pilot who had crashed in the Neston field. Both men were local WWII Air Raid Precautions (ARP) Wardens.

- **Frederick Brixey** was a Lance Corporal in the Wiltshire Regiment (9 months) but had presently been released for special work. In his civilian role, he was a Quarry Safetyman.
- **Albert James Compton** was a lorry driver for the Great Western Railway (GWR) and had been a Warden in Neston for 40 months.

At about 8 p.m. on 7 November 1941, Fred and Albert heard a loud explosion near the Neston Glove Factory at the top of Rough Street in Neston. A British Night Fighter aeroplane had crashed into the ground about 400 yards away from the Glove Factory and burst into flames.

Within minutes, Fred and Albert (who only lived about 400 yards away) arrived at the scene and found the pilot lying down on the ground with his clothes on fire close to the burning plane. They managed to douse the flames on the pilot's clothes and dragged him to a safe spot away from the wreckage.

They tried to revive the pilot, but upon arrival of the doctor, the pilot was certified dead (he had been killed instantly in the collision). A few minutes later, the Senior Warden in Neston, Mr Bernard Light *(see photo)* and two other Wardens had arrived on the scene and immediately telephoned for the Police and the Fire Brigade. In a short time, the Fire Brigade arrived along with the First Aid Party in an Ambulance from Corsham. An RAF Ambulance also arrived later.

Apart from the fact that the aeroplane was completely burnt out, the only other damage found the following morning, was a break in the main water pipe belonging to Messrs. McAlpines who were informed and arranged for the water supply to be turned off.

ARP Wardens were organised by the National Government and provided by the local authorities. The aim was to protect civilians from the danger of air-raids.

The main purpose of ARP Wardens was to patrol the streets during blackout and to ensure that no light was visible. If a light was spotted, the Warden would alert the person/people responsible by shouting something like, *"Put that light out!"* or *"Cover that window!"*

## Chapter 14. Neston - Aeroplane Crash 1941.

The ARP Wardens also reported the extent of any bomb damage and assessed the local need for help from the emergency and rescue services. They were also responsible for the handing out of gas masks and pre-fabricated air-raid shelters (such as Anderson shelters, as well as Morrison shelters). They also organised and staffed public air raid shelters. They used their knowledge of the local areas to help find and reunite family members who had been separated in the rush to find shelter from the bombs.

**Eighty-seven year old Geoff Knapp, retired farmer of Great Lypiatt Farm who was 9 years old at the time of the aeroplane crash, remembers the exact spot where it exploded onto the ground in Neston.**

In Geoff's own words: *"The crash occurred about 400 yards away from the Neston Glove Factory. I used to go to Neston School across the footpath where the aeroplane crashed. I was a bit peeved about having to go to school by the long route along the road as they would not let us go anywhere near the burnt out single-winged fighter aeroplane. At the time, we were told not to mention the crash to anyone and it never appeared in any of the newspapers. The crash site was soon surrounded by soldiers and every piece of the aeroplane was quickly removed. The exact crash location is in the corner of the field where they constructed a duct. This was covered by a drain-cover, (see photo above left) placed over the top of the repaired burst water pipe. The damage to the pipe was caused by one of the engines that had buried itself deep into the ground during the crash."*

*"Halfway up Rough Street, you will see a wooden stile alongside the Old Well House [post code SN13 9TR] on the sharp bend in the road (see photo). Climb over the stile and then follow the footpath westwards along the edge of the field.*

*In the far corner of the field to the right of the stone and wooden stile (see photo above right) you'll see the drain cover. It's right alongside the ditch where the stream now flows along in the ditch. The large drain cover marks the exact spot where the plane came down."*

In 1941, the two rescuers Fred Brixey and Albert Compton took about 5 minutes to reach the site from their homes opposite each other at No's 3 and 30 at the east end of Elley Green.

# Chapter 14. Neston - Aeroplane Crash 1941.

[**Note 1**: The Elley Green house numbers are different today. In 1941, No.30 Elley Green was opposite No.3 at the east end of Elley Green on the Lypiatt side. Today, No.30 is at the west (opposite) end of Elley Green alongside the entrance to the Leafield Industrial Estate.]

**10 November 1941:** A letter was sent to the Officer in Charge of the Chippenham Control Centre by the Head Warden, Corsham, Captain F.C. Slater of 60 Pickwick Road, explaining the incident. In his report, Captain F.C. Slater stated that the pilot was, *'found lying on the ground close to the burning plane.'*

**18 November 1941:** A separate report by Sergeant Cyril F. Smith stated that,*' Warden [Albert] James Compton of 30 Elley Green, Corsham, together with Mr Frederick Brixey of 2 Velley Green, Corsham, were on their way home when they saw this machine come down. They got to the scene of the occurrence in five minutes, and pulled the pilot out of the wreckage, his body then being under the fuselage.'*

[**Ed: Note 2:** Sergeant Cyril F. Smith's report was wrong in four places:
(1). Frederick Brixey's address was wrongly recorded as No. 2 Velley Green; it *should read* No.3 Velley Green. (2). Fred and Albert were *at home*, not *on the way home* when the accident happened. (3) The body was *not under* the fuselage. (4) Warden *Albert James* Compton - not Warden *James* Compton]

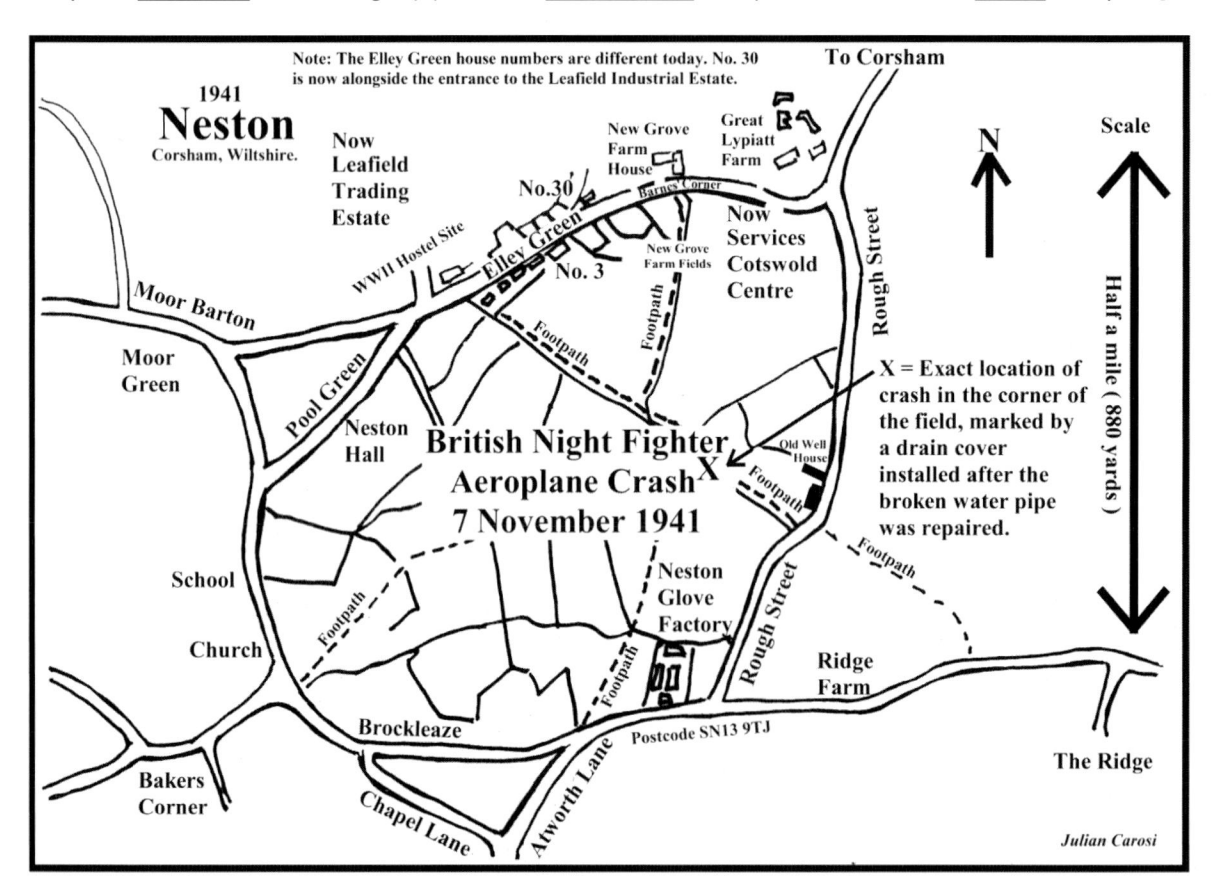

**19 November 1941:** In his report, M.F. Awdry, Controller for Civil Defence Chippenham & District, stated that: *'From the reports I have received there seems no doubt that an act of Gallantry was performed in rescuing the body of the pilot from under the burning fuselage of the plane, where there was a great possibility of explosion from the petrol tank and ammunition.*

*The promptness with which the Wardens obtained the necessary Services and the efficiency with which they did all in their power to preserve the life of the pilot, are deserving of high praise; I therefore respectfully submit their names for award or commendation.'*

## Chapter 14. Neston - Aeroplane Crash 1941.

**5 March 1942:** A letter from Sir Robert Knox of Treasury Chambers in Great George Street London, stated that there was a conflict between the report by Sergeant Cyril Smith which suggested that the body was pulled out from <u>under the burning fuselage</u>, and that of Captain Slater, which stated that the body was found <u>on the ground</u> close to the aeroplane.

As the Treasury Chambers believed that the flying clothing of the dead pilot was only slightly singed, Captain Slater's report was seen to be the correct version (i.e. the body was found <u>on the ground</u> close to the aeroplane).

**10 March 1942:** A Case No. 1865A was raised to see if the incident merited a gallantry award in favour of Fred and Albert. At this stage, because of the conflict of evidence, the decision (or not) to award a Commendation to the two rescuers, required additional evidence to be provided to the Air Ministry from Fred and Albert.

**17 March 1942:** The following statement was provided by Albert James Compton of 30 Elley Green.
*On Friday 7.11.41 at about 9. p.m. I was indoors by the fire, when I heard a crash outside. I went outside, looking towards Neston Glove Factory. I saw a large fire burning. Meeting Mr Brixey, who had also heard the crash, we went to the scene of the fire, and found that a British plane had crashed. The pilot was <u>lying by the fuselage outside the plane</u> with his clothes on fire. Mr Brixey and myself pulled him clear from the plane to a place of safety. Ammunition was exploding all the while around us. We put out the pilot's burning clothes and found he was dead. Mr [Bernard] Light, our Senior Warden, then came on the scene and phoned for Police, Ambulance, Firemen, etc.*
The statement above was witnessed by Sergeant Cyril F. Smyth at 1600hrs 17.3.42.

**19 March 1942:** Lt Col Hoel Llewellyn, Chief Constable of Wiltshire and County Air Raid Precautions (A.R.P) Controller, forwarded the above statement from Albert Compton to the authorities concerning the accident. Fred Brixey was now serving with the H.M Forces so a statement from him was not forthcoming. The Chief Constable stated that as the conflict of evidence had been cleared up, he believed that it was not necessary to obtain a further statement from Fred Brixey.

*Above is a photo of Fred Brixey on his motorcycle taken opposite his home at 3 Elley Green Neston.*

## Chapter 14. Neston - Aeroplane Crash 1941.

**27 May 1942:** The discrepancy in the evidence and the missing *'gallantry award'* papers seems to have held up the case, thus resulting in a nine-month delay in making a decision! The gathered evidence was sent by Mr E.B Davies (Office of the Regional Commissioner S.W. Region) to Miss E.F. Wormington but was lost in transit. Copies were requested.

**24 June 1942:** Copies of the five pages of missing evidence were subsequently sent by Miss E.F. Wormington to Sir Robert Knox of Treasury Chambers, to assess whether a gallantry award should be made.

**12 August 1942:** Confirmation was received that, *'The Committee were unable to approve awards to A.J. Compton and F. Brixey but have recommended letters of appreciation should be sent from the Air Council.'* Although it is recorded that the deed resulted in a considerable degree of risk to life to the rescuers Fred and Albert, the official recognition was that they would only receive a *'Letter of Appreciation'*.

[Ed - looking at the statements provided at the time, it is clear that on arrival at the scene, the pilot's body was lying near to the burning and exploding aeroplane and not underneath the fuselage as intimated in the 18 November 1941 report by Sergeant Cyril F. Smith. An RAF Letter (or Certificate) of Appreciation is an Honorary - Non-Monetary recognition. It recognizes individuals for a variety of accomplishments that do not fall under the performance awards category for an act, or service that is above average. I'd like to think that Fred and Albert deserved a bit more than a 'Letter of Appreciation' for their act in trying to save the life of the pilot amongst the explosions and fire from the burning aeroplane.]

*[Wiltshire Airfields in the Second World War by David Berryman.]* Fighter Command had just made a new sector at Colerne within its No.10 Group which had its Headquarters in nearby RAF Rudloe Manor. The first fighter unit to arrive was No.87 Squadron on 28 November 1940 with their Hawker Hurricane Mk.Is.

As well as its role as day fighter defence, its B Flight was also involved in night fighting. Its Hurricanes were painted black overall and were fitted with flame-damping exhausts. In April, Gloucester's No.501 Squadron arrived in Colerne, replacing their Hurricanes with Spitfires which flew covey escort patrols on low-level strikes in occupied Europe. On 18 June 1941 the No.316 (City of Warsaw) Squadron moved from Pembry in South Wales into Colerne with their Hurricanes. They were employed on convoy patrols in the British Channel and they took part in Operation Sunrise, escorting Hamden bombers on a raid. No.316 Squadron moved out to Culmhead in August 1941.

**The Helmore/GEC Turbinlite: A 2,700 million candela searchlight fitted in the nose of a number of British Douglas Havoc night fighters.**

To improve nocturnal air defences, an aircraft-mounted searchlight was created by Wing Commander W Helmore. The idea was that a twin-engine aircraft would carry the Airborne Interception (AI) Radar and a large searchlight (called 'Turbinlite') mounted on its nose.

It would be accompanied by a fighter aircraft known as a Satellite. Once an enemy plane was located on the Radar it would *'close in'* and illuminate the enemy target, allowing the Satellite aircraft to attack.

## Chapter 14. Neston - Aeroplane Crash 1941.

**Ten Turbinlite flights were formed, two at Colerne.**

**Flight No.1454**: Formed on 4 July 1941 with Douglas Boston and Douglas Havoc aircraft equipped with Turbinlite; it was partnered with 87 Squadron. The Commanding Officer between October 1941 - March 1942 was Sqn.Ldr. W.G. Moseby.

**Flight No.1457**: Formed on 15 September 1941 and paired with No.247 Squadron. The Commanding Officer between 15 September 1941 - May 1942 was Sqn.Ldr. J.R. Watson. By 15 November 1941 Flight No. 1457 had moved to RAF Predannack, Cornwall.

*The awesome Helmore/GEC Turbinlite 2,700 million candela searchlight, while bright, was decidedly not the best for aerodynamic design, with a large flat glass surface.*

Aircraft used between June 1941-January 1942 were the Hawker Hurricane IIA and IIB. In September 1941 the squadron converted to using the long range Hurricane IIB, and began to fly intruder missions over north western France.

The Turbinlite scheme was not a success and ended in January 1943.

**Note 3:** On the night of 23 October 1941, whilst on a Turbinlite searchlight exercise at RAF Colerne (two weeks before the Neston aeroplane crash on 7 November 1941), another Colerne aeroplane crashed and was destroyed.

**Hawker Hurricane MK-IIC RAF** *(Copyright © 2019 courtesy of BAE Systems. All rights reserved).*

In the 1939 census prior to the war Joseph Jollife's father John, who lived in Twickenham, was a Staff Officer in the Ministry of Food which must have been quite a responsibility leading up to and during the war, workng as a Civil Servant with the Board of Trade (Mercantile Marine Office).

Twenty year-old Joseph Jolliffe's 7 November 1941 death record in the Chippenham Register shown below, states that he was on a non-operational flight in a Hawker Hurricane MK-IIC and died from multiple injuries. The entry shows his home address at the time as Portman Court, London W1.

Chapter 14. Neston - Aeroplane Crash 1941.

| Registration District CHIPPENHAM. |
| --- |
| 1941. DEATHS in the Sub-District of CORSHAM in the County of WILTS. |

| No. | When and Where Died. | Name and Surname. | Sex. | Age. | Rank or Profession. | Cause of Death. | Signature, Description, and Residence of Informant. | When Registered. | Signature of Registrar. |
| --- | --- | --- | --- | --- | --- | --- | --- | --- | --- |
| 234 | Seventh November 1941. Neston Corsham RD. | Joseph Hugh Jolliffe | male | 20 years | Late of Portman Court London W.1. Pilot officer Royal Air Force | Multiple injuries caused by the accidental crash of a Hurricane 2.c. aircraft of which he was the pilot while engaged on a non-operational flight. | Certificate received from Reginald A.C. Forrester Deputy Coroner for County of Wilts - Inquest held 10 November 1941 | Fifteenth November 1941 | R Norton Registrar |

**Pilot Officer Joseph Hugh Jolliffe aged 20.**

247 Squadron. Service no 101070.
*RAF Volunteer Reserve (RAFVR).
Died 7th November 1941.
Death recorded in Chippenham.
Son of John Henry and Hilda Louisa Jolliffe. John and Hilda (nee Scutt) married in 1915 and had a daughter Mary later that year while living in London.

They then moved to Devon and sons Henry Thomas (10 August 1917), Peter Eric (23 December 1918) and Joseph Hugh (known as Hugh) (7 August 1921) were all born in Plympton in Plymouth.

The three brothers were confirmed together in the largest parish church in Hertfordshire St Mary's Church, Hitchin, by His Lordship Bishop Butt on 8 November 1931.

*J.H. Jolliffe: Brookwood Military Cemetery, Surrey. Grave Ref. 21. A. 18.*

The three Jolliffe brothers went to St Michael's College, Hitchin, in Hertfordshire *(see photo below)*.

This was a Catholic school for boys, which was administered by priests from two religious orders; the Edmundians from 1903 to 1925 and from 1925 to 1968 by the Assumptionists. The school in Hitchin closed in 1968, and moved to Stevenage. Joseph Hugh Jolliffe's death in 1941 was eventually reported on page 28 (News of the Old Boys) in the St Michaels College Magazine Volume XIX Summer 1945.

## Chapter 14. Neston - Aeroplane Crash 1941.

Located 30 miles from London in Surrey, Brookwood Military Cemetery is the largest Commonwealth War Graves Commission (CWGC) cemetery in the United Kingdom. The cemetery contains the graves of more than 1,600 servicemen of the British Empire in the First World War and over 3,470 from the Second World War. Brookwood Military Cemetery lies adjacent to Brookwood Cemetery (The London Necropolis), a vast space which covers 500 acres.

**Note 4:** The Royal Air Force Volunteer Reserve (RAFVR) was formed in July 1936 to provide individuals to supplement the Auxiliary Air Force (AAF) which was formed in 1925 by the local Territorial Associations.

**Note 5: AIR81/6598:** On 24 May 1941 Leading Aircraftman J. H. Jolliffe was previously injured in a heavy landing, in a Hurricane P3588, at 9 Service Flying Training School on 24 May 1941. (ref: C16755895).

**Note 6:** The RAF Casualty File relating to the loss of BD939 at Neston on 7 November 1941, are in the process of being transferred from the MOD's RAF Historical Branch to The National Archives and should be available for viewing by the public later in 2019.

**GREATEST EVER RAID ON BERLIN. Giant Bombers Battle Through Freak Storm.**
On the same night that the night fighter plane crashed into the field in Neston, Friday 7 November 1941, the *Sunday Post* and *The People* newspapers on Sunday 9 November 1941 reported the following:

**Sunday Post 9 November 1941:**
**GREATEST EVER RAID ON BERLIN. Giant Bombers Battle Through Freak Storm.**
The greatest air armada of giant bombers ever sent out from Britain dropped tremendous bomb loads on Berlin and other German cities on Friday night *[7 November 1941]*. It is estimated between 300 and 500 aircraft were engaged.

They flew through the worst possible weather, through thunderstorms, and in severe icing conditions. Yet large numbers of our biggest bombers, four-engined Stirlings and Halifaxes, as well as Wellingtons and Whitleys, reached the German capital, which was the chief target. They heavily bombed their objectives, often after waiting for a hole in the clouds. Cologne and Mannheim were among other towns bombed.

It was over the interior of Germany [that] a sudden phenomenal change in the weather struck our raiders. Many of them had already attacked their targets when the storms broke. But these conditions, unforeseen when the huge-scale offensive was planned a few hours before, trapped our bombers and 37 are reported missing.

It can be assumed that many of our planes were forced down by icing-up or from lack of petrol. Reports of landings have come from Sweden and France.

173

# Chapter 14. Neston - Aeroplane Crash 1941.

**The People Newspaper 9 November 1941:**

**FREAK STORM HITS RAF ARMADA.**
**The largest force of bombers ever sent by the RAF OVER GERMANY SUDDENLY RAN INTO FREAK WEATHER ON FRIDAY NIGHT WITH THE RESULT THAT 37 OF OUR PLANES WERE LOST. MORE THAN HALF OF THESE WERE FORCED DOWN BY THUNDERSTORMS AND THICK ICE.**

By far the biggest force, including many heavy bombers, hammered Berlin. Though the temperature was as low as minus 34 degrees, they forced their way through the storm to bomb their targets successfully.

**DOWN ON THE SEA:** Some of our planes, it is known, came down in the sea while making for home, but there is no reason to doubt that others landed safely in German-occupied territory. The men who came home told of the phenomenal weather on the way to Berlin.

*"I went to the astro-dome to take some sights,"* said the observer of a Wellington, *"and to keep my hands free I wore only my silk inner gloves. It was agonising just to touch the sextant. The pain bit into my fingers as though they were being scalded. When I went to pick up my leather gloves they were frozen stiff as a board. I saw long icicles on the bottom of the pilot's oxygen mask. He broke one off and threw it at me to show that he was keeping cheerful enough. Another navigator on the Berlin route found cloud thick and flat like a woolly blanket. Moisture inside the aircraft froze and there was frost on my chin like a beard,"* he said.

**IT IS THE WORST RAID BERLIN HAS EVER KNOWN:**

Cologne and Mannheim bore the main weight of attacks which included many other German cities and towns. When the bombing was done, many of our planes found that their battle with the storm and ice had so reduced their petrol supplies that they had to make a dash for neutral territory. One came down in the Vosges district of France, the crew of three being saved. A four-engined bomber, presumably a Stirling, made a forced landing on the south coast of Sweden. The crew of eight were unhurt. They saved all their belongings and then set their plane on fire. A third RAF plane unloaded its incendiaries harmlessly in a field In Switzerland, preliminary to an attempt to land. Three more British planes flew over Oslo and dropped their remaining bombs before making forced landings near the city. Four of the airmen were captured and another two were found dead.

*End of Newspaper Reports.*

*[Ed: It would be fitting if some sort of discreet memorial - maybe a simple brass plaque - could be placed at the crash location in Neston to remember the 20 year-old Joseph.]*

> *In memory of 20 year-old*
> **Officer Joseph Hugh Jolliffe** *(101070)*
> who died here at this spot in Neston, in his
> Hawker Hurricane Ser. No. BD939 Mk-IIC RAF in
> the service of his country.
> **On 7th November 1941**

## Chapter 15. Neston - Charlie Barnes and his three cows!

*[Ed: Interview with retired farmer of Great Lypiatt Farm Geoff Knapp on 10 February 2019]:*

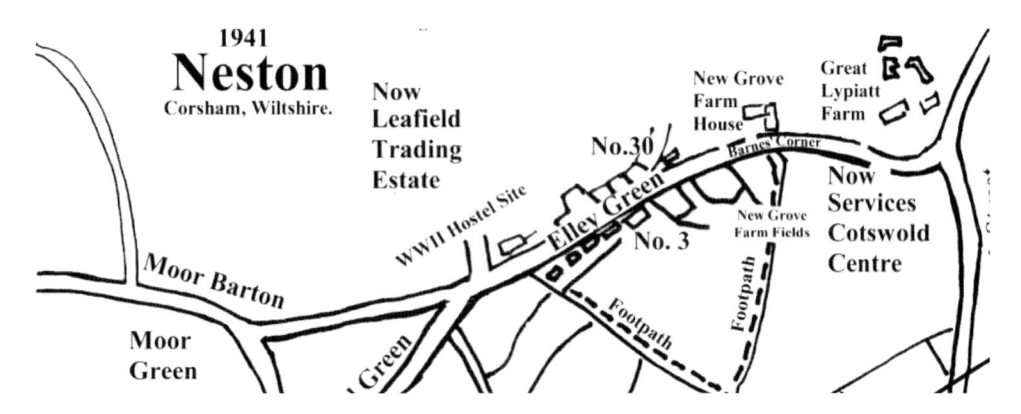

In the early 1900s, George Pargiter Fuller, MP (8 January 1833 – 2 April 1927) known locally as G.P Fuller, established a number of smallholdings on the Neston Estate. The aim was to help local men who were unemployed and later those who had retuned from the Great War, by providing them with some form of productive employment. In 1916, this small nucleus of neighbouring farmers formed a group called the 'Atworth and District Agricultural Society Ltd'.

This enabled the group to buy agricultural products in bulk, therefore saving money by using economies of scale, i.e. the more they bought, the cheaper it was. In 1917, they amalgamated with the Corsham Allotment Society and later in 1918 with the Melksham Poultry Association. At the beginning, they stored their products in a barn at Atworth, then later into larger premises alongside the A4 Melksham roundabout on the Bath Road in Melksham. Until 1975 the co-operative was known as Wiltshire Farmers Ltd. then the 'West of England Farmers Ltd'. In 1989 they merged with West Midlands Farmers (WMF). In 1999 WMF and Midland Shires Farmers formed to become Countrywide Farmers. In 2018, Countrywide Farmers went into administration.

**Eighty-seven year old Geoff Knapp, recalls life in Neston after WWI:** *"After the Great War, G.P. Fuller, MP helped returning soldiers and unemployed local men to set up smallholdings on his land to make a living. G.P. Fuller also had a saw mill at the back of his home Neston House on the road to Atworth. If anyone was unemployed in Corsham, they could always get a job in the saw mill. He was a superb person."*

Geoff Knapp *continues: "One particular smallholding was worked for many years by Charlie Barnes (Charles George Barnes), who was originally a stranger to Corsham. Charlie hailed from the Isle of Wight, and having arrived at Southampton with his three cows tied together by a halter, he started to looking for work by walking north with his cows trailing behind him! He eventually arrived at Corsham after calling in at every farm on the way up; he was fed, along with his cows by the friendly farmers. When he arrived in Neston, G.P. Fuller allowed Charlie to set up a small-holding called New Grove Farm adjoining the Lypiatt Cottages - alongside the sharp bend - a spot later known locally as Barnes' Corner. Once he was settled, his wife Henrietta and daughter Vi joined him in their new home.*

*Charlie's father (also from the Isle of Wight) joined him later, and between them, they helped to provided Neston with milk for many years, delivered on his bicycle which had a little carriage attached to it like a sidecar. The churns and measuring cups where stored inside the sidecar."*

## Chapter 15. Neston - Charlie Barnes and his three cows!

Charlie Barnes' smallholding was mainly across the road from his house, and consisted of three small fields that lay behind Fred Brixey's house at 3 Elley Green. He also had another field where he kept his cows on the north side of Elley Green. *[Jennifer Oatley] "He used to use the garden path at Yew Tree Cottage to access his cows in the field behind our house.* When the bend at Lypiatt Cottages was flooded in the 26 June 1935 storm at Corsham, Charlie and his wife took in a number of children who were stranded there because of the flooding, after being kept in at school because of the storm. They gave the children a meal whilst they waited for a hay cart to be sent from Great Lypiatt Farm to rescue them.

*New Grove Farm Neston.*              *Barnes' Corner in Neston.*

Charlie's daughter Vi Barnes was the Doctors' receptionist for a time, in the Porch Surgery, High St Corsham and sang in the Neston choir. She also became the Divisional Superintendant of the local Ladies' Division of the Corsham's St John Ambulance and lived at *Bakers Corner* where Charlie later moved to in Neston. Charlie believed that to attain a long life - snuff and cigarettes were the answer! Charlie's wife Henrietta passed away on 17 Dec. 1945 leaving £759 in her will (£23,000 in today's money).

*Photo courtesy of Dennis Cole/Deborah Morgan shows Neston Church Choir (c1955). Left to right:* **Back Row includes:** *Jack Nash, Thelma Chapel, Margaret Watts, Unknown, Mr Spence (Vicar), Margaret Gilbert, Shirley Freegard, Walt Shepherd.* **Front row:** *Mrs Chapel, Gaynor Jefferies, Ethel Shepherd,* **Vi Barnes,** *Pam Bryant, Joyce Shepherd.*

# Chapter 16. Neston - Glove Factory

**NESTON Glove Factory:** *Photo shows the empty factory following a fire in December 2018.*

[Ed. The Glove Factory at Neston seems to have had its fair share of serious fires over the years. But you've got to hand it to them; they still managed to keep people in employment for many years.]

**1906:** Local landowner Mr G. P. Fuller wanted to provide some work for those ladies who did not wish to go into service. In 1906 he established the Neston Glove Factory in an existing barn at the top corner of Rough Street in Neston. Those employed there were known as leather dressers. The building was originally used as a coach house in the care of Harry May. Later, sheepskins were 'dressed' there in preparation for glove cutting.

**1911:** Samuel Davis is believed to have been an owner of the property when it was known as *'Davis, May & Co.'*. His company first appeared on page 168 of the 1911 Kelly's Directory.

**1916:** The site was now known as the 'Neston Glove Factory' and at its height was employing 60 people in the factory and 60 outworkers.

**1929:** *The Wiltshire Times and Trowbridge Advertiser - Saturday 7 September 1929 - reported the following STRIKE AT NESTON GLOVE WORKS:* 'It is interesting to recall the very small beginning of the Neston Glove Works, which originally commenced in a barn in Boyd's farm by the men employed there. Even though a number of the working men put money and great effort into the venture, it was only just about surviving. The late Mr G. P. Fuller then took over the business to see if he could help provide an additional industry in the neighbourhood. By his help, the factory was built with sheds and power and gradually increased until nearly 200 (including outworkers) were employed.

Surprise was caused on Saturday when about eighteen glove cutters, wheelers and pieceworkers engaged at the Neston Glove Company [factory], ceased work at 12.50p.m. The dispute concerned the number of apprentices used in the factory. From what we can gather, there was a question of wages or working conditions in dispute. The men were brought out by their Unions, because the employers wanted to use more apprentices than was allowed - i.e. one apprentice to five skilled men. This is the first time any trouble has arisen at the factory and it is hoped that happy relations which have existed for so many years will soon be re-established again and peace reign in the industry.'

## Chapter 16. Neston - Glove Factory

**1930:** In the 1930s to 1950s the Neston Glove Factory was producing superior leather gloves for ladies and gents and had contracts with many of the mail order companies of the day, such as [Great Universal Stores] GUS, Kay's and Dent's. There was a national depression in the glove trade and in some districts this was being interpreted due to the Government's attitude towards Safeguarding in the industry. *[Safeguarding was a term used in the United Kingdom and Ireland to denote measures to protect the health, well-being and human rights of individuals, which allow people — especially children, young people and vulnerable adults — to live free from abuse, harm and neglect.]*

The Neston factory employed local Corsham people, either on the premises, or in work at home, and fully two-thirds of these had been stopped from working. It was hoped that the suspension would only last for a month and that it would be possible to resume normal activities on 2 January. In the meantime the loss of employment was a great blow to the district.

Mr G. H. Laurence questioned the representative and said that he had nothing to add to a statement which had appeared, and the relation of *Safeguarding* of the firm's business was a matter of opinion. There was depression in other industries and unemployment in them (to some extent) had led to trade in the glove business becoming slack. But there was no cause of alarm, for as far they could see, the stoppage would not exceed a month. It was further stated that during the time that the *Safeguarding Act* had been in operation, it had stimulated the glove trade to allow more workers to be employed. But this meant that more workers were now affected because of the downturn in trade. More than had been the case on previous occasions when the factory had been on short-time working. Buyers were hesitating about purchasing till they had seen what foreign lines were available and how far these would affect homemade goods. There was another glove factory recently started in Corsham where trade was more flourishing but it may be that this factory was not affected by *Safeguarding*, if it produced a different class of goods than those produced at Neston.

In the 1930s the Neston Glove Factory had a cricket team, and they practised in the lunch hour in the orchard close by.

**1940:** *The Wiltshire Times and Trowbridge Advertiser - Saturday 3 February 1940 reported the following: THREE FIRES IN ONE DAY. Serious Neston Fire:* Three Fires occurred in the district during Monday, one of them involving the Glove Factory [at Neston] where the damage was so serious that many workers were not able to be employed.

The first call was to the famous Flemish Buildings in the High Street, where a chimney was found to be blazing furiously. Thankfully, Capt. A. P. Methuen and Chief Officer A. J. Hobbs were able to control the flames by means of extinguishers.

In the early evening, a second call was received from a gardener's cottage, occupied by Mr J. Waite, opposite Pickwick House. Mrs Waite had smelt burning for some hours and when her son made an investigation via a hole in the wall she decided that expert assistance was necessary. Chief Officer Hobbs and three firemen found that the trouble was caused by a stove in the stable where soldiers were billeted. A joist running parallel with the beam which held up the roof of the bedroom, was almost burnt through and had to be cut away.

The third call came after the firemen had been home little more than ten minutes. This was the most serious fire in the district for more than 20 years and involved the Neston Glove Factory. Soon after 9.30 p.m. P.S. Treen discovered the fire and immediately notified Mr H. C. Moss, Director of the Company,

## Chapter 16. Neston - Glove Factory

who lived nearby. Mr H. C. Moss quickly raised the alarm. P.C. Axford was soon on the scene, together with the Corsham Brigade.

Fanned by the wind, the flames spread rapidly and despite the gallant efforts of the firemen, the cutting shop, webbing shop and leather store soon became a raging furnace. Meanwhile, the Chippenham Brigade had been summoned and under Chief Officer Clarke got their hoses into play with water from a nearby reservoir. Gradually, the fire was under control. Great assistance was given by the Police, Special Police and Military, who removed valuable papers and books from the offices. The firemen were able to save a portion of the premises, especially a large hall containing nearly 100 machines.

By 1.30 a.m. the brigades were able to return to their stations, with certain Corsham men being left there on duty all night. Originally, the cause of the fire was unknown. Mr Moss stated that the Company had six months orders on hand and unless alternative premises could be found, between 100 and 150 workers would be out of work. The damage was estimated at about £1,000 [£40,000 in today's money!]

*The following letter from Mr Harris appeared a week later in the Wiltshire Times and Trowbridge Advertiser - Saturday 10 February:* THE FIRE AT NESTON GLOVE FACTORY: 'Sir: May I be allowed to correct some misstatements that have appeared in print regarding the fire at the Neston Glove Factory on the night of the 29th.

The Chippenham Fire Brigade needs no word of praise from Corsham for its efficiency, but it is just to its Captain to say that the promptitude of his appearance at the scene, after the telephone call had gone through, was the major factor that saved the Glove Factory.

The local Fire Brigade men of Corsham, despite failure of telephone calls and the state of the lanes, were promptly at their Station only to find that their fire engine, which has done yeoman service over a long period of years, would not start. To save time Mr Hobbs and several of the men went ahead with hose, pump, and fire extinguishers, hoping to mitigate the severity of the blaze until the arrival of their own engine and the Chippenham Brigade. Incidentally, there was no shortage of water.

The Corsham Fire Brigade has a long and honourable history and ever since the Fire Brigades Act of 1938 was passed, the Parochial Committee has been urging their foster parent, the Rural District Council, to supply the equipment needed to enable the brigade to continue its useful work. Alas, the *best laid schemes of mice and men will oft go astray;* the complications of many authorities and indecision, perhaps inevitable, have held up all progress. It is now believed that definite steps have been taken, with the full approval of the Home Office, to place this brigade in a sound position to act as an effective subsidiary unit.

The writer is sure that the *esprit-de-corps* of Corsham firemen of the past will not fail in the future, and that continuity of good service, with some re-organisation of personnel, will be maintained. Further, may word of praise be given to the repair staff of the Post Office Telephone Service. Its men have been untiring in their efforts to repair the damage to poles and lines done by our extraordinary and severe weather. Had our line to Chippenham not been working - it was out of order earlier in the day—it is doubtful if the Glove Factory could have been saved. Yours faithfully, Ethelred House, A. H. HARRIS, Corsham.'

**1947:** White, 'shammy' leather elbow gloves were made in the Neston Glove Factory and sold to ladies attending the future Queen Elizabeth ll's wedding in 1947.

# Chapter 16. Neston - Glove Factory

**1948:** *Neston Glove Factory photo (courtesy of Mrs Kim Goodridge (nee Hardiman).*

Kim's father Walter (Wally) Hardiman is second from the left. Glove Factory Manager Mr Moss is the tall gentleman eighth from the left. Wally Hardiman lived at 32 Elley Green, and along with his wife Dorothy, housed four Jewish evacuees at different times in their house. These were evacuated from Germany during WWII with the help of the Factory owner Mr Moss who was Jewish himself. One of the evacuees was a German clockmaker named George Wiel.

**1953:** *The Wiltshire Times and Trowbridge Advertiser - Saturday 21 February reported the sad news of a WOMAN'S SUICIDE Depressed, for No Apparent Reason:* 'No reason why a forewoman at the Neston Glove Factory, whose body was found in a static water tank in the factory grounds, should have taken her life, was forthcoming at an inquest at Chippenham on Saturday afternoon. The Wiltshire Coroner (Mr Harold Dale) returned a verdict of suicide while her mind was depressed on Miss Margaret Ida Bowden, aged 43, of 90 East View, Whitley, Melksham, who was found drowned on Thursday afternoon. Miss Bowden's father, with whom she lived, stated that until about a month ago his daughter appeared to be in good health. She then became depressed but refused to see a doctor. For the first three days of last week she seemed to be a lot better and showed symptoms of picking up well. She had no worries. She had a good mother and father, and a good home. They knew of nothing to worry her. If she was worrying about her work she never said anything at home. On Thursday she seemed better than she had been for some months, and was quite jolly. She had not had the flu, but witnesses agreed with the Coroner that she had probably been *run down* at this time of the year.'

**Said There Was Nothing Wrong**

Harry Light of Moor Green, Corsham, who works at the Glove Factory on three afternoons a week, said he had known Miss Bowden for 40 years. During the past three weeks he had noticed that she had been crying, but she assured him that there was nothing the matter. There was no trouble at the factory to account for her depression. She often seemed deep in thought. He would ask her if she was all right. At first she would not reply. Then suddenly she would say: "*Did you speak to me?*" He noticed on Thursday that she had been crying, but in reply to his question, she said there was nothing wrong. Later a search was made as she was missing, and he dragged her from the water tank. For half-an hour until the Police and Ambulance arrived he applied artificial respiration but could not resuscitate him.

## Chapter 16. Neston - Glove Factory

Answering the Coroner, Mr Light said Miss Bowden's duties would not take her to the tank. It was between 20 and 30 ft. across and contained some 7 ft. of water. She would be going out of her way to get in there. Dr. K. A. Colenso said the body had been in the tank for some time. The shock of immersion on such a cold day would accelerate death. There were no marks of violence, and death was due to drowning.

**Depressed, for No Apparent Reason.** Mrs Dorothy Light, of 3 Neston, employed at the Factory, confirmed that lately for no apparent reason. Miss Bowden had been depressed. She cried quite a lot. Miss Bowden spoke to the witness at her machine twice on Thursday afternoon. The witness asked her how her mother and sister were; they had been ill. She also asked her if she had a headache, as she often had one, and she replied she did not. Miss Bowden was trembling, but in reply to a question said she was not cold. P.C. Burchell said that when he arrived with Police Sgt. Hayward at 4.07 p.m. the body was just being taken out of the tank. There was no sign of life but artificial respiration was used in the Ambulance until the hospital was reached. The tank was surrounded by wire 3ft. 6in. high, except where the tank joined a smaller one. There was no possibility of her having fallen in. The Coroner said it was quite clear that Miss Bowden died from drowning and that lately her spirits had been low. She evidently got depressed and low, but would not see a doctor. If she had done so he would probably have told her she would be better off doing something rather than staying at home. **R.I.P Miss Bowden.**

**1965:** Following closure of the factory, the buildings were taken over by Mr Brixey, who had worked for Dowty [in Atworth] as an engineer. Later there was a new owner, Bob Sibley, who dealt in plastics and tyres. **Note:** Mr Brixley could possiby be related to Frederick Brixey see *Neston - Aeroplane Crash 1941*.

**2014:** Over the years, there have been several plans for the site, but all have come to nothing. In February, full planning permission was granted to convert the three Glove Factory buildings on the site into 10 residential dwellings. However, this permission lapsed with no works taking place. At this time the buildings were being used to store plastic toys and ten tonnes of tyres.

On Monday 7 April the factory buildings at Brockleaze containing ten tonnes of tyres and plastic toys for recycling were destroyed by fire, and an investigation was commenced as to the cause. Thus another hundred years of local history disappears and will be unknown to those who come after. Seven fire crews spent the night tackling the huge fire.

*Photo courtesy of Gazette & Herald 2014.* The owner of the former Neston Factory said that youths trespassing on the site were a common problem.

The buildings were left empty, unsecured, unprotected and rapidly declining. The cause turned out to be arson.

Both of Corsham's fire crews were called to the fire just after 7pm, after the items inside caught fire, causing thick plumes of black smoke which were seen for miles around.

## Chapter 16. Neston - Glove Factory

Site owner Bob Sibley said at the time: *"I leave all the doors open now because every time I put locks on the doors someone comes and takes them off, and I had all the electric wiring stripped out 18 months ago. It had to be started deliberately, simply because in this weather we just wouldn't get the heat that would make them go up. Kids have been a problem there breaking in and smashing windows for a long time, it's just a playground for them."*

Planning permission had been approved to convert the Factory into ten flats, by Mr Sibley, but he was unsure when work would now be able to start. He said: *"According to the Fire Brigade the building is unsafe, so there is a lot of work to go on there."*

**2016:** In October another outline application for complete demolition of the buildings and replacement with 10 dwellings was submitted.

**2017:** The 2016 application was refused in February 2017. The application was resubmitted in July and withdrawn in November.

**2018:** In April a further planning application was made that would retain the two storey building in order to convert it to one dwelling, albeit with considerable alteration, but demolish the remaining structures, (against the wishes of the Senior Conservation Officer), and erect 5 detached houses in their place. Outline Planning Permission (with conditions) was granted in September. The building that burned down in 2018 on the 28th December is the building that would have been converted to a dwelling, and so another hundred years of local history has disappeared and is lost to future generations.

Caroline Ridgwell, Senior Conservation Officer with Wiltshire Council has said of the site, *"The age of the buildings and their former use as a Glove Factory gives significance to the site due to the aesthetic, communal, evidential and historical value. The buildings and site however, are non-designated heritage assets, (the area does not have a local list), that hold architectural interest and yield evidence about former industries and local employment that were once commonplace but are now far less so."*

*2018: Once again, another fire rages in the old Neston Glove Factory.*

## Chapter 16. Neston - Glove Factory

[*Gazette & Herald 3 January 2019: Glove Factory Fire*]: FIREFIGHTERS battled a blaze last Friday [28 December 2018] at Neston at the former Glove Factory in the village. Crews from four stations dealt with the fire in the disused building in Rough Street.

Fire fighters from Chippenham, Melksham, Bradford on Avon and Bath brought the fire under control after villagers alerted the emergency services when they saw huge columns of black smoke. The fire ripped through the building, leaving parts of the structure unsafe. The fire was under control within three hours of the outbreak at around noon on 28 December.

*2018: Fire rages in the old Neston Glove Factory and leaves it a wreck once again.*

**ANOTHER CORSHAM GLOVE FACTORY IN PAUL STREET:**

Photo shows Paul Street Glove Factory early 1950s. Standing left to right: Sheila Sawyer, Irene Tilley, June Muzelle, Betty Ballen, Joan Green.

Sitting left to right: Unknown ?, Maureen Kelly, Philomena South, Ruby ?

*Photo courtesy of Annette Wilson and Mike Wilson from their book, 'Around Corsham and Box'.*

## Chapter 16. Neston - Glove Factory

In days gone past, if you entered Paul Street, the first thing you would have seen on your right, was the green double-fronted wooden garage door. Behind those doors was another Corsham Glove Factory.

In its prime, this little old factory at No. 2 Paul Street owned by Mr Woods, employed up to 60 people and was an important source of local employment, particularly for the ladies of our town. The building was used previously for the assembly of gas masks during WWII. The original bill for water rates in those days was 5 pence per year.

The Paul Street Glove Factory was purchased by Derek Unwin at the end of 1973 for £6,500. He set up an upholstery service there and called it *Derek Unwin Upholsterers*. When Derek sadly passed away, his sons Mark and Tim carried on the upholstery business. **R.I.P Derek.**

If you entered those doors, you would have travelled back nearly 50 years, and witnessed a space many times bigger than would seem possible from that small frontage facing onto Paul Street.

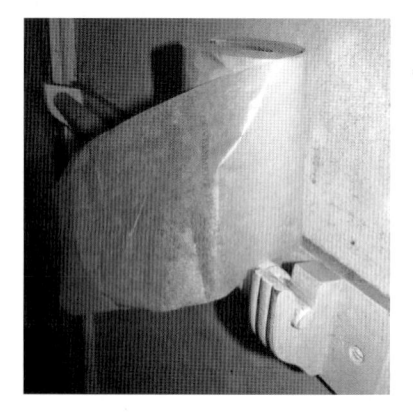

[Ed: When I visited there in 2015 it was like entering the Tardis and travelling back in time. Even the cobwebs seemed 40 years old! And there was even a roll of Government Property Izal-like loo paper (enough to make your eyes water) in the little boy's room. Yikes!]

The factory closed in April 2015 and Mark and Tim moved to new premises in Lypiatt Road where their business is still thriving today (2019).

*Brothers Tim & Mark Unwin in 2015 Paul Street.*   *Dad Derek working away on his sewing machine.*

When Derek passed away, his coat and jackets remained hanging on the wall in the Paul Street factory in memory of him, untouched for another twenty years! His sons Mark and Tim Unwin carried on working in that factory for 40+ years.

If you need any upholstery work done, you can contact Mark and Tim Unwin on their original Corsham Tel. No. 01249-713021.

## Chapter 17. Olga Lehmann's Underground Corsham Murals.

*[Ed - NOTE - the original murals underground are coloured and not black and white as shown here!]*

*Image above © the artist's estate, courtesy of Olga Lehmann's son Paul Huson.*

**Central Ammunition Depot (CAD).**

Between the First and Second World Wars, a new role was found for the old Bath stone workings in and around Corsham and Box. War clouds were gathering in Europe and a safe depository for ammunition was urgently needed to prevent attack by German aircraft. In 1935, following extensive survey of the old underground workings, the War Office decided to construct three huge underground ammunition sub-depots known as the Central Ammunition Depot (CAD). One at Tunnel Quarry in Hudswell, one at nearby Eastlays Ridge near Neston and a third depot deep under the hill at neighbouring Monkton Farleigh on the west side of Box. Originally, it was estimated that it would take four years to complete the refurbishment of the many miles of quarries. The first section - or 'district' - was completed by April 1938. The Tunnel Quarry sub-depot at Hudswell in Corsham consisted eventually of ten 'districts', each with approximately five acres of floor space. This was a massive undertaking which required strengthening the remaining stone support pillars, lining the tunnel roof with asbestos sheeting, constructing roads and supplying services such as electric and water. Giant fans were installed to draw in fresh air and expel the stale, producing a stable atmosphere of 65°F and 80% humidity. Some of the surface fans can still be seen under the grass hillocks beside Park Lane at Hudswell.

At first, the ammunition was lowered down a converted air-shaft by means of a steam winch. Later, when all of the underground storage 'districts' had been built, the ammunition arrived by road and by rail via Thingley Junction and was unloaded at Surface Loading Platforms (SLP), one located at each sub-depot.

## Chapter 17. Olga Lehmann's Underground Corsham Murals.

The huge platform building at Tunnel Quarry can still be seen halfway along Spring Lane on the Basil Hill site. Behind the large doors are three huge slope shafts with conveyor belts to take the ammunition down 90-100 feet into the tunnels and back up again when required. The Tunnel Quarry sub-depot had a standard gauge underground railway, complete with two platforms, while the other sub-depots at Eastlays and Monkton Farleigh employed conveyor belts to connect with nearby railway sidings.

Once underground, the ammunition was originally transported to the respective storage districts by an *'endless rope'* overhead truck haulage system, similar to that used in coal mines. Due to excessive noise and the danger posed by derailments, this system was replaced in 1940 by approximately 7.5 miles of conveyor belts at the Tunnel Quarry and Eastlays Ridge depots.

The Tunnel Quarry included a power station with two huge diesel generators capable of supplying power to a small town and an underground lake for drinking water. Sewerage facilities and flood pumps were also provided. Many war personnel remained underground for long periods to help keep the installation a secret. There was little need to go above ground during WWII.

In 1941 a barracks block capable of accommodating 300 personnel was constructed underground for the workers at Tunnel Quarry. It was described by the Royal Army Ordnance Corps (RAOC) Gazette as 'magnificent', with its communal bars and Mess areas. In February 1942 a new military communications centre for the South-west of England was built in Tunnel Quarry's No1 'district'. Work on the quarry was completed by July 1943, at a cost of £50,000 (£1.6 million in today's money).

Part of the Tunnel Quarry complex was set aside as a subterranean factory for the Bristol Aircraft Corporation, hidden away from the prying eyes and destructive capabilities of the Luftwaffe. It was this section of the Tunnels that in 1943, was graced with the attractive murals painted by Olga Lehmann to brighten up the otherwise drab and gloomy working conditions.  [*Photo by J.Carosi*]

**1912:** Olga was born in a small village called Catemu which was an hour's journey away by horse-drawn carriage from Santiago, Chile. Her mother Mary Grisel Lehmann (née Bissett) was Scottish and her father Andrew William Lehmann (a copper mining engineer) was of French (Paris) descent. Olga Lehmann had a sister and a brother, Monica (Monica Pidgeon) and George (Andrew George Lehmann). Olga grew up in Chile but during lengthy holidays, the family stayed at her paternal grandmother's house in Dulwich, London, where Olga and her sister attended Dulwich High School.

## Chapter 17. Olga Lehmann's Underground Corsham Murals.

**1929:** Back home, Olga continued her education in Chile at the American Santiago College until she was 17 years old.

She later moved to England after being awarded a scholarship to the Slade School of Fine Art at London University in 1929 where she studied fine art under the tutelage of Henry Tonks and Randolph Schwabe.

Olga was taught theatrical design under Vladimir Polunin and portraiture under Allan Gwynne-Jones. Olga's Spanish and Moorish themes which can be seen reflected in her art, were the result of visiting Spain in the early thirties.

Although Olga's initial training was as a portrait painter, she soon converted to mural and large-scale scene painting; it was in this genre that she later made her reputation.

Olga was also inspired by the artist Dick Beck who was a resident at Hogarth Studios. He liked to use a fun illustrating technique using scraperboard, also known as scratchboard - a form of direct engraving where the artist scratches off a dark solid ink covering, to reveal a white or coloured layer beneath. This produced immediate and striking results.

**1930:** Olga worked as an artist for almost six decades, from the 1930s (when she gained a reputation in the fields of mural painting and portraiture) into the 1980s.

**1933:** Her work was exhibited at the Royal Portrait Society. She also designed a series of Newfoundland stamps commemorating Humphrey Gilbert (associated with the founding of that colony in 1583).

**1934:** Olga painted the scenery for La Cenerentola in the Covent Garden Theatre and painted murals in the Palace Hotel, Buxton, as well as murals for St. Helier House Hotel, Jersey.

*One of many striking images painted by Olga Lehmann on the walls of the underground canteen in the WWII Corsham Ammunition Depot (CAD) Tunnel Quarry. Photo by J.Carosi.*

**1935:** Her work was exhibited with the London Group. She designed and painted (along with others) a decoration to cover Queen Victoria Street Railway Bridge to celebrate the Royal Silver Jubilee of King George V and Queen Mary.

## Chapter 17. Olga Lehmann's Underground Corsham Murals.

**1936:** The photo here shows Olga as a 24 year old preparing for her first 'one-man-show' exhibition of her work at the Little Gallery, 2 New Burlington Street, Mayfair, London. By now, she had already achieved a considerable reputation. Olga Lehmann came from a talented family. Her sister Monica Pidgeon was once hailed 'Queen of Architecture'. In her 90's, Monica ran the video-based website 'Pidgeon Digital' celebrating architects of the 20th Century. Olga's brother was the late Professor A G Lehmann, (known as George) a writer on European history.

**1937:** Olga held a 'One Woman' exhibition at the Little Gallery, 2 New Burlington Street in 1937.

She received Commissions for murals in hotels, private buildings, shops and nurseries, along with work for the film industry.

**1939:** One month after the outbreak of the Second World War Olga married Carl (Richard) Huson, editor and publicity director for Argo Records (UK). They had met at a party. Carl was also a journalist and broadcaster with a talent for writing poems. At the time of their wedding, Carl had secured a job as a warden at the Air Raid Precautions (ARP) post in the crypt beneath St. Pancras Church in Islington, London. Carl was anxious to get into the RAF but pending the arrival of his call-up papers he decided to apply for a job with the ARP. During the Battle of Britain, Olga and Carl spent nights in an Anderson Shelter belonging to their neighbour. During the day, they would try to carry on their lives as normal, diving into doorways to avoid the bombs every time the sirens sounded an air raid alert. Olga recalled this as a long wail which one would associate with terror and destruction. When Olga turned up at her studio-flat in Hampstead one day to find it had been bombed, she headed into the rubble and emerged with a few pictures tucked safely under her arm!

Sadly, much of her early work was destroyed. Some of Olga's most deeply compassionate interpretations stem from this period. They went to live in a country house, Sparrows Hall in Saffron in the Essex countryside.

**1940:** This photo from 'The Sketch' 1940, shows Olga putting the finishing touches to her mural in the Wardens' Club at St Pancras Air Raid Precautions (ARP) Headquarters.

## Chapter 17. Olga Lehmann's Underground Corsham Murals.

**1941:** A news correspondent from the Sunderland Daily Echo and Shipping Gazette visiting the 'Hi Gang' musical set at Gainsborough's Islington Studios, perfectly describes Olga as follows:
*"As I was leaving the "Hi Gang" set I saw a slim, curly-headed figure in blue dungarees with a paint pot slung over one arm and a brush in her hand perched precariously on a swinging platform above our heads. The figure descended and introduced herself as Olga Lehmann, artist and mural decorator. Miss Lehmann comes from Chile and is an official war artist recognized by the Government."*

**1943:** Olga gave birth to her son Paul Huson. Olga was approached by David Aberdeen, a young architect who had been at the Bartlett School of Architecture, about painting underground scenes in Corsham. Olga was immediately interested, and along with David, they were whisked down to the Corsham Tunnel Quarry in a War Office car Corsham to meet Mr Claud Henry Tucker O.B.E., then the Business Manager of the Engine Division's underground shadow factory at Corsham Bristol Aircraft Company. After a tour of the Corsham underground, Olga accepted the commission and subsequently, was officially invited by Bristol Aircraft Company owner Sir Reginald Verdon Smith to paint murals in the canteens of the subterranean factory of the Bristol Aircraft Corporation in the Corsham Tunnel Quarry (Spring Quarry). Sir Verdon Smith believed this would brighten up the place and boost the morale of his factory workers, who were producing Centaurus engines for Brabazon Jets.

An arrangement was agreed between Olga and Mr Claud Henry Tucker (a very jovial gentleman), estimating that it would take about a week to a fortnight to complete each underground canteen with the help of her fellow artist Gilbert Wood (1904-1982) who was also employed by the film industry. At the time, they were sharing a Hogarth studio in the Bohemian 'Fitzrovia' area of London. In London, they would frequent local pubs with artists and poets such as Augustus John and Dylan Thomas and characters such as the weird occultist Aleister Crowley. Gilbert was the scenic artist for the 1966 film Alfie, he also illustrated books such as 'The Music Lovers Bedside Book' by Gilbert Wood & Cyril Clarke. Also working as a jobbing scenic artist, he created work for movies during the 40s, 50s & 60s and like Olga Lehmann, much of his work went unaccredited. On her return to London she discussed ideas with her fellow artist Gilbert Wood who loved painting clowns. They considered painting 'prehistoric animals'. Many of the murals at Spring Quarry featured circus clowns. Other themes included circus animals, pre-historic monsters, sports, sailors, mermaids, Alice in Wonderland and sailing ships, etc.

The whole of the underground factory's limestone tunnel walls were painted cream including the bricks. Many of the Spring Quarry murals featured drinking scenes, including one showing Olga and Gilbert drinking together at a fairground. This was certainly Olga and Gilbert representing themselves in their own work? The technique that they used was to *spray-on* the background shapes and then draw the detail over the surfaces with fitches and broad brushes to create a stunning effect. In the evenings, rather than stay in their sparse single-sex *Nissen Hut* accommodation in the workers' above ground quarters, the pair of them would *go out on the town*. They would take a bus into Bath and visit a succession of pubs. Later, they would take a train to Chippenham and then a taxi or bus back to Corsham. The following morning, they would put ladders and planks up and go about the business of painting floor-to-ceiling size Murals. In all, Olga and Gilbert had been commissioned to adorn about six canteens with their murals, and each canteen took about a week to a fortnight to finish. Her lively, decorative murals certainly enlivened the dour interiors, not only of the underground canteens, but also later *above ground* in a nationwide chain of state-run 'British Restaurants'.

Materials had by this time become difficult to obtain. Oil paint was provided from the Factory and the colours used in the murals were also those used in the production of aircraft. Olga told the chairman of

## Chapter 17. Olga Lehmann's Underground Corsham Murals.

the Factory that she believed 'the murals would only survive for 18 months to two years'. The whole project took about eight months to complete. Many of the murals have survived in good condition.

**1945:** Aircraft engine production in the underground complex at Corsham was gradually run down and the factory closed in April 1945. It had used extortionate amounts of public money, production of engines had not been up to speed and the factory got into financial difficulty. The asking price for the factory in 1945 was £70,000 – less than 1% of the actual final building costs! After the War, some of Olga's important commissions included work for films such as The Guns of Navarone, Nemo and the Floating City, The Man in the Iron Mask, Les Miserables and The First Modern Olympics. Emmy awards were collected for some of these motion pictures, now regarded as classics. Her work for the TV soap opera Dynasty was viewed by millions. After World War II, Olga was also involved with graphic designs for the Radio Times and for the film and television industries.

**1947:** Olga beautifully illustrated a book by Juliette De Bairacli Levy called 'Look! The Wild Swans'.

**1950s:** During the 1950s the vast Corsham underground area, with over 60 miles of roads was redeveloped as a bomb and radiation proof Cold War bunker. It was codenamed 'Burlington' to protect the Government, providing a base for the country to be rebuilt should there be a nuclear war. Thankfully, this was never used!

**1979:** The Royal Air Force approached the government for permission to use a small part of Spring Quarry and make a war operations room for RAF Rudloe Manor. The area they were given was one of the canteens that were surplus to requirements. This is the only area where the murals have survived mostly intact. All of the other canteens have been adapted, painted white and used as storage areas: a great loss. It is unclear how many of the murals survive intact today. Some have been documented by English Heritage, some by Rolls Royce Heritage. The fate of the remaining murals is yet to be seen. The RAF Rudloe Manor site at Corsham closed in 2000.

**1984:** Olga's husband Richard Huson dies. After his death, Olga moved to a charmingly converted artisan's cottage in Saffron Walden. She spent her future winters in Los Angeles at Whitley Terrace with her son Paul Huson and his partner William Bast. Whilst there, she would paint the scenery of the Hollywood Hills and socialise with writers, producers and stars of the Silver Screen well into her eighties when she finally became too frail to travel.

**1986:** The BBC showed a documentary film of her work.

**1995:** In December Olga discovers that the Corsham murals had not disintegrated but were still in remarkably good condition after 60 years in the cold, dark, damp and empty tunnels beneath Corsham.

**2001:** Olga painted well into her retirement but with failing health, she passed away in Saffron Walden, Essex on 8 October aged 89. Her ashes were scattered halfway to Avalon in the waters off Santa Catalina Island, near to the Chilean seaside town of Concon.

As a costume designer she had been nominated four times for American TV's Emmy awards, for The Man in the Iron Mask (1976), The Four Feathers (1977), and A Tale of Two Cities (1980) and, in 1984, for The Master of Ballantrae. Her costumes also featured in films like The Scapegoat (1959), The Guns of Navarone (1961), The Victors (1963) and Kidnapped (1971). She also provided numerous illustrations for the Radio Times, between 1941 and 1961.

## Chapter 17. Olga Lehmann's Underground Corsham Murals.

*[Photo of one of Olga's murals in the Hudswell Tunnel canteen by Julian Carosi]*

Her illustrative work was particularly appealing to editors craving a note of light-hearted fantasy during the WWII wartime austerity years. She became a book and magazine illustrator, and worked at landscape painting and portraiture. She was commissioned to design commemorative stamps, painted Covent Garden scenery and was contracted by a paint manufacturer to create murals in hotels, restaurants and shops. Her mural work was represented at major exhibitions, including Mural And Decorative Painting (Whitechapel Art Gallery, 1935) and Mural Painting In Great Britain (Tate Gallery, 1939). Her son, Paul Huson, became a Hollywood writer and producer, and she was thrilled in 1986 to be invited to paint portraits of characters on his TV series, Dynasty II: The Colbys Of California, which were to be hung on the walls of the mythical family's mansion. Her difficulty with Barbara Stanwyck was to make her look 20 years younger than her actual 80 years, while her task with Charlton Heston was to dissuade him from posing with a shotgun in his lap.

Even into her old age, Olga's youthful vivacity never left her, and her diminutive prettiness, vivid red lipstick and red painted fingernails retained the authentic note of the Bohemian London of her youth. The sentence below, from Olga's obituary published by The Guardian on 6 December 2001 is a beautiful description of her personality and of her brilliant and prolific talent.

***'It was clear that her view was; that having an amusing time was the prerequisite of an artist's life.'***

*Another striking image by Olga on the walls of the underground canteen.     [Photo by J.Carosi]*

**SUMMARY:**

**Name:** Louise Olga Mary Lehmann.
**Born:** 10 February 1912.
**Birth place:** Catemu, Valparaiso, Chile.
**Died:** October 26, 2001.
**Place of death:** Saffron Walden, Essex UK.
**Spouse:** Richard Carl Huson (m. 1939–1984).
**Children:** Paul Huson.
**Siblings:** Andrew George Lehmann, and Monica Pidgeon. **Parents:** Mary Grisel Lehmann, and Andrew William Lehmann.

[Ed: **R.I.P Olga**. Our deep, dank and maze-like Corsham underground corridors are still blessed with many of your beautiful images.]

## Chapter 18. Prefab Bungalows - Married Quarters and Hostel Sites.

**PREFABS - PART 1: POPULATION OF CORSHAM EXPANDS:**

Prefabs (prefabricated houses) were a major part of the delivery plan to address the United Kingdom's housing shortage in the build up to World War II. Churchill originally wanted half a million prefabs built across the country as a stopgap measure until labour could be mobilised for more permanent housing. They were expected to last for only 10 years but they proved very popular with some residents> some are still a few lived in today [2019]! The building of Married Quarters, and Hostel Sites in Corsham originally met with considerable protest from the local Parish Council, rightly claiming that: '...*the whole character of this old fashioned township is being rapidly changed*' (National Archives: HLG 80/123).

So why was Corsham chosen to store WWII ammunition and build aeroplane engines? The location of the works was driven by the below-ground facilities; therefore in contrast to many other factory sites which were located in urban locations which had a ready pool of labour, Corsham was geographically isolated. This point is alluded to in a War Office document (National Archives: AVIA 15/ 856): '...*I am certain that owing to its isolated location, Corsham is likely to be the only scheme where Hostel and Married Quarters accommodation will be fully utilised*'.

At the onset of WWII, the Bristol Aircraft Company (BAC) currently employed 32,000 workers at their Filton factory, 20,000 of whom travelled from Bristol suburbs daily. It was proposed that 12,000 of these employees would transfer underground to Corsham and work a two-shift system. In another underground Corsham factory, the Birmingham Small Arms Company (BSA) would employ 3,000 men on two shifts, and the Ministry of Supply (MOS) would employ a further 3,000 men also working two shifts. Hostel accommodation would be provided for 8,000 single men. There would be 2,000 Married Quarters and a further 2,000 employees would be billeted locally. The remaining 6 to 7,000 men would be transported daily from Bristol. *[Page 188 N J McCamley - Secret Underground Cities]*.

For a small town of approximately only 4,000 Corsham residents - the above figures must have seemed preposterous at the time!

*Photo below (courtesy of Sharon Shackleford) shows the Fuller Avenue neighbourhood children.*

## Chapter 18. Prefab Bungalows - Married Quarters and Hostel Sites.

The photo above *(courtesy of Stephen Flavin)* sums up the community spirit that was prevalent in those days. The photo was taken from the roof of Vernon and his wife Hilda Goold's bungalow (No.5) at the south end of Poynder Avenue on the Clutterbuck Road Married Quarters estate (MQ1) in Corsham. This spot is roughly just along from where the top of the Valley Road bus stop is today. The photograph is date-stamped on the back with *'8 MAY 1945'*. The inhabitants are celebrating Victory in Europe (VE) Day [Tuesday] 8 May 1945. It marked the formal conclusion of Britain's war with Hitler. With it came an end to six years of misery, suffering, courage and endurance across the world. If you look carefully in the top centre of the photo, you can see one of the WWII air raid shelters that were scattered around the Married Quarters bungalow estates in and around Corsham - thankfully, these shelters were never used for what they were intended for.

The backs of the modern houses on the horizon in the above photo, are the (then) newly built homes at the top of Pickwick Road on the right as you travel eastwards downhill towards Corsham town centre. The road that travels right at the 'T' junction in the photo was (and still is) Beechfield Road which leads all the way down through the middle of the estate to where the Community Centre and the red-bricked Clinic once were (now the new 'Porch' Doctors' Surgery and Corsham Fire Station buildings).

At the onset, the sudden population increase in Corsham raised quite a few concerns. Would the newcomers return from whence they came from, once their work had been completed in Corsham? If so, who would replace them in the new housing being provided? If they stayed, and the war work dried up, would it cause a major unemployment problem in Corsham? As a major war area, would Corsham get priority help to re-establish itself after the war? Could the underground workings and surface buildings such as the canteens be converted into factories? How did Corsham now fit into the overall planning of the District and County? Would the Grove field be used for additional shops? These were genuine concerns for the local people. In addition to this, because of the increase in the demand for

## Chapter 18. Prefab Bungalows - Married Quarters and Hostel Sites.

accommodation, farmers were reluctant to *let out* their empty cottages because this would eliminate any chances of recruiting agricultural workers for their farms.

Considering the number of underground ammunition depots, the underground Aeroplane Factory and the many military sites in and around Corsham during WWII, there were very few German attacks recorded in the Corsham area. One bomb hit Monkton Farleigh, located to the south-west of Corsham in August 1940; though this was more than likely to have been intended for the Colerne airfield to the north. A few stray bombs also fell in Chippenham (Bumpers Farm) as part of the German bombing raids in Bath. It was rumoured that an unexploded bomb dropped in a garden at the bottom of Station Road.

When you listen to those who lived in the prefab bungalow era in Corsham during the 1930s-1960s, they speak of a 'time lost' when community spirit was at its highest. Everybody was *'in the same boat'*. There were no flashy cars or expensive gadgets to boast about. It was a case of making the best of what you had and helping neighbours whenever you could. The war brought employment to Corsham; it provided new homes for the workers, it gave our small town a purpose that is rarely appreciated (and sadly more often forgotten about) in the modern age. It brought in new people from afar and helped the town to grow into what it is today - a place that we can all be proud of.

**Corsham played a massive part in achieving peace in Europe.** *Lest not forget it—lest not forget it!*

The military development of Corsham during and prior to World War II, not only dramatically altered the local landscape, it completely changed the demographics (the structure of the local population). No census was taken in 1941 due to WWII, but in 1931 Corsham had a pre-war population of just 3,754; in 1941 it rose to nearly triple at 9,268. In the 2011 census, Corsham's population was 13,432; in 2017 the population was estimated at 13,685. Originally it was planned to have 14,000 workers accommodated in eight Hostel Sites, located in and around Corsham, each housing 1,000 persons; plus 1,300 in Married Quarters at Hawthorn; with the remaining workers being bussed in from Bath, Bristol and outlying towns and villages. In the end, only half of the planned bungalow estates were actually fully built because most of the workers from Bristol refused to move to Corsham, preferring to travel in daily via bus and coach.

The small community of Corsham opened its arms to this huge new community, originally made up of 3,000 men brought in to complete the Royal Engineer (R.E.) Government Works at Tunnel Quarry in preparation for the onset of World War Two (WWII). This was very important work, being carried out under the fertile fields and placid green valleys of Wiltshire. Hundreds more men came from Ireland to work in the underground ammunition depots, installing new roads and shoring up the old stone quarry pillars etc. It was envisaged that a considerable number of the men would remain living in Corsham on a permanent basis once the war-work had been completed. Many of the men brought their wives and families with them. Nearly 2,000 of the men took up lodgings in Bath, adding a great deal of income to the local trades' people and landladies. It was estimated that £7,000 in wages (over £300,000 in today's money) circulated each week in Bath and the surrounding area. This went some way to alleviating the ill-based conception that the incoming *'Corsham Workers'* would cause trouble and give the area a bad name. There may have been one or two black-sheep amongst the workers, but overall, they were welcomed with open arms by the Corsham locals.

Many of the men came from distressed areas of the country such as South Wales, Durham, Northumberland and Cumberland. A large number of them had been out of work for years. Some men came with sons perhaps who had never worked before - because there was no work to be had. They had

## Chapter 18. Prefab Bungalows - Married Quarters and Hostel Sites.

become members of a *'forgotten community'* holding grievances against society for their plight. The importance of the human element in providing steady work for unemployed families was completed successfully by the authorities. They promoted a communal spirit and a sense of responsibility by providing homes, food, regular wages and a purpose amongst men who had long been strangers to it through no fault of their own. The men soon began to feel that they were *men once again*, doing a worthwhile job of work. They became self-respecting members of the existing Corsham community which wanted to benefit from the new worker's services and not merely just to see them as statistical units in the tables of Government unemployment returns. The *'social experiment'* at Corsham turned what seemed to be very intractable human material into an efficient labour force for the smooth running of the Corsham Works.

In addition to the above, Corsham provided work and homes for those people who fled Hungary as refugees during the 1956 Hungarian Revolution. The population of Corsham was further added to by evacuees arriving predominantly from London, mainly consisting of mothers and small children. In a matter of a few years, Corsham's population had changed dramatically and changed forever.

See photo: [Ed - My first Father-in-Law John Aibl *(of Czechoslovakian descent and now deceased)* was a 13 year old child evacuee from London. Finding a home in Bathampton and later as a young adult moving permanently into Corsham employed on electrical work underground and later with Blacks Engineering based on the Leafield Industrial site in Neston. He was a gentlemen and a nicer man would be very hard to find.] **R.I.P John.**

The Bristol Aeroplane Company (BAC) at Filton, near Bristol was bombed by the Germans in September 1940. In response, Lord Beaverbrook, the Minister of Aircraft Production, issued an urgent plan to relocate all production below ground, which was endorsed by Churchill. The limitations of time, suitable sites, and wartime resources quickly saw the scheme scaled back to the relocation of Filton's engine plant. In December 1940 Spring Quarry, in the Corsham area was requisitioned by the Ministry of Aircraft Production (MAP).

It was not long before the men employed underground had cemented a good working relationship with the handful of Royal Engineers who were responsible for the overall planning and construction tasks required to turn the miles of underground stone quarries into ammunition depots and an Aircraft Factory. The working men soon improved physically and mentally, both in a moral tone and in their outlook. The regular work guaranteed wages, proper food and exercise. It led to many having put on a stone or two after many years of under-nourishment and lack of exercise. Let us not forget also, the wives and daughters who came with their men-folk to forge a new life for themselves and their families in Corsham. They played an essential part in setting up new homes and integrating into the Corsham community using their own skills and capabilities.

## Chapter 18. Prefab Bungalows - Married Quarters and Hostel Sites.

At the onset of war, over half of the employees recruited locally for the underground Aircraft Factory at Spring Quarry were women. Most had no experience with machine tools but all showed a remarkable aptitude for the work required. The percentage of women workers increased as more were drafted into the industry when more men were taken into the Forces to help fight the War.

© IWM (D 9363) Imperial War Museum Photos.

© IWM (D 9355)

1942: Betty Turner and a colleague at work in the underground factory. Betty was a housekeeper before the war and her job in the factory was as a 'research work inspector'. She was chosen out of many applicants at a government training centre where she trained for 6 months and was 'keenly interested in her work'.

1942: Shop Superintendent Charles Tunstall gives an order for the day's work to a worker as he stands at his workbench and machinery in the underground factory at Spring Quarry.
Clearly visible is the roughly cut stone roof from which hangs standard factory lighting.

© IWM (D 9352)

© IWM (D 9357)

1942: A factory worker stands at the bottom of a large round shaft as a crate is lowered from several floors above at the underground factory.

1942: Ernest Tasker at work on a large piece of machinery at this underground factory. He had worked on the production of shells during WWI.

## Chapter 18. Prefab Bungalows - Married Quarters and Hostel Sites.

**PREFABS - PART 2: HOSTEL SITES AND MARRIED QUARTERS LIST:**

Below is a list of the Hostel Sites (HS). The buildings were simple single-sex accommodation, one-storey structures (prefab buildings). Of the eight sites, confusingly numbered, 1, 2, 3, 8, 10, 14, 15 & 16 only four (Nos. 3, 8, 15 and 16) were completed to the MAP specifications, each to house 1,000 men. The maximum occupancy rates of the four completed (Nos. 3, 8, 15 and 16) were only 60, 570, 600 and 200 respectively. *[Ref: Secret Underground Cities by Nick McCamley].*

|  | Location | Capacity No. of men | Details |
| --- | --- | --- | --- |
| HS1 | Westwells | 1,000. Eventually only housed 60 men maximum. | Buildings all demolished only remaining use is Stephens Plastics Factory. Old road layout can be seen in the landscape there today. |
| HS2 | Gorse Farm | 1,000. Eventually only housed 570 men maximum. Later housed additional staff for RAF Rudloe Manor. | Some buildings remain within the current MOD Rudloe site behind where the Hartham Post Office was), including accommodation blocks, a laundry block, stores and the old *'canteen and welfare'* building. |
| HS3 | Thorny Pits | 1,000. Eventually only housed 600 men maximum. | One prefab building remains. This site is undeveloped. The location of former structures and old roads can be seen in the landscape. |
| HS8 | Potley | 1,000. Eventually only housed 200 men maximum. | Now the Leafield Industrial Estate. Several original prefabs remain as industrial units to the west; plus a few original large storage buildings. |
| HS10 | Kingsmoor later Royal Arthur site. | 1,000 | This site remained in use from 1947 as HMS Royal Arthur; now redeveloped as the Wadswick Green Retirement Homes complex. |
| HS14 | Rudloe | Used to house girls from the Land Army | Redeveloped mainly with council houses in 1963/4. |
| HS15 | Lypiatt | 1,000 | The site is now in use as the 'Services Cotswold Centre' by the MOD. Many of the buildings survive today, including the site's community centre and residential buildings. |
| HS16 | Leafield | 1,000 | This site in the fields between Potley and New Grove Farm house on Lypiatt Road was never built. Now part of the Corsham Rise housing estate built in 2018/2019. |

# Chapter 18. Prefab Bungalows - Married Quarters and Hostel Sites.

Below is a list of the **Married Quarters (MQ) Sites**; bungalows were two/three/or four bed-roomed prefabs for families.

| Site | Location | 2 bed | 3 bed | 4 bed | Details |
| --- | --- | --- | --- | --- | --- |
| MQ1 | Corsham | 140 | 158 | 2 | **Clutterbuck Road Estate**: Redeveloped in 1963/4 as a new build council house estate. Included a Community Centre. |
| MQ1A | Corsham | 52 | 54 | | **Dickens Avenue Estate**: Redeveloped in 1963/4 as a new build council house estate. |
| MQ1B | Corsham | 84 | 92 | 6 | **Kings Avenue Estate**: Redeveloped in 1963/4 as a new build council house estate. Included a school (Regis). |
| MQ2 | Boxfields (North) | 48 | 56 | 6 | Alongside current sports field. Bungalows and shops cleared in 1964. Now undeveloped. |
| MQ2a | Boxfields (South) | 60 | 70 | 7 | Bungalows and four shops cleared in 1964, school and community centre all demolished by 1984. Now largely undeveloped. The Boxfields bungalows stretched from opposite Tunnel Inn and extended all along the road to Rudloe Fiveways and also down towards Thorny Pits. |
| MQ4 | Quarry Hill | | 64 | | Abandoned before construction. |

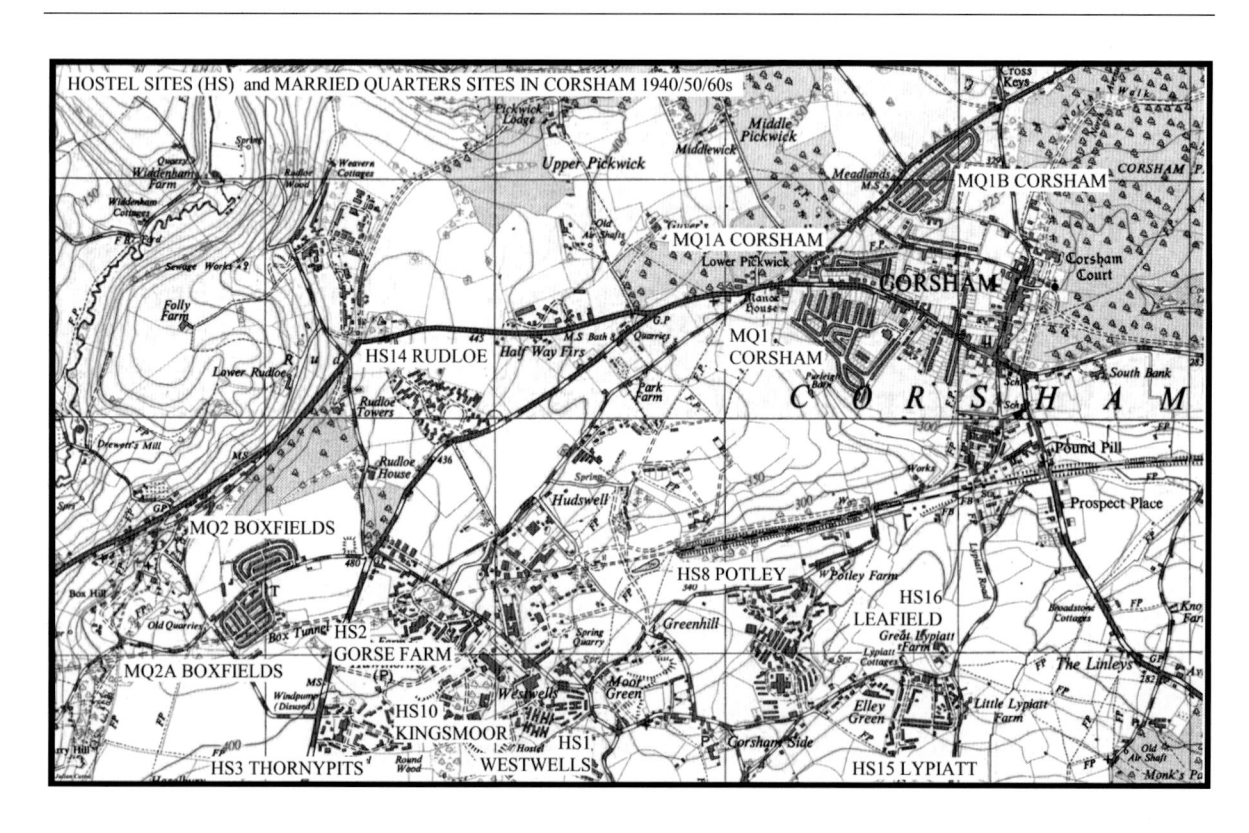

Chapter 18. Prefab Bungalows - Married Quarters and Hostel Sites.

**PREFABS - PART 3: MARRIED QUARTERS & CORSHAM HOSTEL SITES DEVELOPMENT:**

The WWII military development of Corsham began in 1936 with the conversion of the Hudswell Tunnel Quarry into one of three huge Corsham Ammunition Depots (CADs) by the War Office. During the build-up to the WWII war effort, hundreds of prefab bungalows were built in Corsham to accommodate those workers who were brought in to build and run the huge underground armament depots known as Corsham Armament Depots (CADs) and to work in the underground factories e.g. the BAC (Bristol Aircraft Corporation) factory at Spring Quarry. Some of the prefab buildings, such as those at the Thorny Pits Site (HS3) were also later used to house Hungarian refugees at the time of the 1956 uprising. In October 1941, the first bulldozer pushed its way through the wall and orchard down Pickwick Road and made the prefab road called Fuller Avenue. That was the beginning of the three Married Quarters bungalow sites in Corsham. The roads were quickly covered in mud and several Corsham fields were ruined by being transformed into concrete jungles! Cars, bicycles, clothes prams, windows and doors along Pickwick Road became blackened by a sea of mud.

Additional prefabricated huts were put up in Corsham in 1942 for those Bristol workers who were made homeless by bombardment; these sites were later redeveloped as council estates in the 1950s and 1960s. When the prefabs were demolished, some of the remains were transported down to Box and used for building up the land at the bottom of the Box Recreation Ground to level it out for construction of the Box football pitch - which is still well used today.

The 6 March AEROPLANE magazine of 1942, explains the onset of the Corsham prefabs as follows:
*'The structural problems below ground [i.e. creating the underground Aircraft Factory in Spring Quarry] were closely rivalled by others on the surface. Not least of these was the provision of accommodation for part of the huge labour force which will be needed by the factory. The present scheme calls for six sites, each for a thousand men or women, and Married Quarters for another thousand. In the Hostels the beds are arranged two to a room, but if for any reason one or other of the occupants prefers the privacy of a single room, a light partition can be erected to divide them. The second door is already in position. Each tenant has his or her own electric light, wardrobe, cupboard, window, and hooks for clothes. Sheets, pillows and blankets are also provided. Each block has its own baths, foot-baths and showers, and is centrally heated throughout.*

*The Married Quarters are unpretentious little bungalows built in pairs. Each has a lounge, kitchen, bathroom, two or three bedrooms, and a coal-house. The lounge fire heats the kitchen oven and there is an electric grill for cooking the morning rasher. The equipment also includes an electric washing machine. Each bungalow has a good front and back garden and sweeping lawns will, in due season fill the space between the rows. A reasonable rent has been fixed.*

*Schemes that save time, rather than centralisation, have been favoured. For this reason, six canteens have been built for the refreshment and entertainment of the workpeople. Five are comparatively small, the sixth has been made the pivot around which the social life of the 'camp' will revolve, and includes a kitchen equipped with every device for swift service and cooking, and a theatre, which can be used as a cinema [bottom of Westwells Road] or for stage acting, that seats a thousand people. The [canteen] kitchen has electric and steam ovens, steam-heated boilers, refrigerators, bake-houses, and a tea-making plant that looked capable of slaking the tea-thirst of all England. Behind the counter are tiers of hotplates, and in front low metal rails ensure an even flow of customers to and from the serving points in the rush hours.*

Chapter 18. Prefab Bungalows - Married Quarters and Hostel Sites.

*Out of the apparent chaos inseparable from vast engineering and building projects there is gradually growing a new industrial town which, when the war is over and its purpose served, will doubtless disappear as suddenly as it came. And deep below the surface the busy streets of an ancient quarry will once more become dark and silent.'*

Some local objections were received at the time, at the number and style of the new buildings as well as their visual impact against the existing buildings in Corsham such as Corsham Court, the Grove, Mansion House, Ivy House, the Hungerford Almshouses and Wardens House, Flemish buildings and sundry other small *listed* houses. In some ways, sleepy quaint old Corsham had become industrialised in a matter of a few years. Resentment was also generated by the closure of some public rights of way (and not re-opened) and the enclosing of vast swathes of space by the military - much of which still remains under their control today.

On the positive side, the Corsham Parish Council hoped that once the war was over, some of the larger military buildings could be converted for light industry and that Corsham would obtain urban status. The increase in population also boosted the local economy. A large number of local unemployed in Corsham and the surrounding area were also able to find work in the below-ground works, so it was not all doom and gloom as was though at the onset!

[Ed. Some of the old WWII buildings - e.g. the two large buildings top left of the Potley Hostel Site (HS8) aerial photo below - north-east on the Leafield Industrial site are still being used today.
*[Photo courtesy of the Royal Arthur Magazine.]*

## Chapter 18. Prefab Bungalows - Married Quarters and Hostel Sites.

**CORSHAM Y.M.C.A. HUT STOKES ROAD.** Some of the unmarried younger men with pocket money to spend for the first time in their lives and being at a loose end during their leisure time headed for the local Corsham public houses for their entertainment. To alleviate this, sport was promoted with the creation of a football pitch and equipment. Trips to the seaside were also provided. A male voice choir was formed, along with the 'The Tunnel Orchestra'.

*The advert on the right appeared in Vol.1 No.1 of the Corsham, Royal Arthur Magazine in January 1948.*

In addition to competing in a Wilts "Soccer" Football League, the Corsham workers had an interdepartmental League of their own. All these activities were run by the Works Welfare Committee which included a Welfare Officer, and on which the men themselves served as elected representatives. Any grievances were taken to the Commanding Officer Colonel A. Minnis R.E.

**THE Y.M.C.A., CORSHAM**
(150 yards from the Railway Station)

is open from 10 to 11.30 and 17.00 to 21.30 daily.
(Sunday, 15.00 to 21.30. canteen from 17.00 onwards)

Refreshments, Cigarettes, Games and Library

Pianoforte Entertainment every Wednesday from 17.00 onwards

Devotional Service - Sunday 20.30 to 21.00

**MAKE THE Y.M.C.A A HOME FROM HOME**

In order to further solve the social problems of the younger workers, such as drunkenness, and to fill spare time, a Young Men's Christian Association (Y.M.C.A.) hut was built to help solve the leisure hours of these men. The aim was to put Christian principles into practice by developing a healthy 'body, mind, and spirit'. There was some local opposition to the original suggested site, which forced the authorities to build on their own land in Stokes Road. The site finally chosen was not as convenient as that which was originally refused. *[Ed - The hut was on the site where Altus Engineering later stood - now housing.]*

In 1938, the new Y.M.C.A.'s hut Community Service Centre opened on the evening of Friday 19 May. A large company assembled in Stokes Road, Corsham, where the hut had been built by the War Office. Lord Methuen presided, and among others present were Lord Teignmouth. Hon. Treasurer, Western Division of Y.M.C.A.'s; Captain Victor Cazalet, M.C., M-P., the Revs. H. Neville-Smith, G. W. Hodgson, H. E. Jones, Lieut-Col. A. Minnis, R E., Major and Mrs Kean, Captain and Mrs Regan, Captain H. P. Drayson, Mr and Mrs J. Brailsford, Sir John and Lady Middleton, Mr Charles King Smith, J P., Mr N. S. Tucker, and many others. Captain Cazalet unlocked the door of the hut, and declared it open. Lieut-Col. A. Minnis, R.E., said it gave him great pleasure to hand over the building to the Y.M.C.A. from the War Office. (hear, hear) The centre was open to everybody in and about Corsham, and not merely to the men who were employed in the Government works. The hut was constructed mainly of concrete block and brick with pan-tiled roof, Crittal windows, Elm Nab weather-boarded. The main roof was built of half timber trusses and close-boarded. The wing had a Bitumen felt roof with concreted straw insulator and steel channel girders. It stood on nearly an acre of ground with a 106ft frontage onto Stokes Road. The Accommodation provided; Double entrance doors, a Main Hall (34ft. x 20ft.) with wood floor and containing two brickwork fireplaces, gas radiators. Situated off the main Hall were Gent's Lavatories, Ladies' Lavatories, Storeroom, Pantry, Kitchen and Preparation room, containing glazed sinks, and small Committee Room. The Wing Hall (44ft. X 20ft.) was a continuation of the Main Hall and had a composition floor with small raised platform, containing gas radiators and double entrance doors to the rear. Off the wing was situated a Lounge or Card Room (20ft. x 13ft.) with fitted gas radiators. The cost to build the hut was about £500 (nearly £24,000 in today's money). In January 1940, the hut caught fire and was saved from destruction by the neighbours who tackled the fire with buckets of water. One side of the building was badly burnt. After the war, the Y.M.C.A. hut was eventually put up for sale in 1951.

Chapter 18. Prefab Bungalows - Married Quarters and Hostel Sites.

**PREFABS - PART 4: WORK OPPORTUNITIES IN CORSHAM:**

**MINISTRY OF AIRCRAFT PRODUCTION (MAP) FACTORY.**

Construction of the underground factory in Spring Quarry Corsham began in 1941 and was completed in 1942. The factory was used to build aircraft engines, though it never reached full output and was shut down in 1945. Part of Spring Quarry was later converted into an emergency war bunker headquarters codenamed 'Burlington' that would run the country in the event of a war. Thankfully it was never used and is now slowly deteriorating.

Most of the workers had previously been unemployed through no fault of their own for many years. The proposed number of workers for the underground Ministry of Aircraft Production (MAP) Factory at Spring Quarry included 12,000 from the BAC works in Filton, 3,000 in BSA and 3,000 from the MOS (Ministry of Supply). (Nick McCamley 2007).

Canteens were established where the workers could take a break during their working hours. Work carried on apace with three shifts underway each day to keep the Works running 24 hours a day and on track for completion within the timelines set.

The canteen profits were used for the men's benefit and under their own control via their representatives sitting in the Works Welfare Committee. Funds were made available to families when their men became too ill to work.

In several cases, the funeral expenses were also paid to grieving families. A sickness and injury fund was also established to supplement the statutory National Health Insurance Scheme. The Welfare Committee were also responsible for seeing that the men were properly lodged in the Corsham Hostel and Married Quarters sites.

**THE HUDSWELL TUNNEL QUARRY AMMUNITION DEPOT.**

Work on the underground began with the Tunnel Quarry's Corsham Ammunition Depot (CAD) in 1936 and required a huge work force. In January 1938 it was calculated that 3,000 men were part of the overall War Office construction programme at Corsham. These comprised of civilian labourers from the Bath and Portland Stone Company, supplemented by agricultural workers and colliers from the Somerset coalfields.

A larger workforce was added by using the experienced labour of the distressed mining areas of South Wales, Durham, Northumberland and Cumberland.

Although it is thought that the Central Ammunition Depots had been built by the Royal Engineers, in fact, it was a task completed entirely by civilian labour and directed by a very small staff of Royal Engineers.

Contact with the officers and warrant officers of the directing staff, helped to remove from the men's minds many misconceptions about the Army and showed them that discipline and human understanding could be combined.

When each batch of workers arrived in Corsham, they were welcomed by the Shift Manager who addressed them in the following way:

## Chapter 18. Prefab Bungalows - Married Quarters and Hostel Sites.

*"You have been drafted here for the purpose of work. You may not have been employed for some time, therefore we want you to break yourselves in gradually, and if you just 'tick-over' for the first few days we do not mind so long as we see you are interested in your job, and that collectively a fair measure of work is done.*

*Regular attendance is most essential, and we do not want any man to work so hard one day that he is unable to present himself for duty the next day. You have come to live in beautiful surroundings, and we wish you to conduct yourselves properly.*

*When you get your weekly pay, don't go 'painting the town red' but take care of any spare money so as to provide yourselves with new clothes, and send what you can spare to those at home who are probably in need of it. You will be living in new environments and if any of you have had bad habits, now is the time to discard them and set for yourselves new higher standards."* [Secret Underground Cities by Nick McCamley]

---

Below is a photo taken from the top of the Fire Station tower (opposite the Community Centre - now the Corsham Springfield Campus). The first row of bungalows at the bottom, were part of Brunel Avenue which led to the old black wooden Corsham library just to the right of this photo.

The second and third rows are Ethelred Avenue and then Hungerford Avenue.

The road that travels diagonally in the photo left to right was Beechfield Road. In the far distance are the fields where the Newt Pond was once located at the bottom of the valley!

Chapter 18. Prefab Bungalows - Married Quarters and Hostel Sites.

**PREFABS - PART 5: MARRIED QUARTERS SITES (MQ):**

**CORSHAM PREFAB 3-BED 1940s BUNGELOW TYPICAL LAYOUT**

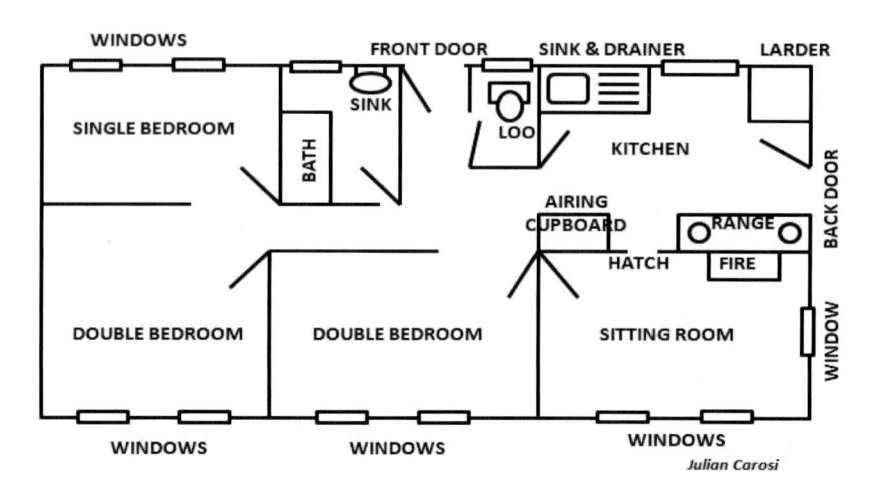

*Julian Carosi*

There was a requirement for Married Quarter's accommodation to be rapidly constructed in Corsham.

The prefab bungalows were described as having three bedrooms, kitchen, living room, bathroom, separate W.C as well as front and back gardens.

In early 1942, commencement of the Married Quarters began. By the end of March 1942, 3,000 accommodation places were also completed in simple single-sex, one-storey structures (prefabs).

There was little resentment from the Corsham townsfolk about the construction of the bungalow sites or the large influx of people, as it was accepted that it was required for the war effort.

But records show that the War Office works did create other problems. For example, the locality quickly became 'seriously short of water' *(National Archives: AVIA 15.856)*. Water was brought in from Chippenham and a large reservoir constructed at the end of Pockeredge Drive. Gas pipes were laid from Bath, concrete roads constructed and sewage outfalls built *(National Archives: HLG 80/123)*. It is possible to see therefore, that the development of Corsham had a domino effect; with each development leading to a requirement for further development. *[Ed: Much like what is happening in Corsham today!]*

The Married Quarters Sites were built at various locations in Corsham and the surrounding area, some as far north as Chippenham and extending west towards Box. Those estates located in Corsham, Rudloe and Chippenham were constructed on previously green field sites. This huge expansion in and around Corsham also necessitated the installation of additional services including water, gas and electricity.

The increased population meant a need also for community facilities including playing fields, allotments, a Community Centre and schools etc. Also required were air raid shelters, shopping facilities, postal facilities, reading and writing rooms, indoor children's playrooms and nurseries etc.

In the early 1940s, to alleviate the burden on the existing schools, the new Regis School was built. It opened in May 1943 and was especially for the children of the married war workers who had been brought into the Corsham area.

Their families were housed in the newly built prefabs alongside the A4 on the Kings Avenue estate (MQ1B), the Clutterbuck Road estate (MQ1) - *(see photo bottom of the next page)* by the Community Centre and the Dickens Avenue estate (MQ1A). Most of these families came predominantly from Bristol but also from other areas such as Plymouth, South Wales and Cornwall.

There was some disparity to start with. The children of existing Corsham residents could start school at 4 years of age, whilst those of the new families were not allowed to start until aged 5.

Chapter 18. Prefab Bungalows - Married Quarters and Hostel Sites.

Below is an aerial photo c1970s of the Regis School as it was originally built in the Married Quarters Site (MQ1B). The school has since been completely rebuilt to modern standards and is now known as the Corsham Regis Primary Academy.

By September 1944 there were 433 pupils on its register. It was an elementary school until 1955 when the older pupils were transferred to Corsham Secondary Modern School; it then became a Junior School.

Below are some of the Clutterbuck Road prefabs.

The Regis School prefab estate was known locally as the 'First Estate'. The Beechfield estate near to the old Community Centre and the Fire Station was called the 'Far Estate' and the Oliver Avenues/Dickens Avenue estate starting behind the Hare and Hounds and down towards the Recreation Ground, was called the 'Middle Estate'.

Chapter 18. Prefab Bungalows - Married Quarters and Hostel Sites.

**Boxfields Married Quarters Estates (MQ2 AND MQ2A).**
At Boxfields, there were a total of 274 prefab bungalows, built on both sides of the (Rudloe to Box Quarry Hill) road; stretching from opposite the Tunnel Inn on one side and extending well along the road to Rudloe Fiveways; also some yards down the Bradford Road towards Thorny Pits.

*[Carolyn Pote]:* In Boxfields, many residents had to rely on occasional door-to-door vendors. Some were disreputable hawkers and peddlers selling inferior goods but the wary householder would avoid these in favour of regular traders who they could rely upon. Salesmen, such as the fishmonger, often called, offering short-life items that needed quick disposal. Hancock's Coal Merchants of Corsham delivered coal to Boxfields from the 1950s. Before that, it was a coal trader from the top of The Firs, Quarry Hill. Mr Smith from Highway Cottage on Quarry Hill delivered fruit and vegetables each Sunday in the 1950s. Threshers from Bathford Hill delivered bread twice a week and milk was also delivered in cans. There were vendors of occasional domestic products like buttons, ribbons and cleaning goods, and, most looked forward to of all, were the treats for children such as fizzy drinks and ice creams. In the late 1930s and early 1940s, an ice cream seller would cycle from Bath to Box to sell his goods door-to-door at Boxfields in a similar way to modern ice cream vans. These ice cream sellers were known as the *'Stop me and Buy One'* men.

*Photo below is of Box Highlands School on its last day Spring 1984, taken by Paul Turner.* Box Highlands School opened in November 1943 and was originally described as a temporary prefabricated building. It opened in November 1943 with 70 children.

From the left in the back row are:

- **Wayne Townsend** - now living in New York since the late 90s.
- **Kerry Miles** - now a teacher in Dublin.
- **Luke Sheffield** - now a senior director with an American IT company.
- **Anne Cleverley.**
- We think the girl with the square satchel leaning in front of Anne is Tamara (Tammy) unknown surname?

At the front are:

- **Richard (Rich) Turner** - kneeling down; now living/working in Swindon for a technology consultancy.
- **Anna Turner** - now working for an international motor company in Gibraltar.

The head teacher at the time of the closure was **Ron Oldale.** The school was moved a mile away onto the Rudloe estate and for a while kept its name Box Highlands.
Then many years later it became Corsham Woodland School, now the Corsham Primary School, Broadwood site.

The Highlands school was demolished.

Chapter 18. Prefab Bungalows - Married Quarters and Hostel Sites.

**1938 CHILDRENS CHRISTMAS PARTY.** On Wednesday 12 January 1938, a Christmas Party for 1,100 children was organised in Bath. The children were accompanied by 500 wives of the Corsham workers. The event took place in the Bath Pavilion which was colourfully decorated for the entertainment. The Christmas Party gave pleasure to children from the distressed areas of Wales, Northumberland, Durham, and Cumberland, the planning of which took two months. The Mayor and Mayoress of Bath (Capt. and Mrs Adrian Hopkins) attended and saw the children consume nearly 15,000 cakes, scones, and jellies and 600 pints of tea.

The hall was bedecked with Christmas trees lit with electric candles and decorations suitable for the festive season. Every child received a present. Parcels, were arranged in 'age' groups, and were distributed by Father Christmas in the person of Mr H. Fordham, assisted by twelve ladies. After tea the children were entertained by the 'Aladdin' pantomime company and by Vera Rice and her pupils, with intervals of community singing conducted by Mr J. Brailsford, the chief organiser of the party. Music was provided by the Tunnel Orchestra, under the conductorship of Mr J. Tucker.

The party was made possible by the men's canteen run by the management of the Corsham works. Altogether £250 (£12,000 in today's money) was necessary to give the children the largest and happiest party they had had for many years. The local paper reported the number as 1,500! *See photo below!*

[Ed: It's very strange to see this photo, as I spent many an hour in this Bath Pavilion Hall as a long-haired *Hippy* in the 60s and 70s watching groups such as Led Zeppelin, James Brown, Fleetwood Mac, Rory Gallagher, Captain Beefheart, and such like.]

The Pavilion certainly presented a sight to make a child's eye glisten, for the gargantuan feast demanded mountains of good things to eat, while the presents - one for each child, amounted to many lorry-loads. From 9 o'clock in the morning the Pavilion was a hive of activity in preparation for this giant party. Indeed, work really began on Saturday, when five lorry-loads of eatables and table equipment arrived in readiness for the great day.

## Chapter 18. Prefab Bungalows - Married Quarters and Hostel Sites.

Not even the greediest boy at one sitting could consume 5,000 fancy cakes, 5,000 buns and scones, 2,000 slices of cut cake, 2,000 mince pies, 800 pints of jellies, 400 lbs. of bread, 600 pints of tea and an iced cake, three feet square, with 'Good Wishes To All' inscribed on it. Tea began at four o'clock. There were over 50 waitresses in attendance. Twenty men from the Works had spent the morning helping to set the tables. The Pavilion must have seemed like a dream come true to those children, many who had never been to a party before. The roof was spanned with evergreens, and there were Christmas trees, lit with coloured electric candles; down the front on either side of the stage stood a Christmas tree, twenty feet high, also filled with lights. Every head sported a coloured paper hat.

The sum of over £100 (£5,000 in today's money) had been spent on presents. It took three vans and a car to bring them from Bristol; while further consignments were bought from Colmer's, of Bath. There were a number of men among the 3,000 workers at the camps, whose wives and children were still at their homes in Wales, Durham, Northumberland and Cumberland. Presents to the children from those homes had previously been despatched to them. Father Christmas (Sgt. Major H Fordham, R.E.), was in attendance. It needed, however, twelve ladies to help distribute the presents to all the children.

-------------------------------------------------------------------------------

Below is a rare photo of *Slippery Jims* also known as *Hilly Fields* (now Valley Road) that lay behind the prefab bungalows on the Clutterbuck Road estate. The whole population of Corsham would descend here after a heavy snowfall to sledge and ski down the hillsides. *[Ed: We couldn't afford a sledge so used an upturned bonnet of an old car, which would seat 4 of 5 of us and project us into the icy stream at the bottom on many occasions.]*

In the photo below (left to right) are Richard (Dick) Moon and John Pyle. Photo courtesy of Dickie Dunmore who took the image as part of his hobby section for his Duke of Edinburgh Award. The bungalow at the top right is in Weaver Avenue leading on to Fuller Avenue and Brakspear Road.

Chapter 18. Prefab Bungalows - Married Quarters and Hostel Sites.

**PREFABS - PART 6: HOSTEL SITES:**

Construction of the Hostel Sites began in 1941 at Westwells which was named as Hostel No.1 (H1). The Hostel Sites were run by the National Services Corporation Ltd. (an agency of the Ministry of Labour) and planned by Alexander Gibb and Partners. As part of the *'Schedules of Measures of Camouflage'* which describes the methods of disguise that were put in place to absorb the new buildings into the local landscape and make them more difficult to be seen by enemy planes above, the flat roofs of the prefab bungalows were divided longitudinally with a 'shadow' side being lightly textured.

Many of the workers enjoyed living in the Hostel Sites which accommodated single persons only. For some, it was their first experience away from home and parents and they relished it. The Hostel Sites included cinemas and ballrooms, at which American swing bands (including the Glen Miller Band) would play and variety shows gave performances. In contrast, some others hated the work and the underground environment; shifts were long and some were too tired to enjoy a social life, and some found working below-ground frightening.

The Hostel Sites required hospitals, stores, recreation halls, welfare centres, launderettes, offices and hairdressers. The Westwells Primary School was situated opposite the Westwells Hostel alongside the Westwells Road. It was used until August 1957 to school the children from the displaced European families until they were re-housed in other parts of the Parish. In the 1960s the school buildings were used for testing purposes by the local Royal Naval Stores Depots (RNSD) of electronic items such as Printed Circuit Boards (PCBs) and in the 1980/1990s it became a Training Centre for the Copenacre RNSD offices. The photo below shows the Westwells School circa 1959/1960.

*Photo courtesy of Anna Higton-Iwaniuk.*

The old Westwells Primary School buildings were later destroyed and in 2011 the site became part of the Ministry of Defence (MoD) Corsham Global Operations Security Control Centre (GOSCC) and Defence Equipment and Support's Information Systems and Services (DE&S ISS) organisation; at its peak during 2011 it employed 2,200 people. Also based on the site were the 2nd Signal Brigade, 10th Signal Regiment and 600 Signal Troop.

## Chapter 18. Prefab Bungalows - Married Quarters and Hostel Sites.

The new MoD buildings were delivered through a Private Finance Initiative (PFI) construction project managed by Defence Estates (DE). Alongside the new offices, is a new living accommodation block to house 180 Service personnel, including those working for DE&S. A sports hall with improved facilities and playing fields were also constructed. The site is a major employer for the town of Corsham.

The Hostel buildings were camouflaged with green paint on the walls and roofs, and there were no road signs in Wiltshire indicating their location. Males and females were segregated within the Hostel Sites, with dismissal if you were caught in the opposite sex's block. Security guards prevented employees from wandering around, and in general most people socialised within their Hostel Sites or the immediate ones, i.e. those living in the Hostels did not generally mix with other Hostels or the locals.

The prefabs were often built out of pre-cast concrete panels fitted onto a concrete frame. They came pre-painted in magnolia and green. They were mainly erected by Irish workers as a temporary solution only intended to last ten years; instead, they lasted twenty to thirty years. Some were built with an asbestos gabled roof; others had a flat bituminous asphalt roof. Some still exist!

During the conversion work for the Central Ammunition Depot (CAD) quarries (mid 1930s to mid 1940s) some of the workers (numbering some 2,000 in total) who were mainly Irish were accommodated at the Thorny Pits Hostel Site No.3 (HS3). Apart from one of the original bungalows, part of a large red bricked building, a few road surfaces and a circular brick airshaft (part of Box Tunnel), nothing else remains on the Thorny Pits site today.

There are very few photographs remaining of the original Thorny Pits Site (HS3) which today is mainly rough pasture land. Below is the last bungalow standing on the Thorny Pits Hostel Site (HS3).

After the war, management of the sites was transferred over to the local authorities and a few years later the freehold sites were purchased by the Rural District Council with all tenancies transferred over to the local Housing Departments.

Between 1962 and 1964 most of the bungalow estates were demolished and replaced by modern council housing. Some of the Hostel Sites were just demolished and have remained dormant.

## Chapter 18. Prefab Bungalows - Married Quarters and Hostel Sites.

*The photos on this page of Thorny Pits Corsham, are by kind permission of John Briggs and Jodie Davies. Above shows Lajos Nagy with an unknown lady above, and below Lajos' wife Margaret.*

Lajos and his wife Margaret were two of approximately 200,000 people who fled Hungary as refugees some time after the 1956 Hungarian Revolution. By April 1957, there were 19,299 Hungarian refugees in the United Kingdom. Lajos and his wife succeeded in leaving Hungary after the third attempt and ended up at the Thorny Pits camp which was then being used as a Hungarian Hostel. Thorny Pits had originally been built as a Hostel to hold 1,000 working men. Lajos and his wife Margaret later moved to Bristol and lived in the St. Paul's area for a time. It is thought that they moved to Newport sometime between 1958 and the 1990's.

There is an interesting British Pathe Video via the link below, of the old Corsham Thorny Pits Site.

https://www.britishpathe.com/video/hungarian-refugees/query/Corsham

Chapter 18. Prefab Bungalows - Married Quarters and Hostel Sites.

**PREFABS - PART 7: POST WAR CORSHAM:**

Victory in Europe Day, generally known as VE Day was celebrated on 8 May 1945. The Victory in Japan (VJ Day) was celebrated a few months later on 15 August 1945, which effectively brought the war to an end. Corsham slowly began to return to some sort of normality. But it took another 20 or so years to replace the crumbling prefab bungalows with modern housing.

Following the closure of the MAP underground Aircraft Factory in 1945, a large number of the Hostel Site buildings remained empty. Some were temporarily used until 1958 to house Polish, Hungarian and East European refugees.

A tentative plan was put forward at the time, to convert the Thorny Pits Site (HS3) into a Borstal Institution (a type of youth detention centre), but this was quickly thwarted, foremost by Lady Katherine Fuller of Neston House, one of the major land owners of the area at that time. This was met with strong local objections, as one landowner stated at the time: *"....for the past fifteen years this area has had most unsatisfactory people in it who have given much trouble and caused the local people much annoyance and disquiet. It would not be fair to them to turn this area into a permanent site for undesirable families"*. [McCamley 2007].

In August 1960, it was announced that the Corsham Ammunition Depot (CAD) at the Hudswell Tunnel Quarry would close. Four years were scheduled to clear the 300,000 tons of ammunition that was stored in the depot. The stocks were sent to small above ground depots. A large amount of the stock was also dumped into the sea. The last box of ammunition left Tunnel Quarry on 4 December 1962. Tunnel Quarry, located beneath Hudswell had held a wide variety of ammunition, with some shells weighing up to 1 ton each.

*Photo 1943 courtesy of Nick McCamley: Shows WAFF girls in the underground plotting room.*

Browns Quarry, a small independent quarry to the north of Tunnel Quarry, was located underneath the former Manor Site of RAF Rudloe Manor. This quarry was converted into the secure underground Command Centre for No. 10 Group RAF Fighter Command.
It included a large wood-panelled hexagonal operations room with plotting table, overlooked by two mezzanine floors. The room was 45 ft high, with no roof supports used.

The site was used as a communication centre both during and after the war. The site was also used as accommodation for some of the mine construction workers and site workers. After the war, many of the buildings were converted into office blocks. The RAF Rudloe Manor site was closed in 2000.

Chapter 18. Prefab Bungalows - Married Quarters and Hostel Sites.

**MEMORIES OF EDGELL'S FISH AND CHIP SHOP (THE CHIPPY!):**

On the Married Quarters Site (MQ1) was the very popular Fish and Chip shop located behind the red-brick built Community Centre opposite the Fire Station and at the bottom of Beechfield Road.

Not much bigger than one of the many single prefabs surrounding it, the *chippy* was established by Mr and Mrs Edgell and later managed by their daughter Marilyn.

**Below are some memories of the *chippy* sorted alphabetically by surname:**

**[Piotr Barbaruk]** If you were really poor, you brought old newspapers and handed them over the counter in exchange for a free bag of scrumps. Those who could actually afford fish and chips must have been from the posh end of the estate ;-)

**[Margaret Booth]** My sister Marion and I used to go along to Edgell's for a Friday night fish supper. They were great fish and chips. Great memories. When the queues were long (which was most of the time!) we used to try and 'push in' by saying out loud to someone (anyone) near the front, 'Thanks for keeping our place'. It rarely worked - and we were often threatened with not being served at all.

**[Julian Bray]** As a small boy of around 5 or 6, my parents allowed me to walk down to the bottom of Beechfield Road to buy the family fish and chips on a Friday evening. After an hour of me leaving home, they came down to find me still waiting patiently outside. I was too shy to go into the shop with people in there and was waiting for it to be empty!

**[Terry Dorney]** I remember it well. And also in the 1960s, every Friday night a fish and chip van would come around Corsham. You could also buy fish and chips in tin foil packs from the local Co-op in the High Street, with the brand name (apologies if the spelling is incorrect) of Mudd Pack!, perhaps a mere coincidence; but those tin foil packs of chips didn't last long!

**[David Edgell]** I can remember my Grandmother Rose Edgell helping out in our Fish and Chip Shop, usually by 'eyeing' the potatoes [i.e. cutting out the little nub sprouts] before the potatoes went through the automatic 'chipper'. I can also remember the really sweet named *Jusoda* orange drink that we had for sale, plus Tizer, and Magnet.

Our shop became really busy when the Bingo crowd emerged from the Community Centre next door.

Every time that I buy Fish and Chips these days for around £7, it takes me back to the early 1960s when a piece of fish cost 10d & chips were 4d, totalling 1s2d, equivalent to less than 6p these days!

Our family had to work very hard to keep our Fish and Chip shop going...... I spent so much time in there, that I probably still smell of fish & chips today.

**[John Feltham]** I lived next door to the Edgell family in Poynder Avenue. Mr Edgell used to cut my hair on a Sunday evening. We used to have a portion of chips occasionally and scrumps.

## Chapter 18. Prefab Bungalows - Married Quarters and Hostel Sites.

**[Stephen Flavin]** I loved the taste of the salt and vinegar. It really does taste better in newspaper. Losing the newspaper was the origin of the nanny State!

**[Robin Gold]** I worked there in the evenings (1972/73), peeling spuds and cutting chips. Thankfully they had a peeling machine over a bath in the garage and a chipper at the side of the shop. Wages were a couple of quid plus fish/sausage/pie and chips, happy days.

**[Terry Hancock]** A bag of chips and a bag of scrumps, then sit in the bus shelter and enjoy, before visiting the Hare and Hounds pub for a blackcurrant lemonade. Great days.

**[Mary Hoar]** At the Wednesday night dances at the Community Centre, I often treated myself by popping along to Edgell's for a bag of Scumpys with my friend Nog; great times.

**[Jeannie Humber]** With written permission from parents, some of us from the Corsham Girls Secondary Modern School regularly walked up to Edgell's on Friday lunchtimes, to have chips instead of school lunch. I remember making a hole in the greaseproof bag after I had finished my chips, so that I could drink the remaining salty vinegar. Mmmm...

**[Paul Kibbey]** We had them as a treat. But having to walk there from the High Street and back home again - with the smell lingering all the while, made me all the more hungrier, even though by the time I had reached home, they had cooled somewhat. Much better once I got a bike. It was 9d for the fish a tanner (6d) for the chips, making the total 1s 3d, I think! At least it was that price after 1962 when we moved to Corsham.

**[Anne Kilmister]** Not long after I moved to Corsham with our three-month old baby girl, I used to walk down to the chip shop with her in her pram to lull her to sleep and treated myself with a chip tea. Great chips.

**[Angela McQueen]** We used to have them as a treat on Saturday lunch time. Loved them.

**[Dennis O'Meara]** I have many memories of Edgell's Chip Shop but the most abiding one is as a 12 year, I walked in one Friday evening to hear John F Kennedy had just been assassinated - Friday 22nd November 1963 to be precise. I'll never forget the shock on everyone's face. I remember sprinting home to 39 Clutterbuck Road in utter disbelief.

**[Graham Peaple]** There were far too many in our family for Mum and Dad to buy all us lot fish and chips. I used to buy them now and then as a treat with my paper round money.

**[Keith Tadhunter]** I used to go around the bungalows to collect old newspapers for the chippy in return for a bag of scrumps.

**[Hilary Jayne Toghill]** On a Friday night, Caroline Charlton and I would go over and peel potatoes there for a free bag of scrumps.

**[Nigel Treloar]** My first memory of fish and chips and in newspaper, adding to the flavour lol.

**[David Webb]** I can remember going there, with my mates every Friday night. On one occasion, one of my mates asked Edgell for 1p worth of chips. We were all laughing. Mr Edgell keeping a straight face, slowly turned around and put a single chip on a sheet of newspaper and then handed it to us over the counter. We did not laugh, but he did! He was a great man for Corsham.

Chapter 18. Prefab Bungalows - Married Quarters and Hostel Sites.

**PREFABS - PART 8: MEMORIES:**

Below is a selection of prefab memories from those who lived there, sorted by (maiden) surnames.

**NAME: Anne Butts.**
**PREFAB ADDRESS: 3 Elm Grove**
**DURATION approx: 1948 to 1964.**

Next-door to us in our semi-detached bungalow at No.1 Elm Grove were Sam Prewett, his wife, daughter Fay and young son Maurice. My Father Jim Hallett worked nights and as soon as he had left for work each night, I sneaked into my Mum's bed to cuddle up to her and keep warm. I remember Mum and I being kept awake by loud rhythmic bumping on the thin adjoining wall, coming from the Prewett's family bedroom wall next-door. It went on and on - getting progressively faster and faster. In the morning my Mum Vera went to see Sam Prewett and asked him if he could move his bed away from the wall as it was embarrassing and keeping us all awake. You can imagine what my Mum thought was going on late at night in the Prewett's bedroom! As soon as my Mum had finished speaking to Sam, he bent over in stitches laughing heartily. When he calmed down, he calmly explained with a grin on his face, that his wife did dressmaking and was making some special outfits and had been working into the night on her treadle sewing machine which they had moved into the bedroom on the other side of the wall. My Mum was so embarrassed. The story caused much fun in our home - and had us all in stitches!

The Guinness family, Mum Sylvia and Dad Bill with children Cynthia and David lived in the semi-detached at No. 5 next-door to us. I remember the Wiltshire family opposite and the Millards.

--------------------------------------------------------------------------------

*Ed: My home, 2 Wardle Road, still occupied whilst building continued around our prefab bungalow.*

## Chapter 18. Prefab Bungalows - Married Quarters and Hostel Sites.

**NAME: Giuliano (Julian) Carosi.**
**PREFAB ADDRESSES: 2 Wardle Road and later 16 Meadland Avenue.**
**DURATION approx: 1953 to 1963.**

**MEMORIES:** When the developers came, we were the last family to be moved off the old Dickens Avenue Married Quarters Site (MQ1A) estate. We were still living in our three-bed bungalow when this photo was taken, as the new Council Houses and roads were being built around us circa 1960. There were six of us living there, my parents, myself and two brothers Domenico and Claudio, and our Uncle (Zio) Tony Bez, my mother's younger brother who slept in the tiny bedroom at the front. My brothers and I slept in one bed, (head to toe to get us all in)!

Today, such a building would be classified as a slum and be demolished, yet we were very happy there and became hardened to the frost lining the inside of the windows in mid-winter. Our adjoining neighbours were Mr and Mrs Stenner and their children, opposite were the Johnsons, next to them was Lizzie Pike (nee Morgan), her brother Tony (sadly passed away) and parents. The street outside ran up to the back of the Hare and Hounds car park, then mostly an orchard. Once, when we were caught by our parents 'scrumping' apples from the trees, our Dad made us go and apologise in person to the landlord. Snells the blacksmith lived opposite us on Pickwick Road. He used to make the local children large rings (hoops) of rusty iron which we would trundle down Pickwick Road with a stick, making enough of a din to wake up the dead!

Our Dad was not what you'd call a skilled DIYer, but he created a magical playground in our small front garden which included a swing, see-saw, double rings and a bar like in gymnastics and a slide. All made out of bits of discarded wood and iron, and most just held together with goodness knows how many bits of wire. Later, we moved for a few years into 16 Meadland Avenue just across Pickwick Road (exactly where Kirby Road is today).

The previous occupant of our prefab, 16 Meadland Avenue was Nurse Slocomb who probably helped many of us old uns into this world. She was a regular sight riding around Corsham with her large black bag balancing precariously on the rear rack.

My strange aversion on arrival in our new home was being frightened by the large rusty stain that ran down the bath under the taps. I never did sit down that end on bath night, when all three of us were 'dunked' at the same time! And we never managed to get rid of the stain no matter how much Ajax we used. I can still see it now!

In the Hilly Fields (now the Valley Road area) behind Clutterbuck Road by the bottom of the old allotments that were once there on the south-facing hillside in the prefab days (1940-1960s), was a pond surrounded by trees and bushes. Roughly situated now - where Ethelred Place, West Park Road and Poynder Road meet up at the bottom of the small hill.

This was a regular haunt for us as children, as the pond was full of newts. We often spent an afternoon there in all weathers, with empty jam jars suspended on string to use as a repository for any newts caught. We used to examine the submerged vegetation for newt eggs which were folded inside the leaves.

To catch the newts we used the flimsy children's seaside fishing nets that were purchased for a few pennies from 'Lords' of the High Street. If you were very lucky, you would catch a Great Crested Newt

## Chapter 18. Prefab Bungalows - Married Quarters and Hostel Sites.

which you could display at home for a few days - sadly they never lived very long in their tiny jam-jars or in the puddles of tap water quickly constructed as make-shift ponds in our back-gardens. These larger newts were devils to capture by hand, as they are slimy and would quickly wriggle away if caught. We also fished (hoping) for bigger prizes in the pond, with a stick and a bit of dangling string with a wriggling worm attached to the end by a piece of old rusty wire. Apart from a snivelling cold in the winter, we never caught much else there! We often took a carrot or two with us on our fishing adventures, as very near to the pond was a field that always had a few horses or donkeys.

The Great Crested Newts are still with us in Corsham and (thankfully) are the bane of planners when any new buildings are proposed near to their territory! Thankfully, they now have full legal protection under UK law making it an offence to kill, injure, capture, disturb or sell them, or to damage or destroy their habitats. This applies to all the newts' life-stages.

According to Corsham's Charlie Bridgman, *"There was a story circulating at the time, that there was once a cottage near the newt pond that got flooded when an old underground tunnel collapsed, whether this was true or not, I don't know."*

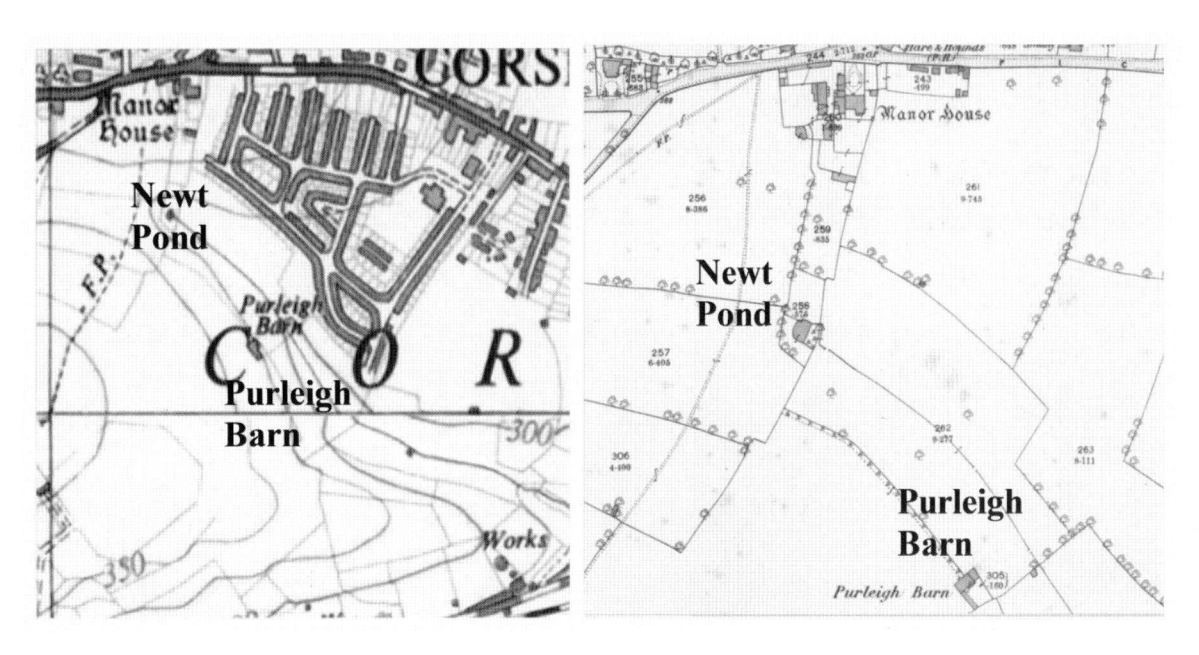

[Ed. The nearest building to the newt pond as far as I know was the old Purleigh Barn a little distance to the south in the valley and the nearest underground quarry (Hartham) is about half a mile away along Park Lane. But……………………………….. in the old maps below you can see the position of the newt pond. It was part of the stream that ran at the bottom of the valley (Slippery Jims). In the older photo on the right, you can just see in the Tythe 263 plot of land, that there was once a fairly large building of sorts next to the pond!] *So, there might be some truth in Charlie's story after all.*

In the days before organised firework displays, we had to make our own entertainment on bonfire night. On the Clutterbuck Road Married Quarters Site (MQ1) estate, there were two expanses of grass.

One at the bottom of my road Meadland Avenue (opposite where the Co-op Garage and shop is now in Pickwick Road) which had two large walnut trees in and the other at the bottom of the estate behind the Community Centre (where the hard-standing all-weather hockey and football pitches are situated today).

## Chapter 18. Prefab Bungalows - Married Quarters and Hostel Sites.

As children, each year we built a very large bonfire on the expanse of grass at the end of my road, and occasionally a rival gang of estate children would build another one behind the Community Centre. This led to competition in sourcing the wood required.

When the 5th of November approached and each bonfire was almost ready, a close guard was kept to prevent sabotage and premature ignition by our jealous rivals. We used to build a den right in the centre of our bonfire for many years until we heard of a child's death by burning elsewhere in the country in similar circumstances.

From thence, our dens were precariously built platforms balanced outside at the very top of the bonfire - much like the crow's nest lookout on an old sailing ship.

Before legislation was thankfully brought in to prevent injury and misuse, we even used to make our own fireworks in copper water pipes by mixing sugar (chlorate) with potassium chlorate or sodium chlorate, found commonly in weed killers which you could buy in bulk in those days, without any questions being asked, in the Chemist shop in Pickwick Road next to Pickwick Papers.

The result was not so much like a firework, but more like the gigantic exploding crow-scarers that the local farmers used in the Pickwick fields!

[Ed: This photo shows me and my two brothers c1956/7 in our prefab bungalow's front garden at 2 Wardle Road, just behind the Hare and Hounds car park.
Left to right:
Claudio Angelo Carosi (youngest), Domenico Roberto Carosi (eldest) and Giuliano (Julian) Adriano Carosi (tallest!)
At the time, we had the nicknames of *'Crow'*, *'Mouse'* and *'Goose'*, a name which some old friends still call me 60 years later!]

On 5 November, people would bring along their own fireworks and share their displays with the large crowds that used to attend the bonfires built on the greens. As the bonfire exhausted itself, neighbours and friends would sit around the bonfire chatting and waiting for their baked potatoes (wrapped in tinfoil) to cook in the burning embers. These events became the main bonfire night displays in Corsham for many years, until legislation came in banning ad-hoc bonfires within a certain distance from roads and houses etc. Nowadays, you can be fined if you light a fire and allow the smoke to drift across a road and become a danger to traffic.

The following morning we would be up early scouting around for 'spent' rocket casings and if you were lucky, unused fireworks that had been dropped or left behind unnoticed.

Chapter 18. Prefab Bungalows - Married Quarters and Hostel Sites.

**NAME: John Cuthbertson.**
**PREFAB ADDRESS: 4 Kirby Avenue then 42 Churchill Avenue.**
**DURATION approx: 1956 to 1958 and 1958 to 1964.**

A family story that has been told over the years concerned me arriving home late from school one afternoon. After school, I had gone straight to one of my mate's house.
His Mum said to me, *"Does your Mum know where you are?"*

I assured her all was well, and that my Mum had told me that I could stay as long as I liked. I was duly invited to stay to tea.

*Photo taken outside 34 Churchill Avenue at my grandparent's house Jim & Agnes Cutter. Right: my Mum, Brenda Cuthbertson (nee Cutter). Left: Mum's sister, Norah McGarry (nee Cutter).*

Unbeknown to me, there was a great search going on for me at home with my family and neighbours and the local policeman all out looking for me.

When I eventually returned home, I was greeted by screams of delight and anger from my Mum. When things settled down, I was told that the local Bobby (Policeman) had been out for hours looking everywhere for me on his bike.

I am told that my immediate response was not one of any great concern.....instead, I innocently asked, *"What colour is his bike"*!!! When the Bobby called round to our house after being told I had been found, I hid behind the settee not wanting to get the wrath of his tongue. I think the modern-day term is *'I was grounded'* for a while following this event. In 1958 we moved to the 'Cross Keys' prefab estate and lived in 42 Churchill Avenue.

I can clearly remember the month of December in 1962 for two main reasons, firstly on Boxing Day it started snowing and I believe it snowed continually for two weeks. It was to become the start of the great winter freeze of 1962/63. On 29 and 30 December 1962 a blizzard swept across South West England and Wales. Snow drifted to over 20 feet deep in places, driven on by gale force easterly winds, blocking roads and railways. The snow stranded villagers and brought down power lines. The near-freezing temperatures meant that the snow cover lasted for over two months in some areas. By the end of the month, there were snow drifts 8 feet deep in Kent and 15 feet deep in the West. The thaw set in and the 6 March was the first morning without any frost anywhere in Britain.

On 29th December 1962 my brother Steven, sister Agnes and I were woken up by our Dad just after 8am to be taken into my parents' bedroom. Mum was sat in bed with a new baby girl. This was our first meeting with our newly born sister Julie. Also in the bedroom was Nurse Massey a larger than life character who was the local midwife. I also recall seeing our 'Cotto' lying on its side blowing out hot air to keep the bedroom warm. Due to the extreme weather my Mum and new sister did not venture out of the house until March. A 'Cotto' was a lidded clothes airier, about 1 metre square by 1.5 metres tall. It had wooden rods laid in the top where clothes were draped over and a lid to keep everything in place.

*John Cuthbertson (aged 11) & Granddad James (Jim) Cutter in Churchill Avenue in 1963.*

Our neighbours to the left were Mr and Mrs Proctor; in those days you always addressed your elders by Mr or Mrs I remember that I struggled (and still do) tying a decent knot in a tie. I used to pop round to Mrs Proctor and ask her to tie it for me as she was a dab hand at that tricky task. Opposite us were the Witt family (Mr and Mrs Witt - June and Dennis with their daughters Susan, Helene and Pamela).

Also on the same side of our road were the Kilminsters and my mate Jon Phillips lived further down the street. My grandparents Jim and Agnes Cutter lived along the road at 34 Churchill Avenue; they later moved on to 3 Charles Street when the prefabs were demolished.

We left 42 Churchill Avenue in 1964 and moved into one of the newly built council houses at 15 Kings Avenue on the corner (opposite the red-bricked Police houses which are still there today).

**NAME: Gillian Davis (nee Reilly).**
**PREFAB ADDRESS: 3 Fuller Avenue.**
**DURATION approx: 1955 to c1966.**

Our bungalow at 3 Fuller Avenue was two doors up from the little Handy's shop that was positioned between Fuller Avenue and Providence Lane (a few yards east of where the Corsham swimming pool building is these days). The shop provided a shortcut route to junior school (Corsham County Primary).

The owner, Mr Hadrell wouldn't let you go in one side of the shop and out the other without buying something! To counteract this, we used to wait until there was a crowd of customers in the shop and then sneak through behind them.

On the rare occasion that I had 3d to spend, I would buy a Cadbury's Flake, or sometimes four Black Jacks for 1d, Fruit Salads, or a tiny tube of Parma Violets for 1d. I would drag my black-and-white checked cloth Scottie dog all the way down to school on Pound Pill - it was no wonder that I was always late.

Our prefab was built in a dip so whenever it rained heavily, the water sometimes came right up to just under the sill of our windows!

## Chapter 18. Prefab Bungalows - Married Quarters and Hostel Sites.

Edgell's Chippy was such a fixture of my childhood, especially when I had 3d/thruppence to buy a bag of chips. The lady serving (Marion Putt? niece of Freddie and Dylis Edgell) would say, *"Want some scrumpies with them?"*

I remember when I was about 7 or 8 years old with no money; I had seen some of the bigger boys and girls from the estate working in the chip shop, so I went in asking for a job.

For a little girl who couldn't reach the counter, let alone see over it, you'd think I'd be *sent packing*; but the lovely Freddie conjured up a job for me.

He sat me at a table (there was an eat-in area to the left of the counter) and plonked a huge pile of newspapers in front of me with instructions to separate the lot into perfectly sized sheets ready for wrapping. I earned a bag of chips and went back regularly to offer my services for this completely fabricated and unnecessary task.

Dylis used to wear her hair piled up high in a lovely bee-hive bun and Freddie was so loud and funny and so kind. The queues in the chip shop were often right out of the door onto the path.

Some years later when I was a little older, I remember being in that queue and being asked by some older kids the vital question, *"Are you a Mod or a Rocker?"* I was terrified to say the wrong thing and then have to stay in that queue with them!

I also remember the Wednesday night dances at the Community Centre a stone's throw away from where we lived. As we were too young to attend, we could never get in, no matter how much we tried. But we *cottoned on* that the bands entered and exited by the door at the back (right next to the Chippie).

We used to hang around there like groupies so we could spot them on their way out, not that they ever had anyone famous playing there I think! My brothers used to go to the Wednesday night dance and I would have been in big trouble if they'd spotted me hanging around at the rear.

*Photo shows the old red-bricked Community Centre (replaced by the Spingfield Community Campus)*

# Chapter 18. Prefab Bungalows - Married Quarters and Hostel Sites.

**NAME: Sheila Williams (nee Groves).**

**PREFAB ADDRESS: 20 & 22 Woodlands, Pickwick.**
**DURATION approx: June 1949 to 28 October 1961.**
**MY MEMORIES:**

*Photo courtesy of Sheila Williams. Taken at the rear of Woodlands estate. Left to right: Judith Whitfield, Malcolm Groves, Anthony Darby, Frances Groves, Sheila Groves, Gillian Groves and Heather Plank.*

Myself, my brother, Malcolm Groves and two sisters, Frances and Gillian had a wonderful happy childhood growing up in a council house in Woodlands surrounded by friendly families and miles and miles of open countryside. During our years there we lived in two bungalows, first number 22 which we moved into in June 1949 (from Potley where my Grandmother, Annie Godsell lived) when I was 2 months old and about 8 years later we moved to number 20. The first one was semi detached and only had two bedrooms so all four children had to share a small room. As our family got larger, we were allocated a bigger detached bungalow which had four bedrooms and it felt like a palace when we moved in with so much space. Whilst we were living in No 22 our Uncle and Aunt (Lesley & Betty Godsell) moved in next door and brought up their family there as well.

My earliest memories around the mid 50s are of playing with my siblings in our garden at No 22, where our Father had built us a railway track around the garden complete with stations, trains and signals. Dad was really good at making things and even made us girls our very first dolls, all handmade out of wood in his workshop garage. He also made most of the furniture in our homes and all these years later I still have a table that he made. Our bungalow backed onto fields and we kept chickens which foraged up close to the fence and sometimes got out into the fields and we had to 'herd' them back ...... We had lots of eggs and Mum used to make some delicious cakes - she really was a great cook.

Dad also grew lots of our vegetables in the garden so we were always having fresh food. We also had a garage and part of this was taken over by a huge aviary and we kept a small flock of budgerigars in a

## Chapter 18. Prefab Bungalows - Married Quarters and Hostel Sites.

variety of colours - I think my love of birds grew from them. Woodlands had two main road entrances and to get anywhere one had to cross the main A4 road although it was not so busy in those days it was still a big deal for young kids. We had to cross the road to get milk from the little Webb's Dairy which was opposite the bottom entrance to Woodlands as well as to attend Regis School or get into the town centre or visit the playground at the Rec. We would also cross the road at the top entrance to visit Newman's Pickwick Store to pick up supplies.

As we got older, we wandered further and further away from home and sometimes spent all day in the surrounding area, perfectly safe. On the edge of a field behind No 20 was a small pond and we spent many hours 'fishing' for Tadpoles and Newts there and taking them home to store in jam jars on our bedroom window sills.

Woodlands photo courtesy of Sheila Williams (nee Groves): Front row left to right: Malcolm Groves, Sheila Groves, and Anthony Darby. Second Row Judith Whitfield with white hair pigtails. Back row: Tallest boy with dark tank top is Maurice Cloud.

The occasion was a 2 June 1953 party to celebrate the Queen's Coronation on the field in the middle of the Woodlands bungalows.

One of our favourite pastimes was to walk to Weavern, down Middlewick Lane and across the fields and woods spending many hours playing and splashing in the river. It's such a scenic spot and I still remember it as a very special place.

Mum did not like us going there though as she used to visit as a child and was caught in a whirlpool which frightened her of *open water* for life. We would often take a picnic which usually consisted of a few apples we had 'taken' from an orchard along the lane - we never did get caught thank goodness or we would have been in deep trouble from our parents, Kathleen and Fabian Groves who were quite strict but always fair.

Happy days and memories to store forever.

Chapter 18. Prefab Bungalows - Married Quarters and Hostel Sites.

**By Malcolm Groves (Sheila's older brother).**

My Dad used to scour the fields with me all day for elderberries and cowslips in the summer and make gallons of wine. My Dad liked a pint now and then; when he visited the Cross Keys, I would be made to sit outside waiting in the porch with a packet of crisps! We had two televisions in our house (which was quite posh!), one which had no sound and the other which had no picture! To watch a programme, we had to have both TVs on at the same time and tuned in to the same channel. When we were living in No.20 (the larger bungalow), all of the bedrooms were at the back, except my small bedroom which was at the front. This meant that after we had all been sent to bed, I could sneak down the long corridor and watch TV from my hiding place behind the settee without my parents even knowing!

The motorbike below belonged to Terry Godsell (Malcolm's Cousin) and seated are Mum Kathleen Groves and Aunty Bet Godsell. From left to right in the photo on the right are Frances, Malcolm and Sheila playing with the large train set made by their Dad. The girl in the far background is unknown.

One way of making a few pennies those days was to take part in the regular pheasant beats all day Saturday and Sunday, organised by Farmer Stafford in the Weavern valley near Pickwick Lodge Farm. At lunchtime, we ate our sandwiches in the first cottage at Hills Green. For two day's of beating, we used to earn either 2s 6p (half-a-crown) or a brace of pheasants to take home with us; I always chose the money! At the side of Woodlands along Pickwick Road and the other side of a very tall wall, was the big house belonging to the Eden's. They had an orchard full of apples which was a magnet to us Woodlands lads. To get over the wall meant climbing up a prickly Holly tree that grew alongside. To climb back was even more arduous and involved clambering up the stone wall using whatever handholds we could find. Another magnet for scaling the wall was the Eden's swimming pool where his young daughters used to spend their summer afternoons! On one occasion when I was 10 years old, I received my just punishment for my 'scrumping' activities and was rewarded with a large gash to my leg whilst descending the Holly tree and falling into some barbed wire; the scar is still visible and just as *angry* today!

We were very often sought out by the local Constabulary for our crimes. On one occasion, we could see the Constable approaching on his bicycle and I managed to hide behind the large fir tree at the entrance

## Chapter 18. Prefab Bungalows - Married Quarters and Hostel Sites.

to the Woodlands estate (that tree is still there today and has grown even bigger). We always called this tree the 'Red Wood Fir' due to the bark's ruddy hue; but my face was much redder than the bark that day as I shook behind it in fear of being caught.

I remember Pat Poolman's grocery van regularly visiting the estate and my Mum would often disappear inside and then come out with the weekly shopping all bagged up. To supplement our diet, our Dad kept chickens in a coup in the back garden. Despite all of his efforts, one night some foxes managed to get through the wire and all we had left in the morning was a pile of bones and feathers!

There were less than 30 bungalows on our estate, which meant that there was plenty of room for us to play football. Mrs Clarke who lived with her son Sidney in a bungalow nearby, would refuse to return our football if it found its way into her garden - which it did on several occasions. In one of the bungalows at the top end of the estate and fronting Middlewick Lane, lived Mr George Davis. He was a regular visitor each week to all of our bungalows, as he was the local Littlewood's Football Pools collector. Another character was Maurice Cloud who lived at No. 30 with his Mum in one of the bungalows near Middlewick Lane. Maurice would wander around forever twiddling a piece of string in his right hand and being transfixed by it. He was very often seen wandering along the High Street in Corsham.

We had a great time as a family living there and we've all managed to keep in touch with each other on a regular basis.

Some of the families living in Woodlands at the time were; Baker, Beard, Bird, Clarke, Cloud, Coleman, Davis, Cullimore, Fletcher, Godsell, Jones, Newman (Steve Newman who managed the Spar Shop in Pickwick), Morgan, Plank, Robinson, Simpkins (managed the bike shop in Pickwick), Teague, Wilmot, Wilson.

**NAME: Colin Hudd.**
**PREFAB ADDRESS:** 20 Dickens Avenue.
**DURATION approx: 1955 to c1962.**

Prior to 1955, our family lived in the small hamlet on the edge of Corsham called Easton, where my Father was employed at Easton Court Farm. One of my favourite memories there was during a hot summer's day, when a cow escaped onto the road. My Father tried in vain to herd the said cow back into its pasture, but it required more than one individual to succeed in this task. Whilst my Father was running back and forth after the cow along the lanes that surrounded the field in front of the farm entrance, he spotted Farmer Flower casually watching proceedings but making no move to come to his aid. My Father spent a considerable time chasing after the cow with little success apart from becoming more heated, tired, annoyed and exasperated by the lack of help from the passive farmer who just stood by and watched. By this time, my Father had had enough, and told the farmer in no uncertain terms what he could do with his job! The wild cow was later captured and returned to the field by the farmer after obtaining assistance from another of his labourers.

My Father having resigned his position on the farm, contacted the local housing authority, (Chippenham and District Council), informing them of our need to be re-housed, as we were living in *tied* accommodation (i.e. accommodation provided by your employer). This resulted in our move to 20 Dickens Avenue, a prefabricated bungalow in Corsham - I was five and a half. Our home was the 10th bungalow on the right hand side, west from the Oliver Avenue end of Dickens Avenue.

## Chapter 18. Prefab Bungalows - Married Quarters and Hostel Sites.

Corsham Regis School was the nearest to our new home. Unfortunately, due to a lack of places being available I continued to attend the County Primary School (where the Pound Arts Centre is today), although walking there was twice the distance than the walk to the Regis School. In the County Primary School photo below, I'm the cute looking one third from the left in the back row!

Our new home was very cosy. In the small kitchen was an oven that was heated by a back-boiler behind the sitting-room fire. Mother always used her electric cooker, so the kitchen oven became redundant. The sitting-room was just big enough to fit a table and four chairs and a small three piece suite. Three bedrooms, toilet and bathroom led off a connecting passage way. Weekly rent cost 14shillings 9pence – 75pence decimal. Our bungalow was built next to an old air-raid shelter that was situated approximately four to five yards between buildings. The previous tenant had enclosed the shelter with walls either end and placed a roof over the top which created an excellent utility room for us.

Winters were much colder than the present day. Central heating was unheard of at these times. An open fire in the sitting room was the only major source of heat with a back boiler for heating the water tank. Our beds would be made up of flannelette sheets, two blankets, an eiderdown and a bedspread. During a severe cold spell, a dressing-gown and coat would also be thrown over.

To take the chill off the bedrooms, bathroom and the toilet, a paraffin heater would be located in the connecting corridor. It was not unusual to wake up of a morning and witness ice on the inside of our bedroom windows, increasing to a considerable thickness over a prolonged period of cold weather, resulting in windows being frozen solid making it impossible to open them! It was not unheard of for a thickness of one inch of ice to build up inside - 25mm. For a working class family during such austere times, money was never plentiful. Both Mum and Dad took on *'side lines'*, for a local company.

Mum would stick sheriffs' badges, decorative bands and coloured feathers to felt cowboy hats, that were later sold at seaside resorts; she also *cleaned* for pensioners who, through old age were unable to do so, (referred to as *home help* by the authorities). Dad, along with my Uncle John would carry out car repairs in our converted air-raid shelter, sometimes working very late hours into the night after doing a full days work with their respective employers.

During the early redevelopment stages of the prefab sites in Corsham, the Calne and Chippenham Council authorities arranged to move familys en-block to create areas for demolition and rebuild. During the World War II years families had developed a strong sense of community spirit on the Corsham

## Chapter 18. Prefab Bungalows - Married Quarters and Hostel Sites.

prefab estates. This was now being destroyed by separating friends and neighbours by moving them to outlying areas such as Chippenham, Calne and other locations when housing became available. Once the bulldozers moved in and demolition of the prefabs began, the great mounds of builders' earth and rubble that piled up became enormous adventure playgrounds. Dens were dug out from the soil and covered over with doors purloined from the demolished bungalows. This was before health and safety practises were thought of. The idea of groups of young children running wild around a building site these days, would cause modern day thinkers to go ballistic!

Families living in Dickens Avenue were: No.18 Dickens Avenue Mr and Mrs Gallagher with daughters Mary and Patsy. No.16 Mr and Mrs Moore with sons Brian, Graham and a younger daughter. No.23 Mr and Mrs Prout with daughters Jacquie, Vivienne and son Dennis. No. 24 Mr and Mrs Johnson with family. While travelling to work Mr Johnson was tragically killed in a motor-cycle accident on the nearby A4 junction with Hartham Lane. No.29 Mr and Mrs George Leamon with daughters Beryl and Jennifer who became close friends of the Hudd family. No 31 Mr and Mrs Walman with daughter Bridget and son Michael. No.35 Mr and Mrs Bill Brown with daughter Diane. No.37 Mrs Moss with her two daughters. No.39 Mr and Mrs Ryan with a daughter and son Tommy. No.41 Mr and Mrs Jenkins with daughters Marlene, Gloria, Debra and Sonia and son Roger.

Families I recall living in nearby Weller Road were Mr and Mrs Lewis with sons Howard and Gareth. And Mr and Mrs Morris with daughter Margery and son John.

On reflection in later life, the community spirit during the 1950s decade was far greater than present day. Although I know many of my present neighbours by sight, only a few are willing to create a conversation - most will not. Too busy with the present day pressures of life I suppose!?

**NAMES: John (Jock) and Josie McMillan.**
**PREFAB ADDRESS: 45 Kings Avenue, 122 Rudloe, 44 Rudloe.**
**DURATION approx: 1954 to 1965.**

Josie and Jock met in their teens and fell in love when they both worked at Mendip Engineering in Atworth. Josie would ride her bike into work from her home in Melksham with Jock commuting from his parent's bungalow at 45 Kings Avenue in Corsham.

When the McMillan family had originally moved down to Corsham from Glasgow, their belongings were sent to Cosham (Portsmouth) by mistake! Because of the lack of places in the nearby Regis School (a stone's throw away from Kings Avenue), Jock had to attend classes two miles away at Neston School where the teachers could not understand a word of what he said, because of his strong Glaswegian accent!

After they married, Josie and Jock spent a couple of years working in Crystal Palace, London where they purchased their first form of transport - a tandem! Josie recalls with laughter when they first tried it out in London. They could not get the hang of steering it and ended up going round in circles before passing through red traffic lights and causing chaos! On one occasion, the London Police purposefully hijacked the tandem and would only return it if Jock and Josie promised to buy tickets to their local Police Ball!

Josie and Jock returned to live for a while with Jock's parents at 45 Kings Avenue in Corsham before moving into their own home on the Rudloe estate at bungalow No.122 Rudloe, roughly around 1954. Their tandem was sent down to Corsham from London.

## Chapter 18. Prefab Bungalows - Married Quarters and Hostel Sites.

*The photo shows Jock and Josie at No.122 (at the bottom of the estate where the flats are now). You can see the Bradford Road entrance at the bottom of the Rudloe estate.*

On one occasion, they rode out together to Weston-super-Mare for *a day at the seaside*, but heavy rain spoiled the outing.

The tandem, along with a very wet Jock and Josie, returned via train to Bath station, followed by a wet ride in tandem back along the A4 to Rudloe. But things were not always smooth in the early days of courting!

On a journey back from a visit to Chippenham, Josie recalls that they had a blistering argument (about something or other) whilst riding back home up Chequer's Hill on the tandem.

Before they had even reached the top, Josie had jumped off the tandem and told Jock in no uncertain terms, *"To ride the tandem back himself"*. An irate Josie made her way back home herself on foot.

Thankfully the lovers' tiff was short-lived, as Jock (now 89) and Josie (86) have been happily married for 66 years and have six children; Robert, Donald, Shirley, Heather, Stuart and Darren. But the tandem continued to have a mind of its own - whilst on their way to a wedding in Melksham, the tandem decided to take a sharp turn at the Great Western at the bottom of Pound Pill and Jock and Josie ended up crashing into someone's front door.

Next door in Rudloe, lived Mrs Corbin a Maltese woman and her lodger a Polish refugee known locally as *Willy the Pole*. Willy, who had long black slick hair and wore knee-length leather boots, was *mad* on pigeons and had cultivated a large number of them in a make-shift roost in the back garden. Willy spent so much time tending his pigeons that one day it caused an argument with Mrs Corbin. The argument reached such a fever pitch that *Willy the Pole* strangled all of his pigeons in a fit of temper. A couple of days later Josie spotted somebody on the roof next door. It was *Willy the Pole* collecting up his clothes and belongings that had previously been strewn all across the bungalow's roof by an irate Mrs Corbin!

Two years later, Jock and Josie moved into 44 Rudloe (at the top of the estate near to where the MoD houses are these days). The Walsh's who lived next door to Jock and Josie at 44 Rudloe, had a dog which Josie's young daughter Heather doted on. Heather would *sneak out* early in the morning and occasionally *'borrow'* a pint of milk from a neighbour's doorstep in the street behind - and feed it to the dog! Needless to say, the dog would have been thankful - but not so the *milkless* neighbours! Heather was partially repaid later at her 18th birthday party in the Rudloe Hotel when a drunken gatecrasher got himself locked in and caused a bit of a rumpus by waking up the landlord in the middle of the night; resulting in some embarrassment for the McMillan family. Josie and Jock still live at Rudloe, in the houses that replaced the bungalows, with the Walsh family next door again.

The Rudloe Social Club was originally located in a building on the west side of the estate (once used as an Egg Packing Factory and later by Westinghouse to house machinery). Here the residents would learn dancing, socialise with friends etc. When the modern Rudloe Social Club was built on the green, many

## Chapter 18. Prefab Bungalows - Married Quarters and Hostel Sites.

people lost contact with each other, as the bar there was too big and the atmosphere not quite as friendly as it had been in the old establishment. The Egg Packing building had a shop attached to it run by Mr Wyatt. Josie fondly recalls wheeling four of her children in her pram back and forth to the shop and all the way into Corsham Town centre on occasions (two hanging on each side, one inside and one standing at the back). To make ends meet for a family of eight, Josie supplemented the household bills by taking on several part-time jobs: Westinghouse as a cleaner, Harris' Bacon Factory in Calne, Price's Rubber Factory at the bottom of Quarry Hill (working in the Black Hole, *"with a bloke called Joe"* and pushing tennis balls through a hot steam pipe!), barmaid at the Royal Arthur Naval establishment at the bottom of Westwells, *"where your ears would stand on end with some of the comments made"!* and a cleaner at the Copenacre Naval Stores Apprentices building on the MoD Rudloe site by Hawthorn Post Office.

Jock's first job was as an apprentice engineer in a two-year stint at the Bristol Aeroplane Company (BAC) underground factory at Spring Quarry. Once qualified, he was kept busy, occasionally moving from full-time job to job to look after his family: working later at Mendip Engineering in Atworth, Westinghouse in Chippenham, and Leafield Engineering.

*Here is Jock below with that blessed tandem!*

Jock also played outside left for Chippenham Football Club. He also played the trombone in the Corsham Band before he married. Josie remembers that they did not have much money in those days, yet they were the happiest years of their life together. Everyone was in the same boat - little money, sparse living conditions, little prospect of a better life. Today, neighbours rarely have the same relationships that seemed to blossom naturally in the 1950/60s.

**NAME: Graham Peaple.**
**PREFAB ADDRESS: 1 Elm Grove and 58/60 Kings Avenue.**
**DURATION approx: 1952 to 1965.**

I was delivered into this world on September 20th 1952 at number 1 Elm Grove Avenue by Nurse Slocomb, one of the local district nurses. Already in the tiny prefab bungalow were my parents and five brothers and three sisters. I don't remember anything about Elm Grove as I only spent my first eighteen months there. Conditions must have been very cramped, and I have no idea of the sleeping arrangements. In 1954 we moved to a different prefab, numbers 58 and 60 Kings Avenue which were situated alongside the A4, halfway between the turnings for Hartham and Biddestone on the Regis estate. This was to be my childhood home for the next twelve years. We had a doorway in the middle of our home that converted the prefab block of two into one dwelling. To my parents, it must have seemed like they had won the football pools with the extra rooms we now had.

We were now down to 'only ten' occupants living there; my eldest sister Emelda having recently married and moved to Bath. Having two bungalows meant that our gardens front and rear were the size of two.

## Chapter 18. Prefab Bungalows - Married Quarters and Hostel Sites.

My Dad was a very keen gardener and the front was in constant bloom throughout the year with seasonal flowers and shrubs. To the rear, starting along one side, we had a cooking apple tree, a long row of blackberry bushes, blackcurrant bushes, strawberries, raspberry canes, gooseberry bushes and an assortment of vegetables. My Dad was careful enough to leave space for a lawn on one side for me and my siblings to play on. There was a dry stone wall at the end of the rear garden, over which were two enormous greenhouses belonging to Bert Sawyer, who ran the Cross Keys pub, *just a stones throw away* from us. Opposite the front of the bungalow was our own 'village green' complete with an air raid shelter. Countless hours were spent re-enacting war time battles with my friends in and around this shelter, as did other children in shelters dotted around the estate. The bulldozers didn't get to us until 1965 and our prefab was the last on the Regis estate to be razed to the ground.

**NAME: Lizzie Pike (Nee Morgan).**
**PREFAB ADDRESS: 3 Wardle Road.**
**DURATION approx: 1953 to 1962.**
**MY MEMORIES:** I remember our times in 3 Wardle Road with fondness. We used to play in the adventure playground built in the front garden by Mr Carosi for his three boys opposite in No. 2. None of the other kids had anything like it in their gardens. My brother Tony always said Mrs Carosi always cooked the best chips he had ever tasted; it must have been the olive oil, as my Mum only ever used lard. The first pasta I ever tasted was in No.2. When I went home and told my Mum about it, she didn't even know what pasta was; neither did I, but I've loved it ever since, although my Mum never ever cooked it. Come to think of it, I don't think they even sold pasta in Corsham or Wiltshire in those days. *[Note by Julian Carosi - my parents used to buy our pasta and olive oil once a month from a proper Italian shop in Bath at the bottom of the Wellsway].* I remember the bonfire nights on the waste land opposite our bungalows. It was a huge affair and the local boys who made the bonfires, used to guard them in case the kids from the other bonfire site next to Edgell's the Chip Shop, at the back of the Community Centre, tried to sabotage it. We had the first television in Wardle Road. We used to have the neighbours in when something special was on. But how we all managed to see it at the same time was a miracle, as the screen was only about 12 inches and the picture was always fuzzy. The television screens these days are almost as big as the screen was in the old Regal cinema in town! Nobody had very much spare money and there was no peer pressure as to who had the best stuff like today's kids.

We didn't write Christmas lists or ask for money; instead we got what our parents could afford and we were really excited to get anything. Christmas dinner was so special - even having a roasted chicken was exciting. We had real Christmas trees (mostly purloined from the surrounding woods).

There were no artificial trees or fairy lights. My Mum used to light small candles in holders balanced precariously on the tree; it's a miracle how our little prefab didn't burn down. We used to enjoy making paper chain decorations to hang across the living room. On Christmas morning, we would all be out in our road showing off our bikes or prams etc. even if they were mostly second hand. It didn't matter to us and we never gave it a thought. In the winter, we had frost on the inside of our windows and I can remember seeing my breath in the room when I put my head above the bedcovers. We had paraffin heaters dotted around the house giving off their pungent smell. This, along with our coal fire was just about enough for us to survive! Did all of this make us better persons, stronger, politer people? Yes it certainly did!

Chapter 18. Prefab Bungalows - Married Quarters and Hostel Sites.

**NAME: Maryvonne Dixon (nee) Phillips, brother Jon Phillips and mum Audry Phillips (nee Rawlin).**
**PREFAB ADDRESS: 45 Churchill Avenue.**

Jon Phillips & Grandmother Bee Rawlin.     Mum Audry Phillips (nee Rawlin).      Jon Phillips

*Nurse Maryvonne Dixon (nee Phillips)!*      *Maryvonne and Jon Phillips in the back garden.*

Maryvonne recalls……..I remember waking up in the winter mornings and dragging my clothes into bed with me to warm them up before dressing, and drawing pictures on the ice that Jack Frost had left on the inside of our window panes. Despite having hot and cold taps in the bathroom, we often had baths in front of the fire as a child, with the water being heated up in the clothes boiler! I felt quite privileged having a bathroom and a separate toilet indoors, compared to some of our friends who did not live on the estate, who still had freezing cold outside loos!

One striking memory for me was running home from school with my friend Peter Brooks when it was raining hard with thunder and lightning. I had taken my New Testament book into school to show people and whilst we were running home I accidentally dropped it in the rain. Both Peter and I stopped to pick it up. At that same instant, two forks of lightening struck the ground in front and behind us. Had we carried on running, I am sure we would have been hit. Thank you God!

Chapter 18. Prefab Bungalows - Married Quarters and Hostel Sites.

We used to shimmy up the wall of the air raid shelter near our home and sit on top with playmates Graham Peaple and his brothers who lived nearby. I used to get pushed about in my dolls pram by the older girls as I was so small. One day, a car came around the corner and frightened them. They all ran away and left me stuck inside the pram which by then had been tipped over in the panic. A lot of the kids used to play in our back garden because we had a huge tree and a part of our garden was shaped like a platform. My brother Jon and his mates created a wall of Breeze Blocks around the tree and used it as their *gang's meeting place*. We (the girls) staged *'pretend plays'* on the platform and did cartwheels all around the garden. Mum Audrey, went to Teacher Training and did some teaching at the new Corsham Secondary School. She went on to become a teacher of Needlework and Domestic science and now lives in Trowbridge. My mum cycled everywhere. It was very unusual to see any motor vehicles. I used to chase the dustbin wagon around, as my uncle was one of the dustmen. One day, I fell over and cut my knee quite badly and had to get a lift back home in the dustbin lorry. I still have the scar. *[Ed: Maryvonne went on to become a Social Worker.]*

**NAME: Evalene (Eva) Wherlock (nee) Thornber.**
**PREFAB ADDRESS: 32 Churchill Avenue.**
**DURATION approx: 1950 to 1962.**
**MY MEMORIES:**

The photo here shows left to right: Maryvonne Dixon (nee Phillips), Evalene (Eva) Wherlock (nee) Thornber and Susan Duparcq (nee Witt). Posing on the platform stage at 45 Churchill Avenue, in their 'Strolling outfits' worn for a performance at the Bath Pavilion from the Dorothy Colborne School of Dancing. Susan became the Corsham Library Supervisor.

**Eva's memories:** I lived at 32 Churchill Avenue with my mum, dad and sister Laureen and brother Barry. I remember the windows frosting over on the inside and marvelling at the different patterns on each pane. My goldfish was in a bowl by the window. I woke one morning to find him suspended in a globe of ice! One Mothering Sunday when I was about 5 years old, I remember getting into a lot of trouble after presenting my mum with a bunch of flowers. She knew I had no money, so asked where they came from. I had picked them from a garden up the road, not realising that this was wrong.

Mum knew they had come from a particular garden, I think the man who lived in that bungalow was a Policeman. Mum brought him down to ours, so that I could apologise. Being an avid **Noddy** reader, I was convinced I would be locked up in prison for my misdemeanor, so I hid under my brother's bed. I was found and made to apologise. I have very fond memories of the freedom we had as children, skipping rope in the street, playing *two-ball* against the wall of the bungalows, hopscotch. It was a real community. *[Ed: Evalene became a Reverend in Bristol (her family came to England from India.]*

Chapter 18. Prefab Bungalows - Married Quarters and Hostel Sites.

**NAME: June Witt.**
**PREFAB ADDRESSES: 8 Queens Avenue, Portland Crescent Boxfields, and 63 Churchill Avenue.**
**DURATION approx: 1950 to 1962.**
**MY MEMORIES:**

The wartime bungalows were not intended to last past the end of the war and were erected quickly and cheaply. The outer walls were made of breeze blocks and lined inside with bricks; no plastering over them, so the wallpaper always looked bumpy! The bungalow was cool in summer but very cold in winter.

The winter of 1962/63 is the one that sticks in my mind. Snow fell on Boxing Day and hung about until March. Every day and night we had snow falling, with temperatures remaining below freezing. As the windows were single-glazed with frames made of metal and poorly fitted, frost quickly formed on the inside of the glass during the evening and icicles hung down from the inside ledges by the morning. During that bad winter, it was usual to send our three girls to bed wearing more clothes than they did during the day, plus hot-water bottles.

Our one form of heating was an open fire in the living room. The cold became so intense on several nights that my husband covered our children with our own blankets.

My husband Dennis and I then went to sleep on the fireside rug with coats and other rugs over us, hoping that the fire would last until morning. We loved our bungalow and were sad to leave it.

The A4 nearby to the left in the photo above runs parallel to the telegraph poles towards the Cross Keys. Our bungalow (63 Churchill Avenue) was roughly where the washing is hanging out in the photo.

In the foreground, you can see the foundations for the *new* Queens Avenue council houses being built at the same time as the remainder of the *old* Churchill Avenue bungalows were being demolished!

In the photo above, the gentleman centre left is walking with his child along the path to the A4 that comes out opposite Hartham Lane. The large block of flats in the distance, is Orchard House top of Orchard Road.

Chapter 18. Prefab Bungalows - Married Quarters and Hostel Sites.

**NAME: Tom Wright. PREFAB ADDRESS: 22 Fuller Avenue.**
**DURATION approx: 1956 to 1965.**
**MY MEMORIES:**

My memories as a child growing up in Fuller Avenue, was that of the *freedom to roam*, and trust in people. We never even had a key for the back door for as long as I can recall. Yes, we had all of the so-called hardships of overcrowding, freezing cold rooms etc. but the community spirit was unbelievable. I can recall on one very special snowy Christmas Eve, there was a knock on the back door. My Mum Eileen Wright went to answer it and there was nobody in sight. But there was a large cardboard box left on the doorstep and it was full of Christmas food and goodies that we could only have dreamed of and could never have afforded. The only message on it was, *'To Mrs Wright and Family, from a well wisher'*. My Mum knew so many lovely people, but she never knew who to thank in case it wasn't them. Like they say, money can't buy happiness and I was so happy as a child growing up in the old Corsham Prefabs.

Below is a photo courtesy of Vicky Spear, of children standing in front of one of the Fuller Avenue bungalows. Looming over the bungalow is one of the Corsham Girl's School buildings, now part of the west end of The Corsham School. Between the two bungalows are the coal sheds allocated for each bungalow.

On the flat roof, is the bungalow's concealed water tank. This location these days is at the bottom (east) end of the public car park behind, to the side of the Corsham Swimming Pool.

*The children in the above photo are as follows: 1: Roy Duffey. 2: Michael Farmelow. 3: Christine Higgins. 4: ? Newman. 5: Alice Harney. 6: Jean Knowles. 7: Vicky Spear (nee Harney). 8: Audrey Wright. 9: Audrey McPherson 10: Loraine Farmelow. 11: ?? 12: Anne Golledge 13: ?? 14: Marion Newman. 15: Hazel Duffey. 16: Mary Harney.*

Chapter 18. Prefab Bungalows - Married Quarters and Hostel Sites.

**PREFABS - PART 9: MARRIED QUARTERS AND HOSTEL SITE MAPS:**

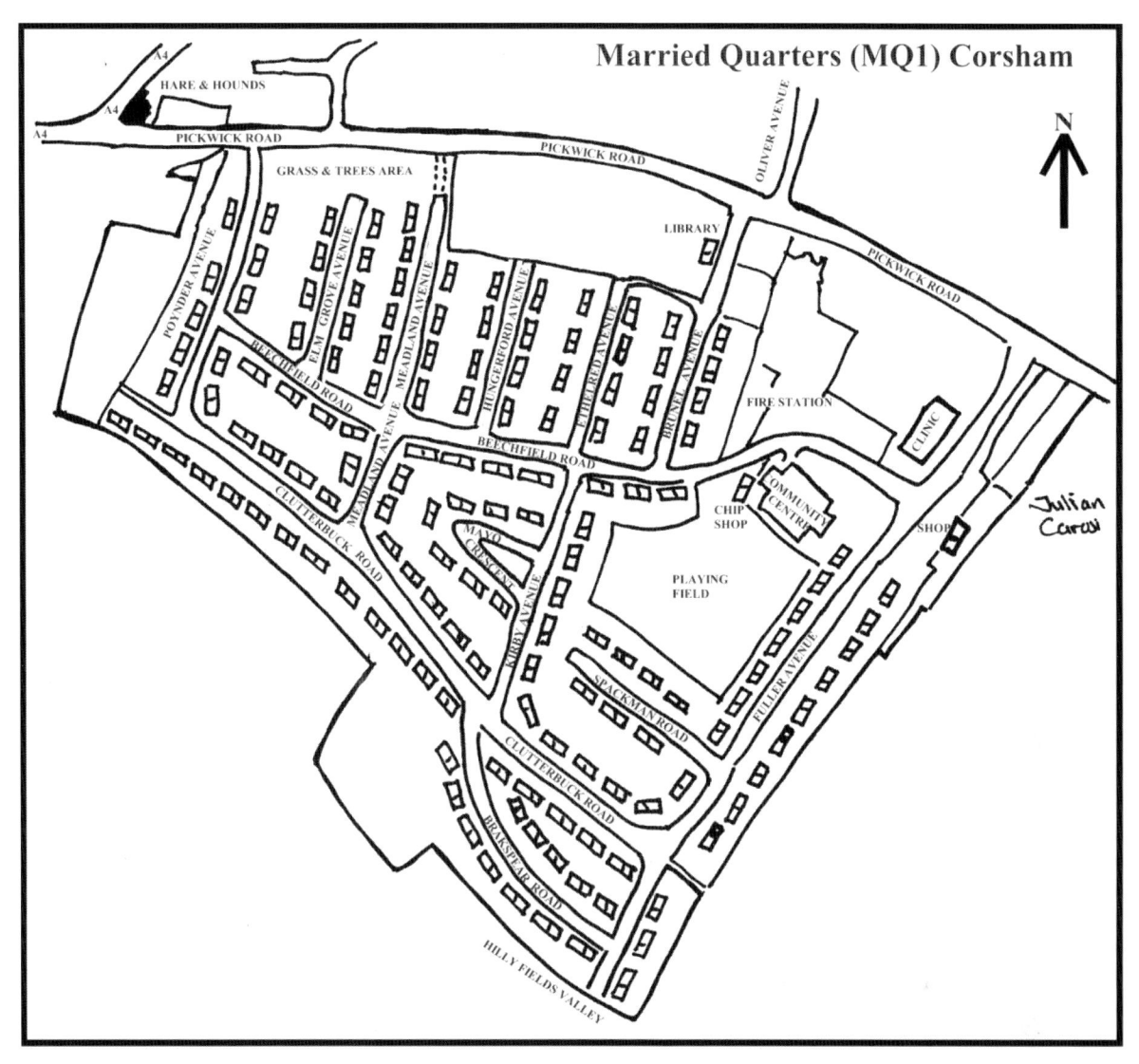

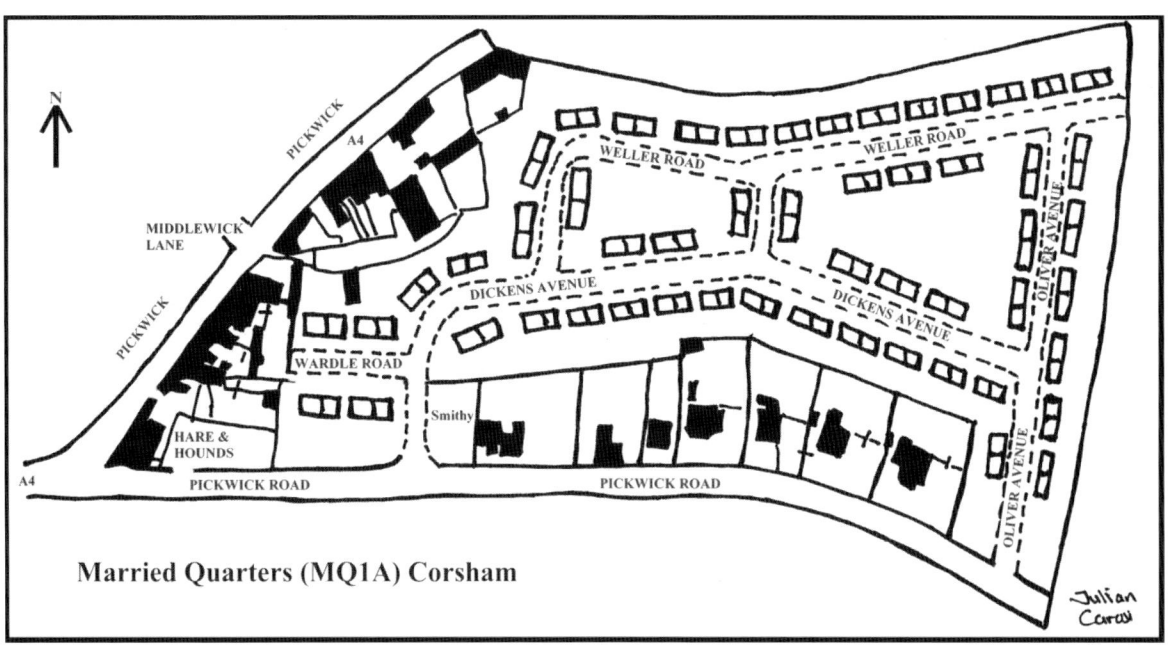

Married Quarters (MQ1) Corsham

Married Quarters (MQ1A) Corsham

Chapter 18. Prefab Bungalows - Married Quarters and Hostel Sites.

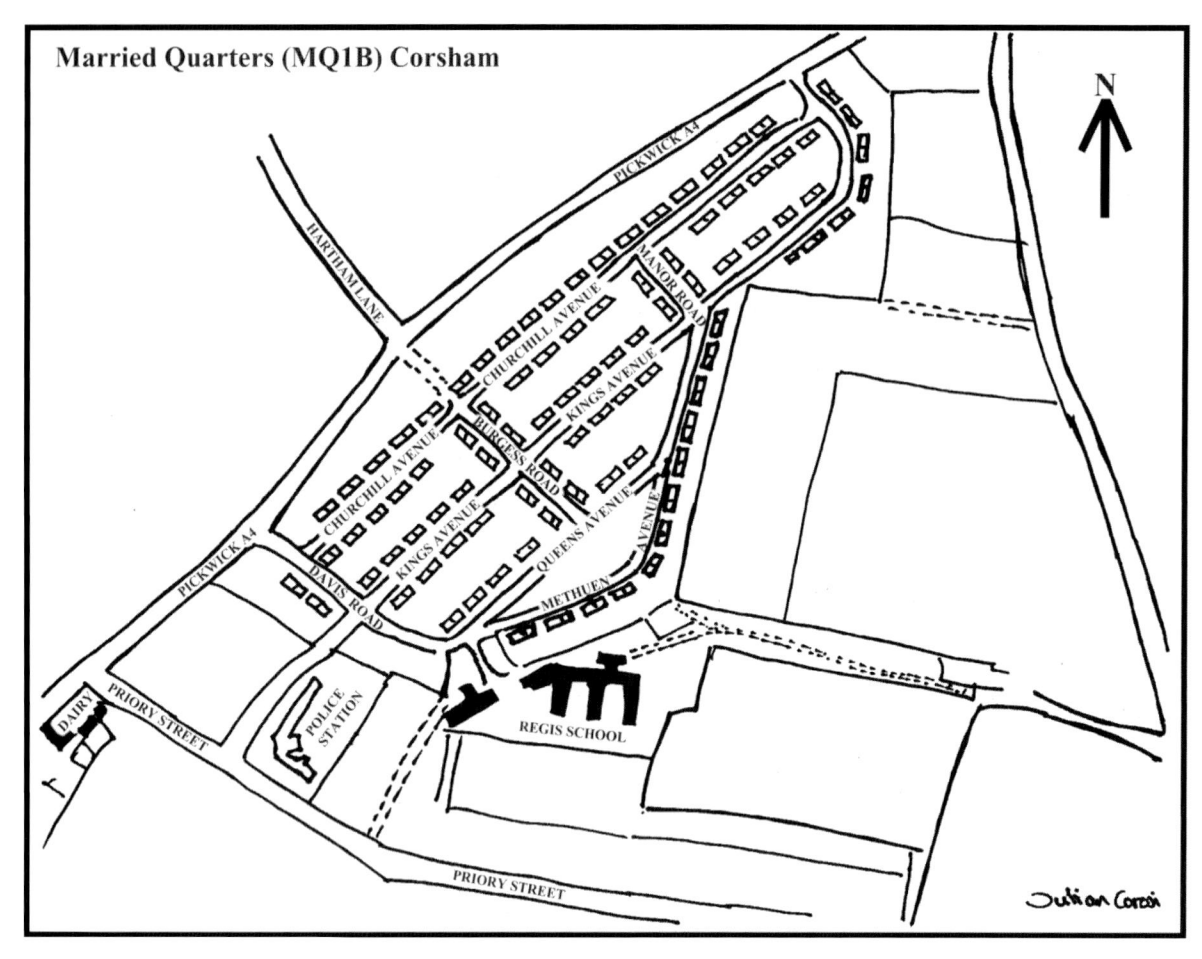

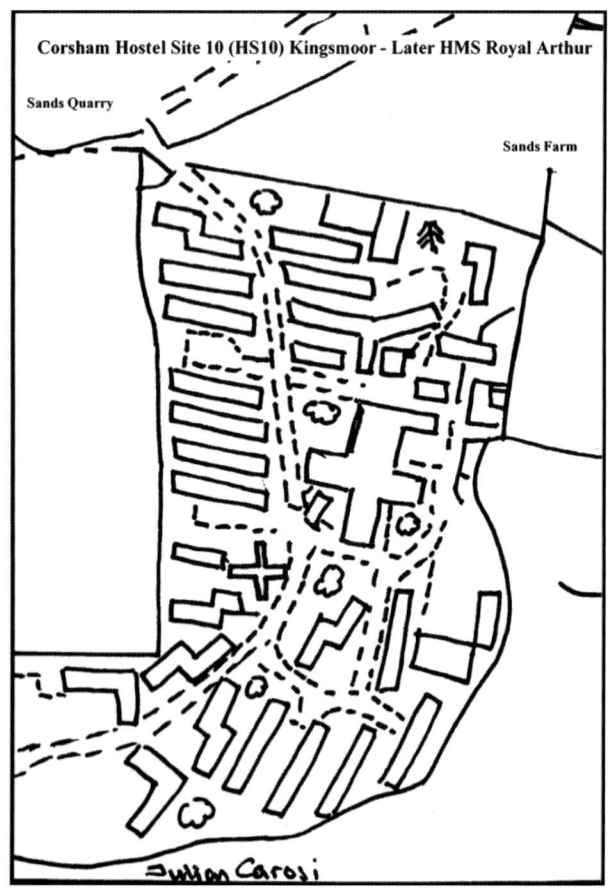

The Married Quarters and Hostel Sites located in Corsham and Rudloe were constructed on previously green field sites.

The Lypiatt Hostel Site (HS15) continues to be used by the MoD and is now the Services Cotswold Centre. Potley (HS8) was redeveloped as Leafield Industrial Estate and Rudloe (HS14), for housing, although the latter had been rebuilt as Married Quarters during the war.

The Kingsmoor Hostel Site (HS10) (ex-Royal Arthur) has been redeveloped and completely rebuilt as the Wadswick Green Retirement Village.

The other Hostel Sites remain undeveloped or have been absorbed into the MoD sites and immediate surrounding area.

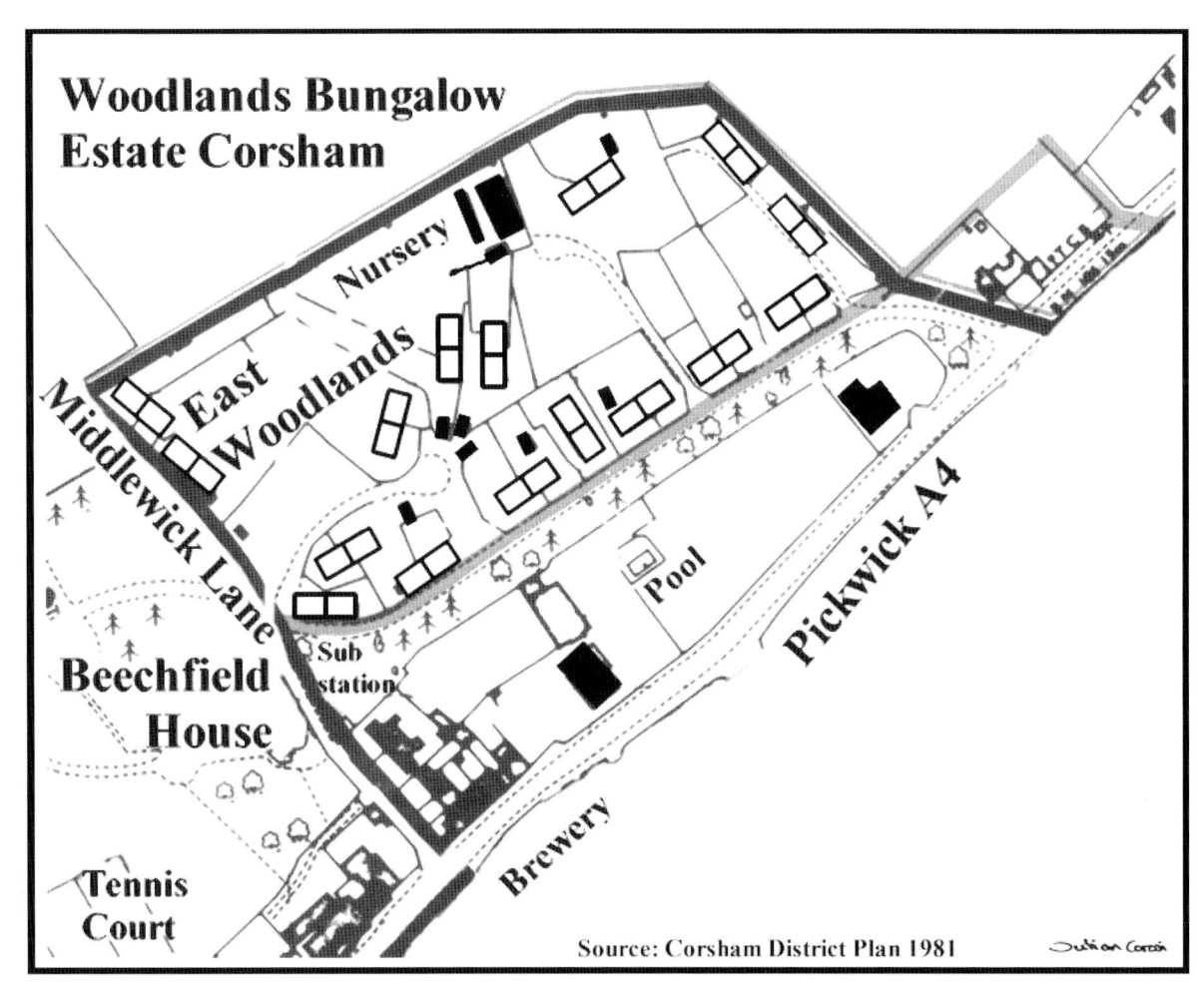

## Chapter 18. Prefab Bungalows - Married Quarters and Hostel Sites.

**Woodlands Bungalow Estate Corsham**

Source: Corsham District Plan 1981

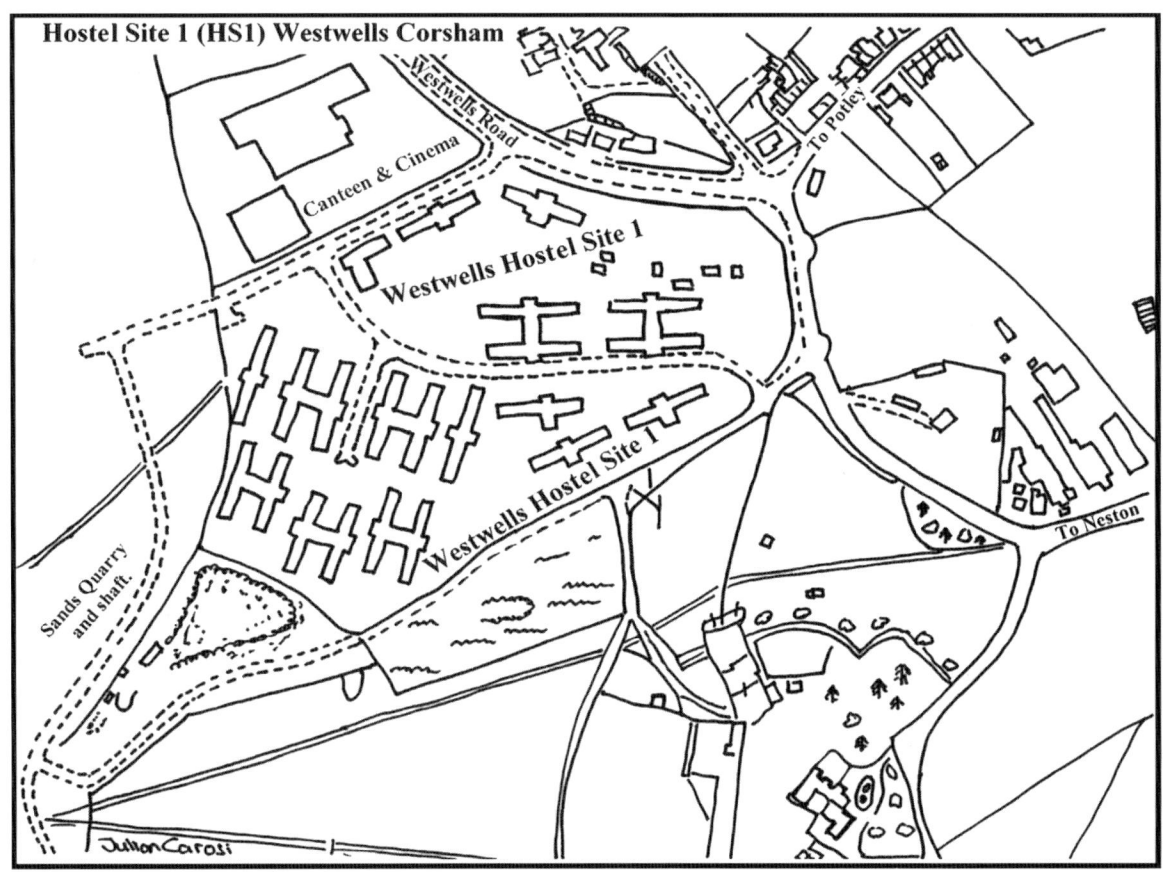

**Hostel Site 1 (HS1) Westwells Corsham**

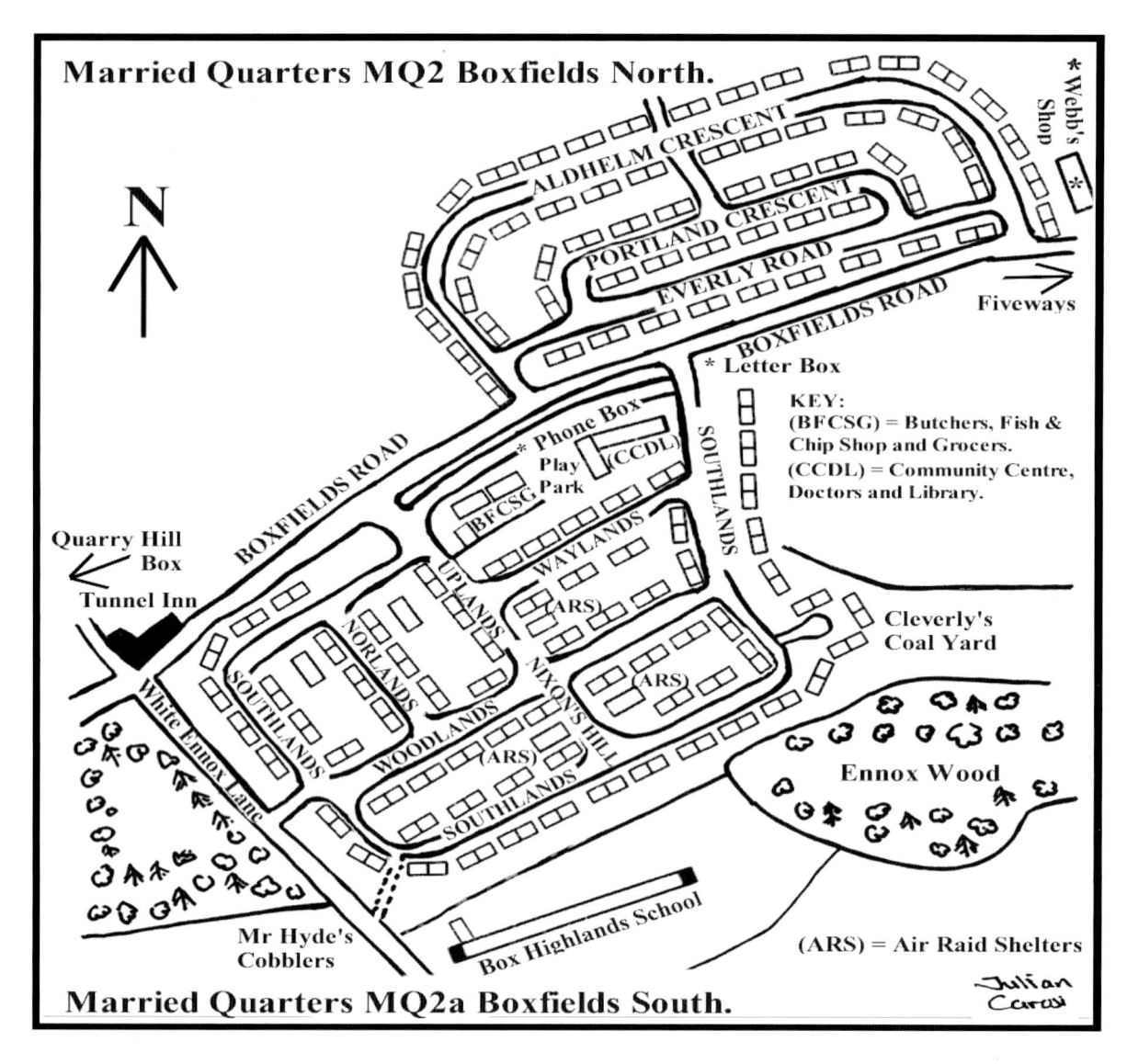

Chapter 18. Prefab Bungalows - Married Quarters and Hostel Sites.

**Married Quarters MQ2 Boxfields North.**

KEY:
(BFCSG) = Butchers, Fish & Chip Shop and Grocers.
(CCDL) = Community Centre, Doctors and Library.
(ARS) = Air Raid Shelters

**Married Quarters MQ2a Boxfields South.**

*Julian Carew*

**Old Corsham Town from the air.**

238

Chapter 18. Prefab Bungalows - Married Quarters and Hostel Sites.

**Additional photos of the Corsham prefabs on the Regis School estate being demolished:**

## Chapter 19. Reverend Edward Gell Corsham's own Unknown Soldier.

**LT. COL. the Rev. EDWARD ANTHONY SYDNEY GELL. DSO , MC ( 23 June 1875 - 9 May 1951)**

This is a story of a Corsham vicar who, although not a death casualty of the Great War, has an interesting history and one well worth sharing. He was that rare breed, a fighting Parson, a combatant Cleric, a man who forsook the cloth for the khaki and who fought in both the Boer and the Great Wars, winning both a Distinguished Service Order (DSO) a Medal for Gallantry (MG) and being Mentioned in Despatches for his bravery in action. Great Britain was fortunate in having so many brave and resourceful men ready to go to their country's aid in the Great War. Edward's role in the selection of the *Unknown Warrior* after WWI is something else that Corsham can be proud of, along with Lord Methuen who was one of the twelve pallbearers. Edward Gell was descended from the Gell family of Hopton Hall, an 18th-century country house at Hopton, near Wirksworth, Derbyshire. His father was a Naval Officer who had seen action in the Far East who, on leaving the service became an Anglican vicar. Edward's story begins in 1875.

**1875:** Edward was born on 23 June 1875 at Hereford. His father was the Church Curate, Francis Gell, born 1825 at Thurland Hall, Nottingham, and his mother was Clara Emma Gell (nee Southan) born 1840 in Gloucester. To ensure his son was not born in Wales, Francis sent his wife across the border to give birth to Edward in *The Green Dragon Inn* at Hereford ........in England.

The nature of his father's job meant that the Gell family were frequently mobile. Rev. Francis Gell was Rector at Llyswen in Breconshire at the time of Edward's birth.

**1881:** The Gell family was living at the Rectory, Lydd in Kent.

**1886:** Edward attended the Sidcot School in Winscombe, Somerset, a British co-educational independent school for boarding and day pupils, associated with the Religious Society of Friends. It was one of seven Independent Quaker Schools in England.

The school based in the Mendip Hills near the village of Winscombe, Somerset, catered for children between the ages of 3 and 18 and covered 160 acres of glorious Somerset countryside.

**1891:** Edward's father was now a Rector of Edburton, Sussex.

**1894:** Edward moved to Corpus Christi College, Cambridge in October.

**1895:** Edward's mother, Clara Emma Gell passed away in Upton upon Severn, Worcester aged 55.

**1897:** Edward graduated from Corpus Christi College with a B.A.

**1898:** At the successful conclusion of his training at a church in Aston, Birmingham Edward was ordained as a Deacon at Worcester later that year.

## Chapter 19. Reverend Edward Gell  Corsham's own Unknown Soldier.

**1899:** When Edward heard of the initial heavy losses being sustained by the British Army in the Boer War [October 11, 1899, to May 31, 1902], he immediately relinquished his clerical duties and volunteered for the front. He enlisted as Trooper No: 7272 in the Queens Own Worcester Yeomanry, one of three Cavalry Companies in the 5th Battalion Imperial Yeomanry, but was shortly commissioned as Quarter Master with the temporary rank of Lieutenant.

**1900:** The London Gazette of 17 November stated the following, *'Cpl. E.A.S. Gell to be Quartermaster with temporary rank of Lieutenant from 6 October 1900'*. When the chaplain attached to the Unit went down with enteric fever [typhoid fever or paratyphoid fever] Edward was put forward to be a *proper* chaplain to one of Lord Methuen's mobile cavalry columns. Methuen had already sent home two chaplains whom he considered too `high church` as they had refused Holy Communion to men who had not been to Confession. Edward stepped into the gap and also whenever it was required, he was acting-chaplain to the Forces. Now he finds himself fighting as a cavalryman during the week and taking church parades on Sundays! He sees himself as a trooper/chaplain - a title he may have given himself! According to the contents of a letter in his file, the officers in the unit were really surprised to discover that they had a *'fully-fledged parson'* within their midst; but his religion didn't protect him from being wounded by a gunshot wound to the head. The casualty returns for the South Africa War show him being wounded at Lindley on 1 June 1900.

The following story concerning Edward came to Rector Roger Clifton in 2005: A distant relative of Richard Tilney of Malmesbury named Col William Tilney was Aide-de-camp (ADC) to Field Marshal Paul Sanford Methuen, 3rd Baron Methuen in South Africa in 1900, where they were both taken prisoner by the Boers. In his memoirs, Col Tilney tells this story about a soldier called Edward Gell:-

*'The time is late 1900 at Krugersdorp District, and to keep the soldiers fit and well races and sports were organised as well as a boxing tournament for the championships of South Africa. The heavyweight final was between a huge Australian and a young Yeomanry Sergeant named Gell. Gell won in the 15th round. After the fight Lord Chesham said, 'Sergeant Gell is one of the men whose name has been forwarded to headquarters as a clerk in Holy Orders, with a view to being made one of the chaplains to Lord Methuen's mobile column.'*

*Photo shows Paul Sanford Methuen, 3rd Baron Methuen © National Portrait Gallery, London*

Col Tilney continues: *"Most of the chaplains who had been sent out from home were of the ritualistic High Church order, and we had real trouble with two, who insisted on Tommies confessing before they administered Holy Communion.*

*Anyone who wasn't on their list, they passed by when administering the sacrament.*

*Feelings ran so high that Lord Methuen sent both of them home and all qualified clerks in Holy Orders who were serving among the troops under his command were asked to send their name to Headquarters to be considered as a potential replacement.*

*There were fifteen in the Yeomanry alone. As I was DAAG, I told Lord Methuen, who was present at the fight, what Lord Chesham had said about Gell".* He replied *"That's the very man we want; send him to me tonight".*

## Chapter 19. Reverend Edward Gell Corsham's own Unknown Soldier.

Edward was not even given time to clean himself up but was taken before Lord Methuen. They discussed the fight - then shaking his hand he told him, "*We will have Holy Communion the day after tomorrow*", and so three services naming Gell as the new chaplain were posted for the Sunday. On the first service that Sunday, 600 soldiers turned out for communion, many had never been to any sort of service before - Gell was bandaged about the head.

When Lord Methuen arrived, he thought they had all got the times wrong. Some of the men, particularly the Australians had never been to a church service before. With such numbers it was obvious, that with no more wine of any kind available, there was going to be insufficient quantities of Communion Wine. But Edward, resourceful as ever, switched the wine by pouring beer into the wine bottles instead. Lord Methuen was obviously very impressed with Edward, and later asked him to become Rector of Corsham.

**1901:** At the beginning of the year, Edward was still serving in South Africa with Lord Methuen's Column in the 1st Division with the 5th Battalion of the Imperial Yeomanry. He may have been wounded again, for he returned to England on 24 May 1901 having resigned his Commission.

**1902:** Edward was discharged from the Imperial Yeomanry, but still retained the honorary rank of Lieutenant, and he also qualified for the Queen's South Africa Medal (QSA) with four clasps (applicable to each battle or campaign), awarded to British and Colonial military personnel, and to civilians employed in an official capacity, who served in the Second Boer War. After his return from the Boer War Edward completed his Master's Degree. Edward married Gertrude Jennie Ryland Bembridge on 3 April at Lillington Church near Leamington, Warwickshire. She was the same age as Edward, being born at King's Norton, Warwickshire, and was the only daughter of the late Rev. Edward Bembridge, formally vicar of Cookley in Worcestershire. The officiating clergy were Edward's father, Rev. Canon Gell, Rev. Canon Flory and the bride's uncle Rev. G.T. Watton.

Lord Methuen who lived at Corsham Court provided Edward with a living and installed him in the new rectory. The Bishop of Bristol inducted the Rev. Edward Gell (formerly curate of Aston, near Birmingham and Army chaplain in South Africa) into the vicarage of Corsham, Wiltshire, on the presentation of Lord Methuen. Edward was introduced to the Corsham parishioners by the 3rd Baron Methuen, known as Field Marshall Methuen of Corsham Court.
*Edward Anthony Sydney Gell* is listed in the display of the Corsham vicars on the wall to the left of St Bartholomew's Church font. Edward was now living in Corsham; the town became the birthplace of three of his children.

| 1872 | Ditto | George Linton |
| 1889 | Ditto | James Dunlap Dunlap |
| 1902 | Paul Sanford Methuen (3rd Baron) | Edward Anthony Sydney Gell |
| 1908 | Ditto | Austin Ainsworth Slack |
| 1912 | Ditto | Henry Blomfield Ellison |
| 1916 | Ditto | Arthur John Winnington-Ingram |
| 1921 | Ditto | Reginald Coombs Hunt |

**1903:** Edward's daughter Olivier (Honor) Mary Ryland Lassalle was born in Corsham 24 January.

**1904:** Edward's first son Philip Ralph was born in Corsham on 30 December.
The Wiltshire Times and Trowbridge Advertiser of 3 December 1904, reported that - an evening 'Lecture on South Africa' in connection with the 'Literary Institute' took place on 1 December in the Corsham Temperance Hall [the Town Hall], when the Rev. Edward Gell, vicar of Corsham, spoke on his

## Chapter 19. Reverend Edward Gell Corsham's own Unknown Soldier.

experiences with the First Division in South Africa. Mr Gell at the time of the early reverses in the South African war was curate at Aston, Birmingham, and feeling that it was his duty to go to the front, and being unable to do so as a chaplain, joined the Imperial Yeomanry as a trooper. On arrival in South Africa, he was attached to the division commanded by Lord Methuen and served through a greater part of the campaign with that General. Mr Gell related many interesting features in connection with the war, his remarks being interspersed with numerous anecdotes. He also described the pursuit of De Wet, having taken part in the attempts made to capture that ubiquitous General. The second part of the lecture was illustrated by lantern slides of many of the incidents of the campaign, the concluding picture being a photo of Lord Methuen, of whom the lecturer spoke in high terms, remarking that Lord Methuen's splendid soldierly qualities made him a great favourite with the men under his command. At the conclusion the Rev. T. C. Sheppard, who presided, proposed a vote of thanks to Mr Gell and this was carried out with acclamation.

**1906:** Edward's second son Edward Francis was born in Corsham on 1 May.

**1908:** Edward began to get itchy feet and his position after six years as Rector of Corsham Parish Church comes to an end. Much to the regret of Lord Methuen, Edward joined the Army Chaplains' Department. On 15 March 1908 Edward became an Army Chaplain Fourth Class (a rank equivalent to Army Captain) serving at Shorncliffe (Cheriton in Kent ) until 1911.

**1909:** Edward's fourth child 'Tony' Thomas Anthony Ryland Gell was born on 31 May at Hythe, Kent.

**1911:** Edward's father, Revd. Canon Francis Gell M.A. of Dawlish, Rector of Ripple from 1893 to 1906 died aged 86 on the 19th July at Dawlish in Devon where he had retired in 1906. He left an estate worth £8,110 *(nearly £ 667,892 in today's money!)* He left £200 *(£16,500)* to each of his sons John Francis Gell and Captain Philip Sydney Gell, his books, papers and pictures etc. to his son Edward Anthony Sydney Gell, property belonging to his wife to his daughters Susan Clara Joyce Paul and Emma Sarah Belinda Sessions, and the residue of his property to his three daughters Susan Clara Joyce Paul, Emma Sarah Belinda Sessions and Mary Berridge, the share of the last named being retained upon trust for her benefit.

**1914:** When the First World War started (28 July 1914 to 11 November 1918) Edward enlisted as a private and rose to command his battalion. On 20 August he left his family in Colchester at '17 The Avenue', Lexden, and landed with the British Expeditionary Force in France - thereby entitling him to the 1914 Star Trio with Clasp and Rose - attached to the 11th Brigade of the 4th Division. This Brigade was made up from the four Battalions of regular troops stationed in the Colchester Garrison at the outbreak of war. By 23 November, Edward had become Chaplain at the 4th Casualty Clearing Station at Lillers and then from 9 April 1915 at one of the Base Hospitals in Le Havre.

**1915:** He was wounded at Beaumont Hamel and in July he was deemed 'unfit for duty' and was sent home on leave to England. However, his actions were to suggest he favoured a more combative role. Whilst on leave Edward resigned as Forces Chaplain on 24 July 1915, and on the same date applied for a Combatant's Commission with the Infantry. Chaplain-General Taylor Smith supported Edward's application and officially recommended him for the role. Another reference on his application form was from the Mayor of Kensington who had raised the 22nd Battalion City of London Regiment. Another was from Lt. General Belfield who wrote *"He is a quite exceptionally good fellow and soldier... on such days*

## Chapter 19. Reverend Edward Gell  Corsham's own Unknown Soldier.

*as we have service he took it and preached very well, on others he fought .... soldiering is his line... strongly recommend him for a commission. He is a gentleman".*

In a letter to his cousin Edith at Hopton Hall dated 13 August 1915, Edward gave his motivation for resigning: *'I have long felt that as an officer in a regiment I could do more useful work from every point of view than I was doing as a Chaplain. I feel that the experience I had in South Africa ought not to be lost at this time when there is a crying need for officers who know something about the work. I am confident from a spiritual point of view I shall be able to do, in reality, much more, and without the handicap which I have felt during this war.'* [From a letter in possession of Brian Gell].

Edward was commissioned temporary 2nd Lieutenant on 27 July 1915 and directed to the 22 Service Battalion (Kensington's) Royal Fusiliers (City of London Regiment), joining them on 13 August 1915 at Tidworth, Wilts, as part of 99 Brigade, 33 Division, where the Division was undergoing its final intensive training on Salisbury Plain. 2nd Lt. Edward Gell returned to France in November 1915 with 33 Division, but on 25 November 1915 his 99 Brigade was transferred to 2 Division. He went into the trenches on the 27 November with the Division 99 Brigade in the Bethune area, already familiar to Edward from his previous work at Lillers.

**1916:** Edward's second son Edward Francis sadly died at his home in Colchester from the adverse effects of chloroform following an operation at home for adenoids and enlarged tonsils.

In August, when Edward was promoted to temporary Second-Lieutenant, the 'Kensington' Battalion moved south to the Somme where it took part in successive attacks in the Fricourt, Bazentin Ridge and Delville Wood areas. On the 27 July 1916 the 99th Infantry Brigade assaulted and captured Delville Wood. The 22nd Battalion had initially provided *carrying parties*, providing food, water and other supplies to the front lines for the assaulting troops, but in the course of the day the whole Battalion was *thrown into the fight*. Edward moved the remaining men he could collect up from Bernafay Wood, (located near Montauban village) and held the south-east flank of Delville Wood against counter-attacks.

**FOR CONSPICUOUS GALLANTRY.** When Edward's patrol was attacked by machine-gun and rifle fire he brought them safely back, and then returned and endeavoured to rescue a wounded man, who was twice hit again while he was dressing his wounds. He repeatedly carried out gallant work, and always set fine example. It was probably for this initiative and action that he was awarded the Military Cross (Liverpool Daily Post - Monday 21 August 1916).

*British & German wounded, Bernafay Wood, France, July 1916.*

On 7 October the ribbon of the Military Cross was presented to Edward by Major-General Walker, officer commanding 2nd Division at Bertrancourt whilst the Battalion was in billets at Mailly-Mallet. On 16 October 1916 Edward relinquished the temporary acting rank of Captain on ceasing to command a Company, but he was promoted Lieutenant on 18 October 1916. After being withdrawn for rest and re-fitting the Brigade was back in the Redan Sector from 25 October 1916 for the latter stages of the Battle of the Somme.

## Chapter 19. Reverend Edward Gell Corsham's own Unknown Soldier.

On the night of 13 November 1916 Edward was wounded in action near Beaumont Hamel whilst he was Second Lieutenant leading 'C Company in the 22nd Royal Fusiliers' operations on Redan Ridge. A machine gun bullet wound to the right thigh, passed through just above the knee and a fractured left tibia - and he was evacuated to Base Hospital. On 18th November 1916 he embarked at Le Havre on 'Asturias' for Southampton and by 21 November 1916 he was being treated at King Edward VII Hospital, Grosvenor Gardens, London. Whilst he was there, he gave his home address as '17 The Avenue, Colchester'. Various Medical Boards, at different locations as his recovery progressed, checked his readiness for return to duty. For example; 29 December 1916 at Weymouth he had joined his family (still unfit for general service), 1 January 1917 (fit for light home duties only), 29th January at Colchester (still only fit for light duties), and 13 February 1917 at Colchester he was classed as fit to return to general service

**1917:** As usual with recovering soldiers, he was posted to a reserve training battalion, the 5th Royal Fusiliers Reserve Battalion at Aldershot, part of the 1st London Reserve Brigade; joining them on 14 February 1917. Additionally, there would have been a leave period at home in Colchester. Since March 1916 the 2/7th Battalion Lancashire Fusiliers had been based at Colchester, but on 28 February 1917 they landed at Le Havre as part of 197 Brigade, 66 Division, and Lt. E.A.S. Gell was with them having been attached to the Battalion.

On 19 October 1917 he was promoted acting Major Lancashire Fusiliers whilst employed at 66 Division Headquarters. On 14 December 1917 he took over command of the 2/7th whilst the Commanding Officer (CO) was on leave. On the 30 December 1917 it was confirmed that the CO. would be returning but only to work at G.H.Q. Therefore, acting Major Gell was appointed temporary Commanding Officer of the Battalion.

**1918:** This temporary command was confirmed on 4 January 1918 when the Commanding Officer Lt. Col. Hobbins was sent back ill to England. With the appointment of a new second in command to the Battalion, temporary Lieutenant acting Major Gell was promoted to Acting Lieutenant Colonel on 19 January 1918 of the 2/7th Lancashire Fusiliers. Edward was actually on leave when the Germans launched their Kaiserschlact (Spring Offensive) on 21 March, but he raced back to the front. For his actions at Vauvillers Edward was awarded a fighting DSO (London Gazette July 1918). The Citation read:-

*'For conspicuous gallantry and devotion to duty. He had just arrived on leave in England when he heard his division was engaged. He hurried back, and after much difficulty, got to them. Within half an hour of arrival he collected about 100 stragglers and attached them to the remnants of his own battalion, his vigour and fearlessness putting fresh life into the defence. Next day when the line was being driven back, he led a counter-attack with splendid dash under very heavy machine gun fire.'*

He was also 'Mentioned in Despatches' (London Gazette December 1918) possibly for his time as a prisoner of war.

On 27 March 1918, Edward was captured.

When Lord Methuen heard that Edward was missing, believed wounded, he wrote to Edward's wife: *'You must be very proud of him, whether as a clergyman or soldier; in either profession he could have reached the top of the ladder....His name rests by itself at Corsham, for he preached the bible and visited the poor. Others may preach brilliant sermons...but scarcely a parson seems to keep in touch with the poor.'* [Letter in possession of Brian Gell].

## Chapter 19. Reverend Edward Gell  Corsham's own Unknown Soldier.

After his repatriation in late 1918, Edward was asked to write a report regarding the circumstances of his capture and whether he had been wounded, not, he was assured with the purpose of apportioning blame, but simply to place on record an accurate account of what had happened.

This is his written report: *"I was on 14 days leave when the news reached me of the German attack of March 21st. Though I still had 7 days leave left, it was obviously my duty to rejoin at once. With great difficulty I reached Divisional HQ at PROYART. The line was retiring fast. I collected somewhat more than 100 stragglers and joined them to the remnants of my own Battalion whom I met in the region of FAUCOUCOURT on the AMIENS-BRIE road. General Malcolm gave me orders to do all I could to stop the enemy and to fall back on the line VAUVILLERS-FRAMVILLERS by nightfall, where I was told to hold on at all costs. At night I dug in on this line. Next day the Germans bombarded our position very heavily preparatory to an attack. The position of my Battalion was just to the north west of VAUVILLERS. Considerable disorganisation was caused among the troops immediately to the north east of VAUVILLERS by the shelling of our own guns whose shells were dropping short. These troops left their positions and in the rush my men on the right gave. I left my HQ and stopped the rush, managing to keep my command in hand. A few Germans got into VAUVILLERS. I led a counter-attack on the village and with some 50 men re-took the position to the north east which had been vacated. We had not been there more than ten minutes when the general German attack began. We held them for about two hours while they came again and again in thick waves.*

*By this time all ammunition was gone and the Germans were rapidly getting around my left flank. I decided that I could do more damage to the enemy by taking my men through the village and touching up with my left than by waiting where I was for more ammunition. I accordingly led them through the village. As I came into the main street, one of my men who was lying against a wall wounded shouted to me to come to his help. I ordered an officer to lead the men to the old position (held previous to the counter-attack to the north-west) hoping that I should be able to get my own man away. I ran up the street down which a machine gun was firing, and knelt beside the wounded man. I think his leg was broken. His wound was spouting blood. I was binding him up with both hands occupied, when I heard some men running down the street. Thinking that they were some of my own Battalion who had been left behind I did not look up until I was conscious of a bayonet close to my chest, while another German was close behind covering me with his rifle"*
**Signed: *R. F. att. Lancs Fusiliers***

After his repatriation on 13 December 1918 Lt. Col. Gell was medically examined at South Camp, Ripon, on 26 December 1918, and sent on two months leave, being ordered to report to the War Office in London ten days prior to its expiration. On 24 February 1919 he was told to report to the Reserve Unit at Dover. His home address during this leave period was given as 22 Arundel Road, Tunbridge Wells.

As a footnote, and though not part of this narrative, it is worth digressing slightly to note that Edward's brother Philip Francis Gell had also survived the war and, as a Major with the 14th Jat Lancers, [also sometimes known as the Murray's Jat Horse, a cavalry regiment of the British Indian Army] in Palestine, also won a fighting DSO. The citation (London Gazette December 1918) read, '*For conspicuous bravery and devotion to duty. This officer led a turning movement in front of a bridgehead, which rolled up the enemy. He sabred three of the enemy and dismounted others with the hilt of his sword. He displayed exceptional ability as a cavalry leader*'. But then, this man, who it is believed, lived his post Army years in Wiltshire/Gloucestershire, is another story!

## Chapter 19. Reverend Edward Gell  Corsham's own Unknown Soldier.

**THE UNKNOWN WARRIOR:**

The idea of the Unknown Warrior came from the Reverend David Railton, MA MC (Military Cross) who whilst under enemy fire, had helped a wounded Officer and two Privates to safety. Whist returning to his billet at Earringham, near Armentières, he passed a small garden. *[The Battle of Armentières (also Battle of Lille) was fought by German and Franco-British forces in northern France in October 1914. ]*

Approximately six paces from the house was a white cross marking a grave. The cross was roughly engraved with the following words, *'An Unknown Soldier from the Black Watch'*. The Reverend Railton remained on the Western Front until WWI ended in 1918. In the meantime, he had written in vain to Sir Douglas Haig, General Officer Commanding (GOC) the British Army in France and Belgium, with the idea that an unidentified body could be brought back to Britain for a symbolic burial.

**1920:** After the war, Reverend Railton was appointed Vicar of St. John the Baptist Church in Margate. In August he wrote to the Dean of Westminster, the Right Reverend Herbert Ryle, expressing his concerns that, *'there could only be one true shrine in memory of the men lost - in Westminster Abbey'*.

He wrote that *'a soldier should be selected from the 300,000 of those British and Dominions soldiers who had no known grave, to represent all those who had fallen'*. The Dean took up the Reverend Railton's idea with enthusiasm.

This subsequently resulted in an announcement being made on 19 October 1920 by the Prime Minister David Lloyd George, King George V and the War Office. The idea of an Unknown Warrior was greeted with enthusiasm from the public and the three armed services.

Brigadier General Louis John Wyatt DSODL GOC, Director of The War Graves Commission for the War Office, (who thought Railton's idea was a *'wonderful gesture')*, was instructed by the War Committee to exhume four unknown soldiers who had died early in the war, from the separate battlefields of Aisne, Arras, Somme and Ypres, one of which would be chosen as the Unknown Warrior.

Lt Col Henry Williams was tasked by the Brigadier on 7 November 1920 to prepare four groups, each comprising of one officer and two other ranks supplied with shovels, a sack and a field ambulance, to exhume one body each from the four battlefields mentioned above.

To ensure anonymity, it was paramount that the bodies should be impossible to identify. In other words, the bodies should be sufficiently deteriorated so that no form of identification was visible on the body or the clothing.

Having disinterred a body, each party was required to confirm by means of any surviving scraps of uniform fabric, boots, buttons or other distinguishing features that it was indeed that of a British soldier. If any personal identification were found, the body was reinterred at once and a further body exhumed.

In fact, the deterioration had advanced so quickly in the muddy fields of France during the space of two or three years, that the selected bodies were 'mere bones' when placed in the sack.

The bodies were transported to the Military Headquarters at St Pol-sur-Ternoise 20 miles west of Arras where each body was received by the Reverend George Kendal whose job it was to double-check that the bodies were British soldiers, and that no identification of any kind remained visible.

## Chapter 19. Reverend Edward Gell Corsham's own Unknown Soldier.

The four bodies where scheduled to arrive back at different times so that the four groups could not confer with each other to identify which battlefield each body had been exhumed from. After delivery of their body, they were dismissed to their billets so that none would know which body had been selected. [Note: Saint-Pol-sur-Ternoise is a commune in the Pas-de-Calais department in northern France].

The bodies were carefully laid out in the temporary Military Chapel at St. Pol. Most people have a vision of this Chapel as being a ruin of some exotic church property when in fact it was just a temporary corrugated-iron Army Nissen Hut. A guard was placed outside to prevent anyone entering the Chapel. Brigadier General Wyatt was informed that the four unidentified bodies were laid out in the temporary Chapel. Just before midnight on the 7 November 1920, Brigadier General Wyatt accompanied by Colonel Edward Gell passed the guards who were stationed outside and entered into the St. Pol Chapel. Inside, the four bodies in sacks were laid out on stretchers, alongside a plain deal shell coffin which had arrived from England the day before. It was impossible to identify the bodies as each coffin was completely covered over with a Union Flag.

On the stroke of midnight (a time steeped in myth and ritual), Brigadier General Wyatt, with closed eyes, simply touched one of the bodies and the Unknown Warrior was selected. Brigadier General Wyatt with help from Colonel Gell placed the chosen body into the shell coffin and screwed down the lid and covered it with a Union Flag. Interestingly, there is no mention at the time of Colonel Edward being a clergyman as well as a serving soldier. The Unknown Warrior was destined to be buried among Kings in Westminster Abbey with a reverence he could never have imagined in life. *[Ed: It's comforting to think that the selection of the Unknown Warrior had some help from an ex-Vicar of Corsham, along with some help from above!]*

Brigadier General Wyatt and Colonel Gell then left the Chapel which was guarded overnight by Sergeant Scot, Sergeant Stevens, Corporal Strong and Corporal Dixon. In the morning, following a short service at the Chapel, the Unknown Warrior started his journey back home to Britain via Boulogne, where two British undertakers, Mr Noades and Mr Sowerbutts transferred the body into a plain two-hundredweight oak coffin made from an oak tree from the gardens at Hampton Court Palace and secured by wrought iron bands. On top of the oak coffin was laid a Crusader's 16th Century sword given by King George V from his own private collection. The simple inscription carved on the coffin's lid in Gothic letters read:

**A British Warrior Who Fell In The Great War 1914-1918**
**For King and Country.**

The Unknown Warrior's coffin was transported over the Channel on HMS Verdun and arrived in Dover on the morning of 11 November 1920. The quayside was lined with people, straining to see the coffin that *could* contain the body of their loved one. It was taken by train to London. On 11 November - two years to the day after the war had ended; the body of the Unknown Warrior was placed on a carriage and drawn by black horses in a procession through London to the Cenotaph. There were twelve distinguished pallbearers: **Four Field Marshals** - Lord Methuen (Paul Sanford Methuen of Corsham), Sir Henry Wilson, Earl Haig and Viscount French. **Four Admirals of the Fleet** - Sir Hedworth Meux, Earl Beatty, Sir Charles Madden and Sir Henry Jackson. **Three Generals** - Lord Byng, Lord Horne and Albert Gatliff. And **Air Marshal** - Sir Hugh Trenchard.

The coffin passed through hushed crowds of thousands of people, many weeping. The new War Cenotaph memorial on Whitehall was unveiled by King George V.

## Chapter 19. Reverend Edward Gell Corsham's own Unknown Soldier.

At 1100 there was a two-minute silence, and the body was taken to nearby Westminster Abbey where it was buried, after passing through a Guard of Honour of 100 holders of the Victoria Cross. In a particularly poignant gesture, the grave was filled with earth from the main French battlefields, and the black marble stone was Belgian.

When the grave was dug in Westminster Abbey, it was found that no other burial had taken place in that spot in the thousand-year history of the Abbey. At the exact time that Britain was interring its unknown warrior, France was doing the same - burying its Unknown Soldier under the Arc de Triomphe in Paris.

In the following days, more than a million people came to pay their respects to Britain's Unknown Warrior (and many more millions have done so since).

**1920:** Returning to Europe, Colonel Edward Gell was placed as 2nd in Command of 52 South Wales Borderers (SWB), then the 23rd Royal Fusiliers and then Officer in Command of the 26th Fusiliers in the Rhine Army as part of the occupying forces, a job he hated.

*By Horace Nicholls - This is photograph Q 31514 of the Imperial War Museum's Public Domain*

Colonel Edward Gell's role in the selection of the Unknown Warrior is something that Corsham can be very proud of.

**1921:** Edward had several leave periods back in England before he was then demobilised in France on 31 March 1921 as Temporary-Lieutenant but granted the right to retain his rank of Lt. Colonel.

Following demobilisation, Edward joined Major General Sir Fabian Arthur Goulstone Ware, KCVO, KBE, CB, CMG (17 June 1869 – 28 April 1949) the founder of the Imperial War Graves Commission, now the Commonwealth War Graves Commission. Edward was appointed Assistant Director of Records from 1 April 1921 with the Imperial War Graves Commission at Chateau de la Tour, Longueness, St. Omer, France. His home address at the time was still given as Tunbridge Wells, Kent.

**1922:** Following a written request by him to the War Office, a response letter dated 23 October was sent to him at St. Omer stating he would be appointed to the Regular Army Reserve of Officers Class 2, Royal Fusiliers, with the rank of Lt. Colonel with seniority from 21 May 1921 (London Gazette 3 November 1922).

**1926:** Edward retired from St. Omer, for reasons of ill health, on 4 April. He was given unpaid leave from 8 June 1926 and later rejoined for duty in July 1926.

**1928:** Having been asked to return to the Imperial War Graves Commission (IWGC), Edward took up a part-time position as the Commission's representative in Italy, based at Bordighera; he worked as a member of the Anglo-Italian Committee which liased with the Italian authorities regarding war grave and memorials work, as Assistant Director of Records, IWGC Representative for Italy.

## Chapter 19. Reverend Edward Gell Corsham's own Unknown Soldier.

**1930:** On 25 June the War Office informed him in a letter that on attaining the age limit of 55 years he would cease to belong to the Regular Army Reserve of Officers with effect from 23 June 1933. It was addressed to Lt. Col. E.A.S. Gell, DSO, MC, Regular Army Reserve of Officers at the Imperial War Graves Commission, Longueness, St. Omer. Whether he actually received the letter at St. Omer or they forwarded the letter on to him, is debatable for Colonel Gell had already retired from St. Omer, for reasons of ill health, on 4 April 1926.

**1932**: Edward moved back to Paris but still worked for the Anglo-Italian Committee. Edward and Lord Methuen remained close friends until Lord Methuen's death in 1932.

**1936:** Edward retired on 31 January after 15 years representing the War Graves Commission. After his retirement Edward moved partly back to England.

**1939:** Brigadier General Wyatt wrote a letter to the *Telegraph* on 11 November 1939, two months after the Second World War had broken out, and on the 21st anniversary of the WWI Armistice.

Brigadier General Wyatt rarely spoke about the selection of the Unknown Warrior, but he did explain in his letter detailing exactly how he chose the body because he had concerns that the facts were not being reported accurately: rumours circulated. People whispered, for example, that the identity of the Unknown Warrior was known from the beginning.

*Brigadier General Wyatt*

Brigadier General Wyatt wrote: *"The four bodies lay on stretchers, each covered by a Union Jack, in front of the altar was the shell of the coffin which had been sent from England to receive the remains. I selected one, and with the assistance of Colonel Gell, placed it in the shell; we screwed down the lid.*

*The other bodies were removed and reburied in the military cemetery outside my headquarters at St Pol. I had no idea even of the area from which the body I selected had come; no one else can know it."*

**1941:** Edward was now living at 47, Chomeley Lodge in Highgate. London.

**1951:** Edward passed away on 9 May at St Annes-on-the-Sea aged 75. He was buried in St. Margaret's Churchyard in the Derbyshire village of Carsington. **R.I.P Edward**.

**1991**: Edward's fourth child Thomas Anthony R. Gell, passed away in April 1991 in Bromley, Kent.

[Ed: Edward was an interesting and brave man, with strong connections to Field Marshal the 3rd Baron Methuen of Corsham Court and with St. Bartholomew's Church at Corsham where he is listed on the wall behind the font. He trained for the clergy and loved his *calling*, but he also found a parallel career with the Army through two major wars. Even after the Great War, he maintained his work for soldiers and their families via his fifteen years with the War Graves Commission.

**Finally, Edward Gell's connection with the selection of the Unknown Warrior is a proud fact for our small town of Corsham to rejoice. R.I.P. Edward.]**

## Chapter 20. Skating on Corsham Lake

**1800:** From the late 1800s to the 1960s, Corsham Lake was regularly used in the winter for skating. The recent warmer winters and the increase in awareness of safety issues have seen its demise as a skating venue. The extent of the lake's surface, the higher winter temperatures and its depth make the lake's ice prone to weaknesses in sustaining many people these days.
**WARNING!**
**The ice is too thin these days and it should no longer be used to skate on.**

Even in the much colder winters of the late 1800s, accidents often occurred on the ice at Corsham.

**1879:** Herbert Spackman's photos of the skaters above (including the humorous superimposing of the bus on the ice) are probably the only photos of skaters on the ice at Corsham Lake at that time. Here is an extract from 'The Spackman Diaries' December 4th 1879: *'An awfully cold day. Went down to the pond (the lake) before breakfast with Lewin, Clara, Sarah, Ernest and Clare and I enjoyed it very much. There were a great many people down there mostly from Bath and Bristol and I saw the place where I fell in last Tuesday'.*

**1842:** A fine young man named Edward Balch, apprentice to a carpenter at Pickwick, near Corsham, was on Monday 10 January drowned whilst skating on the sheet water in Lord Methuen's park. Several persons were present, and used their best endeavours to save him, but without effect, the water being very deep, and the ice very thin at the spot. Dr. Dyke was also on the ice at the time and on the body being taken out the water, did all that medical skill could dictate, but to restore animation was impossible, the body having been under the water for more than half an hour. An inquest was held on the body on the same day before Mr Edwards, the coroner and, from the evidence adduced, it appeared, that among the persons who endeavoured to extricate the unfortunate youth, was Mr J. Hancock, Brinkworth, schoolmaster of Chippenham, who soon became immersed himself, and but for his being an expert swimmer, would also have met a watery grave. The accident it was stated is wholly attributable to the imprudence of a man named Hughes, who overlooks the pounds, and who, drawing a water hatch on Saturday, lowered the water 7 or 8 inches, and thereby rendered the ice *[now hollow immediately beneath the surface]* particularly dangerous. Hughes was very closely examined at the inquest and severely reprimanded for his breach of authority. Hughes had previously intimated to some young men of the town who were skating, that he would stop their sport, and his carrying out his intimation into effect has been the cause of the fatal accident alluded to, besides some other narrow escapes. Verdict: Accidental Death. *[Ed: These days, the verdict would most probably have been manslaughter!]*

**1879:** On Thursday 21 January, skaters were out on the lake, even though the middle of the lake was not frozen solid. There was a boisterous wind and one gentleman was seen skating around the fringe of the ice which was not strong enough to stand the pressure. He was precipitated into the water which was

## Chapter 20. Skating on Corsham Lake

about 15ft deep at that point. Luckily, he was a good swimmer and managed to keep himself on the surface of the water and he subsequently managed to extricate himself.

**1908:** On 5 January, Miss Margaret Clutterbuck, daughter of Mr Hugh Clutterbuck of Middlewick, had a very narrow escape in the lake. Most of the lake's ice was thick enough and skating was in full swing, but certain portions had been marked off as being too thin. Miss Clutterbuck ventured too close to one of the dangerous spots with a result that the ice broke and she was immersed in about 9 ft of icy cold water. Several skaters immediately went to help and removed their coats and threw them towards the lady who eventually managed to grasp one and held firm. Mr F.A. Hake (a manager of the Wiltshire and Dorset Bank in Chippenham) fearlessly jumped into the ice and helped the young lady to safety. Even though Mr Hake was a strong swimmer (he once held the swimming championship for his county), he had considerable difficulty in getting out of the water himself and was only rescued by means of a ladder thrown across the opening. Miss Clutterbuck was taken to Corsham Court to recuperate. Mr Hake warmed up in front of the fire in the Methuen Arms - neither being the worse for wear for their unpleasant experience.

**1916:** On Sunday afternoon 17 December, there was a beautiful sheet of ice on Corsham Lake. This attracted a large number of skaters and sliders and games of hockey and football were enjoyed!

**1917:** *Newspaper item 21 January:* "Some enjoyable skating has taken place on the lake in the park since last Saturday, there being a splendid sheet of perfectly safe ice. On Sunday afternoon there were from 200 – 300 present. The only accident was one of temporary immersion of a gentleman who helped in the successful rescue of a dog from the lake.

**1925:** On Saturday 5 December and the following Sunday, it is estimated that the skaters and the watchers standing on the lake numbered nearly one thousand! Many of the visitor's cars and motor cycles were parked up in nearby Church Square.

**1933:** On the weekend late January nearly one thousand had some of the best skating at Corsham Lake. The ice being considered the best for nearly a quarter of a century. Cars came from every direction, bringing their load of expectant skaters who were making the most of the frost. By permission of Lord Methuen, on Sunday 29 January, a charge was made for parking, and a collection was made on the ice by the Employment Fellowship who later funded a concert and a whist drive for the local unemployed.

**1946:** In early January, many hundreds of people from Bath and the surrounding neighbourhood paid a visit to the splendid lake in Corsham Park. Through the kindness of Lord Methuen, they enjoyed a capital day of skating on the lake; some performing wonderful feats on the ice and there was a quadrille party with a band, who danced in an astonishing manner! Refreshments were supplied by some of the gentry to all-comers, so that the enjoyment was really complete.

**1950:** On the weekend of 28/29 January the lake froze over and a large party of people were seen skating on the lake on Sunday afternoon. There were also a large number of spectators, many who came to Corsham by car to enjoy the skating.

**1963** was one of the coldest winters on record, with temperatures so cold that the sea froze over in places. Corsham Lake was completely frozen over and it was possible to walk safely from one side of the lake across to the other. It was colder than the winter of 1947, and the coldest since 1740. This is thankfully not something that will probably ever happen again. It began abruptly just before Christmas in

## Chapter 20. Skating on Corsham Lake

1962. The weeks before had been changeable and stormy, but then on 22 December a high pressure system moved to the north-east of the British Isles, dragging bitterly cold winds across the country. This situation was to last much of the winter. A blizzard followed on 29 and 30 December across Wales and south-west England, causing snowdrifts up to 6m deep. Roads and railways were blocked, telephone lines brought down, and some villages were left *cut-off* for several days. The snow was so deep that farmers could not get to their livestock and many animals starved to death. This snow set the scene for the next two months, as much of England remained covered every day until early March 1963.

[Ed: As the temperatures warmed up slightly in late March of 1963 we (a gang of Corsham boys) goaded each other to attempt the lake crossing by walking all the way across the ice. The last occasion put a stop to this madness, as one of our party (we'll call him 'D' for now!) fell through the ice near the centre of the lake. We had a premonition that this might happen, as halfway across, the ice started to emit loud cracking noises. Whilst most of us managed to quickly retreat back far enough to safety, poor 'D' disappeared down through the ice. We managed to extract him by lying down in a row across the ice (holding head to feet) and managed to grab his hair to pull him free. The walk back home was just as bad as the poor lad was nigh frozen into a block of ice! The lake very rarely freezes over nowadays.]

*For a bit of fun, photographer Herbert Spackman superimposed a bus on top of the lake's ice.* People would travel from miles around to skate on Corsham Lake. When the evening came, car headlights were shone across the lake to prolong the skating. Entrepreneurs hired out skates to those who needed them.

Accounts of skating on Corsham Lake were common amongst the Corsham folk and there are records of braziers being lit on the frozen ice for roasting sweet chestnuts! *Photo courtesy Stephen Flavin.*

**Pelham Grenville Wodehouse 15 Oct. 1881 - 14 Feb. 1975 (of the Jeeves and Wooster stories).** In shape and size and messuages, Wodehouse's 'Blandings Castle' owes a good deal to his boyhood memory of Corsham, the stately home of the Methuen's near Bath. The young Pelham, spent school holidays with a clergyman uncle nearby and was often taken to Corsham to skate on the lake, and the image of the Corsham Court remained on the retina of his inward eye. *[Richard Usborne, 1976, Wodehouse at Work to the End, p. 126.] Photo below shows the partially frozen lake in February 2019.*

# Chapter 21. Station Hotel

Corsham Station was on the Great Western Railway main line from London to Bristol and was opened when the Chippenham to Bath section was completed in June 1841. The Corsham Station Hotel was built not long after and eventually demolished in 1962. The Station Hotel was situated at the very bottom of Station Road and backed onto the Corsham Station's up-line (London) platform.

The photograph above, of the *'Station Hotel Corsham'* is one of the oldest photographs of Corsham. It was probably taken about 1860 by Joseph Goold (1836-1926). Joseph was the eldest child of Uriah Goold (1789-1860) and Maria Newman Goold (1797-1848) (nee Hancock). Uriah founded the tannery at Pound Pill and was a co-founder of the Baptist Church in Priory Street, Corsham.

*The corner of the Station Hotel can be seen top left centre.*

The Station Hotel was initially also a fully functioning wholesale and retail brewery.

The licensees are listed below.

**William White** 1848-1855
**James Usher** 1855-1874
**William Alway** 1874-1889
**John "Jack" Ogg** 1889-1896
**Fanney Sloper Ogg** 1896-1903
**William Turner** c1907
**Albert Drew** c1910
**Mrs Alice Hancock** 1915-1918
**George Tasker** 1918-1938
**Sydney Tasker** 1938-1946
**Mrs Winifred Tasker** 1946-1952
**Kenneth Tasker** 1952-1962

## Chapter 21. Station Hotel

**1854:** The Corsham Station Hotel was used regularly to hold inquests. One of the earliest being in 1854, on the body of Mr E. Crisp a junior Clerk to Messrs. Randall and Saunders the local quarry firm. The deceased had been walking near the Railway Station on Sunday morning early and had wished the Policeman on duty there, *"A good morning".* When he had walked a short distance from the station towards Corsham, the Policeman heard the sound of a fall and running to see what was the matter, found him lying in the road, his head on the kerb of the foot pavement; he immediately raised him to a sitting position and with assistance got him to the Station Hotel adjoining. A surgeon was in immediate attendance, but life was extinct. It appeared the deceased was subject to fits, which his relatives anticipated would cause a sudden death, an attack of one of such fits having caused a rupture of one of the blood vessels of the head. Verdict. Died from natural causes.

*Aerial view above shows Corsham's Station Hotel bottom centre.*

**1855:** James Usher was now the innkeeper at the Station Hotel and he resided there from 1855-1874. He had previously been the innkeeper at the Pack Horse Inn (now the Flemish Weaver) in Corsham in 1844 as denoted on page 10 of the Pigot & Co.'s Wiltshire Directory of that year *(see image right)*. The Usher's family brewed beer on the Station Hotel site and later moved to Trowbridge to establish the well known Usher's brewery. Some early personal or financial tragedy must have overtaken the family as on the 1881 census they are living in Swindon and James Usher (born in Corsham) is a factory labourer.

```
TAVERNS & PUBLIC HOUSES.
Bear, Ann Goldney, High st
Black Horse, Wm. Buckland, Monkton
Duke of Cumberland, Joseph Moore,
    Market place
Five Alls, Ann Read, Causeway
George, James Douse, Corsham
George, Philip Johnston, High st
Great Western, James Sperring, New road
King's Head, Thos. Uncles, Market place
Lamb, William Cullis, River st
Lamb, Joseph Pegler, Corsham
Little George, William Field, New road
Pack Horse, Jane Holbrow, Calne road
Pack Horse, James Usher, Corsham
Rose & Crown, Wm. Hall, Market place
Royal Oak, Susannah Day, London road
Swan, Stephen Wiltshire, River st
Three Crowns, John Bendrey, Causeway
Three Cups, Richard Fry, Shambles
White Lion, John Beak, High st
Wool Pack, Richard Slade, River st
```

**1865: NOT TO BE SNIFFED AT.** At the Chippenham Petty Sessions, Thursday 7 December, (before J. B. Fuller, esq. (Chairman), Gabriel Goldney, esq., M.P., and the Rev. B. Winthrop), Robert Butler and Thomas West were summoned by John Hoddinot, for assaulting him at the Station Hotel, on the 17th of November last. The complainant [Hoddinot] having being sworn in, deposed that he lived at Corsham and that on the above day a man took out his [Hoddinot's] handkerchief and blew his nose in it; that he was afterwards knocked down by the defendant Robert Butler and then Thomas West fell upon him and knocked him about his head. Mrs Elizabeth Usher, wife of the landlord, said that the complainant and defendants were at their house, when some person took Hoddinot's handkerchief from his pocket.

She did not see Butler strike the complainant, but she saw the complainant John Hoddinot had hold of West's hair. Butler admitted striking the complainant, and West said he struck him because he held his (West's) hair. John Davis said he was present. Hoddinot was very provoking and tried to pick quarrels with everyone present. Butler struck him. A witness afterwards saw West and Hoddinot together. West was down, and Hoddinot held him by the hair of his head. The defendant Butler was convicted of the assault and fined 1s. and costs.

**1874:** Wiltshire Independent - Thursday 6th August:  **CORSHAM WILTS: An Important Sale, of the STATION HOTEL, BREWERY, GARDEN, STABLES, COACH HOUSES, &c.**

MESSRS. PARRY & SON, are instructed by the Proprietor, Mr James USHER, to SELL, by AUCTION, on FRIDAY, August 21st, 1874, precisely at Four o'clock in the Afternoon, at the above-named Hotel, subject to such Conditions as will be then given, all that Capital and Conveniently-built HOTEL AND PROPERTY Called the Station Hotel, situated at the Railway Station, in Corsham, which will include dining rooms, parlour, bar, tap-room, kitchen and scullery, 7 bed-rooms, with W.C., and a club-room of large dimensions; 5-quarter brewery, with capital cellarage, stables, coach-houses, yards, and good garden, well stocked with choice fruit trees.

The Auctioneer would call the particular attention of brewers and publicans to the above property, as the situation is desirable, and the hotel, brewery, stables, &c., so arranged as to do an extensive wholesale and retail beer trade, posting business, &c., &c. Two clubs, the Odd-Fellows and Patriotic, hold their meetings at the house and a good retail trade is done. Possession may be had at Michaelmas next, with the option of taking stock, brewing plant and effects by Valuation.

For further particulars apply to MESSRS. KEARY, STOKES, and GOLDNEY, Solicitors, Chippenham, or at the offices of the AUCTIONEERS, in Calne or Chippenham. Dated Auction, Land, Estate, and Surveying Offices, Chilvester Hill, and Market Hill House, Calne, and High Street, Chippenham, August 5th, 1874.

*The Corsham Station Hotel and bar.*

The Station Hotel licence passes from James Usher to William Alway. William managed the Corsham Station Hotel between 1874-1889. He was born in Yate, Gloucestershire in 1847. William had a background in the licensed trade from an early age as his mother Elizabeth was landlady of the 'Packhorse Inn', Lawrence Hill, Bristol, his brother Fitz was a clerk to a wine merchants, and William himself was a clerk in a Mineral Water factory. William's father Thomas Alway (1815-1855) from Little Sodbury, had been a farmer on the Common in Yate Village, and in Camerton, Somerset.

## Chapter 21. Station Hotel

**1882:** The Station Hotel was a three storey building with front steps leading to an entrance on the first floor, as well as there being an entrance on the ground floor. In 1882 the brick building still had J. USHER painted on the parapet, with the words STATION and HOTEL on either side, although the innkeeper was then William Alway.

Around this time, about 40 years after the station had been opened, the platforms were lengthened. Access to the 'up' platform, for trains going towards London, was via a path and passengers using the 'down' platform crossed a high open footbridge before descending a sloping path. Behind the 'up' platform loomed the imposing Station Hotel with 'PEARCE'S ALES' painted high up on the back wall.

**1881:** An inquest was held on Thursday at the Station Hotel, Corsham, on the body of James Humphries, a fireman on a Great Western train, who was killed near the station. The jury returned the following verdict: *'That the deceased was accidentally killed by his head coming into contact with a buttress on the Great Western Railway.'* [The buttress structure can be seen far centre and was part of the aqueduct.]

**1886:** An inquest was held at the Station Hotel, Corsham, on the body of William Dyke (who had been foreman over Messrs. Pictor's loading crane at Corsham station), who committed suicide on Christmas Day. Mr W. Kemm, coroner for the liberty of Corsham, held the inquiry. Caroline Dyke, the widow told the inquest, that the deceased having had his dinner went upstairs after, with the intention of lying down, as he said. Soon after as she heard him fall she went up and was horrified to find him with his throat cut. She had been married to him for 33 years. For the last 12 months he had been very strange in his manner. Other witnesses were called, including Job Davis, of London, a brother in law of the deceased, who said he had known him for 40 years, and about 15 months ago he had noticed strangeness about him. Dr. Wood said that he had attended him previously for 'delirium tremens' 12 months since and was of the opinion that the brain had suffered from that ever since. The jury returned a verdict of 'Suicide whilst under temporary insanity'.

## Chapter 21. Station Hotel

**1889:** At the Chippenham Sessions of 6 September 1877, the transfer of the Station Hotel's license from William Alway to Mary Alway was refused. The license was eventually transferred from William Alway to John Ogg at the Chippenham Petty Sessions, on Thursday 31 October 1889.

**1891:** William Alway was now living (with his sister Lucy as housekeeper) at Little Lyppiatt Farm, Chapel Knapp, next door to the residence of the retired Isaac Belcher of the Pickwick Brewery.

**1892:** William Alway died in Corsham on 7th September aged 44. At the time of his death he was working at Corsham's Station Coal Depot as a Coal Merchant and Carting Agent.

**1895: DECAPITATED ON THE G.W.R. A MAN KILLED AT CORSHAM.**

Benjamin Pointing, a plasterer, of High-street Corsham, was found decapitated on the up-line of the Great Western Railway. His left hand and right arm were also severed. He had placed himself before the 12:13 express from Bristol. The remains were taken to the Station Hotel where Mr R. Balch, coroner, held an inquest on the body of the deceased. The first witness called was John Bowden, ganger on the Great Western Railway, who stated that he was walking down his garden at 1:45 that day, when he saw something unusual lying on the line. He went to it and found the body of a man lying at the foot of the bank. The head and one arm were severed from the body and lay on the up-line, together with a cap. The man's waistcoat was torn to atoms, as were other parts of his clothing. Raymond Palmer, landlord of the Roebuck Inn, Corsham, said that the deceased came to his house at about 9.30 that morning. He said he felt very bad, and that be thought be should have died before he reached there. He asked for something to drink, and had a quartern of whiskey and a small lemon. To the best of the witness's knowledge he drank once, and then called for a bottle of ginger beer to put into it. The deceased seemed very strange in his manner, but was quite sober. He very seldom came to the inn except when working near. He was as a rule jovial and cheerful, but that morning seemed depressed and not like himself. The engine had no marks on it and the driver knew nothing of the man being killed. The Jury returned a verdict of, 'Suicide while temporarily insane'.

**1896: FIRE AT CORSHAM. DAMAGE ESTIMATED AT £200.** A fire, which was kept within reasonable limits, broke out in the stables adjoining the Station Hotel, Corsham, in July, and the amount of damage done was estimated at £200 *(£18,500 in today's money)*. The Station Hotel, of which Mr John Ogg is the licensee, is in close proximity to the station itself, and some years ago the adjoining premises were used as a brewery. Since then, however, this portion of the building has been converted into stables, the upper fire is said to have originated from sparks from the kitchen chimney, which was on fire, finding their way into the lofts. The Corsham Fire Brigade were quickly on the spot with their fire engine, and Police Inspector Gale also arrived to superintend the operations. Water at a sufficient pressure was unobtainable except by using the engine, and thus the efforts of the Brigade were thwarted to some extent from the outset.

Some four or five horses were safely brought out of the stables. After an hour had elapsed, the fire was got under control. The stables, however, had been completely burned out and only the bare walls remained standing; and the whole of the stables as well as quantities of harness and the stock hay, straw, etc. were destroyed. They are insured, but it is believed that the contents were not.

**1896: TWO DEATHS AT THE PRIMROSE LEAGUE Demonstration at Hartham Park.**

On 22 July in 1896, the Station Hotel manager John Ogg died as a result of an accident at a large Unionist demonstration in Hartham Park, along with a man named Gilbert Davis. The demonstration was organised by the Primrose League members from Chippenham, Corsham and Calne to celebrate the return of Sir John Dickson-Poynder from his *round-the-world tour*. It was the largest gathering of its kind in the area, with reports of up to 10,000 attending. The Primrose League (1883-2004) was an organisation for spreading Conservative principles in Great Britain. The organisation was named after the favourite flower of Britain's first, and so far only, Jewish Prime Minister, Benjamin Disraeli (1804-1881) who held office twice as Prime Minister in 1868 (1st time) and during 1874 -1880. After being elected, Disraeli said, *"I have climbed to the top of the greasy pole"*.

There was another fatal accident that day! Mr Gilbert Davies, a well-known and highly respected Kington St. Michael schoolmaster for many years, was making his way to the demonstration in the early afternoon when the lynch-pin came out of the wheel of his carriage in Biddestone, violently precipitating the passengers into the road. Gilbert sustained fatal head injuries, but luckily the other occupants (who were all from Kington St. Michael), including Miss Evans the school mistress, were unhurt.

John Ogg of the Station Hotel, Corsham, a most accomplished rider, was riding in a gymkhana race when his horse bolted, carrying him beneath a tree. John had been a member of the Demonstration Committee and it was he who had suggested the gymkhana race be included. An eye witness reported how John had lost his reins when going round the bend of the hill and the horse ran out of the course. He was unaware of the existence of a tree due to an umbrella which he was carrying in front of him. His head smashed into the sturdy branch with such force that it broke his neck. He was quickly attended on a stretcher in the pavilion by Dr. Wood of Corsham and Dr. Smith-Batten of Calne but soon passed away.

On hearing the news, Sir John Dickson-Poynder cancelled the planned firework display. Both funerals took place at three o'clock on Saturday 24 July. The funeral of Gilbert Davis took place at Kington St. Michael. John Ogg was interred in Corsham and being a member of the Royal Wilts Yeomanry a number of his comrades, including Lieut. Sir John Dickson-Poynder were present. On Thursday, 6th August, the Station Hotel license was transferred to John Ogg's widow Fanney Sloper Ogg who took over the running of the hotel. Fanney and Jack's parents and two unmarried sisters later moved to Corsham, to help Fanney with her three children and to assist in the running of the busy Corsham Station Hotel.

**THE FATALITY BOX TUNNEL. A BATH MAN KILLED:** In the following month of August, a bricklayer named George Bartlett, about 40 years of age, who lived at Widcombe, met with his death in Box Tunnel. The deceased, who was engaged with other men in repairing the lining of the tunnel, was knocked down and killed by the train leaving Bath at 1.20. Bartlett, who was an old soldier, leaves five young children, whose mother died some time ago. An inquest was held in the Railway Station Hotel, Corsham, before Mr Balch, the Coroner for the district. The poor fellow left his mates about 2.45 p.m., and walked down

## Chapter 21. Station Hotel

the tunnel about 50 yards for a certain purpose. He appeared to have stopped on the 'up' line, and was struck down by the locomotive of the express train. His head was smashed, his left hand cut off and the lower portion of the spine shattered. Death must have been instantaneous, the engine having carried the body about 14 yards before the train passed over it. The remains were removed at once to the Station Hotel at Corsham. The jury returned a verdict of 'Accidental Death.'

**1907:** William Turner is now the new innkeeper at the Corsham Station Hotel.

**1910:** A temporary licence was granted to Albert Drew as licensee of the Corsham Station Hotel.

**1915:** Mrs Alice Hancock is now the licensee at the Corsham Station Hotel.

**1918:** George Tasker is now the licensee. George passed away in 1938 and had been *'mine host'* of the Station Hotel, Corsham for 21 years. He had been ailing for some time. He was 76 years old when he died and left a son and a daughter.

**1938:** The Station Hotel continues to be managed by several members of the Tasker family for a total of 44 years until its demise in 1962. *[George Tasker 1918-1938: Sydney Tasker 1938-1946: Mrs Winifred Tasker 1946-1952: Kenneth Tasker c.1952-1962].*

**1962:** The Station Hotel was demolished and the site became Hancock's Coal Yard for a while. This in turn became a small housing development in the 1990's *(see photo below).*

## Chapter 21. Station Hotel

**1965:** Passenger services were withdrawn from Corsham Station with the end of stopping services between Swindon and Bath in January 1965. Goods traffic had ended in June 1963, though the siding with the loading dock remained in place until 1978. Of the station structures, only the goods shed now remains on the site.

**2009:** The recent growth of Corsham has led to demand for a new station. In 2009, as part of a consultation exercise to investigate the reopening of the station, the District Council conducted a survey which received over 3,000 replies. The battle to reopen Corsham Station continues.

**2015:** The old and much loved cast iron Corsham Station railway footbridge at the bottom of Station Road/South Street was replaced by a splendid new arched 'Green' iron footbridge in the early hours of 22 March 2015.

The new footbridge opened on Friday/Saturday 5/6th June 2015.     *Photo above by Julian Carosi.*

**2016:** The fabulously detailed model of the Corsham Station Hotel shown below was displayed at Hartham House in 2016 and is now held by Chippenham Museum.

## Chapter 22. Stone Quarries - a chronological list.

**This list highlights the importance of how the quarrying of Bath Stone and the legacy that it left behind, helped to shape the towns of Box and Corsham, in Wiltshire.**

| | |
|---|---|
| **200M BC** | About 200 million years ago before the British Isles existed, Bath Stone begins to form. |
| **70-84AD** | The Romans were the first to use Bath Stone for building. |
| **670** | Saint Aldhelm (645-709 A.D.) is reputed to have thrown down his glove at Hazelbury Hill and *'Bade them Digge and they should find great treasure'* meaning the Box Freestone. |
| **700** | St. Laurence's Church in Bradford-on-Avon is constructed from Bath Stone. |
| **1180** | Malmesbury Abbey is also constructed from Bath Stone. |
| **1465** | Quarrying Rights were acquired by Thomas Trapenell and used to build his house Great Chalfield Manor house. |
| **1500** | In the 1500s one quarry at Hazelbury was known as *Castle Dyke Quarr*. |
| **1540** | Leyland in his *'itinerary'* mentions a notable quarry close to Bath, thought later by John Wood to be the Horse Comb Quarry. |
| **1573** | Quarrying Rights were transferred to Sir John Thynne the builder of Longleat House designed by his architect Robert Smythson in 1580. |
| **1663** | A Danish scholar, Oluf Borch, made the earliest reference to an underground Bath Stone Quarry. |
| **1710** | Ralph Allen moved to Bath. |
| **1726** | Ralph Allen commenced buying land on Combe Down Bath. |
| **1727** | The River Avon Navigation from Bath to Bristol is opened. |
| **1728** | Ralph Allen acquired land on the river bank at Dolmead with a view to exporting stone by boat. |
| **1729** | Ralph Allen's tramway, running from Combe Down to Dolmead Wharf is built by John Padmore. Firs Quarry in Bath is opened by Ralph Allen. |
| **1741** | Prior Park, Ralph Allen's show house is completed. Built overlooking Bath, both to show off the qualities of the stone and also his wealth and fine taste. |
| **1764** | Ralph Allen dies. |
| **1800** | Eastlays Quarry between Corsham and Melksham opens. |
| **1801** | The Kennet and Avon Canal Co. open their own quarry at Conkwell with an inclined tramway down to the canal. |
| **1803** | A tramway (by the Kennet and Avon Canal Co.) is built running down from Murhill Quarry (to the west of the village of Winsley) to the Kennet and Avon canal. |
| **1807** | Combe Down Quarry rights were purchased by John Thomas of Bristol. |
| **1808** | An Inclined plane is built linking the Bathampton Limestone Quarry with the Kennet and Avon Canal. |
| **1810** | The Kennet and Avon Canal used to transport quarried Bath Stone is opened.<br>The original vertical winding shaft is sunk at the Travellers Rest Quarry. After closing in 1958 this quarry reopened to give access to the new Hartham Park Quarry and is back in production today. The original boilerhouse chimney can still be seen on the site alongside the Bradford Road in Corsham. |
| **1811** | Extraction of Bath Stone from the Hartham Park Quarry (between Park Lane and Bradford Road) began at the site shortly after 1811, with Hartham Park formed from a combination of three originally separate quarries. |
| **1825** | Cranes were first used in underground quarries from about this date. |
| **1829** | The *Cathedral* Quarry is worked by John Pictor between 1829 and 1850 at the top of Box Hill in Hazelbury Quarry underneath Box Fields.<br>Prior Park House (built from Bath Stone) is purchased by the Right Reverend Dr. Baines for use as a college. |

## Chapter 22. Stone Quarries - a chronological list.

| | |
|---|---|
| **1836** | Prior Park House is badly damaged by fire. |
| **1838** | Box Tunnel is constructed between December 1838 and June 1841 for the Great Western Railway. |
| **1841** | Box railway tunnel is completed. As a result of the excavations it became apparent that there were vast quantities of Freestone un-worked and from this date the quarry industry expanded rapidly in the Corsham and Box areas. |
| **1844** | Work started by Randell and Saunders Tunnel Quarry at Hudswell. This was the original major quarry in the area. A broad gauge railway (the earliest underground tramway) ran into the underground workings. By 1864 it had produced one hundred thousand tons of Bath Stone annually.<br>Alternate names for Tunnel Quarry were Yockney and Hartham Park Stone Co, Corsham Down Quarry, Pockeredge, and Seven Shaft Quarry. |
| **1847** | Seven Shaft Quarry was started by Randall and Saunders. |
| **1849** | The gunpowder stored in Spackman's shop in the High Street Corsham, used for the Box Tunnel excavations exploded, leading to the death of owner Mr Henry Spackman.<br>Earliest underground tramway was built. |
| **1855** | Spring Quarry is opened by Pictor and Sons in 1855-1856, just west of Yule Spring Lane, Corsham. It soon became known as Waterhole as it was wet and flooded regularly. The workings extend westwards into Box Parish; quarrying ended there in 1939. |
| **1860** | The Bath Stone available from Firs Quarry on Combe Down in Bath is exhausted. |
| **1865** | Work stars at Clift Quarry on Box Hill. A gravity tramway took the stone to the west end of Box tunnel. The quarry is now part of the Box Quarry complex and closed in 1968. |
| **1868** | John Alexander Thynne 4th Marquess of Bath, transfers some of his quarrying rights to Job Pictor - thus connecting (i.e. linking) modern quarrying to Corsham and Box. |
| **1874** | Hudswell Quarry near Hawthorn is opened by Randell and Saunders and is connected to Corsham Station by an overland tramway in 1875. |
| **1875** | Old Ridge Quarry in Neston is opened and operated by Pictor & Sons. In the Second World War it is used to store American bombs and small arms. |
| **1866** | The Banker Masons who *dress* the huge blocks of Bath Stone go out on strike for better wages. The hourly rate is increased to 7d per hour. |
| **1877** | Small quarrying companies such as Randell and Saunders, Hartham and Yockney and Pictors amalgamate into the Bath Stone Firms Limited.<br>Pictor's Monks Quarry (known as Eastern Monks) begins production. |
| **1878** | New Ridge Quarry to the west of the Old Ridge Quarry (also known as Monks West Quarry) is started by Messrs Lucas & Allard, trading as the Corsham Quarrying Company. It is later used by the Government for storage in WWI and WWII. |
| **1880** | Randell and Saunders start work at Park Lane Quarry. It closed during the Second World War and the tramways were taken out. It is later reopened and closed once again in 1958. Park Lane Quarry was reopened again in 2012 and is still in production.<br>Brewer's Yard Quarry in the woods at the very top of Box Hill near Rudloe is worked around 1880 and has two distinct levels. |
| **1881** | Between 1881-1930 the hills north-west of Monkton Farleigh village were quarried for Bath Stone, leaving 300 acres of tunnels. Production ceased when the workings were converted to become the largest single underground munitions store in Europe. It was opened to the public as a museum in the 1980s but is now closed and derelict once again. |
| **1886** | A network of tramways around Corsham is completed by this date.<br>The current Monks Park Quarry (known as Sumsion's Monks until WWII) is opened. Apart from a break in production between 1940 and 1952 (used by the Ministry of Aircraft Production), the quarry worked continuously until its closure in 2008.<br>Park Lane Quarry opened at the top of Rough Street in Neston. It became one of the most successful quarries in the Corsham area. |

# Chapter 22. Stone Quarries - a chronological list.

| | |
|---|---|
| **1887** | Up until 1887 most of the quarries were independently owned; seven of these firms (listed below) joined together to become the Bath Stone Firms Ltd.<br>The Corsham Bath Stone Company Limited, R. J. Marsh and Company Limited, Samuel Rowe Noble, Pictor and Sons, Stone Brothers Limited, Isaac Sumsion and Randell Saunders and Company Ltd. |
| **1890** | Longsplatt Quarry, near Kingsdown, starts work; and closes later in 1920; it was originally an open-cast working which later had a slope shaft added.<br>Moor Park Quarry to the south of Sands Quarry is opened by Messrs. Sheppard and Sons and is later sold in 1920 to the Bath & Portland Stone Co. eventually closing in 1952. |
| **1890** | Work started at Sands Quarry in Westwells Corsham. It is closed by 1923.<br>Work started at Westwells Quarry (Moor Park) and it closed later in 1952.<br>The Bath Stone Firms Limited take over all of the Portland Quarries. |
| **1900** | Brockleaze Quarry in Neston, also known as Goblin Pit or Wansdyke, began work. Now used by Wansdyke Security Ltd. for storage purposes.<br>Work began at Clubhouse Quarry in Neston. It suffered from flooding and poor stone. It is used in the Second World War as storage for foreign currency, mainly Polish.<br>Hollybush Quarry opens on the Neston Estate and is worked for two years but the quality of the stone is not very good; leading to its closure on 11 December 1902.<br>After 1900, tallow candles began to be replaced by circular benzene lamps 4 inches in diameter and about 2 inches high.<br>Eastlays Quarry between Corsham and Melksham closes. |
| **1904** | The Bath Stone Firms Limited begin working Pickwick Quarry; it was in use up to 1961.<br>Goods Hill Quarry in Gastard opens but never really produced any amount of stone due to constant flooding of the tunnels. |
| **1905** | Hartham Park Quarry, half a mile west of Corsham, is started up by Marsh Son and Gibbs and was later worked by Yockney and Hartham Park Stone Co. |
| **1908** | Bath Stone Firms Ltd. becomes the Bath and Portland Stone Firms Ltd. |
| **1910** | Until 1942, Copenacre Quarry, then known as Hartham Quarry, was mined for its oolitic limestone .<br>The quarry consisted of two intersecting mines, both owned and developed by Marsh Son and Gibbs until it went bankrupt in 1910 and was taken over by Bath and Portland Stone Firms. |
| **1911** | The Travellers Rest Quarry, Copenacre Quarry and the Pickwick Quarry once separate quarries were all physically joined together and the resulting quarry (Hartham Quarry) was worked by two separate companies up to 1940. From 1945 the Bath & Portland Stone Firms worked the quarry until about 1960. |
| **1912** | Sands Quarry at Westwells in Neston closes.<br>Quarrying begins at Elm Park Quarry at Gastard and is worked with horses and carts. The hard stone produced the curb stones laid by Wiltshire County Council until the 1920s. |
| **1914** | Messrs. Agaric and Co. Ltd. lease a disused portion of the underground quarries of Yockney and Hartham Park Stone Co. Ltd at Hudswell for the purpose of cultivating mushrooms but the industry later moved to Bradford-on-Avon in 1939.<br>Seven Shaft Quarry closes.<br>Hudswell Quarry closes. |
| **1920** | Elm Park Quarry is acquired by Shepperd & Son.<br>Longsplatt Quarry closes down. |
| **1922** | The Ministry of Munitions vacate Ridge Quarry. |
| **1930s** | The industry is in decline, partly due to exhaustion of high quality stone, the general depression of the country, and later, the availability of cheaper reconstructed stone. |
| **1934** | Bath & Portland Stone Company is sold to the Government's War Office. |

## Chapter 22. Stone Quarries - a chronological list.

| | |
|---|---|
| **1935** | The Government were given permission to survey all of the Bath & Portland Quarries in Corsham. Ridge Quarry (owned by the Neston Estate) and Tunnel Quarry at Hudswell were purchased by the War Office on 15 August for £35,000.<br>Eastlays was purchased two months later.<br>Work began to convert them into underground armament depots.<br>Cox's vertical shaft mine at Combe Down in Bath closes. |

*One of the Hudswell Tunnel Quarry slope shafts.*     *Julian Carosi; Box Caves quarry visit in 2015.*

| | |
|---|---|
| **1936** | The RAF was given exclusive use of Ridge Quarry. A forty-four yard endless conveyor is installed in Tunnel Quarry to help remove debris.<br>A large part of Pockeredge Estate is purchased by the War Office - to provide space for the Basil Hill Barracks site to be built and developed by Hoskins & Pond of Newbury.<br>A Sergeants' Mess is also built there.<br>Cow dung and slurry were used to accelerate the growth of lichen to aid disguise from enemy planes! |
| **1937** | The Government War Office purchases Monkton Farleigh Quarry.<br>Copenacre Quarry (also known as Cob, Cobenacre) is taken over by the Government. It was formerly owned by Marsh, Son and Gibb then later by Lucas and Kinnear.<br>Pictor's Monks Quarry is taken over by the Government for use as an ammunition store.<br>Spring Quarry closes.<br>Three people were arrested in Bromsgrove for attempting to pass on forged half-crowns that had been manufactured illicitly in Tunnel Quarry. See Chapter 13.<br>Monks (Pictor's Monks or Eastlays) Quarry closes. |
| **1938** | St. Winifred's Quarry on Combe Down closes.<br>The Hudswell Lift Shafts were completed in June but the electric lifts were not available for another 18 months.<br>Hand steam winches were installed and makeshift cages to enable the ammunition to be taken below for storage. |
| **1939** | World War II begins: Hartham Park Quarry is taken over by the Government for use as storage for Fleet Air Arm stores and Asdic (now Sonar) ranges.<br>On 24 June, a fire destroyed a Royal Engineers (RE) hut at Basil Hill; £2,000 worth of paint and other materials were lost (over £90,000 in today's money). |

## Chapter 22. Stone Quarries - a chronological list.

**1940**  Ridge Quarry is closed. The small Elm Park Quarry near Ridge Quarry, is used for storing lubricating oils and similar materials in drums.

Browns Quarry is converted at great expense into a secure underground Command Centre for No. 10 Group, RAF Fighter Control.

Underground barracks for 300 soldiers were built in Tunnel Quarry but were rarely occupied except by the Women's Auxiliary Air Force (WAAFs) working in Brown's Quarry and for the South West Control workers who operated the underground military telephone exchange.

Lifts were installed at Hudswell by Herbert Morris & Co in December to give better access to Tunnel Quarry. *[Ed - in c1980 following a Saturday morning working in Tunnel Quarry for the Naval Stores Depot, a colleague and I were stuck halfway up in one of the lifts for several hours. The lift had to be hand winched to the surface to release us.]* The two lift shafts entrances have since been concreted over, but are still visible at Hudswell. Eastlays Quarry - CAD Sub-Depot No.2 (halfway between Melksham and Corsham) is being used for storage of high explosive bulk TNT and cordite.

Eastlays was originally called Pictor Monks Quarry.

Spring Quarry is requisitioned by the Ministry of Aircraft Production to house the Bristol Aeroplane Company for production of engines.

**1941**

Ridge Quarry now used as an Ammunition Depot begins to see increased delivery of munitions from America. Ridge receives 3,000 hand grenades from Tunnel Quarry for issue to airfields.

The huge Main Surface Loading Platform (MSLP) at Tunnel Quarry (on the Basil Hill site) becomes operational. This is still visible today from the end of Spring Lane.

The completed Operational Centre for the No.10 Group Fighter Command in Brown's Quarry is handed over to the RAF.

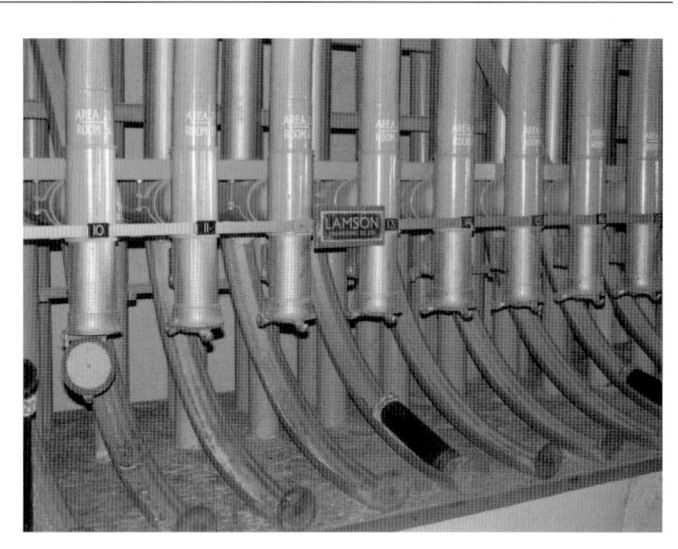

*The photographs shown here were recently taken in Tunnel Quarry Hudswell.*
*Above right is - the Lamson pneumatic tube transport or PTT) system that propeled cylindrical containers through tubes around the Hudswell Tunnel Quarry by using compressed air or by partial vacuum.*
*Below - Aircraft Factory tooling, a huge ventilation duct and the ex-London Underground escalator.*

## Chapter 22. Stone Quarries - a chronological list.

| | |
|---|---|
| **1942** | The underground barracks in Tunnel Quarry are abandoned, as the aerial threat from German bombers had become negligible.<br>A large aircraft factory is built underground at Spring Quarry.<br>Hartham is opened as the Royal Naval Stores Depot (RNSD) Copenacre and also handled films. The Copenacre site is now a modern housing estate with underground access sealed off.<br>On 30 November, a serious fire destroyed the 'Attery' block at Basil Hill which was being used as the ATS quarters. The (ATS) Auxiliary Territorial Service was the Women's Branch of the British Army during the Second World War. Ridge quarry loading platform, top of No.2 shaft is built. The Monkton Farleigh sidings (concrete lined) tunnel used to carry ammunition up to the Monkton Farleigh Depot is completed.<br>The Clubhouse Quarry (a deep underground vault) in Neston is leased to De La Rue as a secure storage facility and used to around 1948 to store East European banknotes printed in Britain by the De La Rue company. |
| **1943** | The Tunnel Quarry, Corsham Armament Depot (CAD) at Hudswell 125 acres is finally completed and contained 3000,000 tons of explosives and cost £4,500,000 to build (£143,000,000 in today's money).<br>Elm Park underground depot closes.<br>The Tunnel Quarry barracks fall into disuse but remain intact until the early 1980s. Electronic lifts are installed to access Browns Quarry and the South West Control room. |
| **1944** | Ridge Quarry ammunitions reach a peak of 31,563 tons in preparation for invasion of Europe. Three trucks loaded with 500lb bombs hurtle down the incline shaft in Eastley Quarry, but miraculously did not explode. |
| **1945** | World War II ends. Moor Park was the first quarry to be decontrolled by the Government.<br>The Bristol Aeroplane Company factory built in Spring Quarry closes. The total cost of building the factory exceeded £20,000,000, with half as much again spent on machine tools. Yet it produced nothing of note. The overspend prompted a House of Commons Public Account Committee Enquiry, the only time that such an enquiry had investigated a Defence project in wartime! Spring Quarry is handed over to the Admiralty under the umbrella of the Royal Naval Stores Depot (RNSD) Copenacre.<br>It was discovered that six-thousand 500 lb bombs in the lower section of Ridge Quarry were stored in unstable condition and could cause an explosion. Most were eventually deep-sea dumped via Barry Docks.<br>The Operational Centre for the No.10 Group Fighter Command in Brown's Quarry is taken over by the RAF Control and Reporting School.<br>From 1945 the Bath & Portland Stone Firms work Hartham Quarry until about 1960. |

*Hoisting and cutting the Bath Stone out of the Monks Park Quarry.*

| | |
|---|---|
| **1946** | The Ministry of Supply *let* parts of Spring Quarry to the Admiralty for temporary storage. |
| **1948** | Samson coal cutters were tested at Moor Park and later used at Monk's Park.<br>Park Lane Quarry reopens after the war at the top of Rough Street in Neston. |

## Chapter 22. Stone Quarries - a chronological list.

| | |
|---|---|
| **1949** | Moor Park Quarry closes. |
| **1950** | The RAF Control and Reporting School home in Brown's Quarry is taken over by the Southern Sector Control for the RAF's Rotar radar system (a shield against Russian atomic bombers). |
| **1951** | Hartham (RNSD Copenacre) Quarry is extended between 1951-54 to double its size. |
| **1952** | Westwells Quarry (also known as Moor Park) closes down. **Subterfuge (codename):** The Government start looking at using Spring Quarry to build a nuclear bunker due to the increase of a Soviet attack. Work begins to quarrying at Monk's Park Quarry. |
| **1954** | **Subterfuge:** The Government estimate the cost of building a Government bunker at Spring Quarry at £1,000,000 (£20,000,000 in today's money). The final cost was £2,500,000 (nearly £50,000,000 in today's money!) In April, the Government purchased the Spring Quarry Freehold along with 100 acres of surface land from the Bath and Portland Stone Firms Ltd. Monks Park is developed into another RNSD storage depot, some 250,000 tons of waste was removed. The north part of Monk's Park Quarry is partitioned off for use by the Admiralty (Royal Naval Stores Department) for storing electronic naval equipment. |
| **1955** | Ridge Quarry is abandoned by the RAF. Army presence remains there until 1964. |
| **1956** | Work begins in Spring Quarry on constructing the Emergency Government Headquarters - later known as the Burlington Bunker. |
| **1957** | The final layout of the Burlington Bunker is established. A new office block is constructed between 1957-1959 at Copenacre to house 400 new staff transferred to Corsham from Risley in Lancashire. Now modern housing. |
| **1958** | Hartham Park Quarry No 2 closes down. The Southern Sector Control for the RAF's Rotar radar system in Brown's Quarry is abandoned. Horses were used underground until this date at Clift Quarry on Box Hill. |
| **1959** | **STOCKWELL**: On 25 January, the Top Secret code name for the Government's underground bunker at Spring Quarry is changed from Subterfuge to Stockwell (which is now intended to be the government's battle headquarters); major work completed and the surface work finished. |
| **1960** | The Bath and Portland Group form. Due to flooding over long periods, Park Lane Quarry at the top of Rough Street in Neston closes. |
| **1961** | **BURLINGTON:** The Corsham underground bunker gets its new code name, 'Burlington' whose prime objective is now a post-nuclear attack role to take over the reins of government if the Cabinet is totally wiped out before it could leave Whitehall. |
| **1963** | **TURNSTILE:** On 25 January the Corsham bunker gets another new code name, 'Turnstile'. |
| **1964** | Hartham Park Quarry closes. Ridge Quarry is abandoned. |
| **1965** | The Royal Naval Codification Authority and Agency is set up above ground at Spring Quarry. In 1986 the organisation (now called the National Codification Bureau) moves to Glasgow. Monkton Farleigh (ammunition) Depot is decommissioned in 1965 and sold in 1976. |
| **1968** | Clift Quarry halfway down Box Hill on the A4 closes. |
| **1972** | It is announced that Copenacre including Monks Park and Spring Quarry RNSD Depots would be closed for fire safety reasons and 900 jobs could be lost. |
| **1974** | It is announced that Copenacre including the Monks Park and Spring Quarry RNSD Depots would not close. Monkton Farleigh and Eastley Quarries are sold to the private sector. |
| **1975** | **CHANTICLEER**: The underground bunker has a new code name, 'Chanticleer'. Concerns were being expressed that the secret bunker's location is becoming too widely known. The Neston Estate purchases Ridge Quarry. All buildings, except the No.2 shaft transit shed were demolished. |
| **1980** | **Project ALBATROSS:** By now, the secret bunker (Code Name Chanticleer) in its current state at Corsham is no longer fit for purpose. Project Albatross is looking at the future of Chanticleer over the next 265 years. In the early 1980s, thieves broke in and dug up the under-floor ducting in the Farleigh Sidings Tunnel and removed all of the copper power cables along the tunnel's length! |
| **1985** | Bath & Portland Stone Firms Ltd. becomes subsidiary of Amalgamated Roadstone Corp. |
| **1986** | Hartham Park Quarry is opened as a museum but closes by the end of the 1990s. |

Chapter 22. Stone Quarries - a chronological list.

| | | |
|---|---|---|
| 1987 | The Western Area Division (CID) MoD Police Unit move to Old Shaft Road Spring Quarry. RNSD Headquarters Staff (Branches 37 and 39) move into Copenacre. Simon Finch reopens Elm Park Quarry in Gastard but work sadly comes to an end following his premature death in a motoring accident that year. | *Photo, 2015 Farleigh Sidings tunnel visit.* |
| 1988 | **PERIPHERAL**: The underground bunker gets a new code name, 'Peripheral'. Eastlays Quarry is now used by Octavian for secure wine storage depot. | |
| 1990: | **PERIPHERAL**: The end of the underground bunker is in sight. | |

| | |
|---|---|
| 1993 | Due to the reduced surface and submarine fleets, RNSD Hartham (Copenacre) is closed. |
| 1995 | Due to the reduced surface and submarine fleets, RNSD Spring Quarry is closed. |
| 1996 | Due to the reduced surface and submarine fleets, RNSD Monks Park is closed. The Monkton Farleigh mine is acquired by Wansdyke Security, and becomes a secure warehouse business for secure storage of documentation. |
| 1997 | Elm Park Quarry in Gastard is opened by a Bath based firm but they failed to quarry stone there. |
| 1999 | **PERIPHERAL**: The condition of the underground bunker has deteriorated so badly that 'Peripheral' is no longer viable. |
| 2000 | Elm Park Quarry is reopened by the Elm Park Stone Company who was successful in supplying high quality stone from the quarry until 2005. Hanson Bath and Portland re-opened Hartham Quarry (between Park Lane and the Bradford Road). |
| 2004 | **PERIPHERAL**: The underground bunker site is declassified and classified items were removed. |
| 2005 | Wessex Dimensional Stone, the company formed by Ian Butterworth takes over the Elm Park Quarry from Elm Park Stone. |
| 2010 | The Portland Stone Firms Ltd one of the last remaining suppliers of the world-famous Portland Stone goes into administration. |
| 2012 | **BURLINGTON:** A book called BURLINGTON is published by Nick Catford and gives a very detailed analysis of the bunker's development including many photos. Park Lane Quarry at the top of Rough Street underneath Neston Park (the estate where the BBC TV Series Lark Rise to Candleford was shot) is reopened by Ham and Doulting Stone Ltd . |
| 2016 | Monks Park Quarry (after lying dormant for 12 years) is back in production, with Hanson UK removing the first stone from the site in January. The Lovell Stone Group (run by brothers Simon and James Hart under the watchful guidance of their father, who is the chairman) takes over the lease of the Hartham Park Quarry from Hanson Bath and Portland in February. |
| 2017 | The Monks Park Quarry site is sold to the Johnston Quarry Group. |
| 2018 | In March, Monks Park Quarry is 'mothballed' by its owners, Johnston Quarry Group after they claimed it had become stagnant. The major quarry group Blockstone takes over the operation of the Park Lane Quarry. The 'Park Lane Base Bed' stone quarried there is unique in the Bathstone market. Found under the top bed, it is far harder and more durable than any normal Bath Stone currently being mined. The stone is uniform light-cream in colour with occasional veins and a slightly larger amount of shell content than the top bed. |
| 2019 | Hartham Park Quarry continues to be mined for Bath Stone by the Lovell Stone Group. |

## Chapter 23. Sylvester, Albert, James (1889-1989) Corsham.

Albert James Sylvester played a very important role as *Principal* Private Secretary in the Government to Lloyd George in 1923-1945 and ended his last years as a local landowner in his home in Corsham.

**1889:** Albert James Sylvester was born in Harlaston in Staffordshire on 24 November, the eldest of three children and only son of Albert and Elizabeth Sylvester. His father Albert was a tenant farmer of modest means, reduced to the role of a brewery farm worker in Burton-on-Trent by the agricultural depression. Through visits to his grandparent's farm young Albert grew to love agriculture, something he later returned to during the latter part of his life in Corsham.

**1903:** One of the subjects Albert studied at Secondary School was Pitman's shorthand. Compelled by family poverty and aged just 14, Albert left school to work in the local Charrington's brewery at a starting salary of six shillings a week. Young Albert gave up most of his leisure time to perfect his shorthand and touch-typing skills, attending evening classes, and often working by oil-lamp much aided by his sisters Eva and May.

1930: Lloyd George, left with Albert Sylvester. ©*National Library of Wales.*

**1910:** Albert migrated to London at the age of twenty and set up his own business as a freelance shorthand writer at Chancery Lane, working as a stenographer *[transcribing speech in shorthand]*. He did a variety of jobs including recording the official records of the House of Lords debates. He went on to win his spurs as a 'champion typist' which enabled him to achieve a high status in all his future jobs. He attained champion speeds of 210 words a minute in shorthand and 80 in typing, and also qualified as a teacher of these subjects and gave free speed (1 hour) demonstrations to the public at various hotels. Reaching 21 years of age, Albert won a competition as Britain's fastest typist; his first official job was to assist a Royal Commission which went out to India.

**1911:** From humble beginnings, young Albert continued to progress to the point when he was now living permanently in London and working as a very competent professional speed typist. Those specialist skills were obviously recognised and sought after by those in high office. In 1910 and 1911 he was a member of the British international 'speedwriting' (fast typewriting) team which competed at the Business Efficiency Exhibition at Olympia and came second to the Americans.

**1912-1913:** Albert went to India and Burma as an assistant reporter for the Royal Commission in the Public Services. On returning to London, he set up as a freelance shorthand-writer in Chancery Lane and had it not been for the First World War, he would probably have stayed there for the rest of his career.

**1914:** When Britain declared war in August 1914, Albert was asked to do some temporary work for the Admiralty, at a salary of three gold sovereigns a week. He went on to play an integral role as Private Secretary to the Committee of Imperial Defence between 1914-1921. Albert had attested *[enrolled as ready for military service]* for military service but was not *called up* on account of his important job.

## Chapter 23. Sylvester, Albert, James (1889-1989) Corsham.

In his political role, Albert would have been at the very heart of all major decisions relating to the War and dealing with all of the War leaders. In respect of World War 1, he typed the First World War Armistice Terms on his own Underwood typewriter and was personally entrusted by the Government to carry those documents to France in his briefcase.

Albert moved into the office as Private Secretary to Colonel M. P. A. (later Lord) Hankey as a stenographer (shorthand writer) and this was the start of his career in political life. Hankey (a British civil servant who gained prominence as the first Cabinet Secretary) was Secretary to the Committee of Imperial Defence and therefore at the very heart of the British war machine. Albert was the first shorthand writer ever to take the notes of a Cabinet Committee - a truly pioneering task.

**1915:** Twenty-six year old Albert wrote a 104 page Underwood Typewriter Manual. It was published by Sir Isaac Pitman, London. The picture in the book is of Albert with his trusty Underwood typewriter.
In the book, his achievements are listed as follows: Two Diplomas of Excellence and Silver Medal (Team Contest) at Business Exhibition, Olympia; Silver Cup (Presentation) Madras; formally Speed Artist: Underwood Typewriter Co. Ltd. ; Underwood (New York) Gold Medal for Speed.

**1916:** Albert became Hankey's Private Secretary. When Lloyd George became Prime Minister he appointed Albert as a founder-member of the Cabinet Secretariat to the newly formed Committee of Imperial Defence and also made him Secretariat of the Imperial War Cabinet.
Previous to this, notes had never been taken at such high ranking government meetings!

**1917:** Albert marries Evelyn Annie Wellman from Kingston on Thames; a Baptist Minister's daughter.

**1918:** Albert was appointed Member of the Order of the British Empire (1918 Birthday Honours List). At the end of the war Albert (with his secondary school education) became an established higher-grade civil servant working with those who had entered as university graduates after competitive examination.

**1919:** Albert was appointed an Officer of the Order of the British Empire in the 1919 New Year Honours List. He continued his service working for the British Secretary of the Peace Conference.

## Chapter 23. Sylvester, Albert, James (1889-1989) Corsham.

By now, Albert had become a well known and very capable Pitman shorthand writer and was responsible for the British stenographic Conference notes. He was assisted by one lady (also a Pitman Shorthand writer) and on some occasions by a third lady who reported in French by means of Pitman's Shorthand. When the report of the League of Nations was presented to the Conference, the whole of the transcribing was finished half-an-hour after the Conference had adjourned.

**1920:** Albert was appointed a Commander of the Order of the British Empire in the 1920 New Year Honours List.

**1921:** Albert leaves Hankey's employment to become *Principal* Private Secretary to Lloyd George at 10 Downing Street. Lloyd George (then Prime Minister of the post-war coalition government) was discredited politically for deserting the Liberal Party and forming a coalition government during the Great War. Albert's only daughter, Joan Maureen Sylvester is born on 12 May 1921 in Wandsworth, London. She was known as Maureen. Albert participated in the extended negotiations which led to the celebrated Anglo-Irish Treaty. Albert is made a Commander of the Order of the Crown of Italy.

**1925**: Photo of Lloyd George left, with Albert Sylvester. ©*National Library of Wales.*

**1922:** On 19 October, Lloyd George tenders his resignation to the King and Albert's role ends. It was a sad afternoon for Albert as he had grown to admire and love Lloyd George and had been made to feel like part of his family. As a civil servant, Albert could be re-employed anywhere. Lloyd George's Tory successor Bonar Law asked Albert to remain on as one of his secretaries at 10 Downing Street. Albert accepted, but found his new 'old school tie' colleagues (who came from the conventional 'Oxbridge' Whitehall establishment) standoffish towards him; with some of them going out of their way to embarrass him because of his association with Lloyd George. On Bonar Law's retirement due to ill health, Albert remained at No. 10 for a short while working for Stanley Baldwin. By now, Albert was amassing huge amounts of money.

**1923:** On 30 June 1923 Albert resigned his Civil Service appointment and re-joined his old Chief Lloyd George (now in opposition) at 18 Abingdon Street on 1 July as his *Principal* Private Secretary and press officer. Albert ran Lloyd's private office in London (which at its peak had a staff of over twenty, including research staff, shorthand typists and messengers). At the time, Miss Frances Stevenson, who was Lloyd George's mistress, was also Lloyd George's Private Secretary. Lloyd George paid Albert a lump sum of £4,500 (£190,000 in today's money) to compensate him for the loss of his civil-service pension rights and a salary of £1000 a year (£42,000 in today's money), which was a considerable sum for the time. It was increased to £1500 in 1926 and reduced by ten per cent in the 1931 economic crisis. In the House of Commons, Albert had his own seat in the officials' box under the gallery. This allowed him (in times of political and diplomatic crisis) to furnish Lloyd George with detailed reports of what was going on.

**1927:** Albert documented Lloyd George's visit to Brazil in December 1927.

## Chapter 23. Sylvester, Albert, James (1889-1989) Corsham.

**1929:** Albert documented Lloyd George's visit to Europe in 1929. In January of that year they sailed by cruise ship along the coast from Cannes to Naples and also travelled by motor car through Belgium and France to the Italian Lakes.

**1934:** Albert, his daughter Joan Maureen and a Miss Wilkes were in a party of six being taken for a Sunday evening trip off Worthing in a speed boat owned by Robert Burglin of Cherbourg House, Kingston, when there was a serious fire on the boat. A petrol pipe near the dynamo had burst causing an immediate flare-up. The fire was half put out using a fire extinguisher, some sea water and lastly, Miss Wilkes' skirt (which she wore over her bathing costume) dipped in water and made to act like a swab. Thankfully nobody was hurt.

**1935:** Lloyd George launches a dramatic New Deal for economic regeneration and a Council of Action for Peace and Reconstruction. All of this was overshadowed by the visit that Albert and Lloyd George made to Hitler the following year.

**1936:** Albert (who was living in Putney) attended meetings (2nd-16th September) between Lloyd George, Hitler, Ribbentrop (the Nazi Foreign Minister) and Hess (2nd Sept) at Wachenfeld House in Berchtesgaden, Germany and is shown the National Socialist sights on 4th September. Lloyd then returned for tea on the 5th with his entourage. Lloyd was accompanied on this trip by a number of other people, including his son Gwilym, his daughter Megan, Dr Thomas Jones (Deputy Secretary to the cabinet), T P Conwell Evans (academic, German speaker, Secretary of the Anglo-German Fellowship), Bertrand Dawson/Lord Dawson of Penn (Royal Physician and author of a report published in 1920 on the provision of medical services nationwide, a report which was influential in discussions later on the setting up of the National Health Service).

Albert, Lloyd's Private Secretary, recorded the events of the trip on silent film where Hitler can be seen in a jovial mood! The film commences with a trip along the miles and miles of one of Germany's newly built concrete autobahns [motorways] one of the best highway systems in the world and at the time, way in advance of other countries. The film can be seen online via the link below. Note; in the film you can see the swastika armbands and one-arm salutes already being adopted by the German military.

https://player.bfi.org.uk/free/film/watch-visit-of-the-rt-hon-d-lloyd-george-om-mp-to-germany-september-2nd-26th-1936-1936

With a hint of disagreement, Albert wrote that after the visit to Hitler, Lloyd George: *'returned to the Grand Hotel in a state of great elation. It was clear to us all that he [Lloyd] had been tremendously impressed by Hitler and to me, at all events, it seemed that he was spell-bound by Hitler's astonishing personality and manner'.* This can clearly be seen in the above film that Albert took. When in Berchtesgaden, Albert stated that he would never forget Hitler's window. It was the biggest window Albert had ever seen. It was enormous. It overlooked the Bavarian Alps with a ravine on the right and Saltzburg beyond. It made a very deep impression on Albert and also on Lloyd George; because when Lloyd returned, he too had a huge window made (to replace two small ordinary windows) and made himself a beautiful outlook. He also removed several trees to improve the view down the hill to his acres of land which he had reclaimed from scrubland himself - and beyond to 40 miles or more into Surrey, Sussex and Hampshire. It was a wonderful inspirational view.

In later life, the view across the Box valley from Albert's Rudloe Cottage home towards the City Bath, would have been in memory of that stunning view Albert never forgot in Berchtesgaden.

## Chapter 23. Sylvester, Albert, James (1889-1989) Corsham.

In fact, Albert later had an extension built at his home Rudloe Cottage that emulated Hitler's view (to a smaller extent). This photo was taken in Rudloe Cottage on 1 April 2019 the day when owners Richard and Jane Body where downsizing and moving out to a more manageable property nearby in Rudloe. The Rudloe Cottage view is magnificent across the Box valley towards Bath and Colerne in the distance.

In his book 'Life with Lloyd George', Albert states that Lloyd George was obviously *struck* with Hitler, 'He is a very great man', said Lloyd, *'Fuhrer is the proper name for him, for he is a born leader, yes, and statesman.'* At the meeting, Albert had asked Ribbentrop if Hitler would mind being filmed and was told that he had permission to do so, and Hitler nodded to Albert in confirmation.

On page 150, Albert describes Hitler as, *'talking with great animation using gestures with great energy, enthusiastically and without the least hesitation. His blue eyes were full of fire. He had a fairly large head and his dark hair dropped over the right side of his forehead emphasising his shaving-brush moustache. He was 46 years of age but looked older and about 5 feet 10 1/2 inches tall and well built in his light pin-point coloured suit'.*

**1939:** Above, is a rare family photo (courtesy of Paul Weaver of New Farm), showing from left to right: Harry Pocock, Albert, his daughter Maureen, wife Evelyn, Joan Pocock and Lillian Pocock all sitting outside together having tea at New Farm in Corsham early 1939.

Back in the office, Albert's responsibilities began to catch up with in him, when following a doctor's examination by Dr. Roberts and Lord Dawson (physician to the British Royal Family and President of the Royal College of Physicians from 1931 to 1937) on 26 October 1939, Albert was told that organically he was absolutely sound, but very much overworked. He was told that normally, he would have been ordered to take two-month's rest, but they were at war. Albert offered to take a week off.

The doctors smiled and recommended a fortnight's rest. Lloyd George was not happy about Albert being reported as being overworked! Albert took 10 days off and spent some time recuperating at New Farm in Corsham before returning on 9 November 1939 to Lloyd George who greeted Albert warmly.

"*Ah,*" said he, "*I can see you are better. I could see that also from your writing [to me]*".

*Maureen at New Farm c1940s (courtesy of Paul Weaver).*

Chapter 23. Sylvester, Albert, James (1889-1989) Corsham.

Farm life and riding horseback in Corsham had restored Albert. The next day, without warning, the Germans invaded Belgium, Holland and Luxemburg.

**1940:** Miss Jean Fowler sold her Gastard House Estate including Gastard House and Chapel Knapp Farm to Albert, who let it out to tenants. The auction was held at 3 o'clock in the Oak Room, Fortt's Resaurant, Milsom Street in Bath on Wednesday 17 July.

**1942:** On page 309 of his book 'Life with Lloyd George', Albert wrote in his dary that *'his [Albert's] wife Evelyn and daughter spent a very peaceful Christmas and appreciated every moment. We are thankful for many blessings. After three and a half years of war, we still had our turkey, and we all took part in preparing and cooking and eating it. L.G. is at Churt . We sent him [Lloyd George] a Christmas card but from him we have not even had his good wishes.'* Churt was Lloyd George's home.

Another famous visitor to New Farm, Corsham in the early 1940s was Frank Wootton from Alfriston Village, East Sussex (see photo), an aviation artist and instrument fitter working with the RAF in Melksham. Frank Wootton OBE PPGAvA (30 July 1911 – 21 April 1998) was famous for his works depicting the Royal Air Force during the Second World War.

Frank became good friends with Mr and Mrs Weaver of New Farm near Byde Mill, Corsham. Frank's mother died when he was still of school-age, and he was raised by his father, a seaman in the Merchant Navy. He was awarded the Order of the British Empire in 1995 and died in April 1998, back home at Alfriston, Sussex.

**1943:** After Lloyd George married his second wife Frances Stevenson in October, Albert often felt uncomfortable, even embarrassed, at the new situation which had arisen. Yet, Albert never displayed any inclination to depart for a new career; both Lloyd George and Frances, clearly considering him nigh on indispensable. Only Albert knew the full details of Lloyd George's personal life with its double loyalty to his family and to his 'mistress' Frances Stevenson (now Lloyd's wife). Albert duly recorded the family rows in his shorthand diary and played an equivocal part between the two sides. There was considerable jealousy between him and Frances, who was also an accomplished secretary for Lloyd George.

**1944:** Lloyd George and Frances had returned to live in their new North Wales home, Ty Newydd, Llanystumdwy. Albert began to resent staying on indefinitely in this remote area of the country and threatened to return to the south-east, feeling that he had been badly treated by his employers – who implored him to remain in their service.

**1945:** Remarkably, Albert served as Principal Private Secretary to David Lloyd George from 1923 until Lloyd's death at Ty Newydd on 26 March 1945 – 22 years running Lloyd George's private office in London (which at one point had over twenty staff). Albert dealt, often on his own initiative, with his employer's massive postbag, served as Lloyd George's press officer and dealt with many constituency cases. Albert

## Chapter 23. Sylvester, Albert, James (1889-1989) Corsham.

often accompanied Lloyd George to public functions (for which he had made meticulous arrangements), attended the Commons (acting as his employer's eyes and ears) during Lloyd George's increasingly frequent absences, and furnished him with detailed reports of events at times of political and diplomatic crises.

His fluent shorthand enabled him to take detailed notes of events, and spasmodically he kept a diary, a practice which he developed more fully and consistently after 1931. Albert was also heavily implicated in his employer's complex, bizarre personal and family life, becoming closely involved with almost all members of the sprawling Lloyd George family, spanning three generations, and experiencing an especially delicate relationship with Frances Stevenson, Lloyd George's secretary, mistress and eventually his second wife.

During the Second World War Albert had become the owner of more agricultural land in Gastard Corsham, Wiltshire *(see advert on previous page)* Chapel Knapp Farm and Gastard House. He never informed Lloyd George of this because there could well have been a jealous reaction. Within days of his master's death on 26th March 1945 at 8.35 p.m Albert was summarily dismissed in no uncertain terms by Frances, now the Dowager Countess.

Frances had resolved to dispense with his services and forbid him from participating in future projects designed to commemorate and perpetuate Lloyd George's good name and memory, including the preparation of an 'official' biography. For the first time in his life A. J. Sylvester, a proud man now aged 55, was out of a job. The man who had been considered indispensable as long as Lloyd George lived was now no loger wanted! It must have been a huge shock for Albert.

In 1945, Lloyd George left a legacy of £1000 (worth £30,000 today) to Albert, *"his loyal and indefatigable secretary"*. Albert, along with Lloyd's close family, was in attendance at Lloyd's death. Albert then earned his living as a member of Lord Beaverbrook's [Max Aitken] staff at the Daily Express on a three-year contract from 1945 until 1948, and spent a further year as unpaid assistant to Liberal Party leader, E. Clement Davies.

Albert's only daughter Joan Maureen (born 1921) married Alun Evans on 25 March 1945 and lived in London with her husband. At the time of Maureen's marriage, Albert was insistent that his daughter's new family should adopt the double-barrelled name of Sylvester-Evans, as he thought it would better aid his son-in-law's career prospects in the Civil Service, rather than only using the surname of Evans! In 1975 Alun Sylvester-Evans, now Deputy Chief Executive, Property Services Agency, Department of the Environment, was made CB (The Order of the Bath, Companion) for his work in the Agency.

**1947:** One of the tasks Albert began to pursue almost at once with great eagerness after Lloyd's death, was the preparation of a semi-biographical volume about his 'old chief', a work eventually to be published in 1947 as 'The Real Lloyd George'.

This was a somewhat guarded biography of his former employer in which he made much use of his own diaries. He was extremely discreet and loyal to his employer. In the book Albert scrupulously refused to write about Lloyd George's marital indiscretions, the details of which he kept to himself until his death. The book did not go down well with everyone, but Albert's reply was to say, *'I have known; a Genius, but, like us all, with weaknesses, and is therefore intensely human. An endeavour has been made to show him in all his moods. This has been done by reciting incidents and leaving them to produce their own effect.'* Several newspapers (British and American) refused to print extracts from the book.

Chapter 23. Sylvester, Albert, James (1889-1989) Corsham.

The first British serial rights of the volume were eventually purchased by the 'Sunday Dispatch' for £500. Arrangements were then finalised for extensive extracts to be published beginning 2 February 1947. During February and March lengthy, potentially sensational extracts from Albert's forthcoming book were subsequently published and gave rise to much interest and general commendation.

The 'Sunday Dispatch' newspaper predictably gave the work maximum publicity, pointing to its unique originality and frankness and drawing attention to some of the more dramatic chapter headings:

**THE WOMAN WHO BOSSED LLOYD GEORGE – LLOYD GEORGE AND HITLER – LLOYD GEORGE'S MARRIAGE TO HIS SECRETARY AT THE AGE OF 80 – THE DIFFICULTY OVER LLOYD GEORGE'S TITLE.**

On the whole the extracts published in the 'Sunday Dispatch' during the early months of 1947 were well received and increased admiration for Albert and Lloyd George. The book was by far the most successful ever published by Cassell and Co. for many years. Within months of publication copies were no longer available. In the wake of the publication of 'The Real Lloyd George', it was mooted that Albert might then be knighted in recognition of his long role as Lloyd George's Principal Private Secretary. During the 1950s Albert himself initiated several attempts to secure a knighthood but once again without success, using his links with Gwilym Lloyd-George, who held cabinet office under Churchill and Eden.

**1949:** Albert retired from political life and moved with his wife to Corsham to farm and manage the agricultural properties previously purchased by him (Court Farm, Chapel Knapp Farm (then Elm Grove Farm) and Gastard House. The *'Elm'* Grove Farm name would have referred to a beautiful row of Elm trees that once ran south-to-north down the hill behind the farm. These had to be felled due to Dutch Elm disease spread by the Elm Bark Beetle in the early 1970s. Being of farming stock, Albert was also a keen fox hunter and often joined in the local hunts.

In later life Albert moved to Gastard House and then to Rudloe Cottage in Corsham (see photo) carrying with him his publicised ambition to publish a full-scale autobiography but this was never realised.

Albert *lets* out Chapel Knapp Farm to a tenant (the Carpenter family who had already been there for 19 years on a Michaelmas tenancy of £150 per annum, but still ran his own smallholding.
*Photo by Julian Carosi: Rudloe Cottage at the top of Box Hill, in April 2019*

Rudloe Cottage is a beautiful large detached house that sits on the very edge of the A4 on the very top of Box Hill. It is a Grade II listed building with the most wonderful and far reaching views across the Bybrook Valley towards Bath and Colerne.

Chapter 23. Sylvester, Albert, James (1889-1989) Corsham.

Chapel Knapp Farm, Corsham. The cottage that fronts the road in this aerial photo has been demolished.

Donald Carpenter was still running the Chapel Knapp Farm at 95 years of age in 2019.

**1951:** Two gypsies, Walter Wells and Joe Sherrard, were each fined £2 (about £40 in today's money) for stealing newly planted trees on Albert's Chapel Knapp Farm. The tenants (Carpenter and Sons) had been subjected to much loss and inconvenience by the thefts in *'Goods Wood'* by the gypsies.

It would not be such a serious matter if *dead wood* had been taken for burning, but growing trees had been cut down. On March 26th, Wells, Sherrard and a third man were seen carrying away two growing trees from the wood and later, the police found them on the fire at the caravan site. P.C. Adcock said Wells had offered to give the owner 5/- for the trees. The Defendants wrote back enclosing postal orders for £2.

**1953:** Albert is appointed a Justice of the Peace for Wiltshire (Corsham).

**1962:** Albert's fellow Wiltshire Magistrates elected him to be their chairman.

**1964:** Having now reached the mandatory retirement age as a Corsham Magistrate, Albert retires.

**1950:** Albert was a Corsham Justice of the Peace (JP) Magistrate for several years.

He was also Vice President of the Chippenham Young Farmers Club, although he would have been in his early 60s at the time!

**1962:** Albert was living in Rudloe Cottage at the top of Box hill when his wife Evelyn died after a long period as an invalid.

**1974:** Albert's life was featured in a BBC TV programme called, 'The Very Private Secretary'. In his old age he was the subject of a BBC television film *The Very Private Secretary (1974)* and also figured in the television series *The Life and Times of Lloyd George (1981).*

**1975:** As Lloyd George's secret life had now became public knowledge, Albert decided to complete a second book in 1975 called 'Life with Lloyd George' (edited by his friend Colin Cross). This book contains selections from Albert's own diary between 1931 and 1945.

This did give valuable information regarding Lloyd George's character and secrets, though it would be a mistake to accept that Sylvester was an impartial witness. There are however diaries and personal

Chapter 23. Sylvester, Albert, James (1889-1989) Corsham.

papers now owned by the National Library of Wales which must provide a unique insight into the personal life of Lloyd George as well as Albert himself.

Albert's note-taking was so prolific, that a major problem in editing Albert's diary for publication was the length of something like a million words that had to be cut down most drastically.

Albert was the only person who spanned both sides of Lloyd George's life. Lloyd George's relationships with both his wife and his mistress were in complete contrast to his public role as a spokesman for Welsh and British nonconformity in general, and as a family man. Albert never did complete the story of his own life.

*View from Albert's Rudloe Cottage towards the City of Bath from the top of Box Hill in Corsham.*

**c1970/80s:** Albert's ambition to publish a full-scale autobiography, upon which he was actively engaged in extreme old age, never came to fruition.

**1977:** Albert retained his remarkable vigour to extreme old age and won a Supreme Award for Ballroom Dancing when he was 88.

**1980:** When reminiscing on the past, Albert recalled that until 1915, there were never any records kept of Cabinet Meetings.

*'Twenty-one gentlemen used to meet around a table in Downing Street and 21 gentlemen went away with their various ideas of what had been discussed, but nothing was ever written down'.*

It was astonishing, but still probably better than having 21 gentlemen all scribbling away like mad at the notes on which they would base their 21 different memoirs on.

**1981:** Albert appeared on the BBC again in a series entitled 'The Life and Times of Lloyd George'.

**1982:** Albert now aged 93, featured in a Radio 4 profile of his life. In extreme old age in his 80s and 90s, Albert had become a media celebrity and a household name throughout the land.

## Chapter 23. Sylvester, Albert, James (1889-1989) Corsham.

*The photo below shows 95 year old Albert leaning on one of his Corsham farm gates in 1984.*

Albert (who never once danced with his wife) continued to learn how to dance. On one occasion (after several lessons locally elsewhere with a young teacher) he visited one of the Corsham Community Centre Dance evenings and stood watching on the sidelines.

Mrs June Witt who was dancing with her husband Dennis, asked Albert if he would like to join in with the dancing. Albert (who was a tad nervous) said that he had left his dancing shoes at home. June asked him to bring them next week.

A week later, Albert appeared once again on the sidelines, watching the dancing. And once again, June asked him if he would like to join in. Albert replied that his dancing shoes were in his car outside. June asked him to get his shoes and to join in. Albert proved to be a willing if not nervous learner; his only difficulty was not being able to get out of a corner.

He was soon taught how to turn and navigate the corners - something which I suppose he had to do in many difficult situations during his long career looking after politicians.

**1984:** Albert was interviewed when he was ninety-five years of age, and recalled, 'Frances [Lloyd's second wife] and I were colleagues for over thirty years. We worked together [as secretaries in Lloyd's office] and never had any quarrel or disagreement of any kind.

You had to work together in order to deal with a man like Lloyd George. He could have a filthy temper.' Beneath the surface, however, the relationship between them [Albert and Frances] was far from harmonious.

In her heart of hearts, Frances, although aware of Albert's strengths and usefulness, considered him to be vain, over-ambitious and touchy. Behind his back she would always laugh at him and his voice which had a strong nasal twang overlaying a marked Staffordshire accent and his tendency to rub his hands together rather subserviently which made him appear, in her view, a modern day Uriah Heep. Albert in turn accused Frances of being prim, stiff, and intent only on providing comfort for Lloyd George and personal self-seeking.

**1989:** Albert lived to the age of 99 and died on 27 October just weeks before his hundredth birthday. Albert James Sylvester - *a country lad done good.*

**R.I.P Albert James Sylvester (24 November 1889 - 27 October 1989).**

## Chapter 23. Sylvester, Albert, James (1889-1989) Corsham.

Albert James Sylvester was cremated on 06 November 1989 at Haycombe Crematorium in Bath (Bath And NE Somerset Council). Date of death 27 October 1989.

*Above is a copy of Albert's Cremation Record from the Haycombe Crematorium in Bath.*

Albert's wife, Evelyn, died in 1962 and they were survived by their daughter Joan Maureen Sylvester-Evans. Albert was cremated on 06 November 1989 at Haycombe Crematorium in Bath (Bath and NE Somerset Council) and his ashes taken were away by his daughter.

**1998:** Albert's daughter Joan Maureen Evans passes away. Her death was registered in Bath.

**2013:** The following articles are from the first Corsham, Gastard News of November 2013 by Donald Carpenter (of Chapel Knapp Farm) and give a further personal insight into Albert's later life.

**Albert James Sylvester CBE JP 1889 -1989:** I have two typewritten notes sent to my father in the late 1940's by Mr A.J. Sylvester. He owned the land that is still my home, Chapel Knapp Farm, Timberleaze Cottage and what are now 5 and 6 Chapel Hill. He also owned Gastard House for some time. He was an excellent and generous landlord taking a keen interest in the farm and the local environment. What is particularly special about Albert's notes is that they were typed on the same Underwood machine that saw the tumultuous events of WW1, for Albert Sylvester was the first person to record the Cabinet meetings in 10 Downing Street. He was summoned there in 1914, from his secretarial work in the Admiralty, and rose to become Private Secretary to three Prime Ministers: David Lloyd George, Bonar Law and Stanley Baldwin. In his time Albert met and worked with the greatest people in the land including Lord Kitchener, Beaverbrook and Churchill. He remained a close companion to Lloyd George working as his Private Secretary – 'recorder and keeper of secrets for 22 years', and he used the same Underwood typewriter throughout his working life. [Ed. One wonders where Albert's Underwood typewriter is now?] Some people in Gastard may still remember Albert Sylvester, for in later years he lived in Rudloe Cottage, where bar one month, he almost reached the great age of 100 years. He started working at the age of 14 in a Staffordshire Brewery but he then taught himself Pitman's shorthand and the skill of touch typing.

He was a truly remarkable person, 'Rising' as he said, from a peasant background to become the most trusted custodian of state affairs in the country. Not only did he attain this distinction but he was also awarded several honours, was a Justice of the Peace, champion golfer, horseman, writer and at the age of 87 a prize ballroom dancer. It was a privilege to have known him.

*Photo shows Chapel Knapp Farm in November 2018*
*[End of Gastard News article].*

## Chapter 23. Sylvester, Albert, James (1889-1989) Corsham.

The following advice was written inside Albert's 1915 Underwood Typewriter Manual as encouragement to his students: *Do not look upon your practice as hard work; treat it as if it were a game worth playing well. If you have the right spirit, you will be inspired and enthused as you feel yourself progressing; your enthusiasm will grow; you will see it; as it were, the blue on the horizon and desire to reach it. Thus, you will forget your difficulties, and will not notice perhaps, what might otherwise be drudgery to you. Every day you sit down to your daily hour's practice, say to yourself: 'Now I am going to try to do better work today than I did yesterday.'* This is certainly a sentiment that Albert maintained throughout his life.

*Many thanks to Kevin Gaskin for providing the idea and framework for this chapter on Sylvester.*

**The Dominion Premiers at 10 Downing Street July 1921; the Meeting of the Empire Conference** *[Courtesy of 'The Sphere '16 July 1921].* **Seated in the front:** The Right Hon. E. S. Montague, M.P., the Right Hon. A. J. Balfour, O.M., M.P., the Hon. Srinavasa-Sastri (in front of whom is 'Cheng' the dog), the Right Hon. W. F. Massey, the Right Hon, A. Meighen, **the Right Hon. D. Lloyd George, O.M,. M.P**,. the Right Hon. W. M. Hughes, K.C., General the Right Hon. J. C. Smuts. K.C., the Right Hon. Earl Curzon of Kedleston, K.G., and the Maharao of Kutch. **Second row (standing):** Mr G. S. Bajpal, Mr G. H. Shakespeare, Mr F. D. Thomson, Colonel S. H. Wilson, Sir M. Hankey, the Hon. C. C, Ballantyne, the Right Hon. Lord Lee of Fareham, Colonel the Hon. H. Mentz, Right Hon. Sir L. W. Evans. M.P., Captain the Right Hon. F. E. Guest, D.S.O., M.P., Sir E. Grigg, the Hon. Sir T. Smartt, and **Mr A. J. Sylvester**. **Standing at back:** Sir C. M. Lambert, Mr P. E. Deane, Mr G. Brebner, Captain Armstrong, and Mr L. C. Christie. **Photo below shows New Farm Corsham where Albert and his wife often stayed.**

## Chapter 24. Town Crier - Charlie Bethel.

*Charlie can be seen in the above photo leading an Armistice parade through Corsham High Street.*

Charlie Bethel born in 1881 was a young man who sought out opportunities when they arose and could turn his hand to just about anything. He loved to be in the limelight and is one of Corsham's most colourful characters. Below are some of his achievements and we are proud of him in Corsham.

OYEZ ! OYEZ ! OYEZ .....Charlie Bethel was a quarryman from Corsham and the official Corsham Town Crier for over twenty years. He had an irritating habit of jumping into peoples' conversations by verbally anticipating what they were going to say. This earned him the name of *'Finisher Bethel'*. He lived in a small cottage in Priory Street with his family and was a staunch member of the Priory Street Baptist Church. He was a regular patron of the Three Brewers pub in Priory Street.

Apart from his job as the Town Crier, Charlie once had a 'Fish and Fruit' round, accompanied by his horse which he kept in the back garden of his Priory Street cottage. Later, he became a Rag and Bone collector. He was obviously a man of many talents, mostly lucrative!

Charlie's 'claim to fame', was attempting to wheel a cubic foot of Bath stone (1 ¼ cwt) 45 miles on a wheelbarrow from Corsham (via Bath, Saltford and Keynsham) to Bristol and back in twelve hours as a result of a wager! The return journey was along the steep and long Box Hill road as it rises towards Corsham from the west - more of this story follows below.

## Chapter 24. Town Crier - Charlie Bethel.

**1902:** In the festivities held at Corsham Park in August, Charlie was the winner of the greasy pole competition which was a race to the top of a long upright slippery pole.

**1904:** Charlie, now 23 years of age and a betting man, could never resist a wager. A group of his friends offered him £5 [over £400 in today's money] if he could wheel a cubic foot of Freestone (i.e. Bath stone) from Corsham to Bristol and back within twelve hours.

Charlie took up the challenge immediately as £5 was a substantial amount of money to be won in those days. One report circulating at the time stated: *'For several succeeding evenings sounds of tapping could be heard from his (closed) garden shed, followed by the emergence of 'Finisher' carrying pieces of Freestone which he secretively dropped into a bed of nettles in his garden'.* To lighten the load, Charlie was believed to be hollowing out the block of Bath stone so as to make it much lighter than it looked! It was still a cubic foot though!

The first attempt was planned to take place on Saturday 1 October 1904. At eight o'clock the hour appointed for starting, rain fell heavily and continued in intervals till midday. One of the conditions of the task was that it should only be undertaken if the weather was permitting. As the conditions were anything but suitable, the journey had to be postponed owing to the inclemency of the weather. A date seven days hence (Saturday 8 October) was set for the second attempt - should the weather be favourable.

At the appointed hour on 8 October 1904 Charlie duly arrived at Corsham Town Hall with the stone block securely wired inside his homemade truck. The distance to be covered in twelve hours was 45 miles, and the route to Bristol was via Bath and Keynsham.

Charlie was a well-known local athlete, having taken part in several walking contests and felt confident of accomplishing the task. A cubic foot of the Bath stone weighs about 1¼ cwt., and the barrow on which it was wheeled was specially constructed by Charlie for the purpose. The wheels being similar to those on a perambulator, with long handles to keep the weight on top of the wheels and off his arms.

According to Charlie's time-table, after setting off at 8 a.m. he planned to reach Bath by 10.20 and Bristol at one o'clock. A stay of about an hour would be made at Bristol to recuperate and to take on refreshments. Charlie estimated that he could be back at Corsham Town Hall by 8 p.m. This was no mean feat, as on the return journey the long uphill stretch along Box Hill would have to be negotiated. One saving grace was that the *home stretch* from Rudloe to Corsham was all downhill. Charlie was accompanied by some local cyclists. To win the wager he was not allowed to go faster than walking pace.

Setting off from the Town Hall in his tennis shoes to the cheers of the spectators, a start was made from Corsham at five minutes past 8 a.m. accompanied by P. Holder and A. Hend; the latter being the representative of those who laid wagers as to Charlie accomplishing the journey. The outward journey went very well, with crowds of inquisitive people to witness the start and amassed at different points along the route, which was why Bath was chosen as a lucrative resting place. The roads were in fairly good condition into Bath, but after leaving the city, a hailstorm was encountered, and Charlie had to take shelter under a tree for about twenty minutes, and on restarting the going was rather slow, not only owing to the slippery state of the roads, but because, whilst waiting attired in his athletic costume, he got cold, and it took him some time to warm to his work again. Bristol was reached at 1.45. But his 'exhibitionist' streak got the better of him and he could not resist informing a curious crowd of his mission. A *'hat was passed round'* and finances were further augmented.

## Chapter 24. Town Crier - Charlie Bethel.

After half-an-hour's stay for refreshments, the return journey to Corsham was commenced. Bath was reached at 5.60 p.m. and a stay of twenty minutes was made - where further sympathetic contributions were gratefully received by Charlie. The going through Bath, however, was slow at some points owing to the crowd of people along the way.

After leaving Bath for the home stretch towards Corsham, Charlie stated that he felt in very fit condition till Shockerwick was reached. From that point to Rudloe the road is steep and all uphill, and he got somewhat fagged. But time was running short and Box Hill had to be tackled at great speed if he was to make it back in time. The Corsham High Street was lined with hundreds of cheering people as Charlie with his barrow pressed through for the finishing line alongside the Town Hall.

Charlie had made the journey in 12 hours **AND FIVE MINUTES**, i.e. five minutes *longer* than the stipulated time. He had therefore just failed to win the wager. He expressed his disappointment and told the crowd that it was his intention to try to do the journey again within the specified time. He believed that under more favourable conditions he would be able to accomplish it.

On the following Monday evening Charlie attended a smoking concert at the Free Trade Club, and was congratulated by Sir J.D. Poynder on his performance. Charlie's expenses in connection with the undertaking was £1 10s., and the amount of a collection made for him was £3 16s (£350 in today's money!) Charlie may have lost his wager, but due to the *additional* collection and the *sympathetic contributions* received on the way, he boasted a total profit of £15 (£1,300 in today's money)!!

[Ed - I could find no further records of a repeat performance by Charlie - methinks he quit whilst he was still ahead. Had Charlie spent less time gathering in monetary contributions from the crowds to line his pockets - he would easily have made it back in time - and he probably knew that!]

**1914-1918:** In WWI Charlie now 33 years of age was a member of the WWI Voluntary Aid Detachment (V.A.D.) WILTS 3 (AMBULANCE) unit with the Corsham Town Hall Hospital.

**1920s:** Joe James told a story about his father who ran the H.R. James & Son hardware store in the High Street. *"My father had a bright idea involving our famous Town Crier, Charlie Bethel. Usually, when Charlie rang one peal of his bell, silence immediately descended on any crowd watching."*
Listeners probably expected the habitual notice of water shortages. But no – this time the pronouncement from Charlie was:

*"Mr H.R. James wishes to thank all his customers for their patronage throughout the year"* .....etc, ending with a seasonal greeting to all. Later, when Charlie came into the shop, he said, *"I done the High Street and Pickwick Road Mr James, and thank 'ee for the ten shillings"*

## Chapter 24. Town Crier - Charlie Bethel.

This little Christmas innovation became an anticipated tradition for the James and Bethel families over the years. It may not have increased turnover in the hardware store, but it certainly added to the Christmas spirit of the 1920's.

---

Charlie held an appointment under the Court Leet, which was established under a charter granted to the ancient and Royal Borough of the then Corsham Regis in the early reign of King John. The office embraced the duties of a Warden of the Pound, Constable, and Ale Taster.

**1922:** During this year, Charlie was fined 5s for allowing his goat to stray along Priory Street! Charlie in his Town Crier role made regular appearances around Corsham, resplendent in his Crier's uniform of three cornered hat, be-medalled velvet coat, knee breeches, and yellow stockings. Few parades took place in Corsham without the 'Finisher' at the head. The origin of the uniform had been a mystery. In fact it had first appeared at a Fancy Dress Ball at Neston Park. One notes that Mr GP Fuller of Neston Park, once served on the Corsham Parish Council as Chairman between 1895-1907. Without doubt, the Town Crier's uniform was a gift to the Council - or Court Leet - from one of their long serving officers!

**1924:** Charlie took part in all of the Corsham Armistice processions as shown in the photograph at the start of this chapter, with Town Crier Charlie Bethel leading at the front in his full regalia and three-cornered hat along with the Corsham Town bandmaster Herbert Spackman.

A newspaper report of 15 November read: CORSHAM UNITED ARMISTICE SERVICE AT THE CENOTAPH AND PARISH CHURCH. All ranks of society gathered at the Cenotaph and the Parish Church on Sunday to do honour to the memory of the brave men who fell during WWI. Following the church service, the procession led by Charlie Bethel the Town Crier, marched through the High Street to the Cenotaph where the 'Last Post' was sounded by Messrs. Pickett and A.J. Rawlings. Field Marshal Lord Methuen inspected the ranks of ex-service men.

**1925:** It seems as if Charlie collected titles like stamps, for in 1925 he was self-proclaimed to also be the 'Haywarden of the Pound' as well as the 'Taster under the Court Leet'.

The photo shows Charlie at the Town Crier National Competition in September 1925 held in Pewsey. He certainly took his Corsham Town Crier role seriously.

**1926:** The competition was held once again in Pewsey. The Wiltshire Times and Trowbridge Advertiser of Saturday 25 September reported the following concerning Charlie:

Although Mr Bethel did not bring away a prize, a London paper gave him the following notice: *'The luckiest, by general consent, was Mr Chas. Bethel, who was the envy of his rivals, not on account of his uniform, his voice, or his bell, but because at Corsham, where he is sort of municipal Pooh Bah, one of his other official duties is to act as Ale Taster to the Court Leet.'*

## Chapter 24. Town Crier - Charlie Bethel.

Some of his competitors seemed to think this gave him an unfair advantage. *'If a man with a job like that hasn't a good voice, who has?'* was their envious remark.

Mr Bethel can claim a good wavelength for the sound of his voice, and when he has an announcement to make, given good atmospheric conditions, can make himself heard from High Street to the outskirts of the town.

W.B. Angliss of Marlborough (last year's champion) was deemed to be champion out of the 13 Town Criers at the Pewsey competition. Charlie Bethel didn't feature in the running, as second place went to W.Y. Barnes of Aldbourne, and third place belonged to W. Abbott of Lyme Regis.

**1927:** In August, Charlie's only son Mr Charles James Plum Bethel, married Miss Eva Bow, youngest daughter of Mr Edward Bow, of Box, Wiltshire, and of the late Mrs Bow. The marriage took place in the United Methodist Church, Redland Grove, Bristol, with the Rev. Mr Urwin officiating.

The bride, who was given away by her father, wore a dress of cream white Crêpe De Chine, with a wreath and veil, and carried a shower bouquet of deep red roses.

She was attended by two bridesmaids and two little page boys, the former being the Misses Peggy and Isabel Watts (nieces), who wore dresses of mauve tulle and mob caps to match, and carried baskets of flowers.

The pages were Masters Charlie Mervyn Robert Hudson Bethel and Artie Henry Charles Pinnell, nephews of the bridegroom, and they wore blue velvet suits with large white pearl buttons and Peter Pan collars and cuffs. They carried silver mounted walking sticks with bows of ribbon. Mr Eddie Bow (brother of the bride) was best man.

The bride's father is a respected signalman of Box. The best man was a guard at Yeovil, whilst the bridegroom was on the railway in South Wales. It was certainly a very colourful wedding!

In September at the Town Crier Championships in Marlborough, Charlie Bethel proudly pointed to his crown on the staff and boasted that he was the only Royal Town Crier in England by virtue of a charter granted by King John. He also reminded them that he held the important office of Corsham's ale-taster.

Twice a year Charlie would sample the ale at the public houses in Corsham. At one time it was quite a good thing he said laughingly.

*"I got quite a large quantity of beer free, but the landlords are getting to know me now; so when I call for a-glass beer they inquire.Be you here as Ale Taster- or a customer today Bethel?"*

When he was acting in the capacity of Ale-Taster the landlords only served him with about a thimbleful.

**1935:** Charlie Bethel now 54 years of age was a long standing member of the Corsham Fire Brigade and along with two other members of the brigade, Firemen J. Martin, and J. Say was awarded a long service medal.

Charlie was the final custodian of the ancient Corsham tradition of Town Crier. How appropriate that his nickname should be 'Finisher'.

## Chapter 24. Town Crier - Charlie Bethel.

**1945:** Charlie Bethel passed away at 64 years of age. The following obituary appeared in the Wiltshire Times on Saturday 17 November:

### DEATH OF MR C. BETHEL. Town Crier and Ale Tester.

The death occurred in Bristol Hospital on Tuesday evening of Mr Charles Bethel of Priory Street, aged 64 - Town Crier, Ale Taster and Special Constable to the Court Leet. Thus passes a figure of pageantry which was a part of old-time Corsham with the picturesque blue knee breeches, canary stockings, patent shoes and three-cornered hat. In his early days Mr Bethel worked in the quarries and in later years for the late Sir F. H. Goldney, Bart., and then Sir Harry Goldney, Bart. He had wide interests. He played football for Pickwick, and was a successful runner, and at many fetes won the leg of mutton offered as a prize for climbing the greasy pole. Some older people will remember that for a wager Mr Bethel once wheeled a barrow from Corsham Town Hall to Bristol Bridge and back between 8 a.m. and 8 p.m.

In the First World War Mr Bethel served in the Corsham Red Cross Hospital, and later at Netley Hospital, Southampton, as a Bed Cross orderly. He was also a keen member the Corsham Volunteer Fire Brigade, and held the National Fire Brigades Association's silver medal for over 20 years service. He leaves a widow with two daughters living quite near, and a son working on the railway In South Wales.

**1949:** The Corsham Parish Council Committee instructed the General Purposes Committee to consider the appointment of a Town Crier, an office which had been vacant for several years. The matter arose on a letter from Mr W. Baker, of 22 Pickwick Road, stating that for the past few years, since the death of Mr C. Bethel, the town had been without a Town Crier, official or otherwise. He felt it was a pity that old customs should be allowed to die out, as for hundreds of years Corsham had had a Town Crier. He suggested a Crier was equally effective, and much more appropriate than a loud-speaker van. Mr F. G. Dyke suggested that if the office of Ale Taster was incorporated, as required under the old Court Leet, there would be no lack of applicants. Remarking that Corsham was too ancient now, without bringing back any more old customs. Mr W. O. Freegard moved that no action be taken, and Mr N. G. Macmillan seconded. Only the proposer and seconder voted for the motion.

Thus ended any chance of a Corsham Town Crier ever appearing again on our streets again.

*Photo shows Charlie Bethel in his prime.*

[Ed: There is a Bethel Road in Corsham, but there is some uncertainty whether it was named after Charlie Bethel, or after Richard Bethel who boarded at the Hungerford Almshouse School; and later responsible whilst in Queens Council for the reform of education and later for the Divorce Act of 1857.

Richard Bethel was created Lord High Chancellor in 1861 with the title of Baron Westbury.]

*[Ed - we like to think that the road was named after Charlie!]*

# Chapter 25. Wine Lodge.

**WINE LODGE PREMISES HIGH STREET CORSHAM.**

*Two photos 'stitched' together of the 'Wine Lodge' and 'Thorne the Chemist' around the early 1960s.*

This large shop on Corsham High Street was often split in half to make two shops. Today, the building, 28 High Street is now occupied by Allen & Harris Estate Agents. The front facade still retains the original pillars. This chapter is about the occupants of this building since the mid-1700s.

**1617:** At a 'Court Baron' of the Lord of the Manor of Corsham, Patents were given out in order to regulate or restrict trades which involved a danger to public morality and order. One of these Patents was the Patent for Inns *[and shops]* that sold alcohol. Under it, one person named Mompesson, and two other persons were appointed Commissioners with authority to give or refuse the licenses. The main business of the 'Court Baron' was the resolution of disputes involving a Lord's tenants.

It appears that Christopher Nott was the first person in Corsham to obtain a licence for a premises called 'The Red Lion', once a separate building on the Methuen Arms site which has long since been demolished.

**1751:** It is possible that the premises on the High Street was surrendered into the hands of the Lord of the Manor on the 23rd October 1751 when Isaac Kingston, John Hancock, Anthony Guy and Samuel Edwards were admitted as tenants.

**1775: SPECIAL LICENCE GRANTED TO THE WINE LODGE.**

The first reference to the premises now known as 'The Wine Lodge' (now Allen & Harris Estate Agents) being licensed that appears in the Court Rolls, is at a Court Leet and View of Frank Pledge with the Court Baron of Paul Methuen, held on the 25th day of October in the Sixteenth year of the reign of our Sovereign Lord George the third by the Grace of God of Great Britain France and Ireland King Defender of the Faith and so forth, and in the year of our Lord 1775, before Henry Merewether Gent, Steward of the Manor.

Chapter 25. Wine Lodge.

On this date, Edward Lee, John Heath and Martha Anne Mary Edwards surrendered into the hands of the Lord of the Manor, all that messuage or tenement brewhouse and garden with the pump and use of the well thereto adjoining and belonging then in the occupation and possession of Walter Kington Taylor, together with a way or road leading from the Street of Corsham over the passage leading from the Street into the said garden and also the north wall of the said garden with the necessary house at the corner thereof and also such part of the west wall of the said garden from the said north wall as far as the same runs to the Aishler part of the said wall being in length thirty one feet.   *[Ed: Well said!]*

The new tenants were Sarah Hulbert Elizabeth Hulbert and Anne Hulbert.

**SCOTTS BOOKSELLER AND DRUGGIST ON CORSHAM HIGH STREET - ROBERT SCOTT:**

**1823:** Robert Scott, was born in Farlam, a civil parish in the City of Carlisle District, Cumbria.

**1830:** Susanna (Susan) Vincent (born in 1821 and baptised on 22nd July in Melksham) widow of the late Mr Morris Vincent of Melksham, moved to Corsham High Street as a bookseller (*J. Pigot. Commercial Directory*).

**1838:** Susan Vincent died, leaving her daughters Susannah Dyer and Sarah to run the bookselling business.

**1841:** Sarah Vincent's older sister, Susannah Dyer Vincent (b. 3rd June 1819) was running a stationers shop next door to Christopher Stantial's tailor shop in Corsham High Street.

**1845:** Susannah Dyer Vincent married Josiah Ranger at Temple church, Bristol, on 4th March.

**1850:** Sarah Vincent married Robert Scott (from London) at Corsham on 27th April (officiated by the Rev. W. C. Bennett).

Robert soon established himself in the Corsham High Street business as a Bookseller *and* Druggist in the premises now named *Scotts*.

**1858:** Robert Scott's wife Sarah (nee Vincent) died at Easton Road, Bristol, on the 19th October.

**1860:** Robert marries his second wife Anna Priscilla Porter at St. John's, Bedminster on 12th July. He was now living at Hanover Villa, Coronation Road, Bedminster and was a Hop Merchant and Maltster.

**1881:** Robert is now a Maltster and Hop Dealer at the Grove, Station Road, Freshford near Bradford-on-Avon.

**1883:** Robert died aged 60 on 21st June 1883 at Winyatt Lodge, in Limpley Stoke.

**CHRISTOPHER and JOHN STANTIAL:**

**1815:** Christopher Stantial married Catharine Long of Chippenham on 4 September. Their son John Stantial was born in Melksham c1816.

**1817:** John Stantial was baptised at the Melksham Independent Chapel on 30 March.

## Chapter 25. Wine Lodge.

**1821:** John's father Christopher Stantial a tailor, originating from Lacock moved his family into Corsham where he took up a shop in the High Street next door to what would become Susan Vincent's, Booksellers and later Scott's Book & Chemist shop.

**1841:** John Stantial married Sarah Taylor at Corsham Independent Chapel on Tuesday 21st December and was trading in Corsham from at least that date as a Chemist and Wine and Spirit Merchants in a shop a little farther along northwards, beyond Henry Spackman's shop (i.e. beyond where Ultra Warm is today).

*Scott's of Corsham (image courtesy of Stephen Flavin).*

**1847:** John's first wife Sarah died leaving one son, Edward Stephen Taylor Stantial born 30 Oct. 1842. One of John's stocked products on sale at the time was *'Perry's Purifying Specific Pills'*, purported to cure gonorrhoea, gleet [a watery discharge from the urethra], stricture and diseases of the urinary organs - yikes!

**1850:** The Rev. W. Jackson married John Stantial to his second wife, Mary Vincent (1816-1893), eldest daughter of the late Samuel Vincent of Melksham, on 23 May at the Independent Chapel in Melksham.

**1851:** In the 1851 census Christopher Stantial still lived next door to Scott's Book and Chemist shop in the High Street.

**1853:** John Stantial had a sideline as an Agent for the West of England Life and Fire Insurance Company.

**1857:** John Stantial and his second wife, Mary Vincent acquired the Scott's Corsham High Street shop from Robert Scott and moved his business there to begin trading (nearly 30 years) as *Stantial* late *Scott*.

**1885:** John Stantial died in Corsham on 16 April.

**1889:** On 10 August, Edward Stephen Taylor Stantial, son of the late John Stantial, Corsham, was elected as Mayor of Pietermaritzburg, Port Natal, South Africa. He had been a chemist at Pietermaritzburg for some twenty-five years.

### BAINES THE CHEMIST - JOHN and FRANCIS BAINES:

**1857:** Francis Baines, son of John Baines the Gloucester Chemist was born in South Hamlet *[now a parish in Gloucestershire, partly within Gloucester city]*, Gloucester and baptised 2nd August 1857. His father John Baines was born in Bradford-on-Avon and became a Chemist and Bookseller in Gloucester.

**1863:** John Baines sells his Dispensing Chemist business at 93, Southgate Street, Gloucester to James Franklin in 1863 and sets up a Chemist shop with his family in Bank Street, Melksham. This sale notice appeared on the back page of the Gloucester Journal - Saturday 25 July 1863.

JOHN BAINES, 93, SOUTHGATE STREET,

IN Retiring from Business, returns his sincere thanks to his Friends and the Public generally for the distinguished patronage he has been favoured with during his residence in this city, as a DISPENSING CHEMIST, and to the Medical Gentlemen in particular, for the courteous and liberal countenance they have afforded him. J. B. respectfully solicits a continuance of those favours for his successor, MR. JAMES FRANKLIN, whom he confidently hopes will prove worthy of their support.

## Chapter 25. Wine Lodge.

**1871:** John Baines leaves Melksham to set up shop in the Corsham High Street and calls it *Baines the Chemist*. He trades there for 10 years when the business is taken over by his son Francis.

**1881:** On 23 May, 23 year old Francis, son of John Baines Esq. of Corsham and Maria George, married Martha Dare Holmes, daughter of [father] Charles Earl Holmes Esq., a Butcher, of 80 Bridge Road, Battersea and [mother] Mary Ann, at St. Mary's, Battersea.

The 1881 census shows that Francis followed in his father's footsteps. He took over the running of his father's Chemist shop in Corsham High Street and traded there for nearly 40 years as, Baines, the *Chemists, Stationers, Booksellers and Wine Merchants* until 1920 when the Baines Pharmacy was purchased by Thomas Rees. The High Street shop was divided in two. One half sold pharmaceutical products and the other half sold wines and spirits which Francis *bottled up* himself.

Francis became a well-respected member of Corsham society and as the only chemist in Corsham at that time, his advice on ailments was often sought. He was secretary of both the Corsham Gas Works and the Water Company. His office was in the small premises next to the High Street shop.

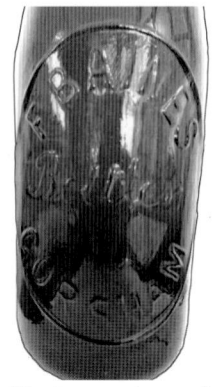

*Photo courtesy of Stephen Flavin, shows original 'F. Baines' Corsham bottle found in a garden.*

**1882:** Francis subscribed to the fund to convert the Corsham Market Hall into the Town Hall in 1882. He became well known as a poultry expert in Corsham and kept white Wyandotte hens; one which laid 588 eggs in three years!

**1883:** Francis and Maria Baines' son Herbert John Baines is born in Chippenham.

**1887:** Francis and Maria Baines' son Frederick George is born in Chippenham.

*Photos (courtesy of Stephen Flavin) shows Francis Baines, Stationer and Druggist. Francis Baines also produced and sold his own photographic postcards of Corsham - including this one of him standing outside his shop.*

**1893:** On page 269 of 'The Ports of the Bristol Channel' book dated 1893, Francis Baines' establishment is described as………………….*Francis Baines, Family and Dispensing Chemist, Wine and Spirit Merchant, - Corsham Stationery Warehouse, High Street, Corsham - Practical pharmacy in the highest phases of its modern development finds an able representative and exponent at Corsham in the person of Mr Francis Baines, who about twelve years ago, in his capacity as a fully-qualified chemist by examination, acquired the business over which he now presides with such vigour and success, and which had been organised between thirty and forty years ago.*

## Chapter 25. Wine Lodge.

*The business is now of a triple character, as indicated by the style and title designated above. The spacious double-fronted shop is appropriately divided into a pharmacy on the one side and into a first-class stationery depot on the other, where in addition to all manner of stationery and fancy articles up to date, Mr Baines does a very substantial bookselling business, including the regular distribution of newspapers and periodical publications.*

*In his pharmacy Mr Baines, who is the only fully-qualified chemist in Corsham, operates in every branch of his profession, devoting the most careful and competent attention to the dispensing of physicians' prescriptions and the compounding of family recipes, and by the use of drugs and chemicals of ascertained purity and standard strength has won the full confidence and esteem of the leading local practitioners and the liberal support of a large and influential family connection. In his third department Mr Baines does a sound and substantial trade as a general wine and spirit merchant, and dealer in all manner of popular mineral waters and aerated drinks, and his house stands high in the estimation of a very large and widespread connection, by reason of the sound methods and honourable principles which have always characterised its business transactions.*

Francis Baines' son Herbert J Baines (b1883), carried on the retailing tradition with two shops next to each other in Pickwick Road, selling grocery and confectionery (*see photo courtesy of Stephen Flavin).* Herbert was also instrumental in starting up the Glove Factory at the corner of Paul Street. Herbert's youngest sister, Winifred, May Baines (b1896) married Richard Knapp in 1928, who farmed at Great Lypiatt Farm, in Neston. Miss Phyllis Dare Baines was the elder sister.

This brings us to Geoff Knapp, son of Richard, who also farmed at Great Lypiatt, and their work has also done much for the town. Geoff has served the Corsham Civic Society for many years and is now retired and living in South Street.

**1895-1897**: John Baines was a member of the Corsham Parish Council a post also held by his son Francis (from 1922-1925) and his grandson Herbert (from 1911-1918) *Ref: 100 Years in Corsham Parish pg. 141.*

**1920:** Thomas Rees *(1885-1932)* purchased the Baines Pharmacy.

**1931:** Martha Dare Baines died aged 72 on 11 July. The mourners included Mr Francis Baines (husband), Mr Charles Baines (son b1881), Mr and Mrs. Herbert J. Baines (son b1883 and daughter-in-law), Mr and Mrs Wilfred Baines (son and daughter-in-law), Mr and Mrs Douglas Aust (son-in-law and daughter), Mr and Mrs R. Knapp (son-in-law and daughter), Miss Phyllis Baines (daughter).

**1932:** Francis Baines died aged 75 on 31 December 1932. He was buried in St. Bartholomew's Corsham churchyard in the same plot No. 2045 is his wife Martha Dare, and their son Frederick George who died on 19 February 1903 aged 16.

Chapter 25. Wine Lodge.

**T. REES' PHARMACY - THOMAS REES:**

**1920:** Thomas Rees *(1885-1932)* purchased the Baines Pharmacy. Whilst he was there, he earned the respect of all who knew him.

Thomas was born at Newcastle Emlyn, Carmarthen, and trained at Edinburgh as a Chemist, qualifying in 1904. For a while he worked at Tiverton, Devon, and during WWI he was a Dispenser at the Bristol Royal Infirmary. He was an active member of the committee in the Bath and District Branch of the Pharmaceutical Society and in his second year presided as its President. He was also a member of the Wilts Pharmaceutical Insurance Committee. As a prominent Freemason, he was a member of the Friendship Unity, Bradford-on-Avon, and the Cumberland Arch Chapter, Bath.

Thomas' grandson John Yapp takes up the story………………….

*'My grandfather Thomas and grandmother Jeanie Briton Rees were the owners of The Wine Lodge in Corsham High Street from 1920 and served the Corsham community as a Chemist for many years. The Chemist Shop was known as* **T. Rees' Pharmacy** *(see photo at the bottom of this page).*

*My Mum [Megan Mary Briton Yapp nee Rees] told me that the Methuen's of Corsham Court would ask for aspirin to be delivered but refused to buy a whole bottle.*

*Thomas ran the Chemist side of the shop and his wife Jeanie Briton and daughter Megan (my mum) ran the Wine Lodge side.*

*Thomas and Jeanie had two children, daughter Megan Mary Briton (my mum) and a son Glyn Davidson Rees (my uncle) who also studied to be a Chemist.*

*Glyn, who had married Doris Leah Wilhelmina Hayman a model from Sidmouth, had his own Chemist shop in Leatherhead but was sadly killed in 1944 during active service with the WWII Pathfinders.'* **R.I.P Glyn.**

[**Note:** The Pathfinders were target-marking Squadrons in RAF Bomber Command during World War II.

The Pathfinders located and marked targets with flares, which a main bomber force could aim at, increasing the accuracy of their bombing.]

## Chapter 25. Wine Lodge.

The photo above *courtesy of John Yapp* was taken behind the Rees Pharmacy in Corsham High Street, and shows: *Thomas Rees 1885-1932, son Glyn Rees (1913-1944), daughter Megan Rees (1913-2005) and wife Jeanie Briton Rees (1889-1984)*.

**1946:** *Photo above courtesy of John Yapp, shows the wedding at St Bartholomew's Church in Corsham, of Horace William Yapp to Thomas' daughter Megan Mary Briton Rees on 23 March 1946.*
**Left to right are:** Vicar François de Chaumont. Woman unknown. Walter Yapp (John Yapp's grandfather). Best man unknown. **Horace William Yapp (John Yapp's father), Megan Mary Briton Rees (John Yapp's mother).** Mr Besley? Bank manager. Bridesmaid unknown. Alice C Yapp (John Yapp's grandmother). And lastly Jeanie Briton, (Butt at that time), John Yapp's grandmother).

## Chapter 25. Wine Lodge.

*Megan Mary Briton Rees can be seen below working in her father's shop in Corsham High Street. Photo below courtesy of John Yapp.*

**John Yapp continues his story...........................................**

*'My grandfather Thomas Rees taught Chemistry at Bristol Royal Infirmary and he never had a student fail an exam. He later ran the Cleveland Bridge Dispensary in Bath before coming to Corsham.*
*When my grandfather died, the business was sold to the FARLEIGH family.*

*After my grandfather had died, my grandmother [Jeanie Briton Rees] married again to Mr Alfred Butt a tailor from Chippenham. They then lived in Box at Redmarley which is opposite the Northey Arms.*

*Alf Butt was tailor to the Methuen Family of Corsham Court. I live in Bristol at Redland and only found out from my mother before she died in 2005, that this is the same area where she was born in 1913 at Redland Grove!'*

*'My mum Megan (called Peggy) Rees can be seen smiling top left in the photo below, attending Mrs Spackman's School in Priory Street at Rose Cottage [now called Dill House] 1923/1924.'*

Teacher Mrs Daisy Spackman:

**Top Row:** Megan (Peggy) Rees, Helen de ? Betty Crouch, Dorothy Bowerbank, Muriel Osborne, Queenie Coates:
**Middle Row:** Marjorie Ody, Peggy Taylor, Sheila Newell, Lilian Fricker, Vera Taylor, ????, Willie Angel?: **Front Row:** Jim Coates, Ron Bidmead, ????, Jack Taylor, Leslie Vowles.

**1932:** Thomas Rees was only 47 when he passed away on Monday 19 September. Thomas had collapsed on Sunday evening, following a walk around Corsham and died at 4 a.m. the next day. He had not been in very good health of late, but on Sunday evening went out as usual to post his letters, and to have a walk around town before returning home just before 8 o'clock.

The help of the Automobile Association (AA) was sought out on Monday to trace and find his son Glyn (now a Chemist at Leatherhead) who was on a motor tour in the Lake District, to inform him of the sudden death of his father. Glyn was found by the AA on Tuesday in Northumberland and left at once. He drove without a break and reached Corsham in the early hours of Wednesday morning.

## Chapter 25. Wine Lodge.

*[Ed. Photo below shows Thomas Rees' grave tidied up 2019 in Ladbrook Cemetery.]* **R.I.P Thomas.**

Thomas Rees' funeral took place on Thursday 22 September at Corsham's Ladbrook Cemetery in 1932.

The interment was preceded by a service at St Bartholomew's the Corsham Parish Church, with the Rev. R. C. Hunt officiating.

The Rev. A. E. Isherwood (Vicar of Staverton), who conducted the Masonic Rites at the graveside, was Chaplain to the Bradford *[on-Avon]* Lodge.

A large number of Freemasons and other friends attended. Mr Lewin Spackman played on the organ, *'I know that my Redeemer liveth'* and *'O Rest the Lord.'* Thomas left behind his wife Jeanie Briton Rees and daughter Megan Mary Briton Rees.

### ROBERT NEWTON GORDON-FARLEIGH:
**1935:** Robert Newton Gordon-Farleigh worked for Eldridge Pope, first in Bournemouth, then in Bath, before moving to Corsham in 1935 and took over the premises from the Rees family on 2 December. It had both an Off and On Licence which meant drink could also be consumed on site. Customers were often seen sitting around in what was called the 'Office', drinking until 10 o'clock and sometimes later at night. Outside the shop was a large clock, with two faces and window boxes on the outer sills which were filled every year with colourful flowers.

The Wine Lodge has an irrevocable licence, dated 1710, which goes with the premises. It cannot be transferred or extinguished and was once regarded as being one of only two in existence.

### CLEVERLEY and THORNE's CHEMIST SHOP:
Later, part of the property was divided into two and let out as a Chemist. Mr Cleverley was the first Manager followed by Mr Cyril Thorne. Housed in an opening between the back section of the Chemists Shop and the hall was a sliding panel that allowed the Wine Lodge and the Chemist Shop to share an old-fashioned 'candlestick' telephone which was passed through a hatch to the person the caller wanted. The number was the same for both establishments - Corsham 2277.

**THE WINE LODGE:** When Robert, Newton, Gordon-Farleigh was called up for WWII duty, Mr Sidnell managed the Wine Lodge. When Robert later returned home injured, Mr Sidnell stayed on for a while to help Mrs Elsie Gordon-Farleigh run the shop.

## Chapter 25. Wine Lodge.

**Daughter Nora Smith (nee Gordon-Farleigh) recalls happy times in Corsham:** *'I was in the middle of a family of seven children, five of whom were born in the Corsham Nursing Home* [across the High Street in Alexander House]. *Mrs Hurst was the midwife there at that time. I can remember being allowed to see the new baby in 1946 on my way to school in the morning. We also used to go up the road to collect our National Health orange juice in the shop near to the park entrance. Mum purchased sweets with the coupons and we were all given three a day. We were not often allowed out on our own, usually going out with my brothers and sister, most often across Corsham Park where we spent many happy hours. When I was older I played hockey, tennis and cricket for Corsham Clubs and my working life was just across the road from home, as my first job was at Lloyds Bank.'*

*Left:*

Robert and Elsie Gordon-Farleigh in their garden behind the Wine Lodge in the High Street Corsham c1940.

*Right:*

Thomas and Jeanie Rees in same garden c1930.

**Nora Smith (nee Gordon-Farleigh) continues her story**.........*'Our house had seven bedrooms: a Lounge, Drawing Room, Bathroom and Kitchen spread over three floors with a nice sized garden behind. Dad grew vegetables and flowers.*

*We also had a large store at the rear and cellars running under the shop and stairs. After we had expanded our cellar (by incorporating the cellar of the Barnett Bros. newsagents shop next-door), in extreme weather the cellars flooded and we used to all head down there to make sure the bottles were stored high enough in the racks to be safe.'*

*'In the early years an errand boy and my elder brothers delivered orders to customers using sack trucks. Then we had two errand boys who did deliveries on a bike with a carrier in the front which could hold a box. Later Dad employed three men to work for us, Harry Brennan, Reg. Gardiner and Douglas Fenney.*

*When Douglas left, Victor Partner replaced him. Then in 1950 he bought a Robin Reliant three-wheeled Van which meant he could deliver to a much wider area. I can remember trips to Aylesbury, Ross on Wye and Cirencester.'*

## Chapter 25. Wine Lodge.

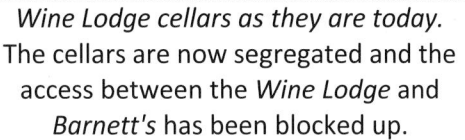

*Wine Lodge cellars as they are today. The cellars are now segregated and the access between the Wine Lodge and Barnett's has been blocked up.*

**1965:** *'Cyril Thorne who rented part of the Wine Lodge premises for his business, moved out and opened a new shop further down the street near the entrance to Michael Tippet's house [Parkside]. Next door to the Wine Lodge, was The Candy Shop run by Wilfie and Addie Shergold. Wilfie was a watchmaker but, sadly, went blind. When he died, his wife Addie sold the business to Ron and Betty from Birmingham. They had a dear little boy Edward who had severe Hydrocephalis [excess cerebrospinal fluid of the brain].*

*They changed the shop to 'Bettinas' cafe. Further along was a bacon butcher run by Mr Lockyer, who had a wife and two daughters - one of which was Marilyn. On the other side of our shop was Barnett bros, they were Newsagents and Bakers. Next was 'Lords' which was run by Stanley Hetherington. They sold toys and tobacco and sweets. Past their shop was Smiths the drapers. This was owned by Ray Smith who was very involved with the Freemasons.'*

**c1966:** After 30 years running the Wine Lodge, Robert Gordon-Farleigh retired and sold the premises to a Devizes company who eventually went bust.

**Robert's son,** Alastair Gordon-Farleigh **recalls his happy times:**
*'When I was very young, we used to get our milk delivered by Mr Dew with his horse and cart. In those days, the high street was a proper metalled road and was the main, very busy thoroughfare through the town. There were frequent traffic jams when Beer Lorries unloaded!*

*The local vicar at that time was Edward M. Hall and several other curates served in my childhood memory. Mr Keith Dimoline, Alan Bevan (who was young and quite good fun for us youngsters and, very memorably, George Scott-Joint who had the most incredible deep singing voice - he sounded like ten Paul Robesons [an American bass baritone concert artist and stage and film actor] singing all at once.'*                                    Photo shows Alastair.

**Robert's son,** Colin Gordon-Farleigh **recalls his happy times in Corsham........**'*As a boy, I knew the lie of the land that made up Park Farm in Corsham, for I spent so much of my childhood playing there. I well remember going home, weary but contented, from helping out at Park Farm during the haymaking season. As dusk gathered after a day spent haymaking, I recall passing by the trees and bidding them a friendly 'Good-night' as if they could understand me.*

## Chapter 25. Wine Lodge.

*After all, I was a son of the soil in many ways and those trees had been with me all of my life, short though it was back then. Whilst walking back from the farm as the sun was setting on another day, I had the woods that bounded Lacock Road on my left, whilst across to my right I could see the lake settling down for another night, the setting sunlight reflecting on the water, turning it into a cauldron of molten gold for a brief scantling of time. Moments like these were magic to a child.*

*Years later, when I lived in Africa, I would remember the sun setting on Corsham Lake as I watched the glorious sunsets that bewitched the African skyline.*

*Several times of late, thinking about the park and the lake, I have recalled Bill Holland who was the game-keeper on the Estate when I was a boy. I don't recall meeting him so much as avoiding him, for his reputation was that if he caught you trespassing where you shouldn't be, then not only would your father get to know about it, and that could have dire consequences, but he would give you a clipped ear as well.*

*That threat did not entirely deter small boys of course, and I often would wander into the woods around the lake and go down by the boathouse to look for fish in the surrounding water.*

*The lake would often freeze right over in the winter in those days. Snow and ice seemed to be with us for week after week back then, unlike the mild winters of today. We were hardier creatures as well, not only because we were younger, but because we grew up to expect it and dressed accordingly. Also, as children, we did not sit glued to a screen, either TV or computer, for hours on end in centrally-heated luxury, but went out to play in the great outdoors as often as we could.*

*Winter, to us, meant opportunities for FUN! I remember some winters when there would be skaters on the ice of the lake. I think that the thing about the lake that I most recall is the dire warnings of my parents not to go near the water for fear of falling in and getting pulled under and trapped by the weeds that reached upward and lay just below the surface.*

*An exciting place to play as a child was in the Dry Arch woods which lay at the farthest extreme of the park with only a field between them and the Corsham to Chippenham road. The woods were so-named because there was a slight bridged area which spanned the Corsham Court's North walk path. As children, the underside of the arch became a great place to play, forming as it did the necessary backdrop to suit the occasion.*

*It could be a fort, a jail-cell, a palace, or whatever our childhood imaginations wanted it to be, and just like so much else in our childhoods it had a touch of magic about it. Not so another place in the park that I recall.*

*Almost hidden in the hedge of one field was an entrance to an underground passage. You went down about eight or nine steps and you were in what appeared to be a bit of a tunnel, although it only stretched for about eight or ten feet at most before it became a drop into some sort of pit or possibly well shaft.*

*I never found out what it was for [Ed. It is an Ice House], but the tales that we made up about it being some sort of secret passage that led either to the vaults of the church or to the cellars of Corsham Court, both relatively close by, were tales that usually managed to scare us witless and thereby ensure that we stayed away from the place for a few weeks until curiosity once more took a hold of us.'*

## Chapter 25. Wine Lodge.

*Colin Gordon-Farleigh at 'The Curiosity Bookshop' in Runcorn - book signing his poetry collections.*

An Evangelist, Hymn-writer, Poet, Singer & Songwriter, Colin Gordon-Farleigh recently retired as a Minister in the Presbyterian Church of Wales, and is now working full-time in a Bereavement Ministry.

His aim in life is to serve the Lord Jesus in any and every way that he can as long as he has the breath.

His media Ministry published a Christian News & Views magazine called 'The Voice', for ten years in addition to his books of Christian verse, all of which came under the publishing division, Voice Publications.

Voice Ministries also had a music division called Sheer Joy Music, now a separate business.

This year [2019] will find him back in Nashville, Tennessee, recording another new Country album.

Colin has written a large number of Hymns and Worship Songs and also a lot of easy-listening, popular songs. He has won many awards for his Country, Jazz and Classical Crossover songs, many of which are available on CD and which can be found in the on-line shop at www.sheerjoymusic.com

*What the old Wine Lodge building in the Corsham High Street looks like today. Exactly the same!*

## Chapter 26. World's Toughest Job - the Corsham Quarryman.

Ed: In my two books *Corsham Revealed* and *Corsham Revealed More*, I have tried my very best to steer clear of providing too much detail on stories about the Bath stone quarries that lie 100 feet beneath Corsham. Such stories are more than adequately covered in fabulously illustrated books such as, 'Bath Stone Quarries' by Derek Hawkins, 'Secret Underground Cities' and 'Second World War Secret Bunkers' by Nick McCamley, and 'Burlington' by Nick Catford.

Having spent what seems like half my free-time in my late childhood, exploring these underground workings, I have a huge admiration for those who manually dug out (by hand) those miles and miles and miles of hard stone tunnels. Nevertheless, occasionally others of my thinking manage to express what is difficult to put into words. The 1934 *Special Correspondent* below, sums up perfectly my admiration for those tough old men of Corsham.

**Quarrymen on the surface displaying their saws c1900**

---

**Daily Sketch 7 May 1934. IS THIS THE WORLD'S TOUGHEST JOB?**

**HOW BATH STONE IS MINED - Working the Bowels of the Earth: Tunnel Three Miles Long.**

**By a Special Correspondent.**

I always thought that coal-mining was man's toughest job. Now I know differently. I spent all day with supermen in the mines of Box which provide Bath with its famous stone. Covering about five miles underground, walking, splashing and skidding my way from 'face to face,' I watched men sawing out huge blocks of stone from down at the roots of the hills.

## Chapter 26. World's Toughest Job - the Corsham Quarryman.

My guide was the foreman. He furnished me with a lamp and told me to follow him into a black tunnel. I expected a lift. Instead I found a gentle incline straight into the heart of the hills. As I floundered along I tried to catch his words, and learnt many things on the way round. The Romans were not the first here, for they found the mines already open and an ideal stone in grain and texture ready at hand to build their beautiful cities.

Our lamps flickered up and down into deep gashes in the rocks. Even while we watched *tremendous pressures were pushing up new mountains*, he said. Sometimes water dripped on to us from seeping rocks. We peered into a well which had its shaft finishing in the backyard of a resident. To get water and air the miners had tapped this well, chancing the possibility of its water level being above them.

### SAFEGUARD AGAINST FALLS

To prevent falls of rock, huge oak wedges were driven into openings in the rocks, for there is no warning when a ceiling falls. The seeping water swells the wedges and takes up the slackness.

One tunnel is three miles long and reaches from one side of Box Hill to the other. Then suddenly round a corner we came down into a working 'face'. An old man was driving a handsaw, a tremendous blade ten feet long. As I listened to the rhythmic rasp of sawing, the labour seemed the toughest and most monotonous I had ever seen. In fact, in the darkness, with occasional streaks of lights shooting across them, the men looked like galley slaves.

Bath stone miners are a special breed in a very difficult job. During one boom period, parties of Welsh miners were brought over to saw out the stone. But they returned very quickly to their soft coal and earth, beaten by the hardness of the rock and stone. There is no machinery used here. Even the raising of a ten-ton block is done by hand on an old wooden, low-geared crane which the Romans might have left behind them. The stone is manoeuvred on to low trams, and heavy horses, with lamps on their heads, haul it to the surface. My guide told me I was walking on an old sea bed, and to illustrate it, showed me the millions of tiny shells, of which the stone is composed.

I mentioned the term Bath brick. How he turned on me! Why *"that stuff"* was neither brick nor stone, but a common composition for cleaning purposes and had no connection whatever with the classic city.

### NO SHORTAGE LIKELY

It was good news to learn that although from the dawn of time man has hacked out his building materials from the hills, there is no likelihood of there being a shortage of stone. The stock of stone at the surface must never be below a million cubic feet or the foreman grumbles that he will not have a stone to sell! At one time when bricks had soared to high prices, stone competed with these and was used even for humble cottages. In Bath itself the local stone must be used for all building purposes so that the old city will for ever retain its classic character.

Hidden away behind the modern buildings one can see architectural gems in small houses. So that Bath stone shall be without flaw or blemish, no explosives was used in mining operations.

*End of the Daily Sketch article.*

# Chapter 26. World's Toughest Job - the Corsham Quarryman.

**17 April 1941- a German bomb falls on St Paul's Cathedral.**

The present cathedral was designed in the English Baroque style by Sir Christopher Wren and finished in 1710, thirty-five years after its commencement.

On 17 April 1941, the first German air strike destroyed the high altar, while the second strike on the north transept *(an area set crosswise to the nave in a cruciform cross-shape)* left a huge hole in the floor above the crypt. Broken debris and masonry was piled high in the Transept. It was repaired using the stone from the same quarry in Corsham that Christopher Wren used over 250 years ago.

*Photos courtesy of The Sphere 17 November 1945.*

The stone was specially selected by the Bath and Portland Stone Firms in Corsham. Nearly 1,000,000 cubic feet of stone was originally used to build St. Paul's so it was important to match the old stone with the new, and to use a stone that would withstand the erosive atmosphere of London.

In the photo, can be seen Mr Bert J. Coles working on the intricate design. Bert had been a mason in Corsham for forty years. Alongside Bert on the right is Mr T. Sheppard a mason of fifty-four years. Both are seen here working in the stonemason's yard at Corsham.

*A specialist task to manually cut the stone.*

*Mr H. Head draughtsman in his Corsham office.*

## Chapter 27. Acknowledgements.

I wrote this second book *Corsham Revealed More*, so that I could share again with you, my love of how Corsham became what it is today. The detail has been gathered together from many sources.

Firstly, I'd like to say a very big thank you to my two proof readers, my partner **Susan Duparcq**, and to **Christine Coutts** who *dotted all the i's and crossed all the t's* for me; without them, the book could never have been finished!

Thank you to all those at the **Wiltshire and Swindon History Centre** at Chippenham for their advice and for helping me delve deep into their comprehensive book, record and newspaper archives. And to **Chris Perry** and his staff at Corsham Print Creative Solutions for a great job in printing this book.

Thank you also to my local fellow Corsham Historian **Stephen Flavin** for some nice old postcard photos from his huge collection and to **James Rowe** a fellow *Corsham* collector. And lastly, but not least, to the **British Newspaper Archive** where I trawled through over 15,000 articles!

Below is a list of the many sources for which I am truly grateful. I have strived to be meticulous in my recording of source detail - and can only apologise if anyone has been missed out.

**Note:** This is a self-publishing and self financed book and not a profitable commercial enterprise.

The acknowledgment listing below is *roughly* in alphabetical order!

**Thank you very much…………to all of you [Ed].**

7bwb-36assn.org : **alchetron**.com : **Archiviostorico**.unita.it : **Around** Corsham' by Corsham Civic Society : Annette Wilson and Mike Wilson from their book' 'Around Corsham and Box' : The **Atlas** : **Aviation**-safety.net/wikibase : **bathstone**.org : **Bath Chronicle** and Weekly Gazette : **BBC**.co.uk : **BBC** News Magazine's Mario Cacciottolo 11 Nov 2010 : This is Wiltshire Paul **Beard** : **Bell's Life** in London and Sporting Chronicle : Wiltshire Airfields in the Second World War by David **Berryman** : **Berkshire** Chronicle : The **Berwick** Advertiser : **Birmingham Daily** Gazette : **blockstone**.com : **Box People** and Places boxpeopleandplaces.co.uk : **Bradford** Observer : Harold **Brakspear** : Corsham Church by Harold **Brakspear** 1924 : A Chronological History of Bath Stone Quarrying, Compiled by Mike **Breakspear** : **Bristol** Mercury : Jane **Browning** : **Bristol** Mercury : **Bristol** Mirror : **Bristol** Times and Mirror : **British** Newspaper Archive : **BroughtToLife**.sciencemuseum.org.uk : Jukie **Bryan** : Dominic **Campbell** : Donald **Carpenter** : **Casardi**, A. (17 April 1957) Report on Hungarian Refugees. *NATO* : Burlington by Nick **Catford** : **cerberusspeleo**.org.uk : **Cheltenham** Chronicle : www.**choghole**.co.uk : **Civil Defence** Gallantry Awards Case No. 1865 : Dennis **Cole** : History of Royal Naval Store Depot **Copenacre** by Pat Whalley : 'Corsham Area Heritage Archive' : **Corsham & Box** Matters Feb-Mar 2014 : **Corsham Civic** Society : **Corsham-court**.co.uk : **Corsham** Facts & Folklore by Pat Whalley : **Corsham Tunnels** - A Brief History by DCSA Corporate Communications : The Women's Suffrage Movement in Britain and Ireland, A Regional Survey By Elizabeth **Crawford** : www.**citypopulation** : en.wikipedia.org : **Corsham Born** and Bred 1 and 2 by Stephen Flavin : **Corsham Facts** and Folklore by Patricia Whalley : **Corsham Memories** From 1910 - Compiled by Corsham Civic Society : **cowtown**.net:80/ : **Derbyshire** Courier : **DE&S Rudloe** Phase 1 Explosive Ordinance Risk Assessment ESG19/026 March 2010 : **Devizes** and Wiltshire Gazette : Dickie **Dunmore** : **discovery**.nationalarchives.gov.uk : Duncan **Curtis** : **Dorothy** Treasurer of the Wiltshire Buildings Record : **Exeter** Flying Post : www.**fire**protect.me.uk : Stephen **Flavin** : Warwick **Franklin** : Kevin

## Chapter 27. Acknowledgements.

**Gaskin** : Corsham Commemorates - Edited by Kevin **Gaskin** : **Gastard** News: The Story of the Unknown Warrior by Michael **Gavaghan** : www.**gracesguide**.co.uk : **Gazette** & Herald : Ruth **Gilhooly** : **Globe** Newspaper : **Gloucestershire** Echo : Mrs Kim **Goodridge** (nee Hardiman) : Alistair **Gordon**-Farleigh : Colin **Gordon-Farleigh** : Nora Smith (nee **Gordon**-Farleigh) : Vera Romain **Gulliford** : David **Gulvin** : Colin J **Hall** 'An illustrated History of Corsham' : The Unknown Soldier by Neil **Hanson** : Wiltshire Community History by Lorraine **Hatt** : The **Guardian** : **Hampshire** Advertiser : **Hampshire** Chronicle : Bath Stone Quarries by Derek **Hawkins** : 100 Years in Corsham Parish by Peter **Henderson** : Jean **Howarth** corsham.the**human**journey.net/ : **Hereford** Journal : **historic**england.org.uk : **Imperial Wa**r Museum : **IMS** Vintage Photos : **Institute** for Fiscal Studies, 2011 : Mervyn **Jackson** : Joe **James** : Dr. John F. **James** : Tim **Jefferies** : **Joint Support Unit** (JSU), Corsham, A Characterisation Study Of The Quarries Nov 2008 : J. GRAHAM **JONES**, 1997 B1990/42 Senior Archivist and Head of the Welsh Political Archive at the National Library of Wales, Aberystwyth : www.**justcars**.com.au : **Kelly's** Directory : Lieutenant-Colonel Peter **Kingston** : **Liverpool** Echo : Ian **Logan** : **London Courier** and Evening Gazette : **London** Evening Standard : The **Lost** Pubs Project closedpubs.co.uk : James **Lowe** fellow Corsham collector : Honour The Light Brigade by William M. **Lummis** and Kenneth G. Wynn : **Manchester** Courier and Lancashire General Advertiser : Cold War Secret Nucear Bunkers by Nick **McCamley** : Secret History of an Industrial Hamlet in War and Peace by Nick **McCamley** : Subterranean Britain - Second World War Bunkers by Nick **McCamley** : Secret Underground Cities by Nick **McCamley** : **milden**hall.af.mil : **MoD** Corsham, Wiltshire Values Study dated March 2010 Issue No.2 : The Place Names of Wiltshire by Allen **Mawyer** and F.M. Stenton : **Medip** Cave Registry and Archive (MCRA) : www.**moneysorter**.co.uk : Richard (Dick) **Moon** : **Morning** Advertiser : **Morning** Post : **National** Archives : **National Archives** Record HO 250/60/1865B : Stephen **Neale** : **Newcastle Evening** Chronicle : **Northampton** Mercury : Air Historical Branch 3 (RAF) **Northolt** Ruislip : Graham **Peaple** : **player**.bfi.org.uk : Carolyn **Pote** : Jennifer **Oatley** : **PERFAR** Population Europ Resource Finder & Archive : Bath Stone A Quarrying History by J.W. **Perkins**, A.T. Brooks and A.E McR. Pearce : Catherine **Pitt** : **Pope's** Bath Chronicle and Weekly Gazette : The **Ports of the Bristol** Channel' book dated 1893 : The Ways of Corsham by John **Poulsom** : Bath Freestone Workings by Liz **Price** : **primary**homeworkhelp.co.uk : **Public Ledger** and Daily Advertiser : John **Pyle** : Andrew **Quinn** MBE :Charlie **Ralph** and son Pete **Ralph**: Steve **Randall** : **Reading** Mercury : Bridget **Robinson** : James **Robinson** : James **Rowe** : **Royal** Arthur Magazine : **Salisbury** and Winchester Journal : Max and Trudi **Salmon** (Lane End Farm) : **Sherborne** Mercury : The **Sketch** : **Spackman** Diaries : The **Sphere** : Corsham **Spotlight** - Corsham Civic Society Newsletter : Mandie **Stone** : **Storyteller**.2day.uk : **Swindon** Advertiser and North Wilts Chronicle : **Sunderland** Daily Echo and Shipping Gazette : **Swindon** Advertiser : A.J. **Sylvester**'s 'Life with Lloyd George' Edited by Colin Cross : Peter **Tapscott** : Songs and other Poems. By John **Taylor** 1828 : The **Telegraph** : Ivis **Thompson** : Wiltshire Place Names by Richard **Tomkins** : **Trowbridge** Advertiser : Mark and Tim **Unwin** : **Usk** Observer, Raglan Herald, and Monmouthshire Central Advertiser : Maz **Wakeman** : National Library of **Wales** : Ronnie **Walker** : **Web**.archive.org : **westcountry**bottles.co.uk : **Western** Daily Press : **Western** Daily Press : **Western** Gazette : Pat **Whalley** : Life And Times Of Neston Glove Factory by Pat **Whalley** Corsham Civic Society : Mr W.A. **Whittock** : **Wikipedia** : en.**wikipedia**.org : en.**wikisource**.org : **Wilts** and Gloucestershire Standard : **Wiltshire** Independent : **Wiltshire** and Swindon History Centre : **Wiltshire** Times : **Wiltshire** Times and Trowbridge Advertiser : Richard Usborne, 1976, **Wodehouse** at Work to the End, p.126 : **Worcester** Journal : **Ww2talk**.com/index.php : John **Yapp** : content.**yudu**.com/

**NWELYAMAID?**

# Chapter 28. The Author Giuliano (Julian) Carosi.

My name is Giuliano (Julian) Carosi; I was born in the Greenways Hospital Chippenham in 1952 and have lived in Corsham all my life. My father Francesco was an Italian prisoner of war who loved this country so much that he decided to stay here after WWII.

My father met and married my Italian mother Fiorenza (Enza) here in England and they set up their first home at 2 Wardle Road, in one of the old prefab bungalows just behind the Hare and Hounds. I have two brothers, Domenico Roberto, and Claudio Angelo and three lovely daughters, Melanie, Isabella Lucia and Sofia Francesca. And two lovely grandchildren George Dalibor and Ella Lucia.

I studied English at the Corsham School and later at Chippenham College. The old black library hut behind the Fire Station *(see Chapter 22 of my first book Corsham Revealed)* was a favourite haunt of mine as a young child. This is where I became enchanted with a love of the written word. The *Famous Five* books by Enid Blyton were one of my favourites in those days and this is where my sense of adventure was kindled. Now, it is Charles Dickens and all of the other Classic novels of the Victorian era.

For a number of years, I was Editor of the National Football Referees' Association magazine *'Refereeing'* and nowadays I run a local Facebook page called *'Mr Corsham'* where I encourage discussion on Corsham's history with the members. My first book *Corsham Revealed* seems to have been a great success and has spurred me on to write this second book *Corsham Revealed More*. I am retired after a long career as a civil servant working in several Government departments in and around and *deep underneath* Corsham.

I live near the cricket field in Corsham with my dear partner Susan Elizabeth in our recentley renovated lovely bungalow. My interest in the history of Corsham began after winning the, *'Know Your Corsham'* history competition in 1979. Since then, I have been gathering facts and stories for many years and discovering the many hidden places during my love of walking along the many public footpaths in and around Corsham. I feel as though I've covered just about every square inch of Corsham in my long years - above and below ground!

I once thought that Corsham was a sleepy little town with very little history of mention. How wrong I was. In my second book, my aim is to share even more of my findings with you. I hope that my book changes the way you perceive our little town. It does for me!

If you would like to contact me, I would love to hear from you.

Email me at: *juliancarosi@corshamref.org.uk*

Regards,
**Giuliano (Julian) Carosi**
2019